IN THE
IMAGE
OF THE
BRAIN

JIM JUBAK

IN THE IMAGE OF THE BRAIN

BREAKING THE BARRIER BETWEEN THE HUMAN MIND AND INTELLIGENT MACHINES

LITTLE, BROWN AND COMPANY

BOSTON   TORONTO   LONDON

First Edition

Library of Congress Cataloging-in-Publication Data

Jubak, Jim.
    In the image of the brain : breaking the barrier between the human
mind and intelligent machines / Jim Jubak. — 1st ed.
        p.   cm.
    Includes bibliographical references and index.
    ISBN 0-316-47555-6
    1. Neural networks (Computer science) I. Title.
QA76.87.J83   1992
006.3 — dc20   91-41771

10 9 8 7 6 5 4 3 2 1

RRD VA

*Published simultaneously in Canada
by Little, Brown & Company (Canada) Limited*

PRINTED IN THE UNITED STATES OF AMERICA

For Marie

CONTENTS

Introduction   ix

Prologue   xiii

1   Paradigms at Play   3

2   Creation Myths   20

3   The Rules of the Brain   45

4   The Nature of Metaphor   75

5   Brainspeak   93

6   Parts and Holes   114

7   The Stuff Thoughts Are Made Of   137

8   Space, the Final Frontier of Meaning?   159

9   The Apparent Reality of the Rising Fastball   183

10   Thanks for the Memories   204

11   Mind, Organize Thyself   216

12   Assumptions, Assumptions   235

13   Survival of the Smartest   261

14   The Mind at Last   278

Notes on Sources   307

Bibliography   319

Index   335

INTRODUCTION

This is a book about science and metaphors. It is a book about how a new way to build a computer, a technology called neural networks, is changing the way we think about machines, computers, brains, and minds.

It is notoriously difficult to tell what someone else is thinking. One of our most common rejoinders in an argument is, after all, "What did you expect me to do, read your mind?" Yet century after century, we have tried to explain what goes on inside our own heads. We have imagined the mind as a nonmaterial thing, separate from the flesh of the body and the neurons of the brain. We have imagined the mind as a machine, perhaps a computer, that is identical to the physical brain. And we have imagined almost everything else in between.

For most of human history, those imaginings were relatively unconstrained by facts. Very little was known about such things as psychology and possibly even less about the workings of the brain. Our time is different, however. We are beginning to know many of the brain's details — not just about neurons but about the chemical receptors that pass signals and the properties of the cables that carry those signals. We've begun to use some of that knowledge to build a new kind of computer called a neural network that is inspired by the brain's biology.

In themselves, neural networks are an intriguing technology. They promise to be immensely powerful computers, perhaps ideally suited to tasks that machines to date have found difficult — vision, for example. The nature and prospects for this technology are part of the story that follows.

But these machines will do more than put a new, extremely versatile computer at our command. Machines that incorporate some of the principles of the physical brain challenge our understanding of what a human being is all about. A successful machine of this sort would certainly raise the possibility that our brains are also machines. Where then our cherished beliefs in free will, individuality, and the like? Must these be discarded or modified beyond recognition if building a neural network is possible?

And what about the mind? A neural network that shows humanlike psychology and humanlike cognition is composed only of parts that lay on the workbench a few months before. The promise — or danger, if you prefer — is that, like the neural network, the mind really is just the sum of its biological parts. That the biology of the brain is the cause of the mind.

Neural network research raises all these questions; as a young science it has definitive answers for none of them. Nevertheless, the kind of machines that seem most likely to succeed and the research directions that seem most promising do suggest the ways in which such questions may be answered. Already it is clear that the answers will not be as simple as anyone expected. The brain may be a machine, but a biological machine may be far different from the machines of physics or chemistry. The mind may be just biology, but that doesn't mean it is either predictable or understandable. The first result of building a neural network that is brainlike, machinelike, and computerlike may be a reexamination of each of those metaphors.

Since I began work on this book in 1988, more than forty researchers have spent time with me explaining their work and the fields that give it context. I would like to extend special thanks to Carver Mead and Federico Faggin, who gave me my first introduction to neural networks. As this book has progressed, I have learned to treasure their balance of enthusiasm and critical caution. Terry Sejnowski, David Stork, Charles Stevens, Walter Freeman, Richard Granger, Christof Koch, and Josh Alspector all helped immeasurably in guiding my early attempts to get my hands around this often amorphous field. I would also like to thank Roger Shepard, David Rumelhart, Michael Stryker, Kenneth Miller, Eric Knudsen, Thomas Brown, Richard Howard, Michael Mozer, Ben Yuhas, Robert Allen, Doyne Farmer, Christopher Langton, Charles Gray, Larry Squire, John Hopfield, Patricia Churchland, Robert Hecht-Nielsen, Bernard Widrow, Carlos Tapang, Michael McBeath, Muriel Ross, Dan Hammerstrom, Shun-ichi Amari, Alex Waibel, Geoffrey Hinton, Anthony Zador, Rodney Brooks, Colin Angle, Paul Mueller, Sylvie Ryckebusch, Tobi Delbrück, Leon Cooper, James

McClelland, Jerome Feldman, and George Lakoff for discussing their work with me. All the errors that follow, in spite of their best efforts, are mine alone.

I am probably no better than most at examining my own mental states, but I feel that the shape of this book owes a great deal to three of my teachers from long ago. David Levin and Alan Howard of the University of Virginia taught me to read nonfiction with care and joy and to understand how belief can shape a community. Ralph Cohen first introduced me to the work of Thomas Kuhn.

This book wouldn't have come about without the encouragement of Lorraine Shanley, who introduced me to my agent, Susan Ginsburg, who was the best advocate that anyone could hope for and so much more, and Pat Mulcahy, then of Little, Brown, who helped me shape this as an intellectual narrative.

It is my everlasting good fortune to share a home with a patient reader, superb editor, and gentle critic — who also makes a pesto sauce designed for those dark nights of final rewriting. To her, my wife, this book is dedicated with all my love.

PROLOGUE: WHAT IS THIS THING, THIS BRAIN?

With an anxiety that almost amounted to agony, I collected the instruments of life around me, that I might infuse a spark of being into the lifeless thing that lay at my feet. It was already one in the morning; the rain pattered dismally against the panes, and my candle was nearly burnt out, when, by the glimmer of the half-extinguished light, I saw the dull yellow eye of the creature open; it breathed hard, and a convulsive motion agitated its limbs.

— MARY SHELLEY, *Frankenstein*

This Friday afternoon the single light over the receptionist's desk makes the surrounding gloom deeper. The big, undivided room that makes up most of Synaptics, Inc., seems deserted or possibly haunted. Shadowy figures occasionally dart from one workstation to another. Suddenly, at the far end of the room, a door opens, splitting the dark with brilliant California sunlight. Lights flicker on overhead. The test is over. On March 8, 1990, Synaptics is one step closer to putting some of the secrets of the biological brain on a computer chip.

But contemplate that chip well, Horatio. Like the skull cast up out of the grave, it mocks us. It says that we can become like gods, building machines in our own image. Our intellectual might can unravel even this mystery of our brain and put it to work for us in computers of unimagined power. Yet this chip also whispers that the mind, that one thing we still believe sets us above the rest of creation, is but a machine. Like a clock or a 1956 Chevy, we are explicable. The chip's creators, Carver Mead and Federico Faggin, understand both implications of their alchemy.

Eighteen months before that test, on October 7, 1988, in one of those anonymous gray and pink, sunlit California/French restaurants in Silicon Valley, Mead had described the machine he wanted to build. This neural network would remember, just like we do. It would learn, just like we do. It would perform a task better with experience, just like we do. It would form new concepts, have new thoughts, just like we do. And just like our own brains, it would be nothing more than billions and billions of dumb neurons connected by wires.

All this talk about what would amount to a part of an artificial brain sounded utterly down-to-earth. Faggin talked about development cycles and market potential. Mead lamented the difficulty of finding exactly the engineers he needed. Faggin spoke with the weight of years of experience, like the man who had in fact developed the first microprocessor, the electronic device that made the personal computer possible. Mead spoke like the man who has had a hand in creating virtually every tool used in designing today's most complex computer chips.

But Mead and Faggin also sounded like raving visionaries. They believed a chip of the kind they would build could, years in the future, pack the computing power of ten Cray supercomputers and cost ten thousand times less. A conventional computer that did everything our brain does would be equivalent to ten million Crays and would consume all the electricity produced by a big nuclear power plant. The chip they had in mind would use just a few watts. It would be an entirely new kind of computer, doing an entirely new kind of computation.

Project leader Tim Allen and the rest of the team scurrying around Synaptics as the lights come on don't seem a match for that task. Only seven people work here, all but one — a poor outcast from the Massachusetts Institute of Technology — recent graduates of the California Institute of Technology, Mead's home base. Janeen Anderson, a soft-spoken woman in her late twenties, runs Synaptic's chip tests from a workbench jammed with delicate machinery and crowded next to the drill press. She seems the oldest after Mead, fifty-eight, and Faggin, fifty. The youngest, John Platt, can often be found perched on his chair, drawing diagrams. He describes his job as "scribbling mathematics on the board here."

Nevertheless, even before this test, this tiny staff had already built neural network chips that worked. Borrowing from the basic architecture of the brain, they had connected a network of artificial neurons with wires that stood in for the brain's dendrites and axons. In the brain signals are passed from neuron to neuron across tiny gaps, synapses, where the signals are often modified. In these chips transistors connected by wires represented the neurons. The floating gates of the transistors held a tiny electrical charge that could be modified to strengthen some paths and eliminate others, duplicating one theory of how the synapses in the brain work. Initial signals came into the chip through an array of light-sensitive receptors. It wasn't too big a leap to think of them as the light-sensitive cells in the eyes' retinas. In a primitive way these networks could see objects and find edges. Some versions could even learn.

Those efforts seemed to show that Mead and Faggin were on the right track. As Mead says, and says so frequently it almost seems like a prayer, "The brain is an existence proof. We know it's possible to do these things because the brain does them." But the brain only grudgingly gives up its secrets. Even so, Mead believes we may be able to examine it, figure out how it does what it does, and then build a machine that uses some of those same principles. "We're just starting to get the tiniest little hints about those organizing principles," Mead says, but he and Faggin believe even those tiny hints will be enough to inspire the products their company wants to build.

Of course, as both matter-of-factly note, they don't want to — nor do they need to — put an entire brain on a chip. The first product out of Synaptics will be a single computer chip that can read the numerical code on the bottom of a check. That optical reader will *only* mimic some of the principles of the eye and the visual cortex.

Ah, the intellectual challenge — and the hubris. When they began, they knew that no one really knew how the biological brain worked. Faggin and Mead believed that all the principles necessary to build their chip were known. But it was quite possible that they would be wrong, that someone would have to solve basic questions about how the brain was put together on almost every level — from that of individual neurons to the way that brain areas worked together. And according to neuroscientists working on the brain, the task was even more complex than that. It faced questions about psychology, language, evolution, and learning that had been asked, without satisfactory answers, for two thousand years.

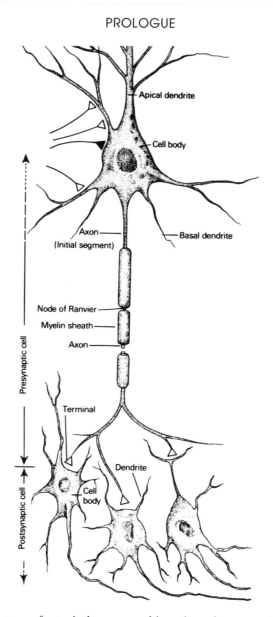

The main features of a typical neuron and its points of contact with other cells. Excitatory terminals are indicated by white triangles, and inhibitory terminals by black triangles. The terminal branches of the axon form synapses with as many as 1,000 other neurons. Axons vary greatly in length; some may extend more than one meter. Most synapses join the axon terminals of one neuron to the dendrites or cell body of another neuron. Thus, the dendrites may receive incoming signals from hundreds or even thousands of other neurons.

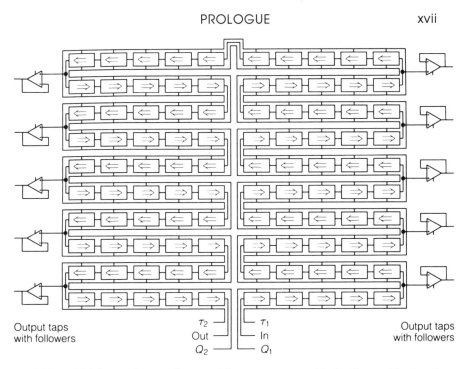

Output taps   Output taps
with followers τ_2 ⌐ ¬ τ_1 with followers
                    Out ⌐   ⌐ In
                    Q_2 Q_1

This artificial neural network, turned into a computer chip by Carver Mead and
John Lazzaro, captures one of the properties of the ear of a barn owl. Wires,
transistors, and capacitors replace dendrites, axons, and cell membranes.
Reprinted by permission from Mead, *Analog VLSI and Neural Systems*, Addison-Wesley
Publishing Co., 1989. Copyright © 1989.

But that was, after all, part of the allure of this puzzle. Why
was the brain so much more efficient than any computer? It was a
challenge to set any engineer's blood running. It was at least part
of what drove Faggin. Faggin knew he was a pretty good engineer.
He had been one of the first to see that a single microprocessor
could run an entire computer. While the IBMs, the Honeywells, and
the Sperrys — the companies that built the room-size mainframes
that dominated the industry — laughed at this idea, he left Intel
and built his own company, Zilog, Inc., around the new device, and
it had made him rich. As microprocessors and computers got
smaller and more powerful everyday, Faggin could see ways to
make computers ten times faster, a hundred times faster, a thousand times faster, just by extending current technology. Yet he was
also beginning to feel the wall where basic physics would put a stop
to this geometric progress. It seemed to him that when computers

reached that point, they would still be unable to do some of the things the brain did so well. Maybe it was time to look at the brain itself.

It is tempting to dismiss this as just another example of Silicon Valley oversell. Even when they finish this chip, all that Synaptics will have created is a better check reader. Sure, it packs a retina and two neural networks on one chip, but it will show little of the complex nature of the brain. Yet Faggin remembers selling his first microprocessors: "The computer people all laughed. 'This is a joke,' they said. 'This is not a computer; this is a toy.' The first people to use it didn't care what it was. They said, 'Give me something to solve my problem.' Those were the early users."

And so the first major use for his microprocessors was in pinball machines, not computers. "We all saw the personal computer coming," says Faggin, "but gas pumps?" The first use of a neural network computer chip is just as unprepossessing. (The first commercial product using this chip is now in beta testing, the last step before full-scale manufacture in 1992.)

"You know," he says, waving his hands to indicate all of neural network technology, "this is the next frontier, maybe better call it the last frontier. It's not going to happen today, or this year, but it is going to happen." Faggin knows he will be able to put the equivalent of 100 million synapses on one chip within ten years. That's still a long way from matching the brain — about 10 million times smaller, he figures — but it's on the way. "I think we will be able to build the first truly intelligent machines. For the first time in history we know something solid about how the brain works and we have the technology to build something based on the brain's principles."

Multiply Synaptics a dozen, a hundred, a thousand times. There's Nestor, Inc., in Providence, Rhode Island, Nobel Prize winner Leon Cooper's company, and Robert Hecht-Nielsen's HNC Inc. in San Diego. There's also Adaptive Solutions Inc., which opened its doors in 1990 outside Portland, Oregon. Intel Corp. has a neural network project. So do Ford and Motorola and many of the Japanese heavyweights. All this is a far cry from 1985 when Kevin Kinsella, a La Jolla, California, venture capitalist, decided it was time to start a company to build a neural network computer with little more to go on than a few academic papers on a brainlike way to find the shortest route for a traveling salesman among twenty-five cities and some intriguing theories about how the brain created memory.

Maybe it's just fatigue that makes them contemplative, but some nights, even as Synaptics inches toward its goals, Faggin and Mead feel the pull of the brain's mystery. One evening Faggin lingers long after dinner in what might be San Jose's most expensive restaurant. Faggin and Mead had come here propelled by their "need" for abalone.

Faggin says, "I'm in awe. The brain is so amazing — that the single cell could be such an incredible information processing device." He shakes his head. He seems in love with what he's making and the process of finding out how to do it. His words tumble out softly and with a strong Italian accent, despite his more than twenty years in Silicon Valley. Exploring the details of the brain hasn't destroyed its mysteries for Faggin. Building a machine that captures part of its behavior hasn't diminished its beauty.

That is one of the strange results of contemplating this chip and the brain. Even as the chip seems to say that the brain is just a machine, the effort to understand how to build that machine reveals more and more of the brain's complexities and mysteries. The explorers fill in more and more of their map, but the landscape seems still grander and more sublime with each step. And the brain may well have the last, cosmic laugh. The farthest edges of neural network research have begun to suggest that if the brain is a machine, it is a machine like no other, one that it may be possible to duplicate but never really to understand.

IN THE
IMAGE
OF THE
BRAIN

1
PARADIGMS AT PLAY

Normal science, the activity in which most scientists inevitably spend almost all their time, is predicated on the assumption that the scientific community knows what the world is like.

— THOMAS KUHN, *The Structure of Scientific Revolutions*

Have you ever noticed, how some scientists in neuroscience, when they get to a certain age, want to understand the whole picture, because they're suddenly faced with the possibility that they are going to die and not know? In fact, they are going to die and they are not going to know. So will their grandchildren and their great-grandchildren. That's one of the realities of working in neuroscience — that you're going to go your whole life and not really understand a heck of a lot more when you're done. You've just got to trust that in some future decade the understanding will come.

— ROBERT HECHT-NIELSEN, neural network designer

Many of the scientists standing around the exhibit hall have the slightly troubled look of third-graders on parent–teacher night at P.S. 87. With proud glances, hangdog smiles, and shy mumbles, they greet the milling crowd for two hours each evening during the three days of the 1990 Neural Information Processing Systems (NIPS) conference. "Oh, is this your work?" says one Ph.D. to another.

They've hung their papers, page by page, on two dozen bulletin boards. Crowd around and read something called "Flight Control in the Dragonfly: A Neurobiological Simulation." Got a question? Ask the authors standing at your elbow. Think the data is flawed? Tell the researchers to their faces. MIT undergraduates, rising assistant professors, the biggest names in the field, all get the same space, all vie to attract the passing throng. The atmosphere is part carnival midway and part Saturday afternoon at the corner garage, where the mechanics and the enthusiasts chew over who makes the best four-barrel carb.

Numbers have made this carnival necessary. Ten years ago you could have held an international conference on neural networks in a space not much bigger than the olfactory lobe. Today more than 2,000 show up for the biggest professional meetings. Even NIPS, a conference with a reputation for carefully screening papers, attracted more than a thousand submissions this year. With just forty oral presentations scheduled, almost none of the submitted papers has a chance to be heard at the public sessions. These poster evenings give the authors of the next 150 best papers a chance to show their stuff.

They also lay bare the currents, rivalries, and controversies that swirl through this scientific community. At first, the diversity is overwhelming. But then, diving deeper, schools begin to emerge. Swim even deeper, though, and for a moment you understand that all these presenters share a single revolutionary understanding of the brain, of psychology, of linguistics, of machine intelligence; that neural networks really are a new way of thinking about human intelligence and the world. But you are only able to catch a glimpse before you have to give up the dive. Back at the surface that unifying vision is once again swept away in a sea of detail.

But there's not much else to do at this conference, banished to the outskirts of Denver in a place called the Technology Center, so why not saunter by the posters? A photograph of a dolphin catches your eye. We trained this dolphin on a matching test, says Patrick Moore of the Naval Ocean Systems Center in Hawaii. From a group of objects floating in water, the dolphin was asked to pick out the two seemingly identical objects using its sonar. But the dolphin didn't seem to think any of the objects were similar, not even the two cylinders that the humans running this experiment thought were identical. The researchers were convinced that the dolphin was getting it wrong, Moore says, until they realized that the cetacean could detect the different amounts of nickel in the stainless steel of the otherwise identical cylinders. Moore is training a neural network to duplicate the dolphin's abilities using recordings of a dolphin's clicks.

In the middle of the floor, Dean Pomerleau of Carnegie-Mellon University is showing a videotape of ALVINN, the Autonomous Land Vehicle in a Neural Network. A totally male crowd watches ALVINN driving a Chevy van down a street with a center line, down another unmarked road, and over an unpaved road. It learned how to do this, says Pomerleau, by first watching a human drive in these different situations. Right now it goes at speeds of up to twenty miles an hour, faster than any automated vehicle has ever driven before. We're still working on getting the speed up, he adds. The "guys" seem hypnotized. "You mean you get to ride around in the back and nobody's driving?" one asks.

Beatrice Golomb guaranteed her poster a steady stream of the curious when she plugged it that afternoon. Four or five especially noteworthy posters are spotlighted after each oral session in what amounts to a two-minute teaser. SEXNET learns to identify gender from facial images, she said during her time. In fact, the machine does slightly better at the task than her coworkers in Terry Sejnowski's lab at the Salk Institute. "Which," Golomb notes, "probably indicates that those lab workers should get out more." From ninety photos of University of San Diego students — sans facial hair, jewelry, and apparent makeup — the machine learned to tell men from women with only an 8 percent error. Humans using the same data made mistakes 11.6 percent of the time. For Golomb, building a neural network that can learn abstract concepts like maleness and femaleness, without ever being told anything about people or sexual characteristics, is just a way to learn how networks categorize. She's interested in more practical applications.

For example, neural networks could diagnose congenital medical disorders such as William's syndrome, also known as infantile hypercalcemia, which initially reveals itself in very subtle facial clues. The clues to William's syndrome, which is associated with a slightly elfin appearance in young children and deficits in some areas of intelligence such as arithmetic ability, are so subtle, and the syndrome itself so rare, that doctors often fail to recognize it in their patients. A neural network trained on photos of children with this syndrome could catch patterns that human doctors might miss.

Ron Keesing, a newly minted Stanford graduate now working at the California research center recently founded by Ricoh Co., Ltd., the Japanese copier maker, is wrapped up in a hairsplitting discussion of evolution. His coauthor, David Stork, is out scouting the other posters, leaving Keesing to explain how their neural network both learns and evolves. "Well, it's not Lamarckian; it's Darwinian," he says, somewhat wearily. Keesing and Stork have applied a computer science technique called a genetic algorithm to the complex task of figuring out how to match the structure of a neural network with the job it's supposed to do. Most neural networks are built with an informed guess about what structure will work best and the hope that the network's ability to learn will make up for any problems in the choice of the initial structure itself. Stork and Keesing start with a guess at structure and then simulate a Darwinian survival of the fittest in their computer. They "build" numbers of their "best-guess" networks in a computer simulation, allow them to produce "offspring" with random mutations of their original structure, give them learning rules, and set them to a task. In any generation those that learn to perform the task reasonably well are allowed to survive to produce part of the next generation of machines — which will also mutate, learn, perform, and die or survive. The machines gradually evolve new internal structures that are better and better suited to performing the task at hand. Keesing's visitor is hung up on allowing learning to influence evolution. "There's no place for learning to influence survival in Darwin," he says. "That's Lamarck and he's been discredited." Patiently, Keesing begins his explanation again.

The diversity on display is immense and intriguing, although after one or two circuits of the exhibit hall, the diversity itself becomes the issue. Everybody here is working on something called a neural network, but what exactly is a neural network? Visit enough posters and the term seems to have so many meanings that it threatens to have none at all.

In the broadest sense neural networks are a potentially revolutionary reimagining of the relationship between biological brains and electronic computers. In the 1940s, during the early attempts to build and understand electronic computers, Warren McCulloch, Walter Pitts, John von Neumann, and others created a metaphor based on what was then understood about the human brain. The brain seemed to do its work with a vast array of units, called neurons, that sent electric pulses when they were stimulated. The brain's information was carried, they supposed, in those off/on pulses.

Traditional computation and traditional digital computers have borrowed very little from that analogy other than a general sense that there is some biological basis for using zeros and ones, off and on, as the way to represent information, and the term memory for the machine's storage capacity. The metaphor — the computer is like the brain — though, served as a quick way to understand the essential similarity of the new electronic machines, the much older brain, and the traditions of mathematical logic. All of these things, the metaphor said, are formally similar.

Neural networks, on the other hand, either simulated in complicated computer programs or actually built out of silicon, draw far more inspiration from the biology of the brain. They are built out of units, simple electronic processors often called neurons in homage to their biological predecessors, connected to each other by wires that mimic not just the nerve fibers between neurons, called dendrites and axons, but even the synapses, the gaps across which neurons connect. Like the brain, neural networks have immense numbers of processors, often thousands, hooked together in *parallel* so that they can all work on a problem at the same time. In contrast, traditional computers are *serial* devices. Their single processor tackles only one minute step in a problem at a time.

Neural networks don't share the traditional division between software — the program that tells the computer what to do — and hardware — the physical machine that executes the instructions. According to neural network researchers, the brain doesn't make this distinction. In the brain and in neural networks, the pattern of connections between the neurons is both hardware and software: the shape of the network and the relative strength of all the individual connections produce the computed answer. In an artificial neural network, either the shape of the network can be predesigned to suit the kind of problem at hand, or the network can be built with connections that it will modify as it gains experience with the problem. In the latter case the network learns from experience how to modify these connections to produce the right answer. Then, by analogy with the biological system, neural network scientists say that their system learns. Or if the learning is extended over generations of networks, they say it evolves.

Neural networks replace the symbolic logic and programming of traditional computers with learning and evolution. That is indeed the great promise of these "brainlike" machines. If the right neurons are hooked together in the right way and information is presented in the right form — all rights that are often wrong without a great deal of work — the neural network can learn how to identify the gender of a face, tell a good candidate for a mortgage from a bad one, or sniff out small amounts of explosives in airline luggage. No one has to write a program that defines femaleness, connects all the good things that should be on a mortgage application, or lays out all the different kinds of explosives and their characteristic X-ray profiles. Neural networks can learn from example to identify female faces or good mortgage risks or suitcases containing bombs.

Neural network researchers are trying to find out exactly how much they have to "pay" for the learning and evolutionary powers of neural networks. The traditional digital computer is what is called a universal computer. We write software that enables it to emulate whatever machine we need to solve the problem at hand. To go from calculating the gross national product to playing chess we don't need to build a new machine. Instead, a software program enables the traditional computer to simulate a chess-player or an economist.

The brain, evidence suggests, isn't a universal computer, or at least major parts of it aren't. Instead, over time evolution has taught the brain how to look at the world and how to efficiently solve problems when survival depends on efficient solutions. Evolution has molded the brain into a thing very different from the electronic digital computer. Want to do word processing or analyze a scene? The very same digital computer can do either. In the brain, however, parts of those tasks are performed by a collection of special-purpose networks, each one modified for an individual task. We have networks for vision and for sound. Specialized parts of those networks find edges or separate sound frequencies. Generations of experience taught the brain what features it can seize on in the physical world that will help it solve a problem. Then evolution encouraged the construction of specialized networks that can manipulate just those features. Neural network researchers wonder if they too will have to evolve specialized networks for each task they want to perform. Trying to imitate evolution with deadlines measured in months instead of millions of years is a fairly daunting prospect.

Although neural networks are a kind of artificial intelligence, neural network researchers and those who work with symbolic artificial intelligence form distinct communities. The distinction is perhaps most concrete in the language and signs each group recognizes. Traditionally, artificial intelligence, the effort to create intelligent machines, has equated intelligence with the conscious part of our mental processes. Machine intelligence in this tradition takes its inspiration from how we solve chess problems or parse sentences. A grammar in any language is an example of this approach. Words are symbolic markers. You or I speak a language by obeying a series of rules that as a set uniquely determine each situation. Artificial intelligence of this sort has been been immensely successful in writing programs that enable machines to perform some very complex tasks that are part of what we recognize as conscious thought.

On the other hand, neural networks so far have been most successful at just the kind of mental processes that we can't describe in words — at finding a pattern in a mess of noisy data so that we can pick out a Dalmatian puppy even in a shadowy forest, at categorizing things so that we know what is a cat and what isn't, even though articulating rules that define "catness" is extremely difficult, at completing a pattern from just part of the data, so that we can remember Greg's face, birthday, occupation, and address given just his name.

Both the artificial and the biological neural networks do this kind of thing in a way totally unlike the way Deep Thought, at the moment the world's best chess-playing computer, plays chess. There are no explicit rules that define "cat" in the neural network. No search through a decision tree of all possible matches to "remember" that Greg's eyes are blue. All there is in a neural network are neurons and the connections between them. Somehow the pattern of those connections represents Greg, and the connections link blue eyes, May 23, self-employed, and Georgia together. Intelligence is a property that emerges from the interaction of all these very dumb little neurons. It is somehow resident in the whole.

The language this neural network community speaks doesn't emphasize rules or logic. Instead, it elevates the terminology of a relatively unknown Canadian psychologist named Donald Hebb. In 1949 Hebb suggested a way to connect the firing of neurons in the brain with memories and learning. Two neurons firing together would cause changes in the synapse between them. Those changes would strengthen that connection, making it easier for those two neurons to fire together in the future. The network would thus become biased toward specific patterns that had been created by the correlated firing of sets of neurons. Out of this, Hebb suggested, the brain could build memories and complex networks capable of various cognitive tasks. No one had ever seen a Hebb synapse, of course. And no one would until forty years later.

Hebb's vague but amazingly prescient insight has been turned into a mathematical touchstone that shows up in virtually every neural network research paper. The Hebb synapse is just the front end of the neuron. From there an electrical signal, of a strength determined by the changes in that synapse, travels toward the main cell body of the neuron. The cell body sums up all the signals it receives from all the synapses on its far-stretched arms. If the sum is large enough, the cell body fires, creating an electrical signal that heads for the synapses between this neuron and others in the network. Mathematically, this addition is expressed in a summing function that stipulates which signals get added, which ones subtracted, and how they are transformed into an outgoing signal.

Both the Hebb synapse and the summing function are parts of the central distinguishing metaphor of this field, that is, that neural networks are like the biological brain. But what does this metaphor mean? How are neural networks like brains? Sketching in the bounds of the metaphor is made just a bit more difficult by the vagueness of our understanding of the brain itself. It's like saying that neural networks are like "abxyces" and then realizing that no one has ever seen an abxyce except miles away on a fog-shrouded mountain. In practice, it is not the exact content of this metaphor but the approach to the questions it raises that creates a relatively unified agenda that can be called neural network research.

It is clear from walking around the poster session at the NIPS conference that the very act of naming this field has created its own centripetal force that keeps together some potentially very unlike things. Neural networks, for example, are now a *commercial* category, a hot button designed to sell things. The term has become a media buzzword, and companies and researchers have recognized that calling something a neural network is a way to make it seem new, improved, ground-breaking. In the 1970s the Defense Department anointed symbolic artificial intelligence, programs that would manipulate symbols following logical rules, as *the* way to solve problems. And it backed up that opinion with millions of

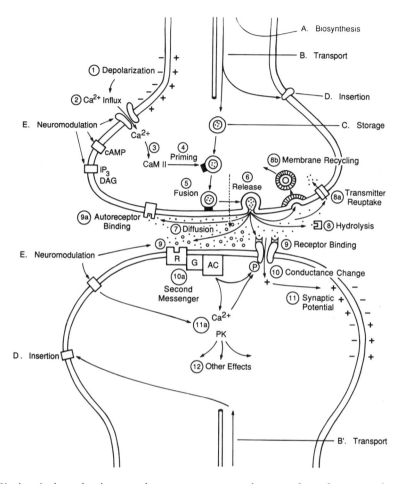

Biochemical mechanisms at the synapse support the metaphor of computation, producing results that neural network researchers say are "like" addition, subtraction, and multiplication. Steps A–E include the metabolic machinery that keeps the cell going. Numbered steps 1–12 show the biochemical steps that make up a signal. Depolarization (1) at the membrane leads to a rapid influx of calcium ions (2), which primes the vesicles (4), fuses them to the cell membrane (5), and finally releases transmitters across the synaptic gap (6). Steps 8a and 8b restore the presynaptic terminal to its original state. The transmitter diffuses across the gap (7) to act on the proteins in the postsynaptic membrane (9), causing a conductance change (10) and a consequent potential response (11), which spreads along the membrane. According to Hebb's theory, correlated firing between two neurons leads to changes in the synapse — perhaps increases in the amount of transmitter released or increases in the number of receptors in the postsynaptic membrane — that make correlated firing even more likely in the future.
Reprinted by permission from Gordon M. Shepherd, *Neurobiology*, 2d edition, Oxford University Press, 1988. Copyright © 1988.

dollars. In the late 1980s that same department declared that artificial intelligence of this sort had failed and that neural networks would solve these problems. A little over $30 million has so far backed that opinion. Science that is neural networks can get funded. Science that is not neural networks can't get funded. What would you call your project under the circumstances?

Money isn't an overt presence at this conference. It's the subtle politician who guides the debate without ever stepping into the spotlight. Nobody from such neural network companies as HNC, Nestor, Neurogen, NeuralWare, Intel, Hitachi Ltd., or Nippon Telegraph and Telephone is presenting here. The few people present with commercial affiliations, like Carver Mead of Synaptics, Richard Howard of AT&T Bell Laboratories, and Josh Alspector of Bellcore, are here as researchers, not product builders.

That doesn't mean, though, that money isn't at least in the back of everybody's mind. Research dollars are getting harder and harder to find at American universities. The scramble to impress the traditional funding sources is becoming more and more frantic, the search for new pockets more and more ingenious. The majority of papers and posters delivered at the conference owe some debt to the Defense Department and its various funding agencies, like the Office of Naval Research. DARPA (the Defense Advanced Research Projects Agency) was supposed to flood this field with money. At one point it looked like the figure would be more than $400 million. Nobody's talking about that kind of money anymore, but, still, the $30 million awarded to date isn't too shabby.

Corporate money is also present at the dance. There's direct funding from American companies such as AT&T and IBM and Japanese companies such as Hitachi. In the last two years NEC, another huge Japanese electronics maker, and Ricoh have both set up major research centers in the United States and have lured some neural network researchers with impressive credentials into the fold.

And then, of course, there's a third way. Neither government grant nor corporate contract, it's the one that starts images of sugarplums dancing in academics' heads. Neural networks seem to be on the verge of becoming real products that can make real money in the real market. At least, that's what the increasing number of researchers who have started their own companies suggests. In addition to Hecht-Nielsen's HNC, Leon Cooper's Nestor, Mead and Faggin's Synaptics, there's Dan Hammerstrom's Adaptive Solutions. Rumors at the conference say that Stanford's David Rumel-hart and the Naval Research Laboratory's Harold Szu have just made the jump.

The odds are against any of these companies. Nestor, after all, has been around since 1975 and has yet to show a profit. But there's new hope in the air. By no means are all the problems solved, but these companies are betting that maybe, just maybe, we now know enough to build that first car that learns to adapt to its driver or the first robot that can pilot its way across an ever-reshuffled factory floor.

If that's true, some scientists will become very rich and some will become very famous. There are Nobel Prizes at stake here, perhaps for work already performed and certainly for work now being done — even if no two researchers in the field agree on which work. There will be — there already may be — real winners and losers here, and the results will be measured in prestige and money. If you know how to read the waters, you can see the rivalries, many based on important intellectual issues and others based more on style and personality, flowing through the proceedings of this conference.

As important as who's in attendance is who's not. The California Institute of Technology, Stanford University, and Carnegie-Mellon — all heavy hitters in cutting-edge computer technologies over the last decade — are well represented. MIT, however, is a curiously subdued force, even though it has one of the country's best and most visible programs in artificial intelligence. And where's Boston University and Stephen Grossberg? Grossberg has built his school into a leader in the field, and he edits one of the major neural network journals. Is his absence, and that of MIT, the result of history, ideology, ego, or all three?

MIT remains a stronghold of traditional artificial intelligence. In 1969 MIT's Marvin Minsky and Seymour Papert wrote *Perceptrons*, a book that is widely and by and large unfairly blamed for having held back the development of neural networks for ten or fifteen years. It's easy to make too much of MIT's absence at the NIPS conference, but there is widespread hostility to neural networks in many academic programs working in certain traditions of artificial intelligence, linguistics, psychology, and computer science. To its critics the field promises too much and delivers too little.

The absence of Grossberg, his colleagues, and his students is tempting to interpret, too. Egos are at war over neural network history. Grossberg was one of the few researchers devoted to the field during the dark ages of the 1970s and early 1980s. Credit is clearly due his pioneering work, but that work is difficult and dense, some say intentionally so. His neural network architecture, the ART family as it has developed over the years, is one way to build a network. Is it a central way or just a dead end? It is certainly too early to tell — as it is for such competitors as backpropagation, Hopfield networks, and Kohonen associative memories.

That hasn't stopped the effort to stake out the high ground of history. After two decades during which no one wanted to call his or her work a neural network, now everyone wants to claim a central role in the development of the field. For example, three people — Yann Le Cun, Paul Werbos, and David Rumelhart — all claim to have invented the backpropagation algorithm, currently the most commonly used rule for telling a neural network how to learn. Everyone wants to be the ape that climbed down from the tree and became Homo sapiens's parent. Nobody is claiming Australopithicus as a child. "I think that in itself this field is frankly better than any soap opera," says Robert Hecht-Nielsen, who runs HNC, one of the bigger commercial neural network companies. People are battling, not just for commercial success, but for their place in the story of neural networks, he notes.

By no means have all the battles over the correct direction for the field been fought and settled. The metaphor that creates this scientific community also divides it. Neural networks may be like the brain, but how much like it? In what ways? Everyone recognizes that neural networks aren't identical to the brain, but virtually no one agrees on which similarities matter and which ones don't. Some researchers say that biologically plausible detail is crucial to building successful networks. Yale's Tom Brown, for example, packs hundreds of synapses into his model of a single neuron, arguing that this is the best way to discover neural networks' true computational powers. Another camp thinks this is silly — these are machines, not collections of living cells. The abstract principles of the biological networks are all that is important. David Rumelhart, for example, explicitly calls the nodes of his network "neuron-like" elements. As he readily admits, his network uses principles that are clearly biologically implausible.

The disagreement sometimes gets a little impolite. Talk to

Brown for more than thirty seconds and you'll be told that almost no one in this field knows any biology, that almost everyone's theories about the neuron are wrong, and that, consequently, almost every network that has been built is unbiological and will never compute anything worthwhile. Then wander to the corner where the neural network chip group from AT&T has hung its poster. All this talk about biology is only of metaphysical interest, says Richard Howard. We know that biological networks are massively parallel and that's about all we need to know. Everything else comes down to engineering.

Want more disagreements and more dismissive comments? Well then, wander the hall after Larry Jackel from that same group has given an oral presentation summarizing what he thinks are the most promising neural network chips now being developed. Carver Mead is ever polite, but he has strong opinions, too. Those chips are interesting; they're good accelerators for plugging into a traditional computer so that you can run a software simulation of a neural network faster. But they're no more real neural networks than the accelerator board you can buy now at Computerland and plug into your PC. Of course, there are people who say, with a sniff, that Mead's chips are very clever actually, but they just compute sensory information. They're not real neural networks, you know. And then, of course, there are the people like Hecht-Nielsen who claim not to understand what the big deal is about building a neural network chip in the first place. You can build a perfectly good software simulation of a network that will run on a traditional digital computer. All these chip builders seem to want to do is strap a piece of meat on silicon, he says. Of course, that didn't stop HNC from signing on to build a neural network chip for the Department of Defense.

In all this turmoil we can see a revolution in progress. Neural networks are part of a potential revolution in how we think about the brain, about intelligence both artificial and biological, and about computers and computation. They are "like" the brain in ways that the traditional computer is clearly not. It is increasingly obvious that the brain is a very different thing than we imagined when the metaphor ran the other way and the brain was thought to be like a computer. Yet this is by no means a completed revolution. The community is divided over the content of the metaphor and even over how to pursue this science. In questioning the role of biology in neural networks, researchers are asking very basic questions about what experiments to pursue and even what "facts" to look for.

Of course, every other Tuesday one or another technology claims to be revolutionary. To put some real content into that claim, you have to grab at least one idea from Thomas Kuhn's 1962 book, *The Structure of Scientific Revolutions.* Kuhn's theory on how to write the history of science is certainly the only one to have emerged from the academic village into the popular marketplace in the last thirty years. Check the bibliography of any popular science book and if you find any work of historiography cited, it will be Kuhn. His basic terminology and premises have become part of the vocabulary of popular science writing and of scientists themselves. We all now speak of paradigms of science. We all now distinguish between normal science and a scientific revolution. We all now pay at least some attention to the way scientific revolutions are not simply the triumph of truth over falsehood, but also the result of emotional and psychological events that raise up one world view and cast down another. Paradigms are in an important sense not provable or falsifiable.

If Kuhn had a dime for every time someone misapplied his idea of a scientific paradigm, he'd be a very, very rich man, but that doesn't make his insight any less useful. Using this framework neural network history can be seen as part of a paradigm shift taking place over the last forty years. However, unlike the typical paradigm shift he outlines, one that occurs inside a single field of science and in fact most often occurs within a small community of twenty-five or so scientists, this one is vast and vague. It involves what seem to be widely disparate fields of science — disciplines as dissimilar as computer science, neurobiology, and linguistics.

Neural network science is a strange beast with two natures. In one it is a method of computation and a theory about how to solve problems like those the brain has solved by adopting some or all of the brain's methods. In the other it is not a body of knowledge but a tool to gain that knowledge. To a neurobiologist, for example, neural networks are less interesting as machines that solve computational problems than as tools that can be used to model the brain. Theories that couldn't be tested in real brains, especially not in human brains, could be tested in these brainlike models. In the model it is possible, for example, to measure the effects of small changes in the network, such as the effect of disabling just one type of synapse. Carefully collected neurobiological measurements can be fed into a model to see if they are sufficient to explain the way the brain grows and functions.

And this is true not just for neurobiology but for other sciences such as psychology or linguistics. For the first time in these fields, it is possible to connect the fine structure of the brain with behaviors or the nature of language. In its own domain neural network research asks, What is the brain like? In these other domains it makes it possible to ask, How much of the way we are derives from the physical structure of the brain?

Of course, the traditional formulations of all these sciences haven't melted away, and the researchers who adhere to them haven't meekly surrendered their vision of truth. As these scientists rightly understand, a way of looking at the world and our intelligence that goes back to Aristotle is at stake and is not to be lightly abandoned. Especially since the older vision may be right. They have counterattacked, revised, reinvigorated. In some encounters they have held their own; in others they have been routed. In still others their opponents have retreated in dismay. It is clear that at this point no one can predict the exact way that the neural network paradigm will be constructed.

The neural network paradigm may be limited to just a small part of computer science, shared among the community that builds computer vision systems, for example. Or it may reconstruct many sciences, forming a new vision for neurobiology, linguistics, computer science, psychology, and other fields. The paradigm may eventually be shared by an immense community, as the paradigm of quantum physics is, or by a relatively small group of researchers. This kind of reconstruction of the Temple of Knowledge is already visible in the growth of a new discipline called cognitive science, which clearly states its intention of synthesizing several of these fields.

This paradigm shift, whatever its final shape, could finally prove even more complex than what we describe as the transition from Newtonian to relativistic physics. It is not confined to a single science. It might be more exact to say that this is about a meta-science, a revision of the world view underpinning a number of sciences. Physics has dominated the science of the first three-quarters of this century. Relativity and quantum mechanics have reordered the way we see the universe, and in the process they have demonstrated the success of an atomistic, mechanistic, mathematically rigorous science. Biology and psychology, and to some degree computer science and linguistics, have no equivalent foundation. Evolution, for example, judged by the standards of physics, is hardly more than a guess. What are its mechanisms? A hundred years after Darwin, we still can't explain how the first wing came to be. Psychology can describe mental states, but we have no idea what causes schizophrenia, assuming that this category really is a single disorder, or why apparently similar brain lesions result in such different behaviors. An entire level of explanation is missing. We cannot point to the mechanisms that produce memory or the ability to recognize a face.

But over the last thirty years, we have discovered hints of these mechanisms. Neurobiologists have learned how to make recordings of the activity of single brain cells so that they can see what stimulus is paired with what response. Psychology has crafted careful experiments to test how seemingly abstract mental processes, like the way we categorize objects, are related to the qualities of the world and the brain. Computer science has provided ways to study the workings of systems so complex that we lack the mathematics to understand them.

These hints have accumulated to the point where they seem to form a possible explanation for the way the brain works. As the details are filled in, this explanation promises to provide a theory of the kind that physics has and that most of the life sciences have always lacked. It says that the brain is composed of billions of simple units, neurons, and billions of equally simple connections, and that behavior, psychology, thought, personality — everything we call mental — results from the local interactions of those units and those connections.

Such an explanation may be wrong in its details or even wrong in its entire program. Certainly, respected scientists from many fields have questioned whether it is too simple a model to produce all the behaviors and psychological states that human beings exhibit. Others have suggested that though it may explain certain kinds of mental processes, especially those at the lower levels of the brain such as the sensory processes, it cannot explain the realm of "thought," the conscious higher processes like language and logic. No one, not even the strongest supporters of this explanation, pretends that it is easy to see how free will, consciousness, personal identity, and the like, emerge from a brain that works like this.

This paradigm will also have to include at least a sketch for the relationship between the brain and the physical world. The machines built so far already show that picking the correct way to represent information from the outside world is crucial. If the brain is not a general-purpose computer, then it is made up of a series of specialized structures that have evolved as "best ways" to get useful information from the physical world, given that world's own specific organization. The task then is to find the right general languages — as well as the tricks, defaults, and shortcuts — that the brain has evolved.

This effort seems to lead inevitably to certain kinds of answers about how the brain got to be the way that it is and how we became the way we are. From watching the way simple units can create complex organisms, neural network researchers wind up emphasizing principles called self-organization, trial and error, and evolution in their history of the brain. All these explain who we are. So, too, do chaos and noise. It's a world view that believes in both a totally deterministic explanation of the brain and undetermined individuals.

To some researchers a neural network is a tool to explore how these two seeming contraries can be true. These researchers want to use network models to explore the dynamics of the brain. To others, neural networks are principally a way to build a different kind of computer. One group seeks to unlock the secrets of the brain, the other to use what we know so far to create an unprecedented kind of machine intelligence. Both groups, though, are revising our definition of what it means to be intelligent — and suggesting a new history of how we became what we are.

2
CREATION MYTHS

Prediction is very difficult, especially about the future.
— NIELS BOHR

Gingerly Bernard Widrow lifts the thirty-year-old machine onto his desk. His office has the dusty feel of a museum, and the slight, graying, soft-spoken Widrow seems both curator and, like the machine, exhibit. In the 1960s Widrow built this machine, one of the first neuronlike computers. In the 1970s he abandoned the field. He renamed his work adaptive signal processing and discouraged students who wanted to write dissertations in the field, fearing that their work would never win departmental approval.

In January 1990, however, when Widrow carries this box onstage at a meeting of the International Neural Network Society, 2,000 researchers, corporate managers, and government officials watch as he flips those aging toggles. To the graduate students, assistant professors, and young engineers in the audience Widrow is a founding father. His machine, the Adaline (an acronym for ADAptive LInear NEuron) still works; the neurons inside the toaster-size box are still capable of learning. Like Widrow, the Adaline has survived to become history.

Carlos Tapang is a member of that audience. His is one of those young faces shining with confidence. He is going to make his own history — with his own machine — and he will be the hero of that story.

The dust hasn't yet had a chance to settle on Tapang's dreams — they are simply far too new. In 1990 his venture, Syntonic Systems, is a homey company, a ranch house in a suburban development west of Portland, Oregon, to be precise. Tapang takes orders for his chip from his kitchen table. In the living room one of his two children watches the Smurfs on TV. A large stuffed Big Bird propped against the wall peers over Tapang's shoulder. Syntonic Systems designs and assembles its products in Tapang's garage. Standard-issue gray room dividers separate his PC-based design system and testing equipment from bikes, grills, and a lawnmower. Corporate security is a Sears garage door opener.

Tapang's life is written in the future tense. His sales literature calls the Dendros I the world's first commercially available neural network chip. Dendros I is indeed available, but only by courtesy can it be called commercial since it would be hard to find a practical use for it in its current form. But just wait, Tapang says. This is only the beginning; neural networks are the future. They are certainly Tapang's future, for better or worse. He's staked pretty much all he has on that prediction.

Widrow and Tapang stand on opposite sides of a great divide, but it isn't age that separates the two men most profoundly. If we could roll back the years and compare the young Tapang and the young Widrow, then it would be clear that changes in the world itself have created the gulf between them. The electronic computer was less than twenty years old when Widrow invented his machine. The field of artificial intelligence had barely been born. No one had yet divided it into camps and set the camps at war with each other. He never thought that if neural networks were right, other forms of artificial intelligence had to be wrong.

Tapang, on the other hand, lives in a fallen world. He believes that an artificial intelligence that uses symbols and an artificial intelligence that uses connections are competitors. He can recite the story of how the leading proponents of symbolic artificial intelligence almost killed off neural networks. He is convinced that his field is now resurgent thanks to pioneers like Widrow, John Hopfield, Terry Sejnowski, David Rumelhart, and Carver Mead. That is the tradition that he calls his own. Whether the history he and so many of his peers believe is accurate almost doesn't matter. Almost. It is the myth that fuels his long days of work and makes him believe in the inevitability of his own success. The myth says that he is riding the wave that leads to the future.

In this history 1969 was the critical year. By then Widrow had built two machines, one with a single adaptive neuron and one with multiple neurons. On the East Coast Frank Rosenblatt, working at the Cornell Aeronautical Laboratory and at Cornell University, had constructed his perceptron, a machine that, like Widrow's, seemed to learn from examples and without programming. The two machines were similar in many ways, but Rosenblatt's could be called more complex since it employed a layer of neurons and a layer of sensory units. In its simplest form, cells in an input layer, which Rosenblatt called a retina, were connected to units in an association layer. This layer was in turn connected to a third layer of response units. Signals could travel in either direction over two-way reciprocal connections. Each association-layer unit was connected to a response-layer unit, which in turn was connected back to that association-layer unit. The perceptron also enjoyed a higher profile in the computer science community than Widrow's machines, at least partially because Rosenblatt had made very strong claims about the machine's ability to solve complex problems.

In 1969 a brilliant former high school classmate of Rosenblatt's decided to take a hard look at those claims. Marvin Minsky, now sixty-four, had a long-standing interest in machine learning. For his dissertation project at Princeton University, he had built a reinforcement learning machine, and from his description of it years later, it clearly belonged to the same family as Widrow's and Rosenblatt's machines. In his book *Perceptrons*, coauthored with Seymour Papert in 1969, Minsky wrote:

> It consisted of forty electronic units interconnected by a network of links, each of which had an adjustable probability of receiving activation signals and then transmitting them to other units. It learned by means of a reinforcement process in which each positive or negative judgment about the machine's behavior was translated into a small change (of corresponding magnitude and sign) in the probabilities associated with whichever connections had recently transmitted signals. The 1950s saw many other systems that exploited simple forms of learning, and this led to a professional specialty called adaptive control.

Minsky and his MIT colleague Seymour Papert, now also sixty-four, were the first trained computer scientists to rigorously examine this kind of network computing machine. Basically, Minsky and Papert decided to look at the crucial problem of "computability," the question of how to tell if a certain kind of machine can solve a certain kind of problem. It was an old and important question in computer science and mathematical logic, and over the first half of the twentieth century, some of the greatest talents in mathematics had refined the question and devised systems for answering it. Minsky and Papert now proceeded to apply those methods to the perceptron.

The results were discouraging. They found entire classes of computational problems that perceptrons seemed by their nature unable to solve. Worse, they concluded, the great advantage of perceptron networks, that they could learn without programming, was illusory, at least when it came to solving real problems. For instance, perceptrons were often said to show emergent qualities such as generalization. Backers like Rosenblatt claimed perceptrons could learn how to create categories of similar items from larger data sets. They would place new items in the appropriate general category. Minsky and Papert agreed that

> such phenomena certainly can emerge from connectionist assemblies. The problem is that, for any body of experience, there are always many kinds of generalizations that can be made. An unprogrammed, unstructured network, like one based on the perceptron, can't possibly know what generalization to look for.

Perceptrons was enormously influential at its publication. Here was a mathematical examination of the new field by two highly respected researchers, the cofounders of what would become MIT's Artificial Intelligence Laboratory. Minsky probably knew as much about neural networks and perceptrons as anyone, and he was thoroughly versed in the methods devised by computer science for examining classes of problems and machines. Rosenblatt, Widrow, and other builders of neuronlike machines simply couldn't answer the book's objections. They couldn't refute its critique of single-layer perceptrons, and they didn't know how to build the sort of multilayer networks that they believed could solve this generalization problem. Added to the almost daily reports of new successes in symbolic artificial intelligence, *Perceptrons* made a pretty convincing argument against staking an academic career on neural networks. And in fact, for more than the next ten years very few people did.

Some neural network researchers had little difficulty in attributing a motive to Minsky and Papert's "attack," especially in the 1970s when money from the Department of Defense and corporate

America flowed to researchers who pursued the kind of artificial intelligence that Minsky, Papert, and their colleagues at MIT practiced. It became almost dogma among what remained of the neural network community — and to a great degree that belief is still shared by newer recruits to the field — that the book had been designed to kill off a competitive field and ensure adequate funding for what has come to be called symbolic artificial intelligence.

Twenty years after the event that version of the story was still so strong that Seymour Papert felt compelled to address it. "Did Minsky and I try to kill connectionism, and how do we feel now about its resurrection?" Papert wrote in 1988:

> Something more complex than a plea is needed. Yes, there was *some* hostility in the energy behind the research reported in *Perceptrons*, and there is *some* degree of annoyance at the way the new movement has developed; part of our drive came, as we quite plainly acknowledged in our book, from the fact that funding and research energy were being dissipated on what still appear to me (since the story of new, powerful network mechanisms is seriously exaggerated) to be misleading attempts to use connectionist methods in practical applications. But most of the motivation for *Perceptrons* came from more fundamental concerns, many of which cut cleanly across the divisions between networkers and programmers. [Emphasis is in the original.]

In the words of dozens of television cops and prosecutors, Papert and Minsky had the opportunity and the motive. But the purported victim had actually entered intensive care long before the suspects set pen to paper. Both Widrow's and Rosenblatt's machines were in deep trouble even before *Perceptrons*. By 1969 the wave of breakthroughs that had driven their research to this stage had clearly started to recede, leaving a beach littered with unsolved and perhaps intractable problems. Widrow, at least, recognized the change.

"I completed my doctoral dissertation in 1956," says Widrow, in a field that would now be called digital signal processing.

> I had no idea what I wanted to do, what I wanted to work on. This was at MIT. Another man in the laboratory who had an office right next to mine began to tell me that there's a thing called artificial intelligence, a whole new field. The idea was to build a machine that sort of thinks like a human brain. He told me that there was going

to be a conference at Dartmouth College. This was in the summer of 1956.

That Dartmouth conference has gained a legendary stature as the birthplace of artificial intelligence. By 1955 Allen Newell and Herbert Simon, then working at the Rand Corporation, had concluded that digital computers, at the time all of about ten years old, could use strings of zeros and ones to represent not only any number but also any features in the real world and the logical relations between them. Everything could be encoded in digital symbols, which computers could manipulate.

Seeing the new digital computers as symbol manipulators and not as just number crunchers was a huge leap. But Newell and Simon weren't finished. They also theorized that the human brain and the symbol-manipulating digital computer had a common functional description: both produced intelligent behavior by manipulating symbols of some kind using formal rules. Newell and Simon formulated this insight in what they called the physical symbol system hypothesis. "A physical symbol system has the necessary and sufficient means for general intelligent action," they wrote. "By 'necessary' we mean that any system that exhibits general intelligence will prove upon analysis to be a physical symbol system. By 'sufficient' we mean that any physical symbol system of sufficient size can be organized further to exhibit general intelligence."

At Dartmouth, Widrow was swept up in the thrill of the birth of a new science. "The creators of the field of artificial intelligence were all there. It was an open seminar. People just came and went whenever they wanted," he remembers.

> I became so enthralled with the idea of artificial intelligence that I immediately lost all interest in digital signal processing. So I came back to MIT and I spent about six months thinking about what it was all about.
>
> I couldn't give up this excitement about artificial intelligence, but my experience was in the field of digital signal processing. So I went back to the idea of a digital signal processor that would have some kind of intelligence, a digital signal processor that had the capability to learn and improve itself with experience. I was trying to get something that would be useful in an engineering context in the near term so that I would be able to remain an academic.

Widrow began working on a crucial problem in signal filters. Such filters are designed to separate the message from the noise in signals such as radio waves, telephone conversations, radar images, and TV pictures. In an everyday telephone call, for example, the speaker's voice is converted into digital signals (or in older systems into analog signals — electric currents that in their rise and fall imitate the rise and fall of the voice), ones and zeros that represent pitch, volume, and the like. But that stream of information inevitably gets contaminated by noise, spurious electrical signals from other circuits, random electromagnetic fields, and even from the components of the phone network itself. Signal filters are designed to remove this noise while keeping the signal intact.

But how does the filter know what is noise and what is a signal? The filter Widrow worked on, called a tapped-delay line, solves that problem by sampling each signal at a number of different moments as it passes down a wire, called the delay line. At any one moment the delayed signals represent the current signal, the signal of a moment ago, the signal for the moment before that, and so on. The filter is able to remove noise from the meaningful signal by comparing all these moments. Different weights on each delay tap control how much of each time-delayed signal will get recombined into the final signal. Changing those weights, and the relationship between the delayed signals, controls the response of the filter.

Unfortunately, to set those weights correctly, you pretty much have to know everything about the signal and the noise, including the way each varies over time, to begin with. Statistical analysis of a sample of the signal lets the engineer design the optimum filter. The bigger the sample, the better the analysis and the better the filter. The optimum solution, named the Wiener solution after Norbert Wiener, one of the fathers of modern information theory, requires an infinitely large sample collected over an infinite amount of time. Approximations derived from the study of a large but finite sample, however, can closely approach the Wiener solution.

But if Widrow could design a delay line that learned its own weights and adjusted its own performance over time, he could avoid that laborious statistical analysis. "The idea of an adaptive filter was that it wouldn't require a prior statistical knowledge of the inputs," he says. "It would have learning capability and would be able to adjust itself automatically." The outline of such a machine was pretty simple: it would compare the output signal, after it passed through the filter, to an ideal uncontaminated signal and then adjust the internal weights in the filter until the output and the input signals were nearly identical. Actually building the machine turned out to be less arduous than understanding how it did what it seemed to do.

"Coming out here to Stanford [in 1959] I began to work with Ted Hoff," Widrow recalls. "One fall afternoon, probably in November, it was a Friday afternoon, the two of us were up at the blackboard, going back and forth. I was explaining to him about tapped-delay lines and filters and other adaptive ways to minimize error." The system Widrow described then was cumbersome and time-consuming. To discover the Wiener solution, they first had to create a gradient, an imaginary bowl surrounded by hills. Every point along this quadratic curve represented some degree of error except the one global low point, the Wiener solution, at the bottom of the bowl. To construct the gradient, a signal was sent through the filter. An individual weight was changed, first negatively and then positively. After analysis the points were used to further map the shape of the gradient. Only when the gradient was completely specified was it possible to adjust the weights in the filter to take the signal error down to an approximation of the Wiener solution.

"All of a sudden, out of nowhere, this idea comes for getting a gradient [without measuring and plotting every point]. Just explaining it caused things to pop out and there it was sitting on the blackboard," says Widrow. They had hit upon a mathematical rule, an algorithm, that seemed to generate the Wiener solution. Mechanically applied over and over again, it could produce the minimal signal error. "We had no perception of how significant it was. It was just clear to us that we had really stumbled onto something and we just knew that it was going to work. We had an analog computer right across the hall. Within half an hour we had that algorithm working." That showed that their rule worked, that a machine could use it to arrive at an approximation of the Wiener solution. But so far it only ran on a room-size computer. Only by building a compact machine that embodied their insight could they be certain that the rule could be applied to *engineering* a filter.

"It was the end of the day on Friday and the stockroom had already closed," says Widrow. "So on Saturday, we went downtown in Palo Alto to Zack's Electronic Shop and we bought the parts so we could build an Adaline. I can't remember how much we spent. It was maybe something like $25 worth of parts. We had that working over the weekend. The next thing we did was to build a much smaller one the size and the scale of the one I have in my office."

The Adaline, the machine Widrow built, is now an electronic dinosaur. It was built without transistors, silicon chips, or circuit boards, all of which were then just dreams dancing in the heads of a few engineers. The Adaline looks like a World War II–vintage Philco radio married to a fish tank. Its array of eighteen toggle switches, sixteen dials, and one large meter clutters a panel that hides a tank holding sixteen sealed test tubes. Each test tube contains two wire leads suspended in a solution of copper and sulfuric acid.

"Let me show you how this works," Widrow says, bending down over the machine's toggle switches. In the neural network terminology of today, an Adaline is actually only one neuron with sixteen synapses. The neuron sums the electric currents that reach

The front panel of the Adaline conceals the tanks and electrodes that simulate the action of neurons and synapses. Widrow enters data by hand, flipping up the sixteen toggles in the array on the far right.
Photograph courtesy of Bernard Widrow.

it after traveling down one lead, through the acid-copper solution, and then up the other lead. Changing the balance of copper in the solution and on the leads lets Widrow adjust the machine's synaptic weights.

Adaline isn't exactly a speed whiz, but it does learn to recognize patterns. The sixteen toggle switches on the front of the machine are arranged in a 4 × 4 array. They represent a very simple mechanical retina. Each toggle that is turned to the on position represents a plus point in the pattern that the machine is trying to learn. If the pattern to be recognized were, say, the letter *T* centered in the array, three of the four toggles in the top row might be turned on to represent to the crossbar of the letter, and so would a descending row of four toggles to make up the stem.

Widrow puts in a *T* pattern, flicking toggles up for the arms of the *T* and its body and leaving the other switches down. They represent minus points. "We'll make that [entire pattern] plus." Widrow reaches over to another toggle and flicks it up to tell the machine that the desired output from adding all the points in this entire pattern, both the plus points and the minus points, is + 1. That tells Adaline what goal it's trying to reach.

Now, one at a time, Widrow adjusts the synaptic weights until the gauge shows that the current running through the *T* toggles minus the current running through the non-*T* toggles equals + 1. Each adjustment changes the balance between the copper and the

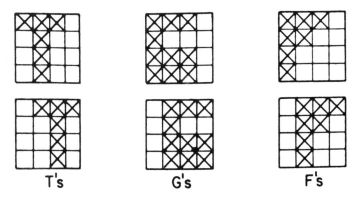

The Adaline must learn that all *T*s are the same and that they are different from *G*s and *F*s. Widrow flips a toggle on for each box with an X.
Drawing courtesy of Bernard Widrow.

acid in the solution in one of the tanks. By changing that balance
in the tanks connected to the minus toggles, he can decrease the
"negative" current they supply to the neuron that sums all the currents. Changing the balance in other tanks lets him increase the
"positive" currents. Widrow is looking for some combination of
positive and negative currents from all sixteen points that will add
up to $+1$, the value he has told the machine will represent T.

When that's complete, he moves on to J. "We'll make J
minus." He goes through the same tuning sequence until the gauge
shows that the balance in the tanks has been changed so that the
currents add up to -1. Theoretically now, any T, not just the
one centered in the array that Widrow initially entered, will
produce $+1$ and any J will produce -1. In calling all Ts $+1$
and all Js -1, the machine demonstrates a simple kind of
generalization.

However, the machine now has two patterns, and getting the
J right has probably interfered with the balances that initially
produced the right answer for T. Flicking back and forth between
the two patterns, Widrow adjusts synaptic weight after synaptic
weight, always getting the two patterns closer to the desired $+1$
and -1 on the gauge. "When you're teaching something new, you
sort of disturb what's already there. You have to recalibrate."

The process is tedious, and the result seems trivial, but when
first devised it set off a rush of creativity in Widrow. Soon to
come were ground-breaking theories, including the still essential
Widrow-Hoff rule, that established basic procedures for solving
problems on this kind of machine. And then Widrow set to work
on building a machine with more than one neuron.

The theories were essential and far more important in retrospect than the Adaline itself. Even though this is a simple machine,
it still wasn't easy to figure out exactly how it worked. For example,
at first the machine would learn quickly from relatively few examples, but gradually the pace would slow. As far as Widrow could
tell, it might even be impossible for the Adaline to learn the one
best answer.

Widrow knew this was a critical problem. A computer that
never reached an answer near the Weiner solution was at best a
very large paperweight. And how would you know you had presented enough examples and done enough adjusting to bring the
machine to an answer close to the Weiner solution? The results

from trial and error weren't comforting. Say Widrow gave the machine six patterns to learn, two *T*s, two *G*s, and two *F*s. The two patterns in each category, the two *G*s, for instance, differed only in their position — one was just slightly to the left of the other. The machine's job was to recognize both *G*s as the same letter, but also recognize that they were different from the *F*s and the *T*s. And then learn the same task with the other two letter pairs.

As far as Widrow could tell, fifty presentations of each pattern reduced the error to a minimum close to but still above zero. Adding another fifty presentations didn't seem to reduce the error at all. From his work with filters and their gradients, Widrow thought he understood what was happening. As the Adaline approached the bottom of the gradient, the point that represented the Weiner solution, it had a tendency to miss the absolute bottom and ride slightly up one side or the other after every adjustment of the weights. "Instead of going to the bottom of the bowl, what you do is jiggle around it in the form of an oscillating motion. Even if you do get to the bottom of the bowl, where the gradient is truly zero, when you measure it, the measurement doesn't come out zero because of noise. So it tells you to go somewhere else. So you never stay at the bottom of the bowl." Widrow could train the Adaline all day, all week, all year, and he would still never produce a result that was clearly the one best answer.

What he needed was a formula that told him roughly how many times he should present his patterns before he would get an acceptably small error. One way to calculate an estimate of the distance from the ideal Weiner solution turns out to be to divide the number of training patterns by the number of weights. Making the number of training patterns equal to ten times the number of weights, for example, reduces the error to just 10 percent. "I've found from experience that that's a good number," says Widrow, "but we don't have a theory, even today, that really explains why."

Other researchers were reporting equally intriguing results and building machines with their own promise. Rosenblatt published a description of his machine just months before Widrow and Hoff. The two machines embody very similar ideas in very different hardware. In the Adaline a human being sets switches to input information. In the perceptron photoreceptive cells "see" the information. In the Adaline the answer is read off a series of dials by a human. In the perceptron the results are registered by a response layer. The hearts of both machines are extremely similar: a unit that sums the electrical currents it receives and learns to produce the right answer as the strengths of individual currents are adjusted by changes in some form of weight mechanism that can increase or decrease the current flowing through an individual connection.

Rosenblatt is certainly a major character in the early history of neural networks, but it's hard to avoid cloaking him in cliché — the romantic victim of the attack on the perceptron. His death in a mysterious boating accident on the Chesapeake Bay in July 1971 — the boat was found floating empty — just adds to the aura.

Rosenblatt's writings make an interesting contrast to those of Widrow and Hoff and to Widrow's recollections. As similar as their machines were, Rosenblatt and Widrow reached their goals by totally different paths, paths that still represent divergent approaches to neural networks. Rosenblatt drew inspiration from biology. He was looking for mechanisms to connect psychology to the neuronal structure of the brain. Widrow was inspired by artificial intelligence and its emphasis on adaptive learning. His articles with Hoff are for an audience of engineers and solidly within the engineering tradition of their time.

Rosenblatt brought his training as a psychologist and an interest in the biology of the brain to the perceptron. He didn't believe that the brain computed logical functions. Instead, it was a learning associator that discovered from experience how to connect a stimulus from the outside world to other similar stimuli. The brain and the perceptron were designed to create categories.

Rosenblatt's psychological approach may explain why it was the perceptron that Minsky and Papert chose to analyze. Rosenblatt's training led him to make claims for the perceptron that Widrow didn't attach to his machine. Along with Rosenblatt, Minsky and Papert saw in perceptrons something the engineers didn't see. The two MIT researchers, in fact, took Rosenblatt's psychological claims seriously. Perceptrons, they wrote, *are* a new method for finding order in data and a possible underlying explanation for psychology, but, they concluded, that method and that explanation are wrong.

The engineers, Widrow's audience, were also critics, but mostly on pragmatic grounds. The bulk of Widrow's peers saw his work as just one method among many competitors for solving problems in pattern recognition. And in that competition the lack of mathematical proofs of what happened inside the machines was devastating. "There would be a conference on pattern recognition, but there were fifty different ways of doing pattern recognition," says Widrow. "You had these two screwballs, Rosenblatt and Widrow, who wanted to talk about learning techniques. Other people had other ways. And they would say, 'You can't prove anything. You can't prove it's phase optimal.' It's not this and it's not that. It was just really tough. You couldn't prove what it was doing. You didn't know what it was doing. You didn't have enough experience and knowledge." What Widrow and Rosenblatt had, for all intents and purposes, were black boxes that produced startling results for for some data and couldn't handle other input at all. And no one could tell when they would succeed and when they would fail, or why.

But if the engineers saw neural networks as just one more way to solve problems in pattern recognition, Minsky and Papert didn't. To them neural networks weren't just another set of tools. In its basic assumptions about the nature of intelligence and its questioning of the analogy between biological and machine computation, neural network technology was a challenge to the very basis of their field, to the edifice of mathematical logic that gave meaning to the universe of symbolic artificial intelligence.

Minsky and Papert weren't troubled by the claim that perceptrons could learn to improve their performance. A perfectly legitimate field of engineering, adaptive control, built machines that learned. Nor were they troubled by the possibility that these simple machines could compute some functions. What did trouble them was the claim that these machines didn't need any programming or structure. Perceptrons, it was said, could begin without structure and by observing the world not only learn how to structure themselves, but somehow divine the principles that structured the world. Worse yet, if you took apart a functioning neural network, you wouldn't be able to find any rules. These machines, their proponents claimed, could produce true statements about the world without any rules, without any knowledge of the rules, without any of the basic laws of logic. That was simply not possible. One hundred years of logic, philosophy, and mathematics said it wasn't.

Around the turn of the century it had seemed possible to

mathematicians and philosophers such as Alfred North Whitehead, Bertrand Russell, and Gottlob Frege to develop a completely formal foundation for mathematics and then to erect a completely formal, logical system on this base. Such a system would escape the devils that had tortured Western philosophers such as Locke and Kant. If all our knowledge of the external world came through our senses, how could we claim to "know" anything? The British empiricist tradition culminated in philosophers like Hume who claimed that all we could know were sensory impressions, which were often the basis for false conclusions about the world. Kant had held out for our ability to truly know the world, but that had required him to postulate certain innate truths. A completely formal logic could exclude questions like these and appeals to those external sources of our knowledge as the basis for proofs about mathematical truths. It could escape the seemingly endless philosophical arguments about the source of truth and the relation of perceived categories to mental forms. Whitehead and Russell's *Principia Mathematica* (1910–1913) is one great monument to this formal, symbolic logic. The electronic computer is another.

But work by Kurt Gödel, supplemented by papers from Alan Turing, Emil Post, and Alonzo Church, showed that the quest for complete formal closure was doomed. In 1931 Gödel, then just twenty-five, proved, in his incompleteness theorem and its corollary on consistency, that any formal system equivalent to that of Whitehead and Russell must, *of necessity*, be incomplete. Gödel showed that there must be undecidable propositions in any such system that cannot be proved or refuted using any of the system's rules. His corollary states that consistency itself is one of those undecidable propositions.

Turing confirmed Gödel's theorem, but he also showed that while a completely formal system was impossible, specific formal systems could be remarkably powerful and expressive. Turing, Post, and Church independently developed specific formal systems that were complete in that, while they could not prove or disprove all propositions, they could formally prove all theorems that were provable within that system. Turing's formal structure, called the Universal Turing Machine, manipulated the symbols of logic in the form of ones and zeros on a strip of paper. Using just those ones and zeros, and enough tape, Turing's machine could express any theorem produced in any logical system. The exact content of these tokens of logic didn't matter, certainly not to the machine. Nor did the context in which they occurred or the original nature of the formal system the machine was duplicating. No matter how that original formal system expressed its logical proofs and theorems, Turing's machine could find a way to simulate it in ones and zeros. In that sense, Turing's machine was universal, a chameleon that could transform its raw materials of ones and zeros into any formal system.

Much of modern computer science and many of our analogies for thinking about the brain fall out of that simple formulation. Already implicit in Turing's machine is the modern computer's definition of a program, which distinguishes operations — formal manipulations of symbols — from the symbols that correspond to real quantities. For a deterministic machine to calculate any function, for example, there must be content tokens — say, the integers 5 and 6 — and operation tokens — say "add."

Also implicit in Turing's machine are the modern computer's division between hardware and software, and the emphasis on changing software programs rather than hardware circuits to address different problems. The Turing machine is also already serial, operating one step at a time, and recursive. This recursive principle, that any big problem logically consists of a series of smaller problems, each of which may itself consist of another series of smaller problems until some final kernel is reached, lies at the heart of symbolic processing and the way artificial intelligence languages are structured. Until challenged by biological constraints, such as evidence that the brain could use no more than one hundred steps to perform a wide range of basic cognitive functions like object recognition, it also was a dominant model of how the biological brain worked.

Turing's machine is to a degree an idealization that assumes the availability of an infinitely long tape of instructions and infinite time. Duplicating some logical functions in ones and zeros may simply take too long to be practically useful. But that is a question of utility and not of capability. What Turing guaranteed was that given enough time, any specific Turing machine can duplicate the behavior of any other Turing machine. Any individual Turing machine is thus a universal computer capable of proving anything that could be formally proved in the formal system it mimicked.

In *Perceptrons* Minsky and Papert applied this framework to the perceptron. Is it a universal computer? they asked. No, they concluded. They showed, for example, that perceptrons are limited by the size of their input arrays and by the resolution of those arrays. The reliance of perceptrons on arrays with a finite number of input points renders them unable to compute global functions, such as completeness or connectedness. How can a bounded array tell if a figure is complete outside that array or connected off the array? But Minsky and Papert also confirmed parts of Rosenblatt's work, offering multiple proofs for his perceptron convergence theorem, a crucial underpinning since it proved that the network would eventually converge on an answer.

But the perceptron had a central flaw, *Perceptrons* implied. No computational system could simply look at the world and discover truth statements. Where was this machine's foundation in logic? How could we be certain that anything it computed would be true? What Minsky and Papert demanded was not just a machine that solved problems but a proof, as rigorous as that provided by decades of work in symbolic logic, that the methods followed by such a machine would yield statements that were provably true. Symbolic logic may not be perfect, they implied, but what did the perceptron offer besides a machine that sometimes solved certain kinds of problems?

Widrow and Rosenblatt didn't have much to say in rebuttal. They had just begun to discover some of the basic computational principles of their machines. Those principles indicated that more powerful machines that could answer some of Minsky and Papert's objections were possible. Unfortunately, they also suggested that the necessary machines would be impossible to build.

From trial and error Widrow knew that the Adaline was a very limited device. It could only distinguish accurately between patterns that were linearly separable, that is, patterns that had no points in common. Mathematically, the Adaline creates a hypercube, an imaginary multidimensional space. Its weights create a hyperplane, a multidimensional plane that divides this hypercube. Tuning the weights, learning, moves this hyperplane until it separates the vertices of the hypercube in a way that represents a correct categorization. A single Adaline, it was clear to Widrow, could not construct a hyperplane to separate categories if they contained overlapping elements. Rosenblatt's perceptron had a similar problem.

Completely independently, Rosenblatt and Widrow struggled to break through the limitations of the Adaline and the perceptron. Adding more synapses and weights increased the complexity of the hypercube, but it didn't address the separability problem. Building layered networks of perceptrons and Adalines promised that it would. It should be possible to train one network to create categories and then feed those patterns into another network that would discriminate among those categories by mapping them into a new hypercube. But was there a way to adjust two sets of interdependent weights? Simply adjusting the Adaline for a T and a J was time-consuming enough. Neither Widrow nor Rosenblatt had a mathematical tool to predict how much adjustment was enough or how many layers were necessary for a specific kind of problem.

Widrow tried to build such a machine, but he couldn't figure out how to adjust all the layers. "What we had in the early days," he says, "was an adaptive layer that fed into a fixed layer. We were able to adapt [that first layer] because we knew what was in the fixed layer. But if you allowed that second layer, the output layer, to be adaptive, then we wouldn't know what was in there and we couldn't adapt the first layer because we didn't know what was in the second layer." If the answer was wrong, what weights should be changed? What synapses should be strengthened? The problem became known as the credit problem — what unit was to get credit for an error or a correct answer? Random changes were as likely to set the system off in the wrong direction as in the direction that led to the right answer.

Mathematically, multilayer systems were completely intractable. There wasn't any way to prove that such a network would ever converge on an answer or to determine how long it would take. Minsky and Papert had issued a challenge that neural networks couldn't meet.

So why, twenty years later, has Carlos Tapang so confidently bet his future on this science?

Many, perhaps all, of Minsky and Papert's criticisms of perceptrons still apply to Tapang's Dendros machine. His mathematical understanding of his own network isn't that much more complex than Widrow's understanding of the Adaline. The learning rule he uses to teach his machine is indeed just an extension of Widrow's method for setting weights, although that extension does let neural network builders put together multiple-layer networks. But the field still can't predict an optimum number of neurons for each layer or how they should be connected to most efficiently solve a specific kind of problem. Tapang's choice of an architecture called ART I, a pattern for connecting the neurons developed by Boston University's Stephen Grossberg, is indeed mostly an intuitive one.

And Tapang's description of what goes into Dendros seems an example of the kind of wishful thinking that made Minsky and Papert shudder. According to his sales literature, "As data from the external world are presented to the input layer in the form of bilevel (or binary) signals, the categorizer layer automatically categorizes such input." That neatly sidesteps the issues of how that input will be processed, what codes should be used, and how to construct a linearly separable data set, as well as other of the issues that Minsky and Papert used to hang the early perceptron. In 1988, when they surveyed the neural network field in preparation for the revised edition of *Perceptrons*, they concluded that nothing had changed.

How then to reconcile that conclusion with the indisputable fact that by the end of the eighties neural networks had become the darling of a generation of graduate students, of corporate America, and of the Department of Defense?

The standard, everyone-agrees-on-it version of neural network history concludes that breakthroughs in the technology occurred and that Minsky and Papert were biased observers in 1969 and still are. Those breakthroughs began in the early 1980s — after the ten years of darkness.

According to this version, it was up to an unlikely hero to revive the field. Beginning in 1982 California Institute of Technology physicist John Hopfield, in collaboration with David Tank of AT&T, proved that a network of neurons could work as an associative memory. Borrowing the mathematics designed to predict the behavior of a very peculiar state of matter called a spin glass, Hopfield proved that certain kinds of networks could compute the answer to optimization problems, such as the shortest route among twenty-five cities or how to assign tasks among workers with different skills.

Meanwhile, progress in symbolic artificial intelligence had slowed, this story points out. Expert systems — artificial intelligence programs that simulate how a human expert reasons when solving a problem in automobile repair or mortgage lending —

had achieved some proficiency, but seemingly simpler cognitive tasks such as vision or speech recognition were turning out to be much more complex than originally thought. This approach to artificial intelligence couldn't discover what symbols human beings used to recognize objects or understand speech.

There are some major problems with the popular history. For one thing, Hopfield's work doesn't answer Minsky and Papert's criticisms. He added sophisticated mathematics from spin glass theory, but there is absolutely no connection between that theory — written to explain the magnetic field properties of a peculiar class of solids — and computation or the brain. In fact, the systems Hopfield and Tank first built are very carefully limited exceptions; if the connections aren't completely symmetrical, the network will produce meaningless oscillations. This is hardly a firm theoretical foundation for a new school of computation.

Nor is the "failure" of symbolic artificial intelligence much to the advantage of neural networks. Symbolic artificial intelligence solved real problems in 1982 — something that couldn't then be said for neural networks. And in 1982 neural networks didn't do much better than symbolic systems at the tough cognitive tasks. To this point the standard history can't explain the rise of neural networks. But wait, it says, there were other breakthroughs as well.

In the mid- to late 1980s, the tale goes, neural network researchers finally blasted through the major constraint in their own field. Virtually simultaneously, in 1985 and 1986, three researchers discovered an algorithm, a learning rule called backpropagation, that could efficiently train multilayer neural networks. The new machines used extra layers of neurons to perform exactly those operations that Minsky and Papert had claimed perceptrons would never perform. In the hands of researchers like David Rumelhart, one of its discoverers, backpropagation led to an explosion of neural network machines that could, their builders claimed, learn grammar, learn to read, and learn to recognize objects. In 1988 DARPA, the same Department of Defense agency that had blessed symbolic artificial intelligence a decade before, drew up plans to invest $400 million in neural network research. The king was dead. Long live the king!

But the coronation seemed a bit premature. Backpropagation certainly worked, but it was so slow — and absolutely nonbiological to boot — that it still remained unclear whether machines that used that learning rule could be scaled up to handle real problems. And the field still had no theory for figuring out even the ideal number of neurons in a network, let alone a way of predicting how the numbers in each layer affect the way a network operates.

No, if the battleground between symbolic artificial intelligence and neural networks had remained the one chosen by Minsky and Papert, the contest would be just about as lopsided in 1986 or even 1988 as it was in 1969 — if either side had even seen fit to resume it. Yet today neural networks are hot. They have attracted real money, talent, and thousands of lines of press coverage. The facts demonstrate the revival of the field.

The revival, contrary to the version of history recapped above, seems totally attributable to a shift in battlefields. It doesn't matter that Minsky and Papert haven't been vanquished on the field they chose in 1969. That ground seems increasingly irrelevant, and so does the standard history, which almost totally neglects the likely causes of the neural network rebirth.

First, the now general availability of powerful computer workstations within the scientific community has made it possible to build computer models to substitute for the lack of mathematical theory in neural networks. Widrow had only three alternatives for proving that his neural network worked. He could build it in hardware, which was expensive in time and money and extremely frustrating: if it didn't work, was the problem in the theory or in the engineering? He could hope to tie up the university's only mainframe for a month. Or he could demonstrate it mathematically on paper.

Today any graduate student can simulate a network on a workstation. Walk into a dozen labs at the California Institute of Technology, Stanford, Berkeley, Carnegie-Mellon, MIT, Brown, and Harvard, and you can look at working examples of neural networks solving problems in vision, speech, movement, and other areas. Maybe no one can mathematically demonstrate that any of these networks are optimal solutions, but trial and error is immensely easier and quicker now than in Widrow's day.

Second, neurobiology has come down heavily on the side of neural networks. The brain is the proof that these networks work and that they can be immensely powerful. In Widrow and Rosenblatt's day, the biological underpinning of neural networks was thin indeed, little more than Donald Hebb's 1949 guess (actually an aside in a book about psychology) that the brain learned by modifying the connections between synapses. Results from physiology had shown the existence of complicated neuronal structures and patterns of connection that were obviously intended for something, but no one could demonstrate what. Lesion studies showed that cognitive processes were degraded when the brain was injured in ways that implied a parallel network structure for the brain rather than something akin to the serial central processor structure of the traditional computer. But no one had yet been able to watch a single neuron respond to a specific outside stimulus.

Single-needle studies and techniques that allowed the voltage clamping of individual cells changed all that. In the late 1950s David Hubel and Torsten Wiesel began to apply those techniques to reveal the amazing specificity of neuronal response to shape, intensity, and direction of movement in the eyes of cats and monkeys. By the 1980s single-needle research had started to lay out computational relationships between layers of cells in the brain. The architecture it revealed had little resemblance to that of the serial von Neumann computer. As research showed more and more clearly that the brain really was a network, the brain's structure became a proof that neural networks worked and a glimmering hope that they could solve problems intractable to artificial intelligence. And in the 1980s researchers at several laboratories demonstrated the existence of Hebb's synapse.

Third, even the other tradition — the symbolic tradition — in artificial intelligence had a role to play. As purely symbolic artificial intelligence discovered the need for schemata and frames to create a way for a computer to choose a set of rules appropriate to a specific situation, an alternative emphasis developed within the field. One school, what Herbert Simon calls the reasoning approach, continued to view thinking as a process of logical inference. The other school — Simon labels it search — views thinking as a process of searching among possible problem solutions. This school emphasized building representations that modeled the problem situation and finding efficient strategies for searching among possible solutions. It found support in biology, which had started to show that the brain solved some search problems by building neuronal maps of the external world.

Computation, at least as the brain might do it and as heuristic search wanted to do it, seemed a very different thing than the manipulation of symbols inside closed formal systems. Ambiguity and uncertainty, and approximate matches, appeared to be the stuff of the brain's work. Gödel's theorem may have revealed the impossibility of constructing a formally closed logical system, but there is no evidence that the brain was ever engaged in this endeavor. The brain may, in fact, fall back on an appeal to the world — to something obviously outside the formal system — when it gets stuck in ambiguity. A problem like deciding whether a perceived object is one or many, for example, seems to tie the brain in knots at times. It works its way out not through computation but by a pragmatic shortcut. A particular computationally ambiguous thing is a connected object, the brain sometimes appears to reason, because most objects in the world are connected.

As this other school has grown within the traditional artificial intelligence community, symbolic artificial intelligence and neural networks now seem to have at least the possibility of common ground. Minsky's recent work on what he calls a society of mind is not totally consistent with some neural network research, but his networks-of-agents theory has a flavor that a neural network researcher would recognize.

The first history, the traditional one with heroes and villains and breakthroughs, isn't unimportant, whatever its drawbacks as an explanatory device. That is the history that has turned neural networks research into a field distinct from other branches of computer science. And it is the upward trajectory of that narrative that encourages people like Carlos Tapang to put everything in their lives at risk.

Listen to Tapang talk about creating his machine and you can hear the power of that narrative history. While employed at Intel developing software, Tapang read an article by Hopfield. "I think that was my first exposure to neural networks," he says. Hopfield's article described a network that acted like an associative memory. It could use data that represented only part of a memory to find the complete memory.

In his reading he had also come across another kind of network, a Boltzmann machine. "A Boltzmann machine is basically just like a Hopfield network except that it has a learning capability. So that was my first project." In 1986, working at night in his garage, Tapang built a Boltzmann machine using readily available parts.

A Boltzmann machine is a neural network pattern matcher.

Named after the late-nineteenth-century Austrian physicist Ludwig Boltzmann, who studied the speed with which a gas diffuses, it mimics one of the essential principles of the universe, entropy, the tendency of all physical systems to seek their lowest energy state. A concentrated gas, for example, will always diffuse to fill the available space, lowering its energy state in the process. Presented with a part of a pattern that it has seen before, by trial and error the Boltzmann machine tries to relax into the lowest energy state possible, which represents the complete memory.

But Tapang quickly experienced the problems that had haunted all Boltzmann designs to date. The machine had a tendency to generate false memories, to produce patterns that were related to the correct answer but distorted it. His Boltzmann neural network "was retaining what it had learned, but, you know, it wasn't stable. You would present it with a pattern, okay, and it could stabilize in either of two states, the correct state or a complementary state. Let's say your pattern is 101101. It could stabilize as that or as 010010, the complement."

So Tapang put his Boltzmann machine aside — today it gathers dust next to his skis above the rafters in his garage — and went back to the drawing board. First, he enrolled in a course at the Oregon Graduate Center taught by Dan Hammerstrom. Hammerstrom has since founded his own neural network company, Adaptive Solutions, Inc. The course text was a photocopy of what was soon to be Carver Mead's book on designing neural networks. Tapang finished Dendros I, the first half of his neural network, in June 1988. Dendros II, the rest of the network, soon followed. By this time Tapang had completely succumbed to the neural bug. He quit his job at Intel and began working on Syntronic Systems full-time.

The dream has possessed him. He knows he can build a completely new kind of computer if only he can get the money. He figures he needs just $1.2 million to develop a more sophisticated network with larger commercial prospects. Japanese money materialized in late 1989. A small Japanese engineering house brokered a deal with a larger Japanese smokestack company after talks had dragged out for more than a year. (Tapang believed he was about three months away from a product that would read handwritten characters as this book went to press.)

"I like excitement," Tapang laughs, but he knows he has

taken a tremendous leap, the biggest yet in a path that has brought him from Mindanao to a suburban Oregon housing development. "Yes, it's a big step, and it's even a bigger step for me considering that I've been here in the U.S. only since August 1983. I don't worry because if this thing doesn't fly, I can always look for a job. I don't worry about that. My wife worried at first." Tapang stops for a moment, as if to consider how much he wants to admit, and then adds, "But I think now she's seeing that it's not really crazy after all."

3
THE RULES
OF THE BRAIN

Our goal is to replace the computer metaphor with the brain metaphor.

— DAVID RUMELHART

The importance of categorization is very clear: most of human cognition depends on it. We cannot fully understand perception, memory, problem solving, learning, language, or induction without understanding categorization. But the converse possibility is daunting: perhaps we cannot fully understand categorization without understanding all of human cognition.

— ELLEN MARKMAN, *Categorization and Naming in Children*

Physically imposing, with a long scraggly beard on its way to gray and a disconcertingly direct stare, David Rumelhart looks — and sounds — like an Old Testament prophet. As much as he tries to soften his opinions with phrases like "I believe" or "in a sense," his sentences still have the resonance of truth carried from the mountaintop. It's not that Rumelhart wants to antagonize other scientists. It's just that having seen the truth, how can he not speak it? Pressed, he will reluctantly admit that neither modern linguistics nor cognitive psychology has been a complete waste of time, but still, he says with the urgency of the converted, how can anyone not see that those disciplines are hopelessly confused about what causes behavior and about how to explain it? For the last decade, Rumelhart has been building a model of how the mind works that challenges many of the assumptions at the core of those fields.

Rumelhart and a gaggle of other Young Turks, calling themselves the Parallel Distributed Processing Group, publicly launched their assault on orthodoxy in 1986. Six years earlier chance had brought a number of very smart but very junior academics together in San Diego. The catalyst seems to have been the arrival of Geoffrey Hinton at the University of California at San Diego at a crucial moment in a number of different careers.

James McClelland, a psychologist now at Carnegie-Mellon, had started to pursue neural network models in his own work on the psychology of perception. Drawing on the work of researchers like James Anderson of Brown University, McClelland had begun to build computer models that tried to explain perception and its psychology as the result of many neurons working together in a connected network. "At the same time David Rumelhart had become disenchanted with conventional artificial intelligence techniques. He was not getting things to work," says McClelland. A mathematical psychologist, Rumelhart, too, had begun to look at ways in which the interaction of many simple processors like the brain's neurons could produce observed psychological behaviors. Then Hinton applied for a postdoctoral fellowship at the University of California at San Diego, having just completed a dissertation at the University of Edinburgh on exactly this kind of network.

"Dave and I had this conversation," McClelland remembers. "Dave said: 'Well, look, let's do a book about this stuff, and let's start a group to do a book.' So we went back and invited a group of people to join in." Hinton, now at the University of Toronto, was a key member. So was Paul Smolensky, a physicist now at the University of Colorado. "We had this idea that we'd write the book in six months." McClelland grins. "It took four years."

The group in San Diego was not the first or only one working on this new science. In 1979 a meeting sponsored by the Sloan Foundation had resulted in a collection of papers edited by James Anderson and Hinton called *Parallel Models of Associative Memory*. Every summer between 1980 and 1986 another group, including Hinton, Terry Sejnowski, then of Johns Hopkins University, and Jerome Feldman, then at the University of Rochester, gathered to work on these topics. Sejnowski also checked in with the San Diego group during his annual visits with Francis Crick at the Salk Institute in La Jolla, just north of San Diego.

The San Diego group's book, *Parallel Distributed Processing:*

Explorations in the Microstructure of Cognition, finally appeared in 1986. Today it still feels like a manifesto of belief from a revolutionary cell awkwardly named the PDP Group — certainly not an easy moniker to spray-paint in the halls of respectable academic departments. Like any new revolutionary label, this one papered over a multitude of agendas and beliefs. While sharing a conviction that the macroprocesses of the brain, such as logical thought, perception, and the like, were best explained by looking at the interconnections of hundreds, thousands, or millions of neurons somehow working together, the members of the PDP Group differed deeply over what that explanation should contain. For example, Crick, winner of the Nobel Prize for his part in deciphering the structure of DNA and a latecomer to the group, urged more biological realism than some group members thought was important. "Once Crick started to come, that changed the tenor of the meetings. There was a lot of argument back and forth," says McClelland. "You know, what's the relationship [between connectionism and neurobiology] and what's the analogy?"

Sorting out the exact differences among the members of the PDP Group in 1986 isn't especially fruitful at this date, but this is a good point at which to clear up some confusing terminology. The San Diego group called their work "parallel distributed processing." Anderson and Hinton had titled the work described in their book "associative memories." Feldman coined the term "connectionism." And then there's "neural network," the term that has received the most general use.

"Connectionism," "parallel distributed processing," and "neural network" are all descriptive terms on roughly the same level. They all refer to a general approach to computation that relies on some analogy to the biological system of neurons and synapses. "Connectionism" and "neural network" have come to be virtually synonymous in many circles. Some scientists, especially those with a background in computer science, prefer "connectionism" because it emphasizes the computational method — that computation results from the way nodes are connected — while deemphasizing the biological analogy with neurons. Those from biology generally prefer "neural network" because it emphasizes the biological analogy. Often they are interested in building model networks that examine the biological properties of the brain.

By and large, the term "parallel distributed processing" has fallen out of use, except when it refers to the work of the PDP Group in the early 1980s. Part of the reason for the term's decline is that it is readily confused with "parallelism" or "massive parallelism," an approach to computation that involves dividing a problem among multiple processors in a single machine. "Parallelism" is currently the hottest trend among designers of high-speed conventional computers.

"Associative memory" is a descriptive term on a different level. It refers to a kind of network, one structured to perform the specific task of associating one input with another and then retrieving both inputs when just one is presented to the machine. There are many different ways to construct associative memories. They can be built with traditional digital computers, although that makes executing the task extremely time-consuming. They can also be built using various types of neural networks.

On a still more specific level of terminology, labels specify blueprints for building each type of neural network. Each architecture involves a general road map for connecting neurons and assumptions about the kind of connections that can be used. Some, for example, allow the connections between neurons to function as two-way streets. Others allow only one-way traffic. Each also uses a small repertoire of different types of neurons. Some types simply add. Others add and also use a threshold. Some neurons incorporate a more complicated mathematics by adding a squashing or a sigmoid function. Those network architectures that permit learning specify some kind of learning rule.

An algorithm is simply a rule that tells a human being or a machine how to execute an operation. Anyone who adds, multiplies, divides, or subtracts uses algorithms. In the case of addition, for example, the rules, the algorithm, tell you how to begin. First, place the two numbers to be added one above the other, with the digits — the algorithm also would tell a machine what a digit is — lined up above each other. Second, begin with all the numbers in the rightmost column. One of the most important parts of the algorithm would tell the machine what to do when the numbers in the last column added up to more than nine. It would define a process that in grade school we learned as carrying.

Algorithms can differ in their details and still be essentially the same. It doesn't really change the algorithm if it says to begin addition by putting the numbers to be added in a horizontal row separated by plus signs and ending in an equal sign rather than by placing them in columns. At the moment there are somewhat more than twenty neural network algorithms that differ in meaningful ways. They all involve sets of instructions that tell the network, whether constructed as a computer simulation or as some physical system such as a silicon chip, what weights to add and what to do to gradually move the weights toward the values that will make the network give the right answer. Backpropagation, for example, is an algorithm that tells how to set the weights in a hidden layer of neurons, one in between an input layer and an output layer, by comparing the results at the output layer with the "correct" answer. Many of these algorithms specify the rules that improve the machine's performance with experience, and they are often therefore referred to as learning algorithms.

Backpropagation, just one of the techniques explored in the PDP group's work, presented a method for solving exactly the problem that had stumped Widrow — how to allocate the weights in a multilevel network. At the time they were published, though, the theoretical discussions were cast into the shadows by the detailed descriptions of working neural network machines that claimed to perform nontrivial, computationally difficult tasks. McClelland and Jeffrey Elman proposed a model for speech perception. McClelland laid out a model for reading and with Alan Kawamoto suggested a way for a machine to understand sentences. The tour de force, however, was a description of a machine built by Rumelhart and McClelland that not only learned to form the past tense of English verbs but duplicated, they claimed, the essential details of the way children learn the past tense.

Several members of the PDP Group saw their academic careers soar after the book. Sejnowski moved from Johns Hopkins to his own laboratory at the Salk Institute, and both McClelland and Hinton taught briefly at Carnegie-Mellon before Hinton journeyed on to the University of Toronto. But it was Rumelhart who became the lightning rod. Often regarded with mixed emotions by his peers in the field, who seem to question whether anyone so good at promoting his work and gaining personal visibility (with the funding that tends to go with it in modern science) can be a good scientist at the same time, Rumelhart can't help throwing down the gauntlet to backers of alternative theories every time he opens his mouth. And Rumelhart's challenge, he makes clear, isn't a minor one. He doesn't simply believe that connectionism is a minor correction or addition to current theories in cognitive psychology. No, connectionism is the correct explanation. It supersedes the explanations of linguistics, cognitive psychology, and other sciences in the way Newton's gravity was superseded by relativity and particle physics.

"It's pretty clear, from my view at least, that the von Neumann machine was based on some image of the human mind," says Rumelhart, who moved to Stanford University as a full professor from the University of California at San Diego. "The image was something like the idea of following a set of instructions, sort of like our conscious thoughts. If we have a list of things to do, we do it. We can easily imagine ourselves being a von Neumann machine."

But what about those other processes that we're not aware of? he asks. When we look at an object and recognize it as a chair, we're not consciously aware of a sequence of reasoning or logic. When we construct a grammatical sentence in our native language, we're not consciously aware of referring to sets of rules that generate the correct sentence. According to Rumelhart, the standard assumption in cognitive psychology or artificial intelligence has been that these unconscious mental processes are just like the conscious ones, only that they go on without our conscious awareness. Maybe they are just faster, cognitive psychologists guessed, but they are still sequential, logical, and rule-based, even if we aren't conscious of the rules or even able to articulate them.

"That's the intuition that I think is wrong," he says. "I think that these processes of which we are unaware are very different than those we consciously experience at a time scale of seconds." Understanding the processes that underlie these events requires inventing a whole new language of explanation. He contends that what linguistics, logic, and cognitive psychology have called the laws of mental processes are descriptions of what the brain does, but they aren't causes. "I concede that reasoning feels like, phenomenologically it feels like, we're going through a sequential process where this follows that follows that. There's a sense of connectedness among things. But if we're really going to understand how we go from one step to the next, we have to look at the level below that because that mechanism, that parallel distributed processing mechanism, is the level at which the causality is occurring. It's the level that makes one thing follow another."

Rumelhart believes that our phenomenological sense that reasoning is sequential, logical, and rule-based is misleading. It's an easy but ultimately false step to go from saying that rules, the rules of grammar, for example, are useful descriptions of how we think, to arguing that we know these rules in some fashion and that we make use of them to speak grammatically. Some systems in linguistics and in much of traditional artificial intelligence hold that these rules are indeed the mechanisms for thought. They are explicitly stored in the brain as propositions, although in a form that precludes an easy verbal communication, and they are used to produce and comprehend language, to decode the visual world, and to generalize as well as differentiate. This view of what a rule is and the role it plays in thought is simply wrong, Rumelhart believes.

Think about this analogy with Kepler's Laws, suggests James McClelland. Kepler's three laws describe the motion of the planets around the sun. They accurately predict planetary speed and the shape of orbits. "So now, you get to ask: 'Well, how is it that the planets come to behave in accordance with Kepler's Laws?' It could be that there is a gyroscopically controlled instrument inside each planet that consults Kepler's Laws and makes sure that the trajectory of the planet remains on that path. Or it could be that an interaction of forces has as its outcome the fact that the planets follow these trajectories." In the latter case, Kepler's Laws describe the situation and the data accurately and can even be used to predict future planetary behavior. But the rules didn't cause that behavior. The causal principles lie underneath the laws, which merely approximately predict their effects.

From this perspective, then, all of logic, linguistics, cognitive psychology, and related fields have been about building rules that approximate the underlying causal processes, and not about the causal principles of the mind at all. "Philosophers, logicians, and the like, haven't been altogether wrong when they say that this follows that because of some logical principle," says Rumelhart. But "I take it that underlying all these logical processes are these parallel distributed systems, and where this causality is happening is best described at this lower level. We can get approximations to it at a more abstract level, and when it comes to logic and reasoning and things that happen rather slowly in time, then this approximation is pretty good. But when we're talking about things that happen quickly in time, then this approximation breaks down altogether."

Many practitioners of linguistics, cognitive psychology, and artificial intelligence wouldn't strongly disagree with the general form of what McClelland and Rumelhart advocate. "The initial grammarians who go out and describe a language don't pretend that they are describing the underlying cognitive structure," says Rumelhart. They are setting down rules that will enable them to describe the language. A rule that says that in German, Latin-derived nouns always take the neuter gender form "das" is descriptively true, but, Rumelhart would maintain, that rule tells us nothing about the underlying cognitive structure of a German speaker. Many linguists and psychologists from other traditions would probably feel comfortable with that statement, especially if the "nothing" were modified to "almost nothing." But the next step Rumelhart and McClelland take would probably shatter that mild consensus. The German-speaker didn't learn to speak and understand German by learning grammatical rules like this one, even unconsciously. In fact, language learning, say Rumelhart and McClelland, is not a process of rule acquisition at all. The rules describe the resulting language structure, but they have nothing to do with how the language was learned. Paradoxically, human beings don't need to learn rules to produce behavior that can be described by rules. That behavior *emerges* from the interaction of the fine structure of the brain and the potential organizing structures in the environment.

In 1985 Rumelhart and McClelland designed a machine to test this theory. As an experiment they built a computer simulation of a simple connectionist machine, a neural network, with just input and output layers of neurons. Then they put it to work solving a particularly thorny question: how do children learn a language? Specifically, they wanted to see if the machine could learn how to make the proper forms of the past tense for English verbs from the stem forms. McClelland and Rumelhart gave the machine pairs of verb forms. During learning the researchers compared the machine-generated past tense forms with the correct forms. No changes were made in the strengths of the connections between neurons if the answers were correct. Incorrect answers led to adjustments. The machine wasn't given any rules, however, and it was never programmed with any general principles. It was never told, as a schoolchild might be in second grade, to form the past tense of regular verbs by adding "ed." Lacking any rules, would the machine be able to use what it had learned from examples it had seen to correctly form the past tense for verbs it had never encountered before?

Rumelhart and McClelland thrust their poor machine, unaccompanied, into a linguistic minefield scarred by thirty years of trench warfare. Beginning in the late 1950s Noam Chomsky had used linguistics to challenge the prevailing behaviorist consensus that dominated psychology. B. F. Skinner and other behaviorists had proposed a very simple model of human psychology. According to the behaviorists, psychological processes, including language, were essentially the product of a few basic laws of learning that produced gradual changes in observable behavior. All of the seemingly complex structure of language was really just the result of association, conditioning, and the like. Behaviorism, in fact, wasn't much interested in building or explaining a mental system for language.

In challenge, Chomsky pointed to the way that children actually acquire language. They learn languages with complicated sets of rules called grammars, without either explicit instruction or obvious cues about the nature of those grammars. Children are somehow able to use never-before-encountered words correctly. They seem to create mental classes and rules that generate new language structures. There is simply no way the behaviorists' theory of learning could produce those structures. Association and conditioning seemed inadequate to this kind of learning.

The debate was not just about the nature of language but also about the nature of the mind and the brain. The behaviorists had consciously decided not to pay attention to internal mental states. To the degree they thought about the brain at all, they saw it as an unstructured biological organ that interacted with the world using a few general principles that were the same no matter what the domain of the interaction, be it vision, speech, motion, or whatever. Chomsky argued that domain mattered. Cognition wasn't one uniform process, and to understand it a scientist had to master the specific rules that governed each domain.

Chomsky effectively demonstrated that behaviorist theories of learning couldn't lead to the languages that really existed in the world, but his refutation still didn't explain how these complex linguistic structures came to be. How did children learn the complicated rules that seemed to govern language? Actual observations of children learning a language have driven more than one learning theorist to conclude that learning is impossible. Children don't seem to receive enough information from the adult speakers around them to learn to avoid speaking ungrammatically. Observation quickly shows that many of our commonsense theories about language learning are wrong. For example, explicit parental correction may make parents feel good, but they supply it far too infrequently and inconsistently for it to be the crucial method of language acquisition. A child would be hard put to know exactly what is being corrected and why from most interchanges with adults. Consider this exchange between language researcher M. D. S. Braine and one of his own children, part of a weeks-long effort to change just one usage.

CHILD: Want other one spoon, Daddy.
FATHER: You mean, you want *the other spoon.*
CHILD: Yes, I want other one spoon, please, Daddy.
FATHER: Can you say "the other spoon"?
CHILD: Other . . . one . . . spoon.
FATHER: Say . . . "other."
CHILD: Other.
FATHER: "Spoon."
CHILD: Spoon.
FATHER: "Other . . . spoon."
CHILD: Other . . . spoon. Now give me other one spoon?

All the evidence suggests that in normal life, where children aren't raised by language researchers, parents don't consistently attempt to modify the child's language behavior by responding negatively to incorrect speech. And when they do, the correction gives the child almost no useful information about what was wrong: grammar, semantics, timing, or facts.

According to Steven Pinker, a professor of brain and cognitive sciences at MIT who specializes in language acquisition, if children don't learn from negative evidence, as field research shows, then they can't possibly learn through a logical process like hypothesis testing. It is tempting to believe that during language learning a child could be forming language rules or hypotheses and then testing them, but that would require that a child be able to identify an incorrect hypothesis.

But children and adults *do* learn to speak grammatically, even when using new words and grammatical structures. Some verbs, for example, dativize with a preposition. "John gave the dish to Sam" is as grammatical as "John gave Sam a dish." However, "John donated a painting to the museum" cannot grammatically become "John donated the museum a painting." "But the child has no way of knowing this, given the nonavailability of negative evidence," writes Pinker in his 1989 book *Learnability and Cognition*.

> The fact that he or she hasn't heard the ungrammatical sentences . . . could simply reflect adults' never having had an opportunity to utter them in the child's presence (after all, there are an infinite number of grammatical sentences that the child will never hear). Therefore, the child should speak ungrammatically all his life — or more accurately, the language should change in a single generation so that exceptional verbs . . . would become regular.

Well, as Oliver Hardy might have said had he been a linguist, "Now, you've made a fine mess of things." Not only is it impossible for a child to learn a language, but the continued persistence of irregular verb forms is also inexplicable. All languages more than a generation old should have eliminated all exceptions to become a mass of regular rules. So why then does English still have no regular past tense forms for "come" and "go" (i.e., "comed" and "goed"), instead insisting on "came" and "went"? And how do we learn these forms and the correct context for using them?

McClelland and Rumelhart didn't set out to explain all of language acquisition. Their experiment drew on one well-researched and repeatedly described example of language learning, the past tense. They wanted to see if they could duplicate the observed behavior of children learning to use the past tense without programming any explicit rules into their machine. To pass the test, their model would not only have to acquire the past tense and apply it correctly to verbs outside the training sample. It would also have to acquire the past tense in stages, as biological children do.

Past tense learning in children actually follows three well-documented steps, they noted. In stage 1 children use only a small number of verbs in the past tense. These verbs, understandably, are words children are likely to hear with very high frequency in the conversations around them. At this point children tend to get the past tenses of words correct, whether the verb is regular or irregular, if they use the past tense form at all. The best explanation for this stage seems to be that they are simply memorizing individual words. There is no evidence that children are generalizing from one verb to another.

In stage 2 mistakes begin to appear that suggest that children are using rules. These slightly older children use a much larger number of verbs in the past tense. Most are regular, although a few irregular verbs have been added to those known in stage 1. Children can now generate a past tense for an invented word: presented with "rick" by a language researcher, a child will form "ricked." And children now overgeneralize the "ed" rule, often making the past tense of "come" not "came" but "comed" or "camed."

In stage 3 children form the correct past tense for both irregular and regular verbs. Exceptions to the regular patterns of the past tense make recognized clusters of verbs, such as the *ing/ang* group and the *eed/ed* group. A few overregularizations persist into adulthood, but for the common irregular verbs this kind of mistake is rare.

The basic model Rumelhart and McClelland built on their computer was a very simple two-layer neural network of input and output neurons with 460 completely interconnected neurons in each layer. A combination of active units in the input layer represented each present tense, and another combination in the output layer represented each past tense. The machine was given a set of 506 verbs. To simulate stage 1, the machine was initially trained on only the ten most commonly used verbs in the sample set. To simulate the relatively meager learning of a very young child, it was only trained on these verbs for ten cycles. That is, each verb was presented ten times, with the connections between neurons tuned after each presentation. In stage 2 another 410 medium-frequency verbs were added to the machine's vocabulary, with an additional 190 training presentations for each of these verbs as well as for the original ten. An additional eighty-six lower-frequency verbs were added in a final stage, but without any adjustment of the connections between neurons.

McClelland and Rumelhart believe their neural child accurately captured the real child's stage 1 learning. Through the first ten training cycles, the machine learned regular and irregular verbs with equal accuracy. But beginning with the introduction of the second group of 410 verbs on training cycle 11, the regular and irregular verbs began to diverge, with the accuracy of learning for irregular verbs initially dropping off sharply and then lagging significantly behind. To McClelland and Rumelhart, the regular verbs seemed to be interfering with the irregular ones. However, this interference began to disappear about halfway through the 190 learning cycles of the stage 2 presentation of the group of 410 medium-frequency verbs. By the time all 420 verbs went through all 190 cycles, the machine showed almost errorless performance on all 420 training verbs.

Rumelhart thinks he understands what happens inside his past tense learning machine. He and McClelland put what is called a pattern associator at the center of their machine. As the connections between the network's simulated neurons are adjusted, the machine learns to associate one input pattern with one output pattern. Connections are appropriately strengthened and weakened until activating one pattern of units among the 460 input neurons always causes just one pattern to be activated among the output neurons. This part of their machine is a kind of associative memory similar to that laid out by Teuvo Kohonen in 1977.

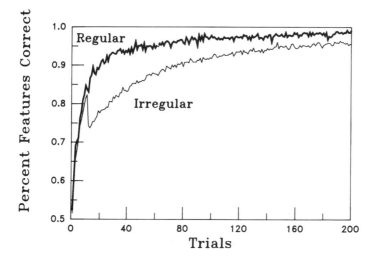

The machine initially learns regular and irregular past tense forms equally well, but with more information the accuracy of irregular forms drops as the machine overgeneralizes. After many more trials the machine begins to once more learn irregular forms accurately.

From Rumelhart and McClelland, "On Learning the Past Tense of English Verbs," in Rumelhart and McClelland, eds., *Parallel Distributed Processing*, The MIT Press, 1986. Copyright © 1986.

How many patterns can a network like this learn to associate? That's a crucial question for Rumelhart and McClelland in practical and theoretical terms. If the network requires an impossibly large number of neurons to handle something like the number of associations a human being has to learn in order to speak, read, and comprehend a language, then it will be impossible to build a working computer simulation. We know roughly how much of the brain is devoted to language. If Rumelhart and McClelland's machine requires more units to handle language than the brain has available, then the theory is, at best, seriously flawed.

As it turns out, the answer to the question of how many patterns the machine can learn has as much to do with the structure of the world as it does with the abilities of the machine. If the environment, the information, entering the machine is completely arbitrary, if each input pattern is completely unrelated to any other, then the machine's capabilities are extremely limited. If the input patterns form what is called a linearly independent set where each input pattern activates no units in common with any other input pattern, then this network of 460 input neurons can only represent 460 linearly independent patterns. If none of the words presented to the network resemble each other, then the network will have to dedicate one neuron to each word. In this case the number of neurons involved in language processing would have to increase by one in both the input and output layers each time we learn a new pattern.

But what if the world as experienced by the machine shows some inherent order? In the arbitrary, linearly independent world, Rumelhart and McClelland discovered, a system with eight input and output neurons can accurately learn only eight associations. But if the environment has even minimal order, the machine can vastly expand the number of associations it can learn with the same number of neurons. In one experiment they asked a network to learn the associations between two pairs of three-digit sequences — for instance, that 2 4 7 is always to be associated with 2 4 8 and that 3 6 8 is always to be associated with 3 6 7.

But the way these three-digit sequences are associated isn't arbitrary. Input patterns in this world always consist of three digits. The first digit is always either a 1, 2, or 3, the second always a 4, 5, or 6, and the last always a 7 or 8. Output patterns are related to the input patterns by a simple rule known to the researcher but not to the machine. In the three-digit output, the first digit is always the same 1, 2, or 3 as in the input pattern and the second is always the same 4, 5, or 6. Only the third digit differs. If it is a 7 in the input, it is an 8 in the output, and vice versa. In a world with this much order, the exact same eight-neuron input–eight-neuron output machine can learn to accurately associate eighteen patterns instead of just eight.

From the Rumelhart/McClelland perspective, order in the environment is not an objective, unchanging quality or quantity. It exists only to the degree that the machine or the brain perceives it. Order depends on two factors. First, the machine must be designed to perceive the specific kind of order exhibited by the environment. If the environment's categories depend on color but the machine is color-blind, the world will seem orderless to the machine. Second, the machine's ability to perceive order depends on the amount of data submitted to it. The difference between a nonrepeating decimal such as *pi* and a decimal that repeats after four digits only exists if the machine is presented with enough digits. Patterns can shift as more information becomes available, and order can emerge at very different scales. The degree of perceived order in the environment can change as the machine learns more data points. Problematic examples of this relationship stud even the everyday world. How, for example, can we say that any line is a straight line? At best, we can be confident that the line segment we see is straight.

In fact, the changing nature of the quantitative relationship between the machine and the world of past tenses is the key to explaining why the machine learns as it does. In stage 1 the machine is presented with so little data — patterns for only ten verbs — that it can find no order in the environment. It treats each pattern as arbitrary. The machine is, if you will, memorizing associations, but since it has so few examples, none of the patterns overlap. As Rumelhart and McClelland wrote, "The child knows, at this point, only a few high-frequency verbs, and these tend, by and large, to be irregular. . . . Thus each is treated by the network as a separate association, and very little generalization occurs."

But as more and more verbs are presented to the machine, the situation changes radically. The new environment is filled with regular verbs that share parts of their pattern. Each regular verb reinforces the associations that lead to the activation of the regular output pattern. With relatively few irregular verbs in the learning set, a characteristic of the verb set the child knows in stage 2, irregular associations are constantly being disrupted by the effort to form regular associations, just as the *T*s that Widrow taught the Adaline were disrupted by the learning of new *J*s. The machine first learns the dominant regular associations, because those are being presented most often. Only when that learning task is accomplished is the machine able to find noninterfering ways to represent the irregular past tenses. Then, like the child, it will go from overgeneralizing "come" into "comed" and accurately learn "came" instead.

Instead of a process that concentrates on the acquisition of rules, learning in the Rumelhart and McClelland network becomes a process defined by the inherent order of the data and the characteristics of the machine that enable it to perceive all, part, or even none of that worldly order. Order exists in the environment, but that order can be invisible if the sample size is too small, and it can be lost in overgeneralization if the sample size is too large.

The most extensive critique of the past tense machine, written by Steven Pinker of MIT and Alan Prince of Brandeis University in 1988, takes the experiment to task on a number of grounds. Some are specifically empirical. For example, Pinker and Prince note that their own analysis shows that the ratio of regular to irregular verbs in parents' speech and children's vocabularies doesn't change during the stages at which overregularization begins to occur. But by far the bulk of the critique deals with Rumelhart and McClelland's claim that they had built a ruleless machine.

The machine itself may contain no explicit rules, Pinker and Prince point out, but its creators introduced them by the way they picked what was input into the system and how they decided what was a right or a wrong answer. "The crucial step is therefore the first one: coding the data," Pinker and Prince wrote.

> If the patterns in the data relevant to generalizing to new forms are not encoded in the representation of the data, no network — in fact no algorithmic system of any sort — will be able to find them. (This is after all the reason that so much research in the "symbolic paradigm" has centered on the nature of linguistic representations.)

Pinker and Prince rightly draw attention to the amount of

coding Rumelhart and McClelland performed before their machine ever saw a word. The machine McClelland and Rumelhart built first sees not words but Wickelfeatures, a version of the Wickelphone scheme proposed by W. A. Wickelgren in 1969. In the original Wicklephone system words are first processed to change the phonemes of traditional linguistics into a code that categorizes each phoneme on the basis of the presence or absence of ten features consisting of consonants and vowels and place of articulation. To capture the context of each phoneme in the code, the encoder also looks at those same features for the preceding and following phoneme. Thus, a single phoneme is represented by some combination of thirty-three features (thirty for the presence or absence of each of ten features in three phonemes, plus three features to represent the presence or absence of word breaks).

But Rumelhart and McClelland's coding didn't stop there. It couldn't. This ideal code was far too complex for the computers of 1985 to handle. Although this coding scheme meant that the machine would need only 1,331 units ($11 \times 11 \times 11$) to represent the linguistic universe, that was still too many to simulate on the available computers. Dealing with that many variables slowed it to less than a crawl. In this design the experiment was simply unrunnable.

So Rumelhart and McClelland had to develop a simpler code. Examining the overlaps in their original scheme, they invented a new code, Wickelfeatures, which captured most of the information using only 460 units.

As Pinker and Prince note, that's a lot of structure for a structureless machine. But it is still not enough structure, they objected. The system that Rumelhart and McClelland built relies almost totally on a phonological code. That code assumes that the relevant patterns this machine needs to know are the correlations between the phonological patterns of the stem and the phonological patterns of the past tense. Thus, "sting" becomes "stung," "fling" becomes "flung," "stick" becomes "stuck." But that means the machine can't learn past tense transformations that aren't related to phonology: "come" becomes "came," but "succumb" doesn't become "succame." Nor can it learn the correct past tenses of two verbs that have the same sound, such as "ring"/"rang" and "ring"/ "ringed." And, Pinker and Prince point out, what about those cases where sound is irrelevant and the past tense form is determined by the verb's derivation from a noun — "high-sticked," for example, not "high-stuck;" "braked" the car, not "broke" the car.

Pinker and Prince summarize the machine's failings: "(1) It cannot represent certain words, (2) it cannot learn many rules, (3) it can learn rules found in no human language, (4) it cannot explain morphological and phonological regularities, (5) it cannot explain the differences between irregular and regular forms," and so on in a list that includes three more specific items. They conclude that the machine demonstrates that "connectionists' claims about the dispensability of rules in explanations in the psychology of language must be rejected."

Rumelhart and McClelland, on the other hand, rightly point out that Pinker and Prince's 1988 critique concentrates on a very simple machine built in 1985 that was intended only as an experiment. The computer power available in that day to simulate this neural network limited that machine to two layers and a relatively simple system of representation. They believe adding hidden layers of neurons would produce a system that more closely matched the results of field research. The point is not that the machine couldn't learn all the rules of language correctly, but that a very simple machine could learn so much. Was the glass half empty, as Pinker and Prince viewed it, or half full, the view of Rumelhart and McClelland?

One way to find out would be to build more machines and throw them at other learning tasks. By the summer of 1985, Terry Sejnowski, another member of the original PDP Group, had taught a neural network to read aloud.

Sejnowski works in a temple to modern science. Baptized with the name of Jonas Salk, the discoverer of the first polio vaccine, and inhabited by luminaries such as Francis Crick, the Salk Institute sits in silent glory on the Pacific coast just north of San Diego. Blocks of white cast concrete house the offices and labs of the institute's researchers. They frame a monumental plaza of white marble that soars off into the ether, hanging at the edge of an ocean cliff. The sea breezes whisper through the eucalyptus and madrona trees, hushing even the occasional tour group to silence. It seems a strangely quiet setting for a researcher so obsessed by language.

Sejnowski isn't a linguist, however, but a neurobiologist with an interest in language. Language is the most visible thing we do that animals don't — what Noam Chomsky has called the human essence. In this sense it is not just a specific, highly structured kind of communication but also a possible description of how we think.

Linguistics and traditional artificial intelligence have often suggested that, at the least, our conscious thoughts behave like language, although artificial intelligence has also insisted on replacing ambiguous natural language with its own computer versions. But how does this "reasoning" behavior relate to the 100 billion neurons of the brain and the countless chemical and electrical events that occur at the biological level? And what biological level is the appropriate substratum for language? Should we look for explanations of language in the workings of the human central nervous

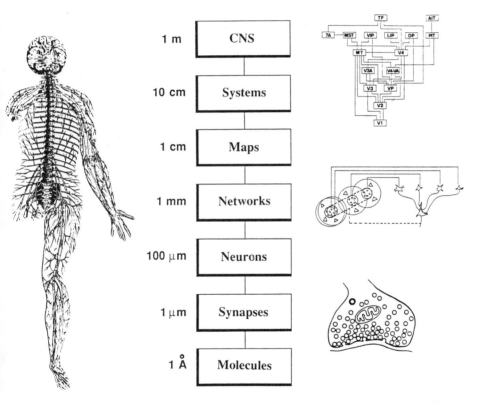

Cognitive phenomena can be explained at many different levels, from the central nervous system (CNS) to neurons, synapses, and molecules. We know very little about the properties at the network level in comparison to the detailed knowledge we have about synapses and the general organization of sensory and motor pathways.
Reprinted with permission from Churchland and Sejnowski, "Perspectives on Cognitive Science," *Science*, 1988. Copyright © 1988.

system as a whole or in its subsystems, or in individual networks, or in the biology of individual cells?

NETtalk, the machine Sejnowksi built with Charles Rosenberg, learns how to pronounce words after seeing written text. Like Rumelhart and McClelland's past tense machine, then, it is a demonstration of the power of neural network theory: see, *this* kind of machine is able to do *this*. But NETtalk is also an artificial biology experiment, destined to be dissected. To Sejnowski and Rosenberg, understanding what and how NETtalk learns was more important than simply building a machine that speaks.

Sejnowski himself speaks a babble of scientific tongues. He's a trained physicist whose Ph.D. dissertation was on modeling the brain. "My first publication was in the late seventies, when I was still a physicist and still approaching the problem the way a physicist would, which is to figure out what the equations are and then try and analyze the equations." But Sejnowski, who despite twenty years of lab work has the clean, athletic good looks of a fraternity brother from a small midwestern college, wasn't satisfied. "That convinced me that the analytical or abstract approach to neurosystems could only take you so far, and if you really want to understand how, let's say, the brain works as a biological system, there really wasn't any substitute to actually looking at it, trying to find out how real neurons interact with each other and what the principles are that neurons are using to compute."

To learn this language, Sejnowski took an intensive course in biological techniques at the Woods Hole Marine Biological Laboratory. After that it was four years of postdoctoral fellowships, first at Princeton and then at Harvard Medical School. "Not only did I get an appreciation of the diversity and the complexity of neurons and neurocircuits, but I also became very committed to that level of analysis."

The need for a new kind of scientific language in biology was proclaimed in the name of the department he joined at Baltimore's Johns Hopkins University, the Department of Biophysics. "In physics you generally are working with very simple systems. You can write down the equations, and you have almost complete understanding of why it behaves the way it does. And no one's ever achieved that for any biological system because the complexity is so much greater. My motivation was to try to come to grips with that complexity, to try to develop techniques for coming to grips with that."

It took Sejnowski and Rosenberg, then a Princeton graduate student, only the summer of 1985 to build NETtalk. As a parlor trick, it was even more spectacular than Rumelhart and McClelland's past tense machine. Show the trained NETtalk an English word and it pronounced it. It began by looking at either the phonetic transcriptions of a child reading or a Merriam-Webster pocket dictionary, trying to match the letters it saw with the correct sounds. At first, NETtalk would babble. It had quickly picked up the distinction between vowels and consonants, but at this stage in its learning, it predicted the same vowel and the same consonant all the time. As the machine learned to recognize word boundaries, the babble got more structured. It became pseudo-words. After about five passes, the machine learned the training set of words and sounds. Accuracy on these familiar words approached 90 percent, and most mistakes involved the substitution of very similar sounds, the *th* in "then" for the *th* in "thin," for example.

NETtalk was more complex than Rumelhart and McClelland's machine, but it clearly resembled it. It began with 203 input neurons that were wired to a layer of 80 hidden units and a 26-neuron output layer. Words were fed into the system through a seven-letter-wide window. As in the past tense machine, the initial coding focused on the characteristics of a single object, the center letter in the group of seven, and the context provided by the other elements in the window. Sejnowski and Rosenberg would have preferred using a bigger window — it would have given them more global information about the word in question — but their computer simply couldn't handle more than seven letters at a time.

For the next two years, Sejnowski and Rosenberg tore apart a machine that had required only a summer to build, trying to see why and how it used its internal connections to learn to pronounce English words from written text. In effect, they wanted to learn its internal language, which they called a representation. The machine pronounced words in a way that could be explained by the rules of phonetics, but it had never seen those rules. What was going on inside that box?

"Charlie's thesis at Princeton, in fact, was a very detailed study of one particular rule, the hard *c* rule," says Sejnowski, who moved to Salk in the middle of the dissection. "The problem is how do you tell whether or not a *c*, say at the beginning of a word, should be pronounced as in 'cat' or as in 'city'? There are correlations with the vowels, correlations of derivations, and so forth.

He did a very, very thorough study, studying the weights and studying the development of the weights as the system was trained and so forth." What Rosenberg and Sejnowski found, surprisingly, was that the network, which employed a third, hidden layer of neurons, didn't always learn the same rule in the same way. Of course, since a connectionist machine doesn't use explicit programmed rules, what Rosenberg and Sejnowski looked at were patterns of activation among the machine's neurons.

A rule-based artificial intelligence program would include something like the schoolchild's mnemonics that we all learn: "*i* before *e* except after *c* or when it sounds like *a* as in neighbor or sleigh." What a programmer would write is a rule that said a *c* sounds like this if it's followed by an *ie*, and that it sounds like this if it's followed by an *a* or a *u*. "But," says Sejnowski,

> there are always exceptions. Every rule has an exception. That's always been a bugaboo to the phonologists who have had to make sense of the variability of English. Sometimes there get to be so many exceptions that you have to rewrite the rules and the rules start interacting with each other. If you have enough exceptions, you begin to create rules for the exceptions, and then you have to assemble a hierarchy of rules so that, you know, the machine applies first this rule and then another.

Worst of all you have to give the machine a way to make decisions when two rules seem to govern one situation. How, for example, would you write a rule that tells a machine how to pronounce both "seine" (sane) and "seize" (seez)? Should the *ei* combinations be pronounced in the same way because they both follow an *s* in a one-syllable word that ends with *e*, or differently because they precede different consonants? Or should the machine be considering another rule entirely, one that depends on the historic roots of these words in German, French, and Latin?

If NETtalk doesn't use this rulelike language, it also doesn't speak the same tongue as the Rumelhart and McClelland machine. Adding a third layer of neurons ensures that. The past tense machine, in its simplest form, associates two patterns. In the front-end layer, the active neurons form a pattern that represents the present tense of the verb. In the back-end layer, the active neurons form a pattern that represents the past tense. Teaching the machine is largely a matter, by no means trivial, of adjusting the weights among the neurons until the correct one-to-one association is formed automatically and every time.

This kind of mapping also lets the machine make generalizations. To a two-layer machine generalization is simply a matter of how much two patterns overlap. Thus, a new input pattern that is similar to a pattern the machine has already seen will yield a similar output. The two will both activate, say, eight response neurons in common and differ in the remainder. The overlap in output pattern says that these inputs belong to the same class. That's how Rumelhart and McClelland's machine learned to add an -*ed* to a regular verb it had never seen before. The already seen verb and the new verb were both represented by input patterns so similar that they mapped to the same output pattern.

But, as Minsky and Papert pointed out in *Perceptrons*, that requires the outside world to cooperate by giving the machine just the right kind of patterns. Certain kinds of patterns can't be mapped by two-layer machines. The "exclusive or" pattern is the classic example. The machine is supposed to learn a pattern of astounding simplicity: to make the patterns that overlap least generate identical outputs. However, there simply isn't any way to get a two-layer machine to respond with a 0 for patterns of both 00 and 11, and with a 1 for patterns of both 10 and 01.

But add a layer in between input and output, called a hidden layer, and the machine has no trouble mapping those classes. Even one hidden unit does the trick. Wire the system like this: each input unit will fire only when it sees a 1. The hidden unit will fire only when it receives two 1s, enough to push it over its threshold of 1.5. If it fires, it will send a negative signal, -2, to the output layer. The output unit fires whenever it receives signals adding up to more than 0.5 from all three units.

Now, consider the results of the different possible patterns. The 00 pattern activates neither input unit, the hidden unit isn't activated, and the output unit receives signals equal to 0. It doesn't fire. The 11 pattern produces the same result. Each input unit fires, sending signals to both the hidden unit and the output unit. The hidden unit, pushed over its threshold, fires, sending a -2 to the output, which cancels the two 1s sent by each input unit. Zero again.

Both 01 and 10, on the other hand, produce a 1 in output. Neither pattern pushes the hidden unit over its threshold, but the output unit receives a 1 from either the left or right input neuron, pushing it over the 0.5 threshold it needs to fire. Voila! "exclusive or."

Hidden units are unfortunately just that — hidden. It's easy to grasp logically what they do when the input is just four binary patterns and there's only one hidden unit. But what about in a machine like NETtalk, which begins with written text and consists of 203 input units, 80 hidden units, and 26 output units?

The answer was neither very reassuring nor particularly simple. Sejnowski and Rosenberg had built NETtalk so that it started as a blank slate. At the beginning, before it learned anything, the network had no predetermined structure, except for the fixed representation of the inputs and outputs. The units representing neurons were arranged in what is called a homogeneous network — each unit was connected to all the other units in exactly the same way, although the weights of the connections started out with different randomly chosen values. Sejnowski knew that biological neural networks aren't connected this way, but he wanted to build a tool for understanding the way the brain functions. Building a

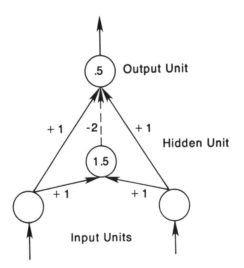

A simple network for creating the "exclusive or" with a hidden unit.
From Rumelhart and McClelland, "On Learning the Past Tense of English Verbs," in Rumelhart and McClelland, eds., *Parallel Distributed Processing*, The MIT Press, 1986. Copyright © 1986.

brainlike structure was, he thought in 1985 and still thinks in 1990, premature:

> When you come into the world, the brain already knows something about vision and something about language structure and language categories. A lot of our knowledge of what's in the world comes through genetic learning, the gradual evolution of the species. The problem is that we don't know how it's organized in the brain, how vision is organized, how language is structured. By making minimal assumptions, we can use the network to discover some of those structures.

Sejnowski and Rosenberg trained their machine until it reached its optimum accuracy rate of about 78 percent recognition on an unfamiliar text. Then they examined the weights, what units were firing together, and especially what the hidden units were doing. Next they erased NETtalk and trained it again. Time after time, the hidden units grouped themselves in ways that seemed to mean something. To Sejnowski and Rosenberg it was logical that the groups were somehow helping the machine reach answers, or at least better answers. But if they wiped the machine clean and trained it again to the same level of proficiency, the groups that formed among the hidden units were often different. "We found that every time you ran NETtalk, you got a different set of weights, but somehow they're all equivalent," says Sejnowski.

The meaning of some of the clusterings seemed clear. One always represented vowels and another consonants. Others showed up that didn't correspond to any linguistic categories that Sejnowski or Rosenberg knew. Some seemed to represent small groups of five words with some trait in common. According to Sejnowski, "They are well-defined separations. It's clear that there are many distinctions like that that the network is using. What linguists have codified and what we're consciously aware of may be just the tip of the iceberg" of the categories that the network and maybe the brain use.

Sejnowski has spent a lot of time thinking about what NET-talk was telling him about how it, and maybe the brain, interacted with the world. On one level you can think of NETtalk as a map, he says. Start with a very simplified world external to the neural network. "Draw a little picture, a map. Here's a lake and here's a path, and maybe here's a bridge, and there's a house sitting here.

This is the world you want your neural network to learn. The goal is a machine that will recognize a lake, a path, a bridge, and a house." Sejnowski's map is a very simple, very literal one, but the elements could just as easily be the words in a sentence or the letters in a word, or even Wickelfeatures.

One way to build a network that represented a map — and certainly the most obvious one — would be to dedicate a single neuron to each object in the map. Input units would detect features in the outside world — roofs, windows, doors, straight sides, right angles — that they transmit to an array of dedicated neurons. Positive input from the roof, window, door, straight sides, and right angle detectors would add up to activating the house unit. "I have a neuron dedicated to the lake and when that neuron is activated, the machine knows it's looking at a lake," says Sejnowski. "If you're looking at the house, then this neuron is activated. So here's a house neuron. Here's a lake neuron. Some people build networks like this." And some neuroscientists have claimed that there is biological evidence that some cells in the brain work this way. They have been called grandmother cells after biological experiments that seem to show that specialized cells in the visual system recognize just an individual face, your grandmother, for example.

But using a single neuron to represent each "fact" the network knows uses up every neuron in the brain far short of capturing everything we know. Sejnowski and Rosenberg took another approach, one that built on the overlapping structures of the real world. NETtalk doesn't organize itself around single units that represent single objects. It uses groups of units in its representation, what Sejnowski calls distributed representation. Continuing the map metaphor, he says, "Here's a group that represents lake, right? Here's a group that represents house and you see that some are in between. These are the ones that represent both." The "fact" is represented by the entire pattern, and individual neurons can belong to many different "fact patterns."

Distributed representation can draw on increasingly strong support from biological research. Early study of biological neurons had concentrated on invertebrates like squids and sea slugs with large neurons arranged in simple networks. It discovered invertebrate "command" neurons, single neurons that when stimulated to swim, say, would coordinate a large array of other neurons to produce this action. Initially, vertebrate neural networks were thought to work in the same fashion. All the signals from a population of neurons would be summed by a single neuron, which would then coordinate other neurons that would control such actions as simple eye movement. But further research seemed to show that that picture was wrong, at least for vertebrates and for many invertebrate neural circuits, too. Experiments in the neuronal basis for vision in vertebrates, for example, showed that large populations of up to 100,000 neurons were involved in simple eye movement, and that chemically deactivating a group of these 100,000 neurons would misdirect the eye's movement in a way that was most simply explained if all the neurons were somehow participating in that task. It seemed that even simple brain events required the collaboration of large populations of neurons.

Being on the side of biology is probably some solace in the darkest nights of the network builder's soul, but in practical terms it makes an annoying headache into a migraine. Representation is clearly much trickier than Rumelhart and McClelland's machine assumed. How did groups of neurons "mean" a specific thing? NETtalk uses what Sejnowski has come to call relative representation, that is, groups of neurons with memberships that differ from learning trial to learning trial and yet somehow represent the same "fact." "The network may have decided to group five words by accident," he says, "but once it has decided to group these five words, that grouping determines other representations. The particular representation you pick has a lot of arbitrariness in it, but the way things fit together is very precise." The fit has to be precise, because, for NETtalk to work, those representational groups have to fill up all the possible space where a word from the outside world could wind up. No word can be allowed to fall through the cracks. "Just think of a two-dimensional space that you have to cover with little bloblike regions," Sejnowski says. "It is pretty arbitrary where you put the first blob, but once you start doing that, the rest have to fit together filling the whole space and not overlapping too much." Adjusting the borders gets tricky, too. Some overlap between clusters is fine; it represents the fuzziness of categories and the way some blend into each other. Too much prevents the machine from making necessary distinctions. A blob defines a category, and its relation to other blobs suggests the relationship between categories.

Sejnowski's observations suggest that the internal structure of the network and the code it uses to represent the outside world are not preordained by the external world. "Well," says Sejnowski, "it has to reflect the outside world, but there is a lot of freedom." All iterations of the network may have to use consonants, but they don't all have to create the same arbitrary group of five phonemes used by the forty-seventh run of NETtalk. He says,

> The lesson, I think, has to do with the complexity of the world. If the world is an incredibly complex place, your representation has to reflect that. All the fine, nitty-gritty detail. The network, if it solves the task, had to do that, and figuring out how it did that becomes the problem. This big iceberg under the surface of the water, which we're not aware of consciously, how it represents things, appears to have a lot of flexibility in it.

The machine and the brain appear to have at least an initial choice among all the possible patterns of representations, NETtalk seems to say, and that choice then becomes part of the conditions that design the rest of the structure. These representations work to allow the network or the biological organism to successfully interpret and interact with the environment, but they are not the only representations that can be derived from that environment.

All versions of the NETtalk network, and by implication all brains, don't share the same fine structure of representation. "There's a lot of similarity, enough so we can communicate," says Sejnowski, "but how we actually represent an object may be very different. If you take an expert on X rays, the way he represents an X ray is very different from the way that you do. They see all kinds of things that you see as smudges and blobs. They'll have names for them. They'll have ways of describing them. That will reflect their internal representation that they've built up over experience."

But if the external world doesn't determine the pattern of representation, then how can we discover the representations that NETtalk and the brain use by analyzing the external world? The researcher in human psychology or the builder of artificial neural networks can't derive all the necessary details by simply observing how people talk and then working backward, Sejnowski says. "That works for the highest levels. It may be that there are some representations that are so important and so significant that no matter what system you use, whether it's a neural network or a symbolic representation or a biological brain, it's a good way to do it." But he believes that isn't true for all levels of the system.

This question comes remarkably close to restating Pinker and Prince's, and Minsky and Papert's, objections to neural network machines. The problem, all four critics say, is not that neural networks can't generalize or create categories, but that they can't create just those few meaningful categories. Given any set of data, the neural machines can create an almost unlimited number of ways to link items in that set.

This isn't a problem unique to neural networks, however. It is one that has puzzled researchers trying to explain how children learn and philosophers who want to know how anyone knows anything. In one thought experiment philosopher W. V. O. Quine imagines that a linguist visits a foreign country whose natives speak an unknown language. The linguist points to a rabbit passing by, and a native speaker says, "Gavagai." Quine argues that pointing and naming can never produce a uniquely correct translation. "Gavagai" could mean rabbit or white or good-to-eat or object in the sun. Each hypothesis is testable, of course. The clever linguist can keep pointing to other objects and asking questions. But, Quine argued, there is simply no way to ask enough questions to produce just one unique meaning for "Gavagai."

Stanford psychologist Ellen Markman compares that situation to the problem of explaining how children learn categories. Much recent evidence shows that children do learn categories and at a very early age, probably before the age of eighteen months. It's unlikely that the child of that age can perform the kind of sophisticated hypothesis testing and extensive questioning that characterize the fruitless efforts of Quine's linguist to pin down meaning. At that age the child is far less informed about the world than even Rumelhart and McClelland's machine. What about the rabbit matches up with the label "rabbit"? Whiteness? Long ears? Furry animal? Indeed, what kind of features should the child pay attention to? Should he or she look at the whole animal, part of the animal, or perhaps the entire scene? A more sophisticated and experienced observer could use logic to draw conclusions about "rabbit" from other objects and labels, but at this age experience is severely limited and any but the most rudimentary kinds of logic seem unlikely.

We have to conclude, Markman writes in *Categorization and*

Naming in Children, either that young children have hidden powers of logical inference or that they form categories by using some
other mechanisms. They might, she notes, come equipped with
assumptions about the kind of features that are important or even
predisposed toward specific definitions of a category. The child
may not have to test all the hypotheses that Quine's linguist must
consider, because the child's brain may simply already know that
some kinds of hypotheses aren't worth testing. For example, Steven
Pinker, in his own work on learning, theorizes that an assumption
of uniqueness — a built-in belief that each word structure in a language has a unique function — may be crucial to a child's ability
to learn language. A child, Markman postulates, might even have
a similar uniqueness assumption that eases the task of linking a
label to a thing.

Neural network critics, researchers who study childhood
learning, and NETtalk may all be pointing in the same direction.
It is hard to see how a network — or a brain — with no knowledge
about the structure of the world, with no knowledge about what a
feature is or what might be important, can come to a meaningful
understanding of the world. Yet as the dissection of NETtalk
certainly demonstrates, it is equally hard to tell what among all
the features of the world is important for the machine or for the
brain.

Hard, but maybe not impossible. Maybe we can't figure out
the complete iceberg, but perhaps the visible portion is enough to
get a machine started on the right track. When we analyze how
human beings perform a task like reading handwritten zip codes
or understanding speech, do we learn enough to build a machine
capable of doing the same thing? A team of researchers at AT&T
has a very practical way of answering that question.

4
THE NATURE
OF METAPHOR

Remember the early pictures of airplanes? People were trying to make machines fly by using flapping wings and so on. Technology doesn't work by direct analogy that way. Seven-forty-sevens don't have titanium feathers and they don't flap their wings, but they fly.

— RICHARD HOWARD

If you wanted to fly, would you begin by building a bird? Richard Howard asks. If you wanted to read zip codes, would you build a brain?

Howard, an abrupt and verbally aggressive man, thinks the answer to both questions is a clear no. The machine that his research group at AT&T Bell Laboratories is building to read zip codes will not need to work much like the brain does. He doesn't even care if his system is a neural network or not.

"Recently, somebody, and I forget his name, unfortunately, made an analogue of a pterodactyl. I think it was to see whether they could really fly, land, take off, and had the right strength-to-weight ratios and so on," says Howard, craning across the table as he shapes the now extinct flying dinosaur with his hands in the air. It was the "best model he could [build] of the pterodactyl so he could learn something of how they might have worked. That was a nice piece of engineering if you want to understand how the biology worked. But I'm not interested in doing that at all."

At AT&T's research center in Holmdel, New Jersey, Howard and the neural network group he heads pride themselves on their devotion to the practical. No metaphysical or philosophical arguments about how much biology *should* go into a neural network or how to connect symbols to meanings. "It's strictly a pragmatic argument. What do you have to put in to solve the problem?"

Howard believes that what you must put in has two parts. It has to include an analysis of what features the machine needs to solve the problem, and it must have a structure designed to detect those features. Learning from raw data on unstructured networks was the initial siren call of neural networks, but according to Howard, even early researchers in the field should have known better. All biological neural systems begin with the extensive manipulation of sensory information by highly specialized networks. Human visual systems, for example, perceive objects in the world as edges, segments, movements, contrast, and so on. But those features are only accessible to the human sensory system because of a neuronal structure designed to respond to them. Detectors for these features "don't exist in the eyes of the starfish or the scallop. So you could never train one of those animals to recognize digits," says Howard. "They just don't have the preprocessors to handle that."

Howard doesn't want to build a complete brain, or even a duplicate of one tiny part of it. His machine should borrow just enough from the brain so it will read handwritten zip codes. That task seems simple only until Howard carts out the actual data — 7,000 handwritten zip codes from the U.S. Postal Service. There are fat numerals and thin numerals. There are stubby 7s and 5s with the tops cropped off. There are 6s with tails that come right through the downstroke, or is that a 4? There is a 2 that looks like an *i*, if it is a 2. There are a few European 1s with their crossbars, but no European 7s.

Logic suggests one way to tackle the problem zip codes pose. Break down the numerals into their constituent pieces — their diagonals, end stops, curves, and so forth. A 3 thus becomes a collection of curves joined in a specified way, and logically, all 3s share these features. That is precisely what makes them 3s.

This view seems so natural, so commonsensical, that it masks the assumptions it makes about the world and about how the brain knows the world. It assumes that "threeness" is defined by a core of features. All 3s share these features; all non-3s don't. It also assumes that the conscious logical analysis we use to arrive at this list of features produces the same list of features the brain uses. This second assumption requires us to say either that the brain's processes are at least approximately logical and conscious or that whatever nonlogical and nonconscious processes the brain uses produce the same list that our logical and conscious cognitive processes do. This second assumption is roughly equivalent to saying that the brain can consciously analyze its own processes. The machine that Howard set out to build is a very concrete test of the validity of each of these assumptions about the brain.

There's no need to build a neural network to do this logical analytic process, although putting a neural network on the job does promise to speed things up. Existing methods tackle a problem like this through statistical analysis. Studying the data, you look for features that in combination will predict the numeral accurately. The crucial part of the method requires finding meaningful

Even something as simple as the numerals in a zip code has tremendous variation.
Reprinted by permission of the MIT Press from Le Cun, et al., "Backpropagation Applied to Handwritten Zip Code Recognition," *Neural Computation*, 1989. Copyright © 1989.

correlations between a specific combination of features and "three-ness," for example — a long computation that requires counting the presence of each feature and then seeing what combination of features best predicts a 3. Just locating one feature won't provide a very accurate prediction. You have to combine features and then test to see what combinations work best.

"You can do that by conventional statistical methods," says Howard, "but that's a very difficult kind of approach, even though people have done it." Instead, Howard asks a neural network to learn some of these correlations. The network itself organizes the actual piles of noisy data. Of course, Howard still has to tell his machine what features to look for and what to discount, and he has to "define" each feature for it. "If I haven't done it well enough, it won't solve that problem. I won't know ahead of time until I actually do the problem whether I got it right."

"Right" is itself a pretty tricky term. "People are always asking what our accuracy in handwritten characters is," Howard says. "That's a meaningless number" unless you're comparing data of exactly the same quality. For example, is this the handwriting someone uses to fill in a 1040 income tax form or a parking ticket? "You pick a problem that you can solve with a conventional technique, and you see if you can do a better job by a technique that is inspired by some of these ideas. And that's the only metric [for judging success]. The only value this field is going to have is whether it solves problems or tells you something [about computation]."

That attitude makes Howard and his team a good representative of the commercial side of neural network research. At companies like AT&T, Ford, and Nestor the focus is on finding better solutions to discrete and well-known problems such as reading zip codes, diagnosing engine problems, or detecting forged checks. The task, therefore, is to beat known performance benchmarks. Each generation of the AT&T neural network, for example, inches toward that goal. Some versions are on chips, but most are simulated in software and then rejected long before they get cast into silicon. A chip is a much more attractive commercial product, but software is easier to modify. Why wait a year for something to come back from the foundry to discover it needs major changes?

Howard may not want to get hung up on philosophy or mysticism, but from the outside it seems that all these versions —

Howard calls them iterations — ask a very mystical question. How much does a machine that attempts to solve a problem the brain can solve have to resemble the brain? In fact, that may even be the crucial practical engineering question. In scaling down the hardware from the size of the brain to the size of his neural network, will Howard have lost the essence that gives the brain its power? Does the brain have principles that can be abstracted from the system in which they are embedded and used by very different kinds of systems — an electronic computer, for example? If the brain's power comes from its wholeness, it may only be possible to build a machine that is as powerful as the brain if we build a brain.

We have only imperfect tools for answering these questions. All our studies of the brain or some subsystem of it are conducted by our own brain and from inside our own head. Here we are applying a tool, whose methods are not perfectly clear to us, to decipher its own behavior. When a researcher asks, "What does the brain experience in reading zip codes?" we are cut off from all except the conscious part of our cognitive processes. All we know about how we do these tasks is some conscious impression. There is no guarantee that our impressions or memories of how we perform a task have anything at all to do with the way that our brain actually does it. We can study our own neurobiology for clues, but then we still have to connect the "facts" we discover with a system of cognitive cause and effect.

Howard and his team members, including Hans Peter Graf, Larry Jackel, and Yann Le Cun, build their machines in cluttered cubbyholes in the upper reaches of an awesome hive. Plunked down in the green fields of southern New Jersey, the anonymous modern buildings of AT&T's research center might have been airlifted in late one night at the command of some far-off planner. The whole complex turns inward. Floor after floor of offices looks down on a central court with company restaurant, greenery, and mingling areas.

This neural network project is science by a team of specialists. Graf is the team's chip builder, the one responsible for turning any ideas into silicon if doing so should prove desirable. New talents join the group to solve problems. Yann Le Cun, for example, who joined the group in 1989 by way of Geoffrey Hinton's lab at the University of Toronto, brought new methods for hierarchical, structured learning.

There aren't any biologists on this team, and indeed this is biologically minimalist network building. The brain may be the inspiration for the effort, but the project draws on only two insights from biological systems. "You learn that massive amounts of fine-grained parallelism are useful," says Howard. "That's at the hardware level. The other thing you learn is that you can make systems that learn by experience using a relatively simple set of rules."

Understanding learning is indeed the ultimate payoff here — far more important than the zip code reader itself. As software programs grow so monstrously complicated that finding the almost inevitable bugs becomes just barely possible and requires hundreds or thousands of hours of effort, the need for an alternative way to instruct computers, such as learning, grows.

This particular effort to understand learning seems incredibly expensive and time-consuming itself. There is no apparent way to tackle the design of a zip code reader except by trial and error, what engineers call build and test. They build a version, see how it works, and then make changes.

Howard and his team are also engaged in a kind of translation. They want to build a commercial computer chip. To do that they must think in two languages — that of the brain and that of silicon.

Any scheme for connecting the system's neurons, for example, has to respect the differences between brains and computer chips. The brain's neurons are densely connected in three dimensions. A single neuron will connect with as many as ten thousand other neurons both in the same layer of the brain and in layers above and below it. Silicon technology, on the other hand, is essentially two-dimensional. Connections within a layer, on a single chip, can be extensive, complex, and dense. But connections between layers involve moving information from chip to chip, and here information encounters a bottleneck. No matter how much processing power is packed on a chip, all information leaving the chip has to pass through one of a few hundred pins. That's no problem for a serial computer, which only performs a single computation at a time, but for a parallel computer attempting to mimic the brain, it's a severe handicap.

In the brain the number of neurons that can be involved in a single computation can easily extend into the millions. In the artificial network, Howard believes, the number of neurons that can be involved in a single computation must be limited to the number that can be crammed on a single piece of silicon. There simply isn't enough room to pass even one thousand partial answers back and forth so that the two chips can work together.

Other designers have attempted to solve this problem by using a multiplexing bus, a connection between the two chips that sequences the information that must pass off the chip. In effect, the bus creates a queue of outgoing information that gets sent off-chip one busload at a time. But that means the designer must be able to segment the problem and write software to coordinate the departure of information, its possible storage, and the need for it on other chips. "People don't know how to do that," says Howard.

Fortunately, the translation to silicon also gives the designers some advantages they can exploit. The brain has to stack its neurons in three dimensions because signal transmission through dendrites and axons is so slow. And the brain needs so many neurons, connected so densely with each other, for the same reason. "You're never going to be able to make a system with nearly as many neurons and synapses as you get in the biological system. But each artificial one will operate ten to the fourth [10,000] times faster. So you're now in a position where you can trade off speed for total numbers."

Unfortunately, none of this says anything about how to tell a 3 from a 4. Much of what Howard and his team use to tackle their problem comes from a discipline called machine vision and in particular from a field called pattern matching. The system that the team presented to the 1988 NIPS conference sums up their first approach to combining this knowledge with a neural network.

This machine is basically a pattern matcher that uses neural networks to do the matching. In general, pattern matching attempts to create a pattern that uniquely defines a category, all 4s, say, and then tries to match that pattern to new examples. The machine calls these positive matches 4 and either simply rejects mismatches or tries to match them with other patterns. Thinking of pattern matching as a stencil you might use to paint your house number on your mailbox gives you the flavor of the technique.

To create a pattern matching machine, first you have to design the stencil. What should the shape of each hole be? Remember, it has to be cut so that it will define only one thing or category of thing. You don't want to cut a hole that looks like both a 4 and a 9. After you cut the hole, instead of dabbing paint into it, you use it as a recognition template, sliding it over the thing you want to examine. Oh, the numeral underneath fills up all the parts of the hole, so it must be a 9. Or, no, it leaves this section of the hole blank, so it isn't a 9. The template will give you only two results: a positive or a negative match. If the match is positive, you know what the pattern is. If it's negative, you only know what the pattern isn't. To find out what it is, you have to put that pattern under other holes cut in the stencil. For each pattern you want to recognize, you have to cut one characterizing hole.

The stencil analogy exposes some of the problems involved in creating a pattern matcher. If our brain does pattern matching, it does it without our conscious involvement in the process. We don't consciously experience the steps we go through that tell us that one 4 is like another. To create an accurate pattern matching machine, however, a designer has to make all those steps explicit. The machine is dumb; it knows only what we tell it. The process of building a machine that actually recognizes zip codes is really a discovery of all the steps our brains must follow to perform this task.

Most of the steps are incredibly mundane and completely obvious once you understand exactly how monumentally ignorant of the world this pattern matcher is. For example, it doesn't have any intrinsic way to separate the significant from the insignificant elements in the images it sees. A spot of white where by accident no ink was laid down on one of the 4s is clearly insignificant to us; it's not part of the pattern. The 4 is still a 4. But the machine can't know that. Like Quine's linguist hearing "Gavagai" and seeing the rabbit, this machine doesn't know what in the scene is relevant information and what is noise. Unless the designers add a rule that tells the pattern matcher "This is noise, ignore it," or add a system that eliminates that noise by filling in that spot, the machine is bound to consider the spot as a crucial part of "fourness" along with everything else it sees.

The traditional pattern matcher thus has two stages. In stage 1 the machine applies various kinds of cleaning and normalizing rules that get rid of dust, spots, and most extraneous noise. It also normalizes the image at this stage, which involves shrinking or enlarging each image until they are all the same size, eliminating differences in rotation, and so forth. In stage 2 the machine compares the stencils with the images, often over and over again. The neural network zip code reader that Howard's team initially built used traditional cleaning and normalizing methods to accomplish the first stage. The team then tried to have the machine learn what kind of matches were the best at predicting the identity of handwritten digits.

Learning now? Well, just one more step. With most of the noise gone, it's time to try to recognize important features. These, finally, are the raw material the neural network will use. The machine uses feature extractors called templates, which are similar to the cutout stencil of our analogy. Each template measures 7×7 pixels, far smaller than the 20×32 size of the whole image. Unlike our stencil example, individual templates aren't designed to match a complete numeral all at once. There is simply too much variation in the way 4s or 6s are written to make a complete numeral match possible. Instead, each template is designed to detect significant features such as the end of a stroke. Starting from one corner of the whole image, the template is placed over the image. It registers a plus if the image matches its pattern and is then moved to a new location just one pixel away. The template also has a negative cutout. If a line segment falls into this area, it cancels a positive response from the other cutout.

As the template is moved over the image, at each point it will have answered either "yes" or "no" to the end detector. The yes answers are recorded on a feature map, which measures the same 20×32 pixels as the original image itself. This map, then, becomes a record of each location where that template has found the feature it was designed to detect.

The AT&T machine begins its search by employing forty-nine feature templates and thus a possible forty-nine maps. It doesn't generate all forty-nine possible feature maps from these templates, however. Some responses are combined with those from other templates to create combined maps, where each point is only a yes if two feature detectors both say "yes" at that point. These combinations are designed to more efficiently and accurately detect specific features that the designers think are important in categorizing the digits. All the combinations result in just eighteen feature maps.

So far, not a single neural network technique has been employed in the system. Only those eighteen feature maps are finally read by the neural network. A first layer in the network reads the maps. (Actually, each map is mathematically expressed as a vector, which is fed into this layer.) A final layer of ten units, one for each possible digit, expresses the machine's best guess at a category. In between, a hidden layer of units, like that in Sejnowski's NETtalk, forms intermediate categories that help the machine make its final choice.

This part of the process is learned, not programmed. The hidden layer, which is crucial to formulating intermediate concepts, starts off as a completely connected system of neurons with randomly chosen weights. Using feedback from right and wrong categorizations, the machine learns how to adjust the two sets of weights between the layers. In setting and resetting those weights, the machine is gradually learning how important any combination of features is in deciding what a specific numeral is. For example, in learning how to identify a 7, the machine may learn to emphasize the detection of three end points. It may put the same high degree of emphasis on the presence of a descender, but it may put less emphasis on those features that characterize the descender. After all, in the examples it sees that descender can be either perpendicular or diagonal, straight or curved, uninterrupted or crossed by a bar. One or the other of those should be present, but the absence of one in particular should not affect the identification. On the other hand, it is hard to imagine a 7 without three end points.

This version of the learning system was able to read the zip code numerals with an accuracy of 99 percent if 14 percent of the images were rejected as unclassifiable. If no images were rejected, the machine missed on about 6 percent of the examples.

Deciding what feature templates to include and what ones to combine requires knowing a tremendous amount about the problem. But Howard feels it still requires knowing much less about the problem than would be required to actually solve it. "I still can't tell you how to do these things [recognize handwritten digits] exactly by formula. What I can do is give the network the very best set of hints I can and all the help I can — everything I know about the problem — and get it into the easiest possible shape that I can and let it do the statistics for me."

He adds, "It's a change, to have machines learn by example rather than learning by being told exactly what to do. I think that's the revolution, that concept of training things by example."

The guts of this network, the part that performs the learning, is very simple. The entire system does contain thousands and thousands of lines of code, but "most of those, when we strip it away, are things that format data, are things that move data around," says Howard. "When you strip away all the data-handling part, the bookkeeping parts of the problem, there's a few lines of code that do the learning. And that's it."

Howard and his team did try stripping away that preparatory code, but the results with raw data weren't promising. Accuracy nosedived by a factor of five. Constructing a neural network employs two biological analogues, evolution and learning, and, Howard notes, it's important not to confuse the two. Teaching a properly structured network to categorize from examples is analogous to learning. Structuring the network so that it can detect features that are appropriate to the problem is analogous to evolution. Human beings learn how to recognize numerals, but they begin with a visual system that has evolved over millions of years. "People who start out with a fully connected network without any structure and expect it to learn from scratch are embarking on the evolutionary process. And we don't have the computational power to do that." It would require, Howard says, running a program and altering it once for each generation over some period that corresponded to real biological time.

Howard's team did find a way to improve the performance of the zip code reader in their next generation. The older system had to reject about 14 percent of the digits to attain a 99 percent accuracy on the rest. The next system rejected only 12 percent to attain the same accuracy. The extremely counterintuitive improvement? Make the machine sloppier.

Newcomer Yann Le Cun and his colleagues from the earlier team added two more hidden layers to the one hidden layer in the earlier version. Presumably, this gives the more recent network lots of material for forming higher-order features that aid in categorizing the digits. This addition also eliminates the need to handcraft combinations of features used in the earlier network. The machine now creates many of its own feature detectors. It is also a much bigger neural network, with 1,256 units and 64,660 connections.

Oddly enough, the increased exactness comes from a machine built with an intentionally engineered "fuzziness" in its "vision." The earlier machine, which used vectors to translate the feature maps into the input for the neural network, kept very precise records of space. It assumed that it was important to know exactly where every stroke ended, exactly where every curve began. The new version lives in "sloppy space." First, it undersamples the input grid. Points that are two apart in the input will be only one apart on the maps created in the hidden layer. Second, the learning rule used for adjusting the connections between neurons says, "Don't worry about where a stroke ends, just count all stroke ends the same." Instead of adjusting all the weights between all the units in this layer independently, depending on whether an individual neuron has seen a feature, all the weights in each of the twelve 8×8 neuron feature detectors change in unison when a feature is detected.

From layer to layer in this neural network, the world gets blurrier and blurrier. Undersampling and constrained weight change govern the second hidden layer, too. Here the input is the response of the first layer of feature detectors. This hidden layer has exactly the same number of feature maps as the previous layer, twelve, but each map contains only sixteen units instead of sixty-four. Again, the weights among the units in each of these twelve maps are constrained to remain equal. Again, some positional information is lost.

Hidden layer 3 has only thirty neurons, each one connected to every neuron in hidden layer 2. This last hidden layer is in turn fully connected to the ten units, one for each digit, that form the output layer.

Now, why does this system outperform the earlier iteration? Size might be one answer. Having more units might increase the system's computational power, as might adding more layers. It seems logical that giving the machine more material and opportunity to form intermediate combinations might improve accuracy and power. Le Cun and his colleagues say that some of the representations in the hidden layers are suggestive of the kinds of biological feature detectors first found by David Hubel and Torsten Wiesel in the visual systems of cats and monkeys.

Le Cun has a rough and dirty idea of what's going on inside the box: "The first layer is essentially forming edge detection, and the third layer is combining these edges to form more complex features like corners and angles and that kind of thing. But, in fact, we don't really know what this network is doing. It's doing something that it finds useful, but we didn't tell it what that should be."

Le Cun looks up from sliding a 7 in front of the video camera mounted on the workstation. Recently the team discovered that the machine is able to read hollow numerals, a 7 in outline, for example. Howard is excited; getting this kind of generalization out of the network is a verification of the approach. But Le Cun seems strangely downcast by this piece of success. "It has never trained on these hollow numbers," he says with a slight trace of a French accent. Now it's generalizing correctly, "and there's absolutely no reason why it should."

Le Cun and Howard are stuck with that puzzle. It is one that lies at the heart of many neural network machines. Why should this structure and this knowledge about the world make this kind of result possible? What if we had changed the structure in some way? What if we had used color or kept line width as part of the machine's knowledge? Would the performance have been even better — or would it have quickly deteriorated? Once you've begun asking those questions, there is no logical place to stop. You can argue that you should limit your trials to parameters roughly equivalent to those human beings or other species seem to use in solving similar tasks. But those parameters and the tasks themselves aren't very well understood. For example, studying human hearing led Ben Yuhas to conclude that we hear with our eyes. Visual feature detection, he believes, is essential to understanding speech.

Yuhas is just out of graduate school. In fact, he has just recently gone to work at Bellcore, the research arm of the regional Bell telephone companies. But that doesn't stop him from shaking his head sadly at most of the existing approaches to speech recognition. Speech recognition research goes wrong when, in an effort to understand how we turn sound into meaning, it immediately looks for symbols and ways to manipulate symbols, he says. "Traditionally you get it [speech] down to some alphabet of meaningful symbols and then write rules to manipulate them." Most computer scientists working on the problem have looked to linguistics for their understanding of speech. "It is symbolic, phonemic, and rule-based," Yuhas says.

Unfortunately, that characterization is wrong, he believes. Linguistics characterizes language as a closed, formal system. Using the symbols of the language system and its rules, a speaker can comprehend and generate all statements that are possible in that system. Yuhas thinks that has very little to do with speech as it exists in the real world. Speech isn't a closed system. It is inherently ambiguous.

We comprehend speech by combining information from a number of different information sources, he theorizes. By itself, each source provides imperfect information. The key to building a machine that recognizes speech may not be figuring out a more precise system of phonemes and the rules that translate them. Understanding speech may be as much due to seeing as it is to hearing phonemes. To recognize speech, a machine must be able to extract the appropriate information from many sources and then use the relationships among those sources to eliminate ambiguity, according to Yuhas.

To a degree, Yuhas arrived at his approach by chance. At Johns Hopkins he inadvertently acquired an extensive body of hard clinical data and some radical theories about computation at the same time. In Moise Goldstein's laboratory he was exposed to the problem that deaf people have with regulating the pitch of their voice. Since they can't hear themselves, they often talk either too loudly or too softly. Goldstein wanted to see if some kind of visual feedback could solve this problem. "I was in that environment when Terry [Sejnowski] was talking about the Boltzmann machine."

It wasn't the architecture of that particular machine that intrigued Yuhas but the avenues it opened up for attacking speech from another direction. "I was very interested in perception. Maybe we could explain some of the issues of artificial intelligence without immediately jumping to the symbolic level." Certainly it might be a way to get around at least one or two of the stumbling blocks to speech recognition in artificial intelligence. In particular, it might be a way to solve the problem of understanding speech in noise. The field, it seemed to Yuhas, had gotten bogged down in mechanics. Researchers were trying to find better ways to segment speech into phonemes or other units and then to manipulate these segments. The assumption was that if enough processing of the right kind could be done to phonemes, speech recognition would result.

He found that a questionable assumption. "In really young infants, if you give them two video screens and only one sound track, the infant will attend to the screen where the images [such as lip movement] match the sounds. There seems to be a very close relation between the auditory and visual parts of speech. We fuse [the two modes] at very early levels in the brain."

But Yuhas didn't know exactly what visual features the brain matched with what sounds of speech. The conventional solution would have been a careful statistical study that decomposed the signals and finally derived the necessary and sufficient visual alphabet. Yuhas decided to use neural networks instead.

The electrical engineering faculty at Johns Hopkins wasn't amused. "I was the first person in the department to do neural networks," he says, and initially, the faculty turned thumbs down on his Ph.D. thesis proposal. It was the project's reliance on computer simulations rather than mathematics that disturbed many of them. "What's the difference between running something on a computer and doing a whole set of equations?" Yuhas asks. After half a year of discussion the proposal was finally accepted unanimously.

The network Yuhas built is founded on a simple research observation. In a noisy room normal-hearing subjects tested on isolated words from a limited vocabulary get only 13 percent of the words right. Allow those same subjects to see the speakers, and performance shoots up to about 90 percent.

Using a neural network to make the connections between visual and auditory information is crucial, Yuhas says. A symbolic approach to artificial intelligence quickly bogs down in the attempt to create a complete symbol set. The researcher taking this approach must construct not only a phoneme system but also a system of visual symbols. And on the visual end there isn't even any agreement on what constitutes a visual unit. No one knows precisely what in a speaker's face we use as cues in recognizing speech. The one symbolic approach Yuhas knows about, that built by Eric Petajan for the recognition of isolated spoken digits, encodes both acoustic information and binary visual images of the speaker's mouth into symbol strings, with rules of combination and rules to settle conflicts.

With anything but a small vocabulary, the symbolic system ties itself in knots. To turn the visual and acoustic information into symbols the machine can use, the program must first reduce the information to categories. That in itself discards features that hold information. As the system progresses the problems multiply. It has to make a decision on how to combine and interpret each phoneme and visual symbol pair before moving on to the next. Necessarily ambiguous images and sounds have to first be fitted into precise categories before they can join the system's symbolic scheme. Once the images and sounds have been so encoded, a series of rules take over that say either "Yes, these two symbol systems agree," or "No, they don't." If they don't agree, other rules tell the system how to break the deadlock.

And what kind of symbols should such a system use? Yuhas says the speech recognition community isn't even agreed on the degree to which speech contains symbolic or subsymbolic structures. Visual signals of speech are even more problematic. Many of the sounds we make are clearly associated with the visible movements of lips and teeth. Others, those associated with the glottis and the velum, are invisible. Yuhas knew from other studies that phonemes such as /b/ and /k/ that are produced in visually distinct ways are among the most easily confused acoustic classes. Visually indistinct phonemes such as /p/ and /m/ are among those least likely to be confused when only presented acoustically. The evolution of our biology and speech seems to have matched ambiguous acoustic cues with distinct visual information and vice versa. The two may form a complementary set of signals that reduce ambiguity and increase comprehension.

Developing the visual signals for the network was the toughest part of the project. "There was this laser disk created at Hopkins" of video images of a single speaker's mouth, says Yuhas. After a few modifications, that became the visual training set. Yuhas had to pick representative examples of phonemes and mouth movements from the many repetitions on the disk. To avoid a speaker's natural tendency to shorten or drop phonemes in fluent speech, he picked only stressed vowels in isolated words. Segmentation, too, had to be carefully controlled so that the only acoustic signal considered by the machine was the one that matched the visual signal: neither could slop over into the next sound or image.

Despite these difficulties, the neural network approach gave Yuhas one key advantage. He didn't have to figure out what meaningful visual features to code. Say the speaker pronounced an /m/. A glimpse of teeth, lip movements, muscles tightening and relaxing all in various degrees matched that sound. Which of those, or indeed what combination of them, is the listener using to understand the acoustic signal better? Is it crucial that the speaker curls the left side of her lip or that the listener sees three teeth instead of four? To produce a set of symbols that an artificial intelligence can use, the researcher has to pick the right feature set.

Yuhas let his neural network do the picking. He established a rectangular area of interest centered on the mouth and simply fed a 20 × 25 pixel gray-scale image into the network. Using a network with five hidden units and nine output units, one for each of the nine vowels in the data, he trained his network on half of the 108 samples until it could recognize each vowel simply from the image. The machine never became perfect at this. "The visual categories are inherently ambiguous, too," says Yuhas. But the machine's performance compared favorably with that of two human subjects trained on the same data. It averaged 76 percent correct categorization; the two humans averaged 70 percent after five training sessions and 80 percent after several follow-up sessions. (With continuous speech, the neural network's performance fell to 40 percent correct. Human lip readers score around 54 percent with continuous speech.)

The next stage was a vowel recognizer unit that combined information from the visual and acoustic networks. Each network independently estimated the vowel, visually and acoustically, respectively, and then sent that estimate to the vowel recognizer itself. First, Yuhas trained the vowel recognizer with completely noise-free signals from the acoustic network alone until it achieved 100 percent recognition. Pumping in 12 dB of noise, however, reduced the network's accuracy to chance — about 11 percent. Adding the independent signal from the visual network improved performance markedly. At the 12-dB noise level performance went up to 35 percent.

But Yuhas started to get odd results as he pushed his network to the extremes. Alone, the visual network showed a 55 percent accuracy, but at high noise levels the combination of the two signals was less accurate than the visual signal alone. Clearly, the signals needed to be weighted somehow. Yuhas first tried a weighted average that factored in the signal-to-noise ratio. The network did significantly better at high noise levels and indeed never dipped below the 55 percent accuracy achieved by the visual network alone.

Yuhas also tried to improve the performance of his network by teaching it to weight the signals, somewhat as one of Widrow's adaptive filters did. The network measured the signal-to-noise ratio and tried to produce a noise-free signal. Here Yuhas used a standard neural network computation to measure and then reduce the noise — the squared error. This structure did indeed reduce the squared error measure but produced poorer categorization than either of the other networks. Yuhas found that disappointing but interesting. Squared error had been used to train the network origin- ally. Would some other method produce better results from the training? Could he find another way to link an added layer of units that would improve performance?

Yuhas thinks his approach seems promising. But he has to get a better handle on two issues: first, he needs to know more about what information the brain finds valuable in visual images and auditory signals. Second, he needs to figure out exactly how to combine this information. The symbolic model for language might be the wrong one for understanding how the brain works, but this new vision doesn't seem a whole lot less complicated. An intuitive sense of what language the brain might be using in one specific system isn't sufficient to duplicate that biological system.

5

BRAINSPEAK

To me, the major question of AI is this: What in the world is going on to enable you to convert from 100,000,000 retinal dots into one single word "mother" in one tenth of a second?

— DOUGLAS HOFSTADTER, "Waking Up from the Boolean Dream"

We must, however, acknowledge, as it seems to me, that man with all his noble qualities, still bears in his bodily frame the indelible stamp of his lowly origin.

— CHARLES DARWIN, *The Descent of Man*

Sitting across the breakfast table over muffins and coffee in a Pasadena café a few blocks away from the California Institute of Technology, Carver Mead gradually starts to put himself in the brain's shoes. This is how he would have evolved, Mead is saying, if he had been the human brain.

You've got to understand the brain's point of view, Mead begins. What does the world look like if you are the brain? It's certainly not orderly, precise, discrete, or predictable. It's full of ambiguities. "You're working on data that you don't know how to characterize. They're not regular. They're not well understood. They have regularities in them but you don't know what they are, and they are certainly not in any sense well-understood regularities." Nothing could be more different from the world of the digital computer.

You, the brain, don't have an endless library of computer programs or a rack full of transistors to work with, either, Mead notes. Nor do you have a lot of time to get it exactly right. If your solution for distinguishing between food and an enemy doesn't work, you can't send it back to the design team. You'll be dead. "So what did the nervous system do? It built up things that were easy to build out of the things it had. The stuff that it had was organic chemistry and the distributed energies of nerve channels. And the result is six or seven orders of magnitude more effective as a computer than anything we can imagine building [with digital technology]. Now that has to be telling us something, doesn't it?"

Mead finds it awesomely frustrating. The brain is "the only working system we have to study. But you can't get the blueprints." Indeed, in an important sense, there aren't any blueprints. This is an evolved system, not a designed one. Unlike an engineered system, the brain doesn't necessarily have a single, overall design logic.

But Mead does believe that we can reverse-engineer the brain, to a degree. We can examine it, figure out how it does what it does, and then build a machine that uses some of those same principles — if we never forget that we are engineers studying a brain and not engineers studying the work of another engineer. The brain's power, Mead believes, is derived from its ruthless opportunism. Over the course of evolution, it seized whatever fundamentals of physics and chemistry were available and lashed them together in systems that themselves changed over time. "It obviously has become very, very sophisticated," says Mead, "and we don't yet understand those principles, and we have to understand them. There's this whole other way to think about computation, and we don't have the beginnings of a clue to how it's done. We're just starting to get the tiniest little hints about those organizing principles."

If you were a brain, a very tiny brain about the size of an insect's, how would you go about a basic task like walking? Sylvie Ryckebusch, a fifth-year graduate student, spends her days in Mead's CalTech laboratory trying to imagine her way to solving that problem.

Very blond and very intense, Ryckebusch constructs insects — and leeches and sea slugs and lobsters. Actually, she *recon*structs them, trying to build the simple biological neuronal circuits that control swimming in the lamprey, chewing in the lobster, or walking in the cockroach out of transistors, capacitors, amplifiers and resistors. She believes all these seemingly dissimilar but simple activities share a common underlying structure that can be duplicated using a family of circuits built out of silicon. She's a little impatient today. An improved version of her computer chip is due back from the foundry. It incorporates a scheme that should let the circuit sense the minute imperfections in its own electronic components and teach itself how to compensate for them, much as the biological brain must teach itself to compensate for minute imperfections in its own neurons, she and Mead reason.

Walking should be almost automatic. It shouldn't require constant conscious decisions or even the sending of messages to higher command centers. Yet walking requires constant minor adjustments to match varying terrain. The basic motion constantly adapts to textures, elevations, and pitch. To Ryckebusch all this suggests a simple circuit that produces a repetitive motion that can be modified by feedback from the external world.

Her study of the biological systems that produce this kind of motion seems to support that intuition. Ryckebusch has looked at the simple circuits that produce repetitive motions like swimming in the lamprey or walking in the locust. These circuits, called central pattern generators, all produce a basic repetitive muscle action. That's not an insignificant trick in itself. The pulls and counterpulls of sets of muscles must be locked in a unique sequence, repeated without variation over and over again.

These circuits also seem to respond to limited feedback from the environment that adjusts the motion from moment to moment while preserving the basic pattern. A cockroach's walk, for example, combines a single, repeated pattern, called a tripod gait, with feedback from the surface underfoot and from the position of the legs relative to the body.

"I've been looking at the pattern generator that controls the swimming of the sea slug," Ryckebusch says. "In the real slug, you basically have these two groups of nerve cells that control the dorsal and ventral muscles. The slug swims by making a series of alternate dorsal and ventral contractions. It's very, very simple. The biological circuit has been worked out in quite a bit of detail, all the connections between the nerve cells, as well as the strengths of the connections. This," she says, gesturing both at the circuit diagrams on the wall next to her workbench and to the chips that rest on a shelf above it, "is a simplified version of the circuit."

Ryckebusch has moved on from the sea slug to study more complicated circuits with more sensory feedback. She had briefly considered tackling the circuits that produce flight in the locust for her dissertation project, but the sensory feedback involved in the wing system looked impossibly complex. Walking seems a better bet at the moment. "That's assuming that the physiology of the animal cooperates" when she begins studying the biological neuronal circuits.

To actually build a circuit that will control walking, Ryckebusch and Mead not only have to understand the principles the cockroach uses, but also to figure out how to translate them into the language of circuits. Before they can even begin this task, they have to decide what level of language is important to the meaning of the translation.

The standard "the brain is like a computer" analogy assumes a style of translation. Computers and computer scientists use mathematics as their language. Beginning computer science courses, Mead notes, often start by teaching a short catalog of basic algorithms, mathematical rules for performing elementary logical functions. At its most basic level, successful computation is simply a matter of using one of these rules to combine two or more signals carrying information in the appropriate way. Mathematical functions include sums, differences, multiplications, and divisions. Neurons, we have learned, combine signals in ways that can be seen as analogous to these operations. They sum signals, for example.

Finding neuronal evidence to support their mathematical structures has never been a critical need for computer scientists working in this metaphor. The history of their own discipline made it a marginal endeavor. The analysis of formal systems performed by Turing and others, and especially the Turing machine itself, demonstrated that a formal system of the sort that includes modern computers can simulate all the necessary classes of formal systems. A Turing machine can behave like the brain despite the differences between neurons and computer tape or electronic parts, because the brain was also a formal system.

But what computer scientists, both those working in the Turing machine tradition and those building neural networks, often seem to forget, says Mead, is that computation is just a metaphor for how the brain works. While many neuronal operations can be seen as sums, differences, multiplications, or divisions, those functions are really only convenient mathematical notations for much more complex and very poorly understood biological operations.

Take one process, visual edge detection, that Mead and other neural network researchers have studied intensely. After looking at the cells of the retina and their response properties, and the circuits they form, they have concluded that the eye uses a process that is very similar to taking the second derivative of a function in calculus. The first derivative of a function predicts the maximum and minimum points on the curve defined by the function. The second derivative finds the point of the greatest change in the function as it moves from its maximum to its minimum. The eye apparently finds an edge in the same way: circuits of cells with different responses to light intensity enable the brain to find the points of the greatest intensity change. Often in our world of shadows, corners, and textures, the line of those points makes up an edge.

The eye doesn't calculate a second derivative, notes Mead. It biologically combines signals in a way that resembles the mathematical function, but the computation of a second derivative is a metaphor for the biological process. The actual process in the eye and brain may have other properties that don't precisely match the second derivative. For example, the neurons may saturate — in effect behaving like a circuit breaker that has received too much current — at a certain level of light intensity. Above that light level they may not perform this "computation" at all. The biology of the brain, the mathematics of computation, and the physics of the silicon circuits that Mead uses to build his neural systems are all distinct languages. The key to neural computation, he believes, lies in finding what Mead calls the biological cognates — while always remembering, as any schoolchild struggling with a language knows, that the world is full of false cognates.

Depending on how you do the counting, this is Mead's second or third stint on the barricades of a computer science revolution. Along with Federico Faggin and others, he ushered in the age of the microprocessor. A decade ago Mead's classes and textbook on chip design, written with Lynn Conway, paved the way for putting entire computers on a single piece of silicon. Called very large scale integration (VLSI), the technique required new design tools. These new chips were just too complicated to design with existing methods. Mead's students, often with Mead sitting on the board, built the companies that built the new tools: Silicon Compiler Systems Corp., Seattle Silicon Corp., and Actel Corp.

Born in Bakersfield, California, in 1934, Mead looks like some version of Pan or some other Old World sprite, who grew up in the Sierras rather than in the glens of Arcadia. His sharp goatee highlights the mischief that gleams in his eyes. Speaking slowly and with long pauses that weigh every word twice, he seems a throwback to an earlier time when his family raised cattle in California's Kern Valley.

Now Mead is trying to use the VLSI technology he pioneered to build silicon neural networks complex enough to utilize some of the brain's architectures. Think about vision, he suggests. It starts in the eye with about 125 million rods and cones — the first-stage receptor cells that begin the process of seeing. By the time visual signals are ready to leave the retina, they've traveled through horizontal cells, bipolar cells, amacrine cells, and finally the 1 million retinal ganglion cells that make up the optic nerve. All of those cells have performed computations. They have detected brightness, compensated for contrast, enhanced edges, computed temporal derivatives, and in some animals calculated orientation, distinguished motion, and specified its direction. These are all incredibly useful and indeed essential operations if you want to do more complex things like pick out an object against its background.

Mead's views on the kind of translation an artificial network would require were influenced by his own first exposure to neural computation, more than twenty years ago, at the California Institute of Technology, naturally. "Everybody was looking for the nerve channel," he says. "It was just after the discovery of DNA. So everybody was looking for the molecule to be everything. If you knew the structure of the molecule you knew everything because that's how you got Nobel Prizes." Max Delbrück, who was to win the Nobel Prize for his work in viral genetics, was convinced that the way to understand the neuron and therefore the brain was to figure out the properties of the cell membrane. "So he came into my office, and he said in his thick German accent, 'Does the nerve membrane work like a transistor?'" After studying the membrane, Mead concluded that the theories being proposed were "garbage." Delbrück replied, "Well, then we have to figure it out!"

"You know, many people are still working on that," Mead says, "looking for all the channels in the membrane and trying to characterize them." Trying to understand the nerve membrane is a fascinating pursuit, but silicon chips shouldn't simply duplicate every detail of the biological neuronal system's microchemistry,

Mead believes. The important thing to understand isn't the behavior of each channel, protein, and neurotransmitter in each type of neuron. Instead, he wants to grasp the principles neurons use to represent information.

If an opportunistic biological brain seized the tools it had at hand to solve its problems, Mead, the opportunistic engineer of a silicon brain, should do the same thing with his different raw materials. Mead argues that below a certain level the details don't matter; this can't be a word-for-word translation. The point isn't to fashion a receptor for a neurotransmitter out of silicon but instead to find a basic circuit that can perform the same function in the chip that the receptor does in the brain. It isn't important, for example, whether a neuronal connection is built of nerve fiber insulated by myelin or of the thinnest of wires insulated by silicon, as long as both systems are able to delay the arrival of signals.

Mead finds support for his approach in the variety of the biological world. "The retina in a mud puppy uses totally different neurotransmitters than the retina in a rabbit, but the system principle by which it detects motion is similar. So what we're after is the part that's similar and not all the details," he says. "They're built with all kinds of neurotransmitters, but they all use gain and delay [as ways to modulate signals]. Whether those signals are chemical or electrical isn't the issue. There have to be certain signals and they have to be organized in a particular way or you won't get that behavior. That's what I'm after, the behavior of the system, not the behavior of the specific neuron."

The goal is a dictionary based on function that can be consulted to build neural networks. For example, if you begin with a biological structure that adds two parts of the signal together over a certain intensity range, you can look in the dictionary to find a silicon circuit that will do the same thing.

Building a dictionary of functions requires picking apart the biological system in exquisite detail. Only when Sylvie Ryckebusch understands how a biological system works can she begin to group its processes by function. Take just one box on her sea slug circuit diagram as an example. "This little box represents the circuit which integrates currents and produces pulses," she says. Currents come into the circuit and are summed, added together, in capacitors. Enough current will switch a transistor, generating a current through the rest of the circuit at a voltage determined by the amount of incoming current. "This is basically analogous to a sodium-potassium biological neuron."

At a functional level the biological neuron that the electronics mimic is also a circuit that adds currents and produces pulses. In the brain a nerve cell is surrounded by salt water containing sodium chloride (common table salt), calcium chloride, and a few other salts. Most of these salts exist as ions (positively or negatively charged atoms) of calcium, potassium, and sodium. These ions not only bathe the neuron but also move in and out of it. It is their distribution on either side of the neuron's cell membrane that creates the electrical imbalance that the nerve cell uses as a signal. Sodium and potassium ions, both of which are positively charged, do the bulk of the work involved in creating the electrical signals that travel through the nervous system.

If you look at one of the silicon circuits that Mead designed to perform like this biological one, you'll notice what at first glance seems to be a flaw in this adding device. Even at rest, when there is no signal causing current to flow through this circuit, there is still a tiny electrical charge stored in a capacitor. Surely, that charge will make the addition incorrect. What should be a straightforward $2 + 2 = 4$ can be $2 + 2 = 3.5$ or 4.5 or 2.6, depending on the size and sign of this stored charge. This isn't a flaw, however; it is the way the circuit simulates the Hebb synapse. By changing this charge, the circuit can be tuned so that the addition produces the right answer and the system as a whole produces the desired behavior. If it were a biological system, we would say it learns.

This stored charge is a silicon version of the electrical potential at the cell membrane of the biological neuron, without the chemical messengers and channels that produce that electrical charge in the cell. The biological cell membrane isn't an impenetrable barrier. In reality, each cell's membrane is pierced by countless passages through which substances, including the ions of calcium, sodium, and potassium, pass from one side of the membrane to the other, depending on various conditions. Some of these pores use size to control what passes through them, screening out larger ions and molecules. Others are pumps, powered by the burning of oxygen and glucose in the brain cells, that selectively move one kind of ion from one side to the other. Still others, called channels, open and close depending on the electrical charge on the cell membrane or in reaction to chemicals floating in or near it.

Creating the neuron's electrical pulse requires two other players: diffusion and the electrical charge on the ions themselves. At rest, the cell is slightly negative inside and the fluid slightly positive outside. The difference is about 70 millivolts (0.07 volts). This charge, called the electrical potential, is created by a pump that moves sodium out of the cell and pulls potassium into it. At the same time as the cell is pumping sodium and potassium, other pores allow potassium to passively flow through the membrane. Relatively few pores allow sodium to pass at this moment.

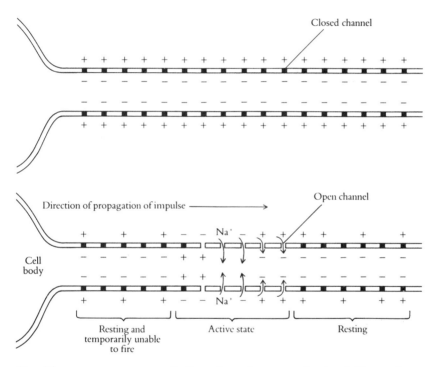

Top: The nerve axon at rest. Sodium channels are mostly closed. Pumps have expelled most sodium ions and brought in most potassium ions. Open potassium channels allow enough potassium ions to exit so that the membrane potential is 70 millivolts positive outside.

Bottom: A nerve impulse travels from left to right. In the middle section, sodium channels are open, allowing sodium ions to pour in. The membrane is now 40 millivolts negative outside. At the extreme left, the membrane is in recovery: potassium channels have opened and sodium channels have automatically closed. Drawing from David Hubel, *Eye, Brain, and Vision,* Copyright © 1988 by Scientific American Library. Reprinted with permission of W. H. Freeman and Co.

The sodium-potassium pump creates an imbalance between the inside and outside of the cell. There are more sodium ions outside than inside. Diffusion would force them across the membrane to equalize the two areas, but the relative lack of sodium pores makes this impossible. Potassium, in contrast, is in a higher concentration inside, because of the pump's action. It therefore diffuses out of the cell to the area of lower potassium concentration.

But the ions' electrical charges have a role to play here, too. Initially, the pump kept the two sides of the membrane in electrical balance since every time it removed a positive sodium ion from inside the cell, it replaced it with a positive potassium ion from outside. But now diffusion is pushing potassium ions out through the membrane, adding more positive charges to the outside solution. Eventually the electrical repulsion of positive charges will equal the tendency of diffusion to push potassium out of the cell. By that time, though, the outside of the cell will be positive, because of the combined positive charge of all the sodium ions (pumped out) and the potassium ions (diffused out), and the inside will be negative. At that moment the outside/inside difference equals an electrical potential across the membrane of exactly 70 millivolts.

Although it's easiest to think of a nerve impulse as an electrical current that flows through the "wires" of the nerve cells, that image is misleading. A nerve impulse isn't a current but rather a series of events. What travels down the nerve cell toward the cell body from the receiving synapses on the neuron's dendrites is a moving patch of change in the electrical charge across the cell membrane. Nothing like an electron or an ion travels down the nerve cell.

As far as any individual nerve cell is concerned, all nerve impulses begin at the synapse. Here the nerve impulse that has reached the end of the axon of the previous cell causes the release of neurotransmitters in the presynaptic membrane. These chemical messengers diffuse across the synaptic gap and fit into receptors on the postsynaptic membrane of the next nerve cell. The effect they have depends on the type of neurotransmitter; each kind of nerve cell has its own specific supply of neurotransmitters, and each neurotransmitter has its own message.

Different neurotransmitters acting on different receptors open channels that allow specific ions to pass through the membrane of the receiving cell. If, for example, a few sodium channels open, sodium begins to flow into the cell, powered both by diffusion into the cell from the higher concentration of sodium ions outside and by the attraction exerted on the positive sodium ions by the negative potential inside. So many sodium ions flow into the cell that the charge across the membrane at this location is temporarily reversed: the positive outside becomes negative in relation to the inside of the cell. This change in charge begins the impulse that will travel down the receiving cell.

Depolarization, the change from positive to negative outside the cell, doesn't last long, nor does it grow forever. The sodium channels are themselves voltage sensitive. As they sense the beginning of depolarization, more and more open until the cell membrane is about 40 millivolts negative outside, instead of 70 millivolts positive. But the sodium channels also have automatic timers that close them after a few thousandths of a second and prevent them from reopening for another few thousandths of a second. Thus, the pulse can't travel back toward its source — the sodium channels in that direction are in a forced rest — and it must travel as a kind of wave, down the nerve cell, as more and more sodium channels in that direction open in response to the membrane's depolarization.

The nerve impulse has a specific form that brain researchers and neural network builders assume is crucial to the way the brain signals information, even if no one knows precisely how. The impulse doesn't take place all at once along the nerve fiber but instead exists as a moving patch that may be as much as an inch long. This patch moves along the nerve fiber at about 0.1 to 10 meters a second, depending on the nerve fiber's specific characteristics. As it moves, this patch encounters other patches, which have resulted from the activation of other synapses. Some patches add their charges; others cancel each other out.

The final result of all these depolarizations is an all-or-nothing decision at the juncture between the cell body, called the soma, and the axon, the cable that leads away from the cell body and carries the pulse to numerous synapses with the dendritic trees of other neurons. The all-or-nothing nature of this decision led to the analogy between the nerve pulse and the off/on electrical signal in the digital computer.

Many more details go into this system — and may have a profound effect on the electrical signal. For example, some presynaptic

membranes release neurotransmitters that are excitatory for neurons with appropriate receptors — they encourage the receiving
nerve cell to generate a nerve impulse. Others are inhibitory —
they try to cancel any impulse generation. Many of these processes
also have thresholds. A weak electrical potential that falls below
this strength will simply die out without effect.

In the analogy of Harvard's David Hubel, the nerve is more
like a gun than a car accelerator. Unlike the accelerator, which
increases the car's speed depending on the force applied to the
pedal, the nerve impulse explodes down the nerve fiber when the
neuron fires, just as a bullet explodes down the barrel of a gun
when the trigger is pulled. Tugging very softly on the trigger results
not in a less forceful explosion and a slower-traveling bullet, but in
the same explosion and velocity. Similarly, the speed of the nerve
impulse is determined by the characteristics of the nerve fiber, not
by the force applied. Nerve impulses can be closer together or farther apart depending on the signals the cell receives (how often the
gun fires), but the strength of each impulse in any individual cell
will be the same as the strength of all other impulses. Information
about the specific event that led to the initial signal thus has to be
carried in the time at which impulses are generated and the rate at
which they are repeated, not in their strength. (This is true of
almost all neurons. A few neurons use graded signals, where the
bigger the initial signal, the bigger the depolarization.) At the synapse, of course, the distribution of specific channels, packets of
neurotransmitters, and receptors can perform other operations on
these signals in the process of turning them from patches of electric
potential to chemicals and then back again. These operations can
reduce the signal's effective strength, boost it, or transform it from
excitatory to inhibitory.

Understanding the process of nerve impulse transmission
gave Mead another clue to how the brain might have solved
its computational problems. He looked at this system as an
information-processing machine. Information coming in one end
had to be received, manipulated, and then transmitted to another
cell. What tools did the brain have for expressing information?
Well, Mead thought, it had the time of arrival of the pulse. That
would obviously affect the results of the addition.

The brain also had space and time at its disposal in this system. Pulses are being passed to even a single neuron from hundreds

or thousands of other neurons. All those pulses don't enter through the same door, either. Some come across synapses that are far out on the ends of the dendritic tree, at the very tips of its branches. Others come across synapses on bigger branches closer to the trunk. Still others are on the trunk itself. All of that affects how long it takes that patch of depolarization to reach the final decision point in the cell body itself. And all along the way these signals mix with each other in an order determined by where they entered the system. Some signals that might have canceled out instead miss each other because of their timing. Others coincide in time and add their effects. Time, then, must be included in the brain's list of computational tools, Mead came to believe.

"If you think about how we do computing, it's actually very, very strange," Mead says. "We decide ahead of time that we're going to represent things with ones and zeros and that the [logical] operators we'll use are NANDs and NORs. Then we build up everything, floating-point numbers, fixed-point numbers, adders, by doing the Boolean [logical] operations that it takes to make a set of ones and zeros turn into another set of ones and zeros according to some rules.

"By doing that we've been able to build a system that is completely deterministic. We can completely understand everything about it. There's enormous power associated with that total determinism. In fact, you know what's going to come out. When it comes to figuring out how to put the Voyager around Saturn or figuring out a bank balance, or controlling the airlines, it's just very, very important to be able to do that. But there is another way to do computation."

The tangible evidence of that other kind of computing litters the workbenches in Mead's laboratory. Tobi Delbrück is hunched over a piece of human retina. Steve DeWeerth has crudely mounted two monkey eyes and part of an ear on a lazy Susan. Of course, there isn't a bit of tissue or a smear of blood anywhere in this lab. These are all silicon circuits of oscillators, transistors, resistors, and wires.

It's possible to look at the software simulations of neural networks that Richard Howard's team is building at AT&T and still feel the kinship with traditional artificial intelligence. That effort still involves programming, transformation rules, and a structured decomposition of the task into logical subunits. It isn't clear that building a neural network in this way makes you think differently about computation or leads to questions about the "source" of behaviors that would seem to require coordinated intelligence.

In Mead's lab, in contrast, very strange ideas about how to produce complex behaviors come out of his way of thinking. Consider the question of how a cockroach walks. The end result requires coordinated motion among six legs, each with a tremendous repertoire of movements: lifting legs to get over obstacles; bending legs to walk on inclined surfaces; changing the force propelling each leg when the surface underfoot goes from tile to carpet.

Ryckebusch's cockroaches will one day accomplish all of these walks without using a brain or any kind of central processor — once she figures out how to add the right sensory modulation to the basic walking pattern. That solution will not require a higher center that puts together a complex solution and then fires a set of instructions back to the cells that command the leg. Her cockroaches probably won't even have a command neuron that could coordinate this behavior. In Ryckebusch's bug walking will simply emerge out of the interaction of all the neurons in the motor and sensory systems.

It will start with the basic walk rhythm created by the pattern generator. You can think of it as the default rhythm — what happens when no sensory feedback enters the system. This basic pattern results from the network's architecture, that is, how the neurons are hooked together. The balance of the connections creates a self-sustaining, repeated pattern analogous to the repeated swings of a pendulum or, since this is a many-neuroned creature, the rhythmic collisions and swings of the steel balls that make up the very popular toy that adorns many executive desks.

In some future generation of Ryckebusch's insect, all the other, more complex walking behaviors of the cockroach will result from perturbations of this pattern. As long as the insect walks along a level surface, for instance, the sensory neurons that detect balance send signals that cancel each other out. They neither add nor subtract anything from the pattern. On an incline, however, that balance is disturbed, so the sensory system does send a signal. It could add to the signal of one of the neurons in that pattern, kicking the signal that it sends to another motor neuron over its threshold. Or it could cancel out an inhibitory signal that has kept a neuron from firing. The end result will be a new pattern, a new walk, a variation in the swing of the pendulum. All this is still in the future for Ryckebusch.

Nowhere in that system is there any table of possible walks, or walk symbol tokens. A "walk unit" is never defined, and it is impossible to point to any one place where the decision about how to walk is made.

Ryckebusch didn't start with the act of walking and try to break it down into categories of walk or units of walk. A walk, she believes, is the result of the interaction between an internally generated pattern and the world. In this case, the world consists of inclines, textures, hardness, and the like. All of these features somehow — the exact how is the next big puzzle in Ryckebusch's research — modify the internal walking pattern. Perhaps the only way to understand this part of the process will be to build a machine that constitutes a best guess at how the biological system works.

The actual biological brain may be an opportunistic jumble of jury-rigged solutions built by blind evolution, but it's a marvel of efficiency compared to these stumbling attempts to duplicate just the first steps in the brain's work. Fortunately, evolution never had to use a screwdriver. Watching the wave patterns on the screen above his workbench in Mead's lab, Steve DeWeerth slowly, very slowly, turns one tiny screw. For a moment the waves almost lock into place, but then the pattern dissolves again. DeWeerth puts down his tool and flexes his hand. The tiny screwdriver keeps digging into his palm. His collection of transistors, resistors, and capacitors, all mounted on a circuit board, won't focus today. In biological terms, his two chips are just a little cross-eyed.

DeWeerth's chips are artificial retinas, networks of artificial neurons and synapses connected by almost invisible wires that do some of what the real human retina does. They can't "see" everything the collection of nerve cell receptors lining the back of the eye can. They aren't sensitive to color, for example. But they can distinguish patterns of black and white and even compare two patterns — just enough "seeing" to perform edge detection.

As primitive as this kind of vision is in comparison to that performed in the brain, DeWeerth would be very happy if his chip worked. Vision — duplicating something like the brain's ability to recognize faces, to tell the trees from the forest, or to read handwritten zip codes — has stumped immensely larger conventional computers, and it's not hard to see why. A single one-second black-and-white TV image is made up of 64 million bits of information. Even a massively parallel computer, such as the last-generation Connection Machine with its 65,536 processors, each much more complicated than the chip sitting on DeWeerth's bench, takes seconds to process a two-dimensional image. Nor are computer models of neural networks programmed on conventional computers any faster. Running on an AT-type computer, a program that modeled one cell of the visual cortex, developed by Rodney Douglas, Kevin Martin, and David Whitterridge of Oxford University, took thirty seconds to duplicate 400 milliseconds of the cell's processing in the brain. The brain can "read" such an image in fifty milliseconds — fifty thousandths of a second — a speed so fast it seems instantaneous. It's the ability to match the brain's real-time processing that makes building a neural network on silicon so potentially rewarding.

When the chip works, the CalTech artificial retina essentially matches the brain's speed. And DeWeerth has achieved that speed in a package that seems close in size to the amount of gray matter the brain may use. Even the limited vision he has attempted isn't currently possible on any commercially available system smaller than a desktop. But DeWeerth has packed it all on a single computer chip with just twenty-two simple processors. As rudimentary as this system is, it seems to be operating at the right order of magnitude, both in the time it needs to produce an answer and in the size of the machine itself.

But DeWeerth and Mead aren't after just a retina. They are attempting to build a two-step pathway, called the vestibulo-ocular system. If we move our head, but want to keep the same objects in our visual field, without conscious thought the brain tells the ocular muscles, the muscles around the eyes, to move them right or left, up or down. By adding another set of chips, representing the ocular muscles, to the retina chips, DeWeerth hopes to mimic the biological system.

It's a crude kind of mimicry, though. His retinas are mounted on a vaguely head-shaped piece of plywood attached to a lazy Susan, which simulates the changing orientation of the real human head. When they arrive from the foundry, the chips representing the ocular muscles will be mounted like eyebrows above the face's two eyeholes. This system bears only the most distant resemblance to biological reality. And to be honest, the retina chips themselves aren't much closer to neurobiological truth. After all, the biological visual system of the common housefly, for instance, is built around 270,000 neurons, not just twenty-two.

But exactly what does one of these silicon neural networks do? Mead's own auditory localization system, based on his silicon cochlea, which models the ear of the barn owl, is a good example of this kind of biological computation.

In one sense, the choice of the barn owl was arbitrary. "It's hard to get a well-studied biological system," says Mead. The barn owl fit the bill. The bird's spectacular auditory system lets it locate a mouse in complete darkness just by sound, and that biological system has been extensively studied by Eric Knudsen at Stanford University and Masakazu Konishi at CalTech.

From their work, Mead knew that slight differences in the vertical placement of the owl's two ears and equally slight differences in the left and right halves of the owl's facial ruff of feathers let its brain calculate the mouse's vertical position. The horizontal axis is computed from the very slight lags between sound waves reaching each ear. If the mouse is dead ahead, its rustlings reach both ears simultaneously. If it is slightly to the left of center, sounds it makes reach the left ear slightly ahead of the right. The difference is only measurable in microseconds, millionths of a second, but it's enough to let the owl silently swoop down on unsuspecting prey.

To build his chip, Mead assumed that the owl's brain uses those time delays to compute the mouse's location. His chip begins with two silicon ears connected to microphones. Each cochlea collects sounds from the lowest to the highest frequencies. Artificial hair cells, analogous to those in the owl's ears, tap into each cochlea at sixty-two different locations. Each hair cell responds to a different sound frequency. A sound that contains frequency A will produce an electrical current in the A hair cell in both the left and right cochleas. Each hair cell is in turn hooked up to a silicon neuron, sixty-two for each side. Two delay lines, representing the two axons from biological nerve cells, run between the A-frequency neuron on the right and the A-frequency neuron on the left. All sixty-two neurons on the right are connected to all sixty-two neurons on the left by pairs of wires in this way.

Another set of neurons connects each delay line of a pair at 170 equally spaced locations. A neuron will send out the strongest electrical pulse when the signals from both sides of the cochlea arrive at the same time. When the sound is directly ahead, the signals will reach the middle neurons of the A-frequency pair at the same time, and they will fire most strongly. All the other neurons along the A-frequency pair of wires will also fire, but with varying and weaker strengths. If the sound comes from the left, the signal will strike the left cochlea first, travel down the delay line from the left A-frequency hair cell first, and meet the laggard signal from the right cochlea closer to the right side of the neural system.

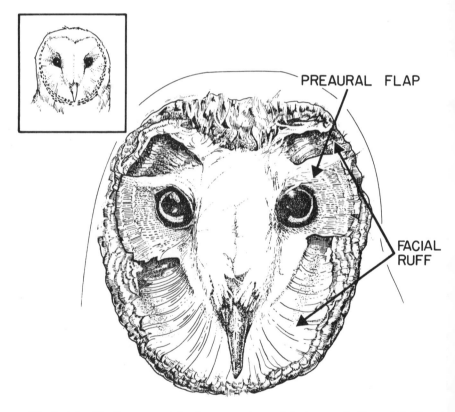

The facial ruff collects sound for the external ear of the barn owl. *Upper left:* The face of the barn owl with all its feathers in place. *Above:* The face of the owl as it would appear if all the overlying facial disc feathers were removed. The openings to the ear canals are immediately behind the preaural flaps. Note the molded contours formed by the ruff feathers.
Drawing courtesy of Eric I. Knudsen.

Each actual location produces a slightly different pattern of electrical signals. Each of these different firing patterns of the chip's sixty-two sets of 170 neurons corresponds to a different position on a map of the outside world, learned by the owl's brain when the owl was very young or, in this case, calculated by a somewhat older Mead.

Mead believes this localization system, built with John Lazzaro, captures some basic principles in the brain's bag of perceptual tricks. He is sure, for example, that time delays are used throughout the brain. Time is a crucial computational building block in the brain, what is called a "primitive." In every brain — no matter the species — the delays, the differing speeds, and the lag between signals carries information from one part of the

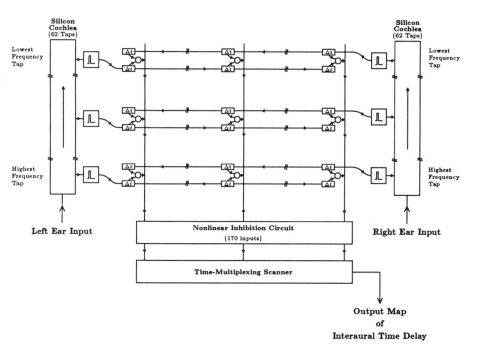

A plan of the silicon model of the time-coding pathway of the barn owl's auditory localization system built by Carver Mead and John Lazzaro. Inner hair-cell circuits (which tap each silicon cochlea at sixty-two locations) and spiral ganglion neuron circuits are represented by the square marked with a pulse. Action potentials from the ganglion circuits travel down silicon axons, represented by the rows of small rectangular boxes marked with the symbol Δt. The small circles represent the 170 neuron circuits that lie between each pair of silicon axons.

network to another, and together these time values make up the operations of the system, the adds and subtracts, that produce the "answer."

But the principles embodied in Mead's chip are by no means universal. The brain's auditory and visual systems, for example, are radically different in the way they deal with a seemingly similar phenomenon like wavelength. As Mead's localization system shows, the auditory system uses all of sound's wavelength components. In the biological ear thousands of receptors are each tuned to a different wavelength. That's why a trained ear can pick out and identify the individual notes of a chord.

The visual system, on the other hand, is very reductionist. It captures only three wavelengths of light, and we can see only seven colors. Nor can we pick apart a beam of light into its components.

Vision has sacrificed all these capacities for a spatial mapping of the outside world that is far more complex than that produced by the auditory system. The 125 million rods and cones in the retina give the visual system the ability to distinguish the minute differences in the scene that lead to our perception of depth, motion, continuous objects, and distances. The visual circuits being constructed in Mead's lab confront an entirely different problem from that addressed by his artificial cochlea, and their solutions must reflect that difference.

The brain speaks not one but many languages, and vision and audition know their own tongues. What we think of as a unitary process, such as speech recognition, is often actually a bundle of languages working together to gather some part of the available information in the outside world. They then collaborate to find a way to extract meaning from it, encode that meaning, and then manipulate it. Often these languages aren't complete. By itself each one is a garbled translation, an ambiguous version of the outside world. The confusion isn't because of some noise entering the system or a faulty neuronal part. It seems instead that ambiguity is the single characteristic that best defines our sensory relation to the world.

The pieces of silicon littering the benches in Mead's laboratory are all sensory systems, the periphery of the nervous system. They are the easiest systems to study, the parts of the brain about which we know the most. It is simple enough to imagine the auditory system of a barn owl as a delay-line circuit, but is the rest of the

brain just a similar set of engineering solutions and specific circuits? Neural networks strongly argue that behaviors such as walking emerge from the interaction of all the neurons connected in a
system. Do things such as thoughts and memories and logic and
generalization and psychology emerge in the same way from the
properties of neural networks in other parts of the brain? And what
happens if we put together systems of systems, networks where
each unit is itself a network? Would these systems start to produce
behavior that we might call intelligent?

6
PARTS AND HOLES

God becomes God when the animals say: "God."
— JOHANNES ECKHART

When would we be willing to call a machine intelligent? Alan Turing asked more than a half century ago. Put a human being in one room and the intelligent machine in another, he suggested. Give them both the same task to perform, such as answering questions or conducting a conversation. Let an outside observer see only the results. If the observer can't tell the difference between the performance of the human being and the machine, then we have to say the machine has achieved intelligence.

Michael Mozer's machine clearly fails this test. Frankly, Mozer himself looks like the last person you would ask about intelligence. Dressed in a black T-shirt and what once must have been shockingly bright madras pants, and toting a backpack, he seems determined to cling to his roots as a California surfer. His routine performed for a largely somber audience at the 1990 Neural Information Processing Systems conference is pure David Letterman, laid-back and self-deprecating. This machine is just something we whipped up, and we think it's kind of neat, his manner seems to say. But, hey, it's no big deal, you know.

But no one needs to take Mozer's word for it. Just listen to his machine itself. Can this machine compose music that sounds like Johann Sebastian Bach's or not? Using *The Notebooks for Anna Magdalena Bach* as basic lessons, Mozer tried to teach the machine to create new compositions in the style of Bach. Rather than analyzing Bach's music and then feeding those derived rules to the machine, however, Mozer taught his device by "ear." It learned by "listening" to examples of Bach's compositions. "Just the right-hand parts, though," says Mozer, who is an assistant professor at the University of Colorado at Boulder. He turns on a tape of the machine's performance.

As Mozer readily admits, it's hard to make a meaningful comparison since the performance lacks any of Bach's complex counterpoint. Phrases sound eerily reminiscent of a Bach minuet for almost a dozen bars, only to dissolve into something basically . . . well, let's say unmusical. Promising figures are repeated once and then twice, as Bach might have done, and then a third time and a fourth and a fifth without significant variation. "You can hear that this still has a way to go," Mozer notes.

Right now the machine's Bach is worse than its bytes, but Mozer thinks he knows how to remedy that. What the machine needs, he feels, is a global sense of the patterns in Bach's music. Adding harmony would help clarify that global picture. Bach's chord progressions follow a very regular pattern, and that order helps to constrain the individual notes within a musical phrase. (This is especially true with classical compositions. Mozart used the global rules of composition during his lifetime to produce his own composition machine. His "A Musical Dice Game" [K516f] consists of 176 bars of music that can be combined according to throws of the dice and a few rules to produce a vast number of 16-bar waltzes.) Such an improved machine might sound more like Bach and be a step closer to passing the Turing test.

But this particular fix isn't a simple one. In fact, it is one of the fundamental problems facing the builders of neural networks and other sorts of artificial intelligence, one of the true chicken-and-egg problems in the field. Instead of chickens and eggs, however, it involves "local" and "global" information. To figure out what local information — what notes, for example — the Bach machine should play, it needs a sense of the global pattern of Bach's music. But the machine can only build this global pattern from local information. All that this Bach machine knows (like the past tense machine, NETtalk, and the artificial cochlea) is some limited part of the world. But without global knowledge it is extremely hard for that local knowledge to mean anything.

But how much of the global picture does Mozer's Bach machine need to know? It certainly needs to know less than everything Bach knew. A knowledge of how to produce children, a body of facts that Bach seems to have mastered well in his lifetime, is probably irrelevant to the machine's ability to compose music, for example.

And even if Mozer could find that balance, and his machine composed music indistinguishable from Bach's in a blind test, would we be willing to call it intelligent? It would still be a machine without intention, awareness, or choice. Even though it is tremendously complex, we could call its behavior a reflex, a conditioned response. Confronted with stimulus A, the machine responds in pattern B after appropriate conditioning. It would have no understanding of its task, or at least none that we could see. None of these qualities is demanded in the Turing test, but as University of California at Berkeley philosopher John Searle objects, the Turing test doesn't really meet our commonsense definition of intelligence. We require that an intelligent being be aware of its own internal mental state, for example.

Even honeybees seem much more intelligent, in these terms, than that yet-unbuilt machine. In 1988 James and Carol Gould trained a number of marked bees to fly to a rowboat in the center of a lake, where they gave them a carefully measured quantity of nectar — enough to keep the marked bees coming back to the boat but not enough to make them "dance" the location of the nectar to other bees in the hive.

After the marked bees had clearly learned the location of the nectar, the Goulds increased the quantity. Now the marked bees danced its location when they returned to the hive, but dance as they might about the abundant food, they were ignored by the rest of the hive. The unmarked bees simply would not pay attention to what, for honeybees, is ordinarily vital information. The majority of the bees failed to follow a reflex.

Of course, it was impossible to ask the bees why they ignored the dance. The Goulds theorized that the unmarked bees simply knew better: they had a mental map of the geography surrounding them, and they knew from that map that the dance had to be wrong. A large source of nectar couldn't possibly be located in the middle of a lake. To check this theory, the Goulds gradually moved the boat with the nectar source closer to the lakeshore. As it neared a position that was more plausible, the number of bees in the hive responding to the dance increased.

Without some access to the bees' mental process, any attempt to decide what mechanisms produced their behavior has to include a large element of speculation. The bees might be mentally aware of what they know and could have concluded that the message should be ignored since it was clearly implausible. We might feel more comfortable with this explanation if the subjects were not bees but human beings. Or maybe the bees only follow a very simple chain of rules without any need for awareness of any sort. Maybe one rule says, "Interpret dance but ignore if location is implausible after consulting map." The rules could tell the bees what global patterns to consider in what circumstances. They could be hardwired into the bee brain. Application wouldn't require any conscious thought: very simple environmental conditions could trigger entire strings of behavior by telling the bee brain what to ignore and what to look for.

As Daniel Dennett, a philosopher of the mind who teaches at Tufts University, has pointed out, we tend to limit our ascriptions of intention to human beings. With machines we assume that if we know how they were designed, we can predict their response to any circumstance. With human beings we add goals and beliefs and desires to the explanation. If we know that Mary wants an ice-cream cone, we can predict Mary's actions. We can also explain human behavior backward in a causal chain from purchase of ice cream to walk to store to request for money from Mom to Mary's desire for ice cream. We have to assume Mary's rationality in this case. The explanation won't work if Mary believes that she can get an ice-cream cone by putting an ice cube under her pillow.

But, Dennett asks, is the intention in Mary or is it an explanatory stance assumed by the observer? We sometimes explain very complex machines, such as a chess-playing computer, as if they had goals and desires. The computer wants to win the game, we say. What would we say about a machine that roamed around the Artificial Intelligence Laboratory at MIT picking up only empty soda cans and carrying them away for proper disposal? Does such a machine show intention? Does it have a psychology? And can we infer anything about the complexity of its internal design from its observable behavior? A talk with Rodney Brooks, the spirit behind this Collection Machine, certainly raises tricky questions about the "intelligence" of seemingly intelligent behavior.

In Cambridge Brooks is getting some very complex behavior out of some very simple machines. They have absolutely no sense — on any level — of what they are doing, and in fact, they haven't mastered any patterns as remotely complicated as those conquered by the honeybee. Often, Brooks knows, the right hand can't know what the left wheel is doing. Brooks knows they can have no intention, no sense of purpose, awareness, or consciousness, because he put none of that in. But their behavior seems to demonstrate all of these characteristics — Brooks's robots behave as if they were intelligent. Are those qualities actually in the machines, or do we simply read them into any behavior that resembles our own?

Brooks, an Australian who presides over a menagerie of walking and rolling machine intelligences, didn't set out to prove anything about the nature of intelligence or the validity or usefulness of neural networks. In fact, while he sees the connection between his work and neural networks, he doesn't claim membership in that camp. He has the pragmatic goal of the engineer. "I want to build systems that work, actually, in the physical world." Conventional robots seemed to have severe limitations, ones that Brooks wasn't sure would ever be overcome. They took too much time to figure out where they were, where to go, and how to get there. Beginning in 1984, he decided to take a different approach, one inspired by biological systems and evolution. In the natural world "more complicated animals are built out of simpler systems," says Brooks. Why wouldn't that be a good idea for building mobile robots?

"I was perturbed by what was going on in 1984, 1985 with mobile robots," he says. "At that time any mobile robots that were around were extraordinarily slow. They would take an image and compute for many, many minutes, and then move a little bit. This didn't seem compatible with moving around in a dynamic world at all. Sitting in the middle of the road while a truck is coming is not a good idea. I was trying to see how we could get responsive actions, reactions almost, into whatever cognitive architecture that we were going to use. I realized that I would need fast feedback loops between senses and actions. I thought I would also have slower feedback loops operating separately."

The initial rough design was a typical artificial intelligence map with boxes representing the various processes that the computer "mind" of the robot would have to perform to move across a room or pick up an object. To speed it up, Brooks designed a parallel organization with lots of loops connecting sensors to motors. Each one of these took information from one or more sensors, fed it to some of the robot's motors, and then checked back with the sensors to see the effect of that action. With these loops hooked up in parallel, they could all act at once — no system had to wait for the results from a long chain of other systems. So far, aside from the unusually high degree of parallelism, this looked like traditional artificial intelligence. At this stage each of these boxes was itself a very complicated computer. It had to be to run the complicated symbolic languages and the rule sets that would decide what to do. Still all very traditional.

"Then," says Brooks, "we started to build our first robot and built a simulation of our first software on a LISP machine, and initially each of those boxes was a LISP program." At that time LISP was one of the standard languages of artificial intelligence computer programs. A complex set of rules that allows a programmer to break down an event into an ordered string of very simple sequential rules, LISP required the power of a complicated computer. At each box information would have to be sent to a central processor powerful enough to execute the LISP program, which would then generate actions that would be sent back to the motors of the robot. Brooks, it seemed, still hadn't conquered the bottleneck of the central processor or the time delays it and LISP introduced into the robot.

But "as we started doing things, we noticed that a lot of those boxes were really simple," he says. Each one took a few inputs and needed to perform only a relatively small number of computations. When two boxes reached a decision at the same time, applying a fairly simple rule usually was all that was necessary for resolving the conflict. "We originally thought that we would have to have a whole arbitration box where two data streams came together. That was hairy stuff." Instead, Brooks simplified the number and kinds of decisions the system could make between boxes. One signal could be inhibited — switched off. Or the signals could be prioritized, with one going first and then the other, a process Brooks calls suppression. Or they could all be let through for later addition.

A tour of the ninth-floor "bug" lab shows that these simplified boxes have mutated into a menagerie of creatures. There's Allen, now six or seven years old and the first robot to come out of the lab. Allen is a simple cylinder mounted on a three-wheeled base. Two rings of sonar, scavenged from Polaroid cameras, give Allen basic information about his environment.

Traditional robotics said that the way to guide a robot around a room was to first create an internal symbolic map of the room inside the robot's head. Sensors on the robot, whether "eyes" that saw visible light or infrared or sonar, would feed in information that the robot would strive to match with the internal map, generating new movement signals as a result of the discerned position. The constant updating of position, the search for a match with the internal map, and then the generation of movement was incredibly time-consuming. And it ran into problems in a dynamic environment. If the room to be navigated changed — a chair was moved, for example — the robot often got confused. It couldn't tell if the room had changed — time to update the internal map — or if its position in the room had altered — whoops, I'm not where I thought I was. Position could be readily confused with new map features.

Allen didn't have an internal map. It was supposed to maneuver around an unstructured room environment without any knowledge of what the room as a whole looked like. "We were not dealing with any a priori knowledge," says Colin Angle, a twenty-three-

Brooks's menagerie: Herbert, the Collection Machine, is on the far left in the back row, between Allen and Seymour. Genghis is on the floor in the foreground. Photograph by Anita Flynn, MIT.

year-old graduate student who has worked on almost all these robots. "None of these have any global knowledge of the room."

The second robot is Herbert the Collection Machine, whose name is a typically Brooksian play on MIT alumnus Danny Hillis's supercomputer, the Connection Machine. Herbert tackles a more difficult task than Allen's. It is supposed to wander around the ninth floor, navigating desks, walls, stacks of books, and the like; find soda cans; pick them up; and carry them back to home base for disposal. Like Allen, Herbert is a cylinder on wheels, but with an added arm for picking up cans. With a set of more precise infrared sensors and a visual sensor that can discover edges, it can navigate, lock onto a can on top of a desk, stop in front of the desk, position itself, reach over and search for a can with its arm, pick up the can, and then carry it away for disposal.

Seymour is the last of this first generation, which are all named after stars of the artificial intelligence field — Allen Newell, Herbert Simon, and Seymour Papert. "The goal was to have it [Seymour] interact with people," says Angle. "The idea was that it was going to live up here on the ninth floor, using its infrared sensors to locate people. When its batteries went low or it needed to open a door, it would roll up to a person and say, 'I'll give you fifty cents if you open the door.' Seymour has never actually been finished, however.

With Allen, Herbert, and Seymour, Angle acts as a gracious if disinterested host. Talk about Genghis or Attila, however, and his eyes light up. These are his babies, the ruthless conqueror series. Genghis is the first walking robot built in the lab, fabricated in a blindingly fast three months. Gone is the cylinder and the wheeled base. Genghis hugs the ground, a six-legged metal insect driven by servomotors taken from model airplanes. Picking up one leg after another, it walks across a special gravel landscape built and enclosed just for its tests. A full-color photograph of the earth seen from the moon covers one wall. As Genghis scuttles across the gray plain, scaling rocks as high as six inches, it reveals its designers' ultimate goals: Genghis is a prototype for a robotic moon explorer.

Attila is Angle and Brooks's current project. "This has been an obsession for two and a half years pretty much full-time," says Angle. In fact, this insect walker is Angle's master's thesis project. Mounted in a vise on a workbench, Attila twitches its legs. Soon, Angle hopes, it will walk. "On Monday, Rod and I were here till five-thirty, and we almost got it to work. Tuesday, we found the bug and all the legs moved to servo position [upright and ready to walk] around midnight. That was the first wonderful milestone, so we broke out a bottle of champagne and went home. Then yesterday, I was here till midnight swapping around the motors, and then I got stuck because I needed some new software. Tonight I think we're going to hack late again. I think we're going to get real walking tonight." The key is finding the right timing pattern that will coordinate the legs. The first one Angle tried froze the robot with all its legs in the same position. The next one lifted three legs at a time, and Attila pitched forward onto its nose.

Attila is the best of all insects — a powerful brute with feeling. The burnished aluminum insect isn't smarter than Genghis, mind you. Its mechanical framework is just immensely more physically versatile, and Angle has added more and better sensors so that Attila is able to gather much more information about its world. Attila can lift its leg to take a ten-inch vertical step. "If it can find

Genghis, a prototype for a planetary explorer, can successfully tackle extremely varied terrain.
Photograph by Anita Flynn, MIT.

footholds, we hope that it can climb nearly vertical surfaces," says Angle. If it should fall over, no matter. It doesn't helplessly wave its legs in the air, nor does it flip or roll over. Angle designed Attila so that it really doesn't have a top or bottom. Flipped on its back, it simply rotates its head and legs 180 degrees, bottom becomes top, and Attila goes on its way. "One of the few things that we can do better than Mother Nature is build rotary joints."

On Attila 150 sensors of twelve different types supply information on the robot's environment. With twelve spring gauges on each leg, Attila feels the hardness of surfaces and their angles. Other detectors let each leg know when it's within an inch or so of something or differentiate between grass and the hard surface underneath. An active whisker probes ahead into space. "We are trying to give it more and more sensory information to act on and to use to build its world," says Angle. Listening to him talk, it's easy to forget that he is just twenty-three. But then he adds, "I wanted it to look cool, too," as he points to Attila's matte-gold legs.

But where does all this sensory information go? It doesn't go into anything resembling a brain or a central processor. As far as "brainpower" goes, Attila is about as dumb as a stump, far dumber than insects that have a central nervous system. Very little information gets passed very far in any of these machines. Certainly nothing happens that's remotely akin to a message or symbol being passed into a central processor for computation and then, after the addition of new information, being returned to the motors and sensors for action. Most units, the boxes of the original design, speak only to a very few nearby boxes. The perplexing thing about Brooks's robots is that they seem to show organized intelligence in their behavior while they contain nothing inside that can possibly be the locus of that intelligence.

Take Herbert the Collection Machine. "There is no internal communication" in the Collection Machine, says Brooks. All the computing units — simple computational devices called finite state machines, which exist in one of a small number of conditions determined by the information fed into them — are directly connected to sensors. The robot has almost no memory. It couldn't construct and remember a map of its world if it wanted to.

And yet this machine behaves as if it were intelligent. "To an observer," says Brooks, the machine looks like "it does this cohesive thing of going around and finding a soda can and taking it

home to where it was switched on. But if it can't remember anything for more than three seconds, how can it remember where
home is? How can it know how to get back?" The machine seems
to have an overall goal, finding soda cans and bringing them back
to home, without any place in the machine where that goal could
be stored, remembered, imagined, or imaged. And it shows order
and sequence in its actions without a central brain to prioritize
movement. The machine stops in front of a desk, lifts its arm, and
searches for a can. How does it know when to lift its arm without
a program to give it a sequence? How does it know to return to
base after it has picked up a can? There is no program, not a line
of code anywhere, that says anything like, "If you have picked up
a can, return to base."

A lot of what we call intelligent behavior is simply a way of
telling an ex post facto story, Brooks claims. "When you're asked,
'Why did you do that?' 'Why did you turn the corner here?' 'Why
did you put the brakes on now?' you have to make up a story.
'Well, there was a car in the way.' Stuff like that. But you didn't
go through that when you put the brakes on. We make up stories
that rationalize our behavior all the time." We cannot assume a
simple correspondence among observed behavior, internal structures, and ex post facto explanation, Brooks says. Brooks, like
Rumelhart, draws a clear distinction between rules as description
and rules as causal mechanism.

"This is meant to be an extreme point in mechanism space,"
Brooks says, "and the message is, Don't believe what you see. You
look at this [machine's behavior] and it looks like it has a cohesive
plan. And it doesn't. So what's the take-home message of that? If
you see an animal doing something, does it have all that [a controller, a map of the landscape, and so forth]? No. Not necessarily.
And that's the message you get from the ethologists. Animals are
not as anthropomorphic as we think they are. And then maybe
people aren't as anthropomorphic as we think we are. A lot of what
we do isn't as rational as we'd like to think it is." A lot of "rational"
behavior results from systems that don't have even an understanding of that term.

The Collection Machine is actually driven by very simple rules
that don't bear much resemblance to anything we could call intelligence. For example, one of the finite state machines is hooked up
to sensors in the mechanical hand that tell it how far apart the

fingers are. "If its fingers are one distance apart, it's got something in its hand. If they're a different distance apart, it doesn't have anything in its hand," says Brooks. Thus, that finite state machine exists in one or the other of only two possible states. And those states, in turn, tell the machine which of two navigation rules to use. One set, nothing in the hand, is designed to keep the machine searching for soda cans. The other set, the hand is full, is designed to take the machine back to base. All the Collection Machine uses to determine its behavior are sensors that detect simple either/or conditions and finite state machines that say, If condition one, do this; if condition two, do that. Add a local infrared map and a simple compass and, presto, seemingly purposeful behavior.

Observing the machine's behavior, watching how it reaches for a soda can, is not a very good indication of how it arrives at its actions. According to Brooks, "There's no internal communication. When the laser scanner sees the soda can and drives the robot up so that it's sitting in front of the soda can, it can't tell the arm that we're sitting in front of a soda can. So what does the arm do? The arm is always looking at the wheels. If the wheels haven't turned for a while, it must be the case that the robot is sitting in front of a soda can; otherwise, the robot would still be exploring. So now the arm comes out. It has seventeen behaviors and it has all sorts of local searches that it does, and it finds the soda can."

The complexity arises not from complicated rules in the individual units or out of complex rules governing how individual units interact. Instead, it seems to emerge from a lot of units doing simple things with simple interactions all at the same time. "There's this whole big word coming around, 'emergence,' which is getting hotter and hotter. I'm interested in emergence as a phenomenon, but we've recently decided it's best not to define it. It's like trying to define artificial intelligence."

Emergence turns a basic premise of artificial intelligence on its head. From its beginnings as an applied science, artificial intelligence has assumed an identity between the complexity of the resulting behavior and the complexity of the mechanisms that produce it. All behavior could be broken down into simple units, simple acts, and simple logical statements. However, those simple statements would be embedded in complex structures of recursive logic that, step by step, would again build up the complex structure. After each simple statement, a simple logical connection would arbitrate between multiple possible pathways. The resulting structure had a complexity that roughly matched the complexity of the behavior. A behavior that required a complex story to explain it required a complex underlying structure to produce it.

Brooks's machines seem to break that connection. The Collection Machine shows complex behavior without a complex internal structure. The absence of much internal communication means that there is no recursive structure with symbolic tokens of action passed from place to place in the machine. Behaviors are the result of local states rather than global recalculations of the state of the entire machine. The overall behavior, a complex pattern of search, recognition, grasping, and return, is nowhere matched in the machine's structure.

Brooks's theory certainly didn't go over too well in 1984 or 1985 or 1986, and it really doesn't go over well even now in some places. Brooks has a copy of a reviewer's very negative comments on a paper he wrote in 1986 taped to his eighth-floor office door. "This paper is an extended wandering complaint," it says, "that the world does not view the author's work as the salvation of mankind. There is no scientific content here. Little in the way of reasoned argument as opposed to petulant assertions and non sequiturs and ample evidence of ignorance of the literature on these questions." Brooks chortles when he notes the ultimate fate of this piece. "It finally appeared in a journal in 1991. It's had a little hard time. I have not changed a word. I refused to change it. It's called 'AI Without Representation,' and it says that all of AI is wrong."

This conclusion may be a little premature, however. Brooks's machines certainly show more global complexity of behavior than can be found anywhere in their structure. Local units interacting with local feedback result in a system that seems to show intelligence and purpose and intention. If we were machine psychologists studying these machines on the basis of their behavior alone, we would be justified in asking where these principles came from.

Still, if we take a step back, we see that these machines clearly depend on an a priori understanding of the task and its solution by their creator. There are no real surprises here. Nothing emerges from the interactions of these local units that wasn't predicted and sought after. As a definition of intelligence, these machines seem too predictable and too engineered.

Is animal intelligence different in kind from the "mentality" of these machines, though, or is it just more difficult to explain?

Compare one of Brooks's machines with a rat performing a similar task. Bruce McNaughton, a psychologist at the University of Arizona, has spent the last decade watching how rats learn to run mazes with different rewards, different learning cues, and different patterns. Comparing the different experiments, seeing what rats learn easily and what is difficult or impossible, starts to establish some parameters for rat learning.

For example, take a rat and train him to find food in one arm of a plus-shaped maze, as John O'Keefe and D. H. Conway did in 1980. The researchers kept the enclosure featureless except for an array of cues, objects scattered around the maze, that they introduced. With the cues the rats rapidly learned how to identify the arm with the food no matter which arm of the maze they were initially placed in. If they were introduced into the maze without any cues, they chose at random. If they were introduced into the maze in the presence of cues, but were confined to the starting arm while the cues were then removed, they were still able to make the correct choice. Even when the start of the run was delayed for half an hour after the cues were removed, the rats were still able to find the correct arm. And forcing them into the wrong arm before letting them free to seek the arm with food didn't hinder their search. From this, McNaughton concludes that rats aren't simply memorizing motor routines — turn right, walk eight steps, turn left — to conquer the maze. Otherwise, forcing them into the wrong arm would disrupt their ability to find a solution. It seems as though they must be creating a map of some kind and remembering it.

The rats seem far more "intelligent" than Brooks's machines. They make maps. They don't simply memorize motor routines — or look to see if their wheels are moving.

But another experiment that McNaughton ran himself suggests a somewhat different conclusion. This one involved an eight-arm maze whose eight arms all radiate outward, like the spokes of a wheel, from a central crossroads. Food was located at the end of only one arm. It took a rat only three to four trials to get this down right.

After the fourth trial McNaughton physically moved the maze to another part of the same room, one separated from the original location by a partition. This new space had only two features in common with the old: the researcher and a 25-watt bulb that pointed into the upper corner of each partitioned space. But here McNaughton reversed the position of each of these relative to the maze and the arm with food by 180 degrees. The rats didn't do well on this maze; in fact, they did everything exactly 180 degrees wrong. McNaughton discovered that they tended to orient relative to the lamp rather than to local features in the maze arms or to an absolute compass direction. He carefully checked how the rats used the lamp. They didn't always run toward or away from it, as they would have if they had been treating the lamp as a stimulus to be approached or avoided to secure food. Instead, when the target was located at an angle to the lamp, they seemed to use the lamp as a landmark for finding the correct arm.

Finally, consider a third experiment, conducted by T. S. Collett, B. A. Cartwright, and B. A. Smith in 1986. Here a rat had to learn to find buried food by using visual cues — several white cylinders standing on an otherwise featureless area. In one run of the experiment the rat had to find the food that was buried equidistant from two identical cylinders. Once the rat had learned this task successfully, the researchers increased the distance between the two cylinders, leaving the food still equidistant from them. The researchers believed that the first trials had taught the rat a map of space. What would the rat do when that map was changed by a proportional enlargement?

The rat double-crossed its observers, who had expected that the rodent would concentrate its search in the area equidistant from the new position of the cylinders, thus maintaining the original proportions of the learned map. Instead, the rat divided its search time between two areas, each one at the original distance from one of the two cylinders.

This kind of mistake, McNaughton concludes, is consistent with a rat that performs a complicated process called vector computation. In simple terms, a vector is a number with size (scale) and direction. Four feet to the northwest or four units along the y axis is a vector. In the case of the rat and the two cylinders, McNaughton believes that the rat initially constructs a map with two vectors, one from each cylinder. Their conjunction gives the location of the buried food. But with the two cylinders moved farther away, the two vectors don't meet at their end points. Instead they each point to a different spot. To find the food, the rat unsuccessfully searches beneath each X that marks the end of the vector. Unfortunately, each is short of the actual location.

The rat's "intelligence" seems less impressive now that we understand how the trick is done. Its behavior is about as predictable as the machine's. With our grasp of the rat's design, we find it easy to confuse him. In fact, the more we find ourselves able to reduce the rat's behavior to rules and principles, the less intelligent we tend to think it is.

Does this mean that we are only willing to bestow the appellation "intelligent" on behavior we can't take apart, analyze, and reduce to rules and principles? If a cognitive process that we once attributed to conscious and logical, "higher" brain centers turns out to be the result of "tricks" in wiring in the perceptual edges of the brain, do we then devalue it? It is impossible to avoid the sneaking suspicion that the answer has less to do with computer science or neurobiology than it does with all the baggage freighting down the word "intelligence."

Brooks's machines are one possible way to generate complex behavior. Very simple parts, without any central controller and capable of only a few simple calculations, can result in a whole that is able to collect soda cans and return them to base. They solve the local/global problem by severely limiting the possible global actions and the available local information. They tell the machine to attend to only a very few things that are keys to the task at hand. The machine hardly has to decide between courses of action or between sets of relevant information. The hardwiring of the system eliminates all that confusion.

But the brain need not be constructed this way and indeed probably isn't. What we have instead is a system that is hardwired at the sensory periphery to process the available kinds of input in specific ways, and then seems to pick and choose between these percepts — applying useful data and ignoring the rest for the moment — at a higher level. Or at least that was the way Michael Mozer thought about it when he built MORSEL.

Mozer joined the connectionist melting pot in San Diego as a graduate student in 1981, and he began working on MORSEL (for multiple object recognition and attentional selection) soon after. He built his network around one of Rumelhart and McClelland's neural network architectures, one they had designed to identify four-letter words from the features of individual letters. His method for representing words as strings of letters was similar to the Wickelphone system that Rumelhart and McClelland had used in their past tense machine. "I didn't know all the abuse that was going to get," says Mozer.

What Mozer wanted to explore was how a network can deal

with multiple objects at once and how it pays attention to just one at a time. To a core word recognition system Mozer added an attentional mechanism, a controller that gates what signals go into the reader by reacting to local activity in the input neurons. At the output end he also added the elegantly named "clean-up" mechanism.

Mozer's model is much more complex than Rumelhart and McClelland's word recognition system, although it performs much the same task at its front end. It isn't limited to four-letter words carefully positioned on the artificial retina — it can recognize words of varying lengths in varying positions. Instead of using just one intermediate stage as the earlier machine does, MORSEL uses five representational stages. According to Mozer, "Much of the architecture is required to deal with the problem of translational invariance — how to recognize a word as being the same no matter where on the retina it appears."

Mozer tried to keep MORSEL true to the way human beings perceive the world. Psychological accuracy was the best way to ensure computational usefulness, he felt. "If we take into account the limitations of human performance and design a psychologically plausible architecture with these limitations in mind, we are likely to end up with a good computational or AI model."

MORSEL starts off with a system that can recognize letters and parts of words. It sees features on a retina. Mozer, who seems genetically incapable of passing up the opportunity for a joke, has labeled this part of his machine BLIRNET. BLIRNET's input comes through a 36×6 point array. Each of the 216 points in the array is equipped with five detectors, one each for oriented line segments at 0, 45, 90, and 135 degrees, and one for the end point of a line. BLIRNET works only with a special font that Mozer designed: all the letters are capitals and all are the same size, covering a 3×3 area in the retina array. Letter strings are sequences in adjacent 3×3 regions.

BLIRNET maps this input to an output array that represents letter clusters. Instead of having to build an output with one unit for each word, the clustering scheme could use overlapping combinations of just 56,966 units to represent virtually any word. Unfortunately, that far exceeded the combinatorial power of the computers Mozer had available when he built MORSEL. He compromised on a much more limited scheme of 540 output units that could represent all the words in a carefully constructed training set of 909 words. It took approximately 300 passes through the complete set (272,700 training trials) to bring MORSEL up to speed.

BLIRNET isn't a very clear reader, it turns out. The basic pattern that enables the machine to identify the word "grate," for example, is embedded in a lot of extraneous activations from units that find something to respond to. Ideally, all the correct target clusters would show an activation of 1, and all the others would be at 0. What actually results is a mix of strengths ranging from a little less than 1, through a big clump at 0.7 to 0.8, all the way down to 0.05, with another big clump at 0.2 to 0.1. Not unexpectedly for a neural network, BLIRNET's response is ambiguous.

It's up to the next level in the hierarchy to remove some of the ambiguity from the perceptual system. A clean-up mechanism, called the pull-out network, disentangles this pattern of partial activations. To accomplish this, Mozer gave the machine some memory and some knowledge of semantics. First, the pull-out network looks to strengthen consistent neighboring clusters and weaken those that are inconsistent. At the simplest level, this means making it impossible for two clusters to be on at the same time if that would force one letter to be two letters at once — a principle that might be compared to what Pinker and Markman call uniqueness. A pattern can't be both GAT and RAT at the same time. In deciding which it is, the machine relies on innate knowledge about the working of the real world outside itself. Simple excitatory and inhibitory connections do the trick. The GAT cluster and the RAT cluster would have an inhibitory connection that would effectively eliminate the more weakly activated cluster.

Mozer also gave MORSEL a very limited understanding of the meaning of specific words. Suppose, Mozer says, the pull-out network had a semantic unit that represented the "to annoy or irritate" meaning of "grate." That unit would be connected to all the clusters that form "grate." Activating any of those clusters would activate the semantic "annoy" unit, which would in turn excite all the "grate" clusters, and so on. Again, Mozer has given the machine an understanding of the world outside itself, this time in the realm called language.

Adding worldly knowledge is great in theory, but in practice it involves nothing less complicated than devising a complete set that will represent all known and unknown semantic features.

Linguists have been engaged in this process for more than a few decades, and they still don't agree on what would be necessary and sufficient to form such a set of features, nor how they could best be linked to individual words, let alone letter clusters. Not wanting to sidetrack MORSEL while he took a century or so to solve the linguists' problem, Mozer resorted to what he readily calls a cheat. Rather than trying to figure out what are the simplest units of meaning, he connected letter clusters of each word with units representing all the meanings of the word. This lets the machine eliminate blend errors, in which it mixes the beginning of one word with the end of another. The two words' different meanings eliminate the confusion.

The pull-out network still didn't solve all of Mozer's and MORSEL's problems. Mozer wanted a more psychological way for the machine to handle what it saw. "People don't just see single words in isolation," he says. "They'll see a whole page of print at once or a whole road sign." A machine that must be spoon-fed one word at a time will never really learn how to read.

But while the cells in the retina may respond to a whole page of print at once, human beings actually only attend to one word at a time. According to Mozer, "Research shows that reading for most people is pretty much a one-word-at-a-time process. People pay attention to this word and then that word and then that word, even though they "see" many more at once. So he decided to give MORSEL "attention," too.

MORSEL's attentional mechanism is designed to follow psychological and neurophysiological evidence suggesting that attention works like a spotlight that focuses on a particular region of the retina. Stimulus information in that region is amplified, and since those activations are stronger, they get noticed more readily. Thus, the brain "sees" objects in this region while "ignoring" objects in other parts of the visual field. In 1984 Francis Crick suggested that this attentional mechanism was located in the reticular complex of the thalamus. Other researchers have since produced results contesting this identification, and indeed, recent results from Wolf Singer and Charles Gray among others suggest a completely different mechanism. (For more on Gray, Singer, and attention, see Chapter 14.)

MORSEL's spotlight is actually a gate that lets activations from the attended region pass from the first to the second layer of BLIRNET. (Activations in the unattended region aren't absolutely inhibited, but they are less likely to result in strong activations in both BLIRNET's layers.) The attention network's task is to focus on areas of the retina that are currently activated by external stimuli, and to focus on only one activation region at a time. Mozer has assumed that to do this his network should pay attention to the area of the strongest stimulus.

All units in the attention network initially start out with zero strength. As units in the retina are activated by outside stimuli, that activation is fed to the attention network, in which there is a one-to-one correspondence with the units in the first layer of BLIRNET. Connections between the units in the attention network are designed to increase the activation strength of units with active neighbors. In effect, any unit that is part of a continuous object will grow in strength faster than an isolated unit or a unit with active neighbors on only one side. As the system runs, units with the most active neighbors will increasingly strengthen each other. Activity in other units will decline from initial levels.

MORSEL is now looking wherever there is an object, and attention will gradually select the biggest or most active object. Mozer calls this data-driven or bottom-up attention. It could be fine-tuned to become a powerful discriminatory device. Certain kinds of features could be given greater activation biases in the attention network. "In MORSEL attention is geared to spatial tasks — connectedness, for example," says Mozer. "It could be focused on other features, whatever other features are useful predictors of attention." If you wanted to design an attention network for a frog, for example, the network could be biased for motion. If you wanted it to attend to square blocks and ignore spheres, it could have an attentional bias for squareness.

Mozer believes that there is a second kind of attention, too, although he didn't try to implement it in MORSEL. "Attention isn't just dependent on the presence of a feature; it also depends on what task you are trying to accomplish," he says. This top-down attention would come from higher levels in the system that tell the attention network what the relevant features or objects of the moment are. This higher-level control could also set the size of the spotlight. In tasks requiring detail work, very small areas would get very focused attention; landscape photography, on the other hand, would require a wider attentional focus. "This wouldn't be that hard to implement on MORSEL," says Mozer.

He may be just a little optimistic about this, however.

Information from higher levels of cognition could certainly be used to modify the connections from each of the five feature types in the first layer of BLIRNET, so that the network would focus on the relevant feature for the task at hand. But that would require Mozer to build these higher cognitive levels, something that no one in the neural network community has yet successfully tackled.

Even though MORSEL is not a complete cognitive system, it behaves in ways that suggest that its three components, BLIRNET, pull-out, and attention, have captured some of the principles of such a system. For example, MORSEL mirrors the extinction that comes with neglect dyslexia.

Mozer first heard about neglect dyslexia while he was pursuing a postdoctoral fellowship with Geoffrey Hinton at the University of Toronto. There he ran into Marlene Behrmann, a neuropsychologist at the university who was working on this particular disorder. In patients with this kind of learning disability, when two words are simultaneously presented in two visual fields, the word in the field corresponding to the brain hemisphere that has been damaged becomes extinguished — it disappears as far as the patients are concerned. They may ignore the left side of a book, the beginning of a line of text, or the initial letters of a single word. All the evidence indicates that they "see" absolutely everything a person without neglect dyslexia sees, but that their brain simply ignores the information coming from that part of the visual field. However, extinction isn't absolute; the form of the words affects the degree. If a single word extends from the "good" field to the "bad," extinction in the "bad" field is less severe. The same is true if two words such as "pea" and "nut" are presented as a single compound word or even as two separate but related words. If the words can form a compound word, patients show less extinction for the left-hand word than they do if the two words are unrelated (for example, "pea nut" versus "cow nut"). "This strikes me as paradoxical," says Mozer. "If the meaning of the words affects their detection, then the patients must have processed the words to some extent. But if they've processed the words to this level, why can't they report them?"

MORSEL shows the same kind of performance when it is "damaged" electronically. In normal operation it gives preference to a three-letter word in the left field in 41.3 percent of trials and to the right in 40.8 percent. But in a version of the system with damage to its left side, the right-side word is almost always chosen because the bottom-up input to the attentional network is damaged for the left half and its support is weakened. Looking at the network, Mozer can still see two blobs of activation, representing the two words, but the left blob is far weaker.

"It's clear from this that the problem in the model is with attention and not with perception," he says. Two other MORSEL behaviors support this. If the words are joined, so that MORSEL thinks it is dealing with one object instead of two, extinction in the "bad" field is much less severe. The connections in the attention network strengthen the whole image, making up for the "bad" field's weaker initial signal.

MORSEL can also simulate the strange effect that conscious higher-level commands have on extinction. People with left-side neglect who were told to report the left-side stimulus first were able to report both left and right stimuli with no extinction. Marlene Behrmann found a similar surprising result with reading: patients who reported only 4 percent of left-side words reported both words correctly in 56 percent of trials when told to report the left-side word first. Simulations with MORSEL seem to duplicate this result.

MORSEL also demonstrated the same preference for words over nonwords as did patients with neglect dyslexia. The patient HR in Behrmann's studies correctly reported 66 percent of words and 5 percent of pseudowords. A lesioned MORSEL reported 39 percent of words and 7 percent of pseudowords.

To Mozer the results are suggestive of principles that extend beyond MORSEL. MORSEL has only one device designed for attention, but in operation it shows more than one kind of attention. The preference the lesioned network shows for words over nonwords doesn't come from the attention network. Instead, it results from the semantic knowledge in the pull-out network and that network's desire to find consistent words. For example, Mozer points out that the "pea" in "pea nut" is attenuated to the same degree as the "pea" in "pea boy." However, the pull-out network recovers the "pea" in "pea nut" because the two words are related.

Analyzing each part of the network in isolation doesn't tell the whole story of the system-wide behavior. Behaviors that we group under a common heading, such as attention, may actually result from more than one mechanism. It might in fact be more proper to say there are several behaviors that can be called attention. Drawing a one-to-one connection between a behavior and a mechanism is a very tricky operation indeed.

At this point Mozer's machine doesn't have much to say about top-down attention. Higher levels would tell the network what should be attended to and what the relevant features of the moment are. MORSEL doesn't address how those higher levels would know what the appropriate features are for any specific occasion. It has only pushed this question up the hierarchy, not answered it. And what does "know" mean to the brain, anyhow? All we can see in neural networks are patterns of connections. Somehow both artificial and biological networks have to move from that kind of physical thing to thoughts about moon, and June, and swoon.

7

THE STUFF THOUGHTS ARE MADE OF

We certainly do not summon up pictures inside our head for they would have to be looked at by a little man in the head.... Moreover, the little man would have eyes in *his* head to see with and then a still littler man and so on *ad infinitum.*

— JAMES J. GIBSON, "Visualizing Conceived as Visual Apprehending Without Any Particular Point of Observation"

If I close my eyes and imagine a purple cow, is something somewhere really purple and cow-shaped?

— DANIEL DENNETT, *Brainstorms*

Daniel Dennett puts it quite succinctly: either minds are just brains or minds are more than brains. And if minds are just brains, then a mental state, what you and I call a thought, is identical to some physical event in the brain. How could it be otherwise? There isn't anything else for a thought to be. There is no mind vapor, no mind essence, no mind spirit. Just the brain.

It's hard to imagine anything more resolutely physical than a neural network. Yet neural networks have "thoughts." The state of the network can stand for a category or concept. These thoughts can only be a combination of neurons.

But identifying a particular neural network thought proves to be surprisingly difficult. What state of the network corresponds to a thought like "Add 'ed'" or "Pronounce 'sēn'"? Sejnowski's NETtalk, for example, shows disconcerting tendencies. On consecutive trials, it could wind up reaching the same conclusion while activating different neurons. NETtalk suggests that even though mental states can only be physical states, two identical mental states don't require identical physical states. But then what does it mean to say that these two mental states are the same thought? (And does the brain work the same way?) What neural networks research needs, it seems, is a theory of thought.

As the 1980s opened, the need for a way to understand the physical basis of machine thought increasingly occupied John Hopfield, a physicist at the California Institute of Technology. Hopfield had caught just enough of the ferment in neural networks and neuroscience to become intrigued. The brain was a puzzling physical system — as a physicist Hopfield didn't even pause to consider any kind of mentalist or vitalist explanation. What tantalized him, though, was not the brain's amazing capabilities as a computer, although that did assure him that the brain was worth studying. It was something else, something harder to put a finger on. The calculations the brain performed had a . . . what? A personality? A flavor? They often began in ambiguity, and yet the result was nonetheless a complete, internally consistent gestalt. And sometimes just a tiny change would throw the whole system into a very different state — almost like the difference between water and ice.

Tall and thin enough for his intensity to have an almost physical edge, John Hopfield doesn't look like a man who thinks much about metaphors. Words don't flow easily from him. He seems more comfortable with numbers, and his work on neural networks is densely mathematical. In the strictest sense, his initial work in neural networks applied the complex mathematics developed to explain a peculiar physical state called a spin glass to model neural computation.

But that strict interpretation doesn't explain the excitement that his work, often in collaboration with David Tank, created in the early 1980s. Hopfield and Tank created a new metaphor. They reimagined the brain — and neural networks — as a landscape that computes. As proof they offered a neural network landscape that could recall all the memories associated with madeleines or plot the best route among thirty cities for a traveling salesman.

A conventional computer tackles the traveling salesman problem as it does every other problem: as a step-by-step series of calculations. For instance, it might add up the distance in each of the possible combinations of cities and then compare all the answers, looking for the smallest number. Unfortunately, even with just thirty cities there are 1,000,000,000,000,000,000,000,000,000,000 possible routes. Algorithms designed to solve this problem eliminate a lot of those possible combinations at the very beginning and save considerable computer time. In fact, it takes a typical microcomputer only a tenth of a second to spit out a solution. Of course, using the algorithmic shortcuts means the solution isn't *the* best answer, only one of the best. In this case, perhaps one of the 10 million best.

In terms of computational difficulty, though, the traveling salesman problem pales in comparison to what is called associative memory, the ability to recall all the combinations associated with a specific entity and then to pick out only those that are appropriate to a specific occasion. The taste of a crumb of madeleine triggers a kind of associational riot at the beginning of Proust's *Swann's Way*. In the narrator's memory madeleines are connected with an old gray house, the little pavilion and its garden, the water lilies on the Vivonne, and indeed all the good folk of the village and their dwellings and the parish church.

Although most of us stop our associative meanderings a good distance short of Proust, this is exactly the kind of thing we do easily every day. We remember Joe's face from his name, and then, should it be needed, we can retrieve his job, his softball ability, his propensity to drink too much beer after the third inning, and more. You can certainly program a conventional computer to do this, after a fashion. One way would be to tag every item associated with Joe when you first add it to the computer's memory. To find all the items linked to Joe, the computer would have to look at every memory it held for this "Joe" tag. As the number of memories built up, you would probably want to structure the memory. All the "Joe" memories would go in one section, and the machine would then not have to search sections holding non-"Joe" memories. In effect, you would have created a "Joe" list.

Of course, this assumes that "Joe-ness" doesn't overlap with any other categories. Adding a new memory, say that of Joe's daughter Kathleen, which might overlap with some of the existing memories and sections, would require a massive reorganization of the entire structure. You might even need to introduce an index of

"Joe-ness" or a measurement of "Joe-context" to let the machine prioritize memories so that you wouldn't have to wade through all your memories associated with Joe if all you really wanted were those related to his hobbies.

Even if researchers don't yet know exactly how the brain completes its associative tasks, it clearly can't work this way. Because the brain's individual neurons are so much slower than the computer's individual processors, it simply isn't fast enough to use this brute force approach. Some very simple math tells us that. By dividing how long it takes the brain to do a cognitive task, such as recognizing an object, by the length of time it takes a neuron to fire and then recover, neurobiologists have calculated that the simple cognitive task of reclaiming the basic associative memories connected to our core gestalt of Joe cannot require more than a hundred steps, give or take a few. Conventional computers require thousands of times more operations than that to do even their primitive tasks of association. How, Hopfield and Tank asked, can the brain as a whole be so effective at recognizing a face, remembering things associated with the taste of madeleines, or reaching for a sandwich?

To understand Hopfield and Tank's answer, you have to rethink your image of a conventional digital computer and adopt a point of view common among computer scientists. Forget about the computer as some electronic version of the mechanical adding machine. A computer's answer isn't a number printed on a piece of paper but a physical state, the sum of all the electrical states in the machine. In solving a problem, the digital machine moves from one state to the next, at each step correcting for variations introduced by the minor imperfections in individual electrical devices, until it reaches a final state, which is then read out as the answer.

In retrospect, Hopfield and Tank's "answer" seems almost obvious, as simple as rolling downhill. Visualize Proust's madeleine computation as an energy landscape with hills and valleys. Each point on those contours represents a partial memory, some combination of associations. The solution, the complete memory with all the associations evoked by the taste of a madeleine, is represented by the lowest point in the deepest valley. Imagine the evoking event, the crumb of cookie or the sight of a church, as a ball released at a point on these hills that corresponds to that event. It will follow the curves of the hills, gradually losing energy as it sinks toward the valley that represents all the associations. Only at that point is the ball quiet and the system at its energy minimum.

Hopfield and Tank's energy landscape is a specialized version of the final electrical state of the digital machine. Instead of a general machine that builds that landscape from scratch, using software rules to constrain the possible solution space each time it wants to solve a problem, Hopfield and Tank start with a specialized, preconstructed landscape. Each time they want to solve a specific *kind* of problem, exemplifying a specific function, they just let the ball roll down the specified hills and valleys.

Their solution depends on one crucial difference between the brain and the computer. In the computer, computational steps are cheap, since the machine is very, very fast and each one takes a very, very short time. Electronic processors, on the other hand, are relatively complicated and, in simple dollar terms, are expensive to fabricate. Dedicating a processor or a series of processors to a

The computational landscape of a Hopfield network can be pictured as a series of hills and valleys. The network computes by following a path to the bottom of a valley. All valleys are approximate solutions; only the deepest valley is the best solution.
Drawing by Ellen Epstein.

specific task would be costly. A well-engineered computer would therefore conserve processors by using them as general-purpose devices that can shift from one task to another. Any loss in efficiency resulting from the use of general-purpose processors would be made up for by the speed of the silicon system.

In the brain the situation is almost exactly reversed. Processors — neurons and synapses — are cheap and, in comparison to the machine world, incredibly abundant. But neurons are slow, and time is the resource that must be conserved. The efficiently engineered brain can afford to use lots of processors and can indeed afford to dedicate processors to specific tasks, such as representing a specific landscape. However, it can't allow any of those tasks to require thousands of steps.

When Hopfield and Tank got around to building a simple neural circuit, their proposed machine showed exactly that kind of trade-off. They started with a very simple and therefore "cheap" processor that would function as their neuron. They noted that a simple electrical circuit, the flip-flop, is a remarkably good example of this kind of energy landscape. A flip-flop circuit has just two stable states, $+1$ and -1, and it always chooses one state or the other, no matter what the inputs supplied to the circuit. In terms of a landscape, the ball will always roll downhill until it rests in either the $+1$ valley or the -1 valley.

What determines where the ball winds up? Changing the strengths of the connections between the two amplifiers in the flip-flop will reconfigure the landscape. The valleys might get deeper, for example. Adding additional external current to only one amplifier will deepen just one valley and also increase the basin of attraction, the amount of downhill that leads into this valley. Each flip-flop is a landscape whose features can be sculpted into higher hills and deeper valleys.

It's easy to imagine how the landscape created by the current and characteristics of the flip-flop can do simple computations such as deciding which of two numbers is bigger. Both amplifiers are given external currents proportional to the numbers. The amplifier with the stronger current will have a deeper valley and a basin of attraction that includes the "neutral" starting point. When the computation begins, the circuit travels downhill to the deeper valley, say the $+1$ state.

Solving a tougher problem requires building a more complex

landscape. A landscape that decides between two potential solutions includes two valleys, each with a depth proportional to the likelihood of that solution being true. A landscape designed to solve a problem with thirty possible solutions needs thirty potential valleys, each with a specific depth and contour. (Actually, this isn't exactly true. Each additional solution adds not just another valley to the landscape but also another axis to the familiar Cartesian x and y. Unless you're really comfortable working in, or even imagining, graphs with thirty axes, however, stick to the simpler three-dimensional approximation. It will give you the general idea.) To build a two-valley landscape, Hopfield and Tank proposed using a circuit with just two possible states, a flip-flop with just two amplifiers, one for each solution. A more complicated landscape requires a more complicated circuit, with an amplifier or a combination of amplifiers, for each potential solution.

Hopfield and Tank noted that optimization problems, which require finding the combination of many interacting factors that produces the best solution, seem especially well matched with this kind of network. One example is the traveling salesman problem. Another is figuring out how to divide the job of reshelving books for a large library among a number of different assistants, all of whom are familiar with different parts of the collection but in different degrees. Hopfield and Tank posed the problem this way: "Jessica can shelve six books a minute in geology, four per minute in physics, and so on, whereas George can shelve one book per minute in geology, eight per minute in physics, and so on. You must assign one category to each assistant." With six assistants and six categories, the number of possible combinations is six factorial, or $6 \times 5 \times 4 \times 3 \times 2 \times 1$ — just 720.

An elementary computer approach simply calculates all 720 combinations and the time each one takes. With only 720 combinations the solution pops out in close to no time. But unfortunately, the time the problem requires increases with the cube. So if a problem with six assistants and six categories takes only 720 nanoseconds (or one nanosecond per combination) to compute, one hundred assistants and categories will take approximately 10^{100} (a one with a hundred zeros) nanoseconds. (There are more complex and effective digital algorithms for solving this particular problem.)

"The computation could be done even faster, however," Hopfield and Tank wrote, "if one could take full advantage of the problem's essence: the fact that the proper assignment of each worker depends on the capabilities of every other worker. Ideally the mutual dependencies should be considered simultaneously." In the system Hopfield and Tank designed, commonly called a Hopfield network, the answer emerges from the interaction of all the computing elements. They simultaneously share information, take provisional positions, change them, and finally arrive at a collective solution.

The two researchers use the analogy of voting at a meeting. At the digital/serial meeting the members vote yes or no in sequence. Each member knows only a few preceding votes and can't change a vote once it is cast. In the collective meeting members vote together, know all the other votes, and can change their own. The decision that emerges reflects a sense of the meeting.

The collective meeting vote on the shelving task isn't structureless, however, Hopfield and Tank note. The shape of the voting depends, to a degree, on our understanding of how the parts of the decision affect each other. In this example it takes the form of a 6 × 6 array of amplifiers in which each row corresponds to an assistant and each amplifier in the row corresponds to a different task. All the amplifiers are connected in a way that reflects the shape of the task: no single assistant can shelve more than a single category and no category can be shelved by more than one worker. Thus, some individuals can't vote for certain candidates — some amplifiers turn off other amplifiers. If the geology amplifier in Sally row is on, all five other geology amplifiers have to be off and so do all five other amplifiers in the Sally row. Each amplifier thus has to be connected to the five other amplifiers in its row and the five others in its column with an inhibitory connection. The array therefore has a total of 360 connections, each of which has two possible states, inhibitory or excitatory.

In the beginning, then, the energy landscape for this circuit consists of 720 valleys of equal depth, one for each possible solution. They are all equally deep initially because all solutions are equally likely. To create the energy landscape for a particular case, an input current equal to the shelving rate for each assistant for each task is fed to each amplifier. Higher shelving rates produce deeper valleys. As some valleys deepen, some inhibitory connections come into play, flattening out other parts of the landscape and increasing the watersheds of some valleys. "In the final configuration the circuit usually settles into the deepest valley," Hopfield and Tank note.

Think about the format of the answer this array produces, and the process may get a little clearer. If each amplifier is a light bulb, the answer will be a 6 × 6 array where six of the bulbs, one in each row, are lit and all the others are dark. Each of these bulbs corresponds to a hypothesis, a statement that is either true or false. In this case, the hypothesis can be simply stated: "This assistant should be doing this shelving task." If true, that bulb should be on; if false, off.

Now, does this system of amplifiers and wires "know" anything about truth and falsehood? Of course not. You would look in vain for anything corresponding to your moral or logical conception of truth. But the system has been given one simple algorithm. We know that the energy landscape with the deepest valley or the most deep valleys is the most likely to yield a solution, and we know that the landscape with the least energy has the deepest valley or valleys. To get a true solution, we tell the network always to choose the landscape with the deepest valley or valleys. The algorithm is simple: measure the energy in landscape A and then measure the energy in landscape B; pick the landscape with the smaller energy number.

To find that landscape, start the system in some random state with any six bulbs lit. Don't worry if the statements they represent are true or false; that state just gives you an energy starting point. Then change one bulb — turn it on or off. That single act will ripple out through the system's inhibitory connections turning other bulbs on or off. But according to our one rule, the system will only adopt that state if the resulting energy level for the entire array is lower than in the original state. If not, the system will return to the configuration with which it started. No matter. Change the next bulb; it will further change the modified state that resulted from changing the first bulb, change the primal state itself, or also be rejected. Try this until no changes minimize the landscape's energy cost any further. That's the solution. The bulbs that are lit at this point correspond to the true hypotheses. For a simple system like this, a few times through the thirty-six amplifiers usually produces the optimal solution.

But only usually. Hopfield's machine isn't predictable, and its truth has a certain "approximate" flavor. Solving the same problem more than once doesn't necessarily produce the exact same solution each time. As Hopfield puts it, the answer, to some extent, is dependent on the history of the system.

It's important to understand why the solutions vary. Unlike many systems of logic, the logic of the Hopfield network isn't commutative. Adding 2, 4, and 6 is not always the same as adding 2, 6, and 4. A sensitivity to temporal flow is built into the nature of this neural network. Like our lives, it is embedded in time. The thing experienced and the thing doing the experiencing are intertwined, since the things experienced in the past can affect the network's reaction to future experiences. The thing experienced is involved in creating the character of the thing doing the experiencing.

At some time scales such a statement seems unexceptional for either a neural network or a brain. For instance, at one extreme, that of evolutionary time, we have little trouble accepting the idea that experience molded the brain over the eons. But at shorter time periods the question is much more perplexing. Does this mean that my trip to the store today changes the way I experience my trip to the store tomorrow? Our commonsense answer to this is ambivalent. In some contexts, we would readily agree, today's trip, which involved an unpleasant argument with the store manager, obviously changes tomorrow's trip. But in other ways the trip seems to remain unchanged. The stop sign is still red, for example, and the distance is still two miles. In what sense am I experiencing the same street from one day to the other? Indeed, in what sense am I the same "I" on the two days? How much have I changed from one day to the other?

Hopfield doesn't provide a way to put these epistemological doubts to rest, but he does provide a framework for understanding why they exist in his system. In the jargon of the sciences that study dynamic systems, a Hopfield network is extremely sensitive to initial conditions.

Again, think of this as a landscape of hills and valleys. An omniscient observer knows which valley is the lowest. The ball seeking the lowest valley only knows local conditions: it only knows if its path is uphill or downhill. In an energy landscape with more than one valley, the ball seeking the solution, the lowest point in the entire system, doesn't know if there is a valley lower than the one it has settled in. Remember, solving the problem starts with a random choice of which units are on and which off. Some random choices will yield the global minimum more readily than others. Some initial patterns will produce a deep, but not the deepest, local minimum very quickly. In that situation the system will reject most changes in off/on units, since most will yield worse energy landscapes. Eventually, a test change might bump the system out of that local minimum, but if that local valley is deep enough, the system will be very stable, even though it hasn't yet reached the absolute minimum.

The energy landscape thus also represents a graph of solution probabilities. Only if there is one and only one valley will the array produce the same answer 100 percent of the time. In any other situation the depth and shape of a valley roughly correspond to the probability that the machine will wind up in that valley, that this solution will be produced. In the case of Hopfield's traveling salesman problem, his 900 neurons can produce the 10 million best solutions in a few trips around the array. More trips, more test combinations, will reduce that number, although not very quickly. But no number of tests can guarantee the one best solution.

The uncertainty intrigues Hopfield. To him it suggests a computational basis for psychology. Two Hopfield networks that work on the same problem but that began with different initial random states would both solve the problem, but they wouldn't necessarily come up with exactly the same solution. The history of each network would affect the result. Each would be an "individual" even though the underlying components and connections were exactly the same in each case. "Psychology developed independently from neuroscience," Hopfield points out. Maybe in the character of the Hopfield network there lies a clue to the neuronal basis of psychology.

A Hopfield network is a machine that behaves in very unmachinelike ways. It suggests that we must either modify our idea of the machine or break with the machine metaphor that has dominated our understanding of everything from human psychology to economics for hundreds of years. The human machine is a key metaphor in the scientific revolution that defines modern times, but it relies on a very specific idea of the machine. To René Descartes (1596–1650) the human body was a clockwork mechanism, or sometimes a water-driven machine. Listen to Descartes describe the muscle reflex that pulls the skin away from a hot ember: the ember displaces the skin, which pulls a thread that stretches to the brain, which opens a pore in the brain, which allows animal spirits to flow and inflate the muscle, finally causing movement.

In our time the machine metaphor remains, but the computer has replaced the clock or the waterwheel as the prototype. We speak of electronic brains, of processing information from a meeting, of needing a weekend to consider that new input. Nor is the metaphor limited to popular culture. The seeming correspondence between the rigors of Boolean logic — which sought to reduce all logic to true/false, on/off, one/zero statements and the operations performed on them — and what was in the 1940s thought to be the electrical on/off binary signals of the brain were part of von Neumann's inspiration for the modern digital computer.

Although the type of machine at the core of the analogy has changed, our view of the defining nature of the machine hasn't. Machines, we believe, are deterministic and predictable; they take the same input — information or raw materials — and reproduce the same result each time.

Neural networks don't seem to be machines like that. If they are machines, then machines are different than we have thought. And if they are not machines, then we need to find another thing to call them and another metaphor for understanding our own bodies and much else in the world.

At the least, a machine like a Hopfield network suggests that the deterministic, predictable model for a machine is really a radical simplification of the way at least some complex systems work. New sciences called chaos or complexity are now saying our scientific methods for understanding the world are suited to only that part of the world that is linear in its organization and where elements have only relatively simple and relatively few meaningful interactions with each other. With a science that is best at solving linear problems, we have seen all problems as linear. But linear systems include only those where the relationship between variables is not complex. When one goes up, so does the sum in some readily predictable way, or maybe the sum decreases in an inverse relationship. But still the change is readily predictable.

But most of the world isn't like that, these new sciences are saying. The patterns water makes coming out of a faucet, the patterns that make up weather, and perhaps the patterns we find in the brain aren't predictable with these simple tools. In fact, they may not be predictable at all in the sense that a linear, clockwork machine is predictable.

Machines that behave like clocks are perhaps just a subset of all machines. They produce a steady, static state from initial conditions. But machines can produce other kinds of dynamics. It's easy to imagine, for example, a system that swings wildly with each adjustment.

Hopfield and Tank knew they were venturing into uncharted territory. Most of the mathematics we have developed for systems with a large number of variables, or degrees of freedom, deal with just the linear part of our world. But the network Hopfield and Tank designed was intentionally nonlinear, just like the brain itself. Their flip-flops, like neurons, aren't linear devices. The flip-flop is stable in only one of two states, never in between. It can be $+1$ or -1 but never 0.5 either negative or positive. Put a current in, and the flip-flop may rest at -1; double it, and it still may be -1. Ten times the current and the flip-flop may switch to $+1$. No matter how much more current is now added, the state never changes. Like a neuron, it is in either of two states determined by some threshold value. Below that value, the neuron doesn't fire. Above it, no matter how far above it, it does.

Hopfield and Tank knew that linking a large number of nonlinear local units in a network that allowed the change in one unit to affect all other units could create a system that would never settle on a solution. Systems like this can oscillate indefinitely, moving with time from one state to another to another to another, and then repeating the cycle endlessly. Or they can be chaotic in a mathematical sense. Rather than settling into single-point solutions or into exactly repeated oscillations called limit cycles, chaotic systems show often complex patterns that are approximations of each other over time.

Oscillating circuits have been discovered in biological neuronal systems. Some researchers suggest that the brain may also use chaotic attractors. But what if we simply want to build a neural network to solve a computational problem?

Hopfield and Tank could live with a probabilistic machine; there are, after all, sophisticated statistical methods for dealing with probabilities. But to solve an optimization problem they couldn't live with one that oscillated or demonstrated chaotic behavior. Hopfield networks must settle to a rest. They assume that the answer is represented by the system coming to an equilibrium, and the answer is read off only when the system reaches that quiescent state. The whole solution method relies upon a gradual decrease in error, a gradual descent toward the best or nearly the best answer. Oscillations or chaotic patterns threatened to drive the system into new valleys just when it was settling to an answer. It might never reach a decision on whether to give Joan a mortgage or have Mike shelve the geography section.

They discovered that their networks wouldn't oscillate if they used only certain connection patterns. What if all the connections between the neurons are exactly the same, and what if they are all symmetrical? Then the network begins to resemble a number of naturally occurring systems — gas diffusing in a room, for example, or the magnetic rearrangement of the molecules in a spin glass.

Drawing on the specialized mathematics developed for spin glasses, Hopfield was able to demonstrate that a symmetrical neural network would indeed converge on an answer. All Hopfield networks, therefore, must be symmetrical or include asymmetry of certain restricted kinds. In the latter case Hopfield and Tank have been able to show that the asymmetric network is effectively equivalent to a symmetric one and thus will also converge on an answer.

Of course, such a network can make no pretense of biological accuracy. It gives up the immense nonsymmetries that seem to be critical to much of the brain's work — for example, it eliminates the precise asymmetries of feedback that are so crucial to a system like Sylvie Ryckebusch's. But at least it works for certain kinds of problems.

In the early eighties Hopfield and Tank were not the only researchers exploring a cognitive landscape. A group at IBM built their exploration around the metaphor of annealing, a common metalworking technique that involves heating a metal and then gradually cooling it to rearrange its crystal structure. The Boltzmann machine drew an analogy with the way a gas seeks an energy minimum in any space. Geoffrey Hinton's work with this type of machine demonstrated one of the first effective algorithms for "teaching" a neural network, which was especially important, says Hopfield, "since it was the absence of a good learning algorithm that made the perceptron craze collapse in the sixties." Like the Hopfield network, all these systems hinged on some easily expressed global measure. Unlike the Hopfield network, though, they begin with an essentially unstructured landscape and build the correct one through learning.

Exploring the landscape of a learning system is a much more dangerous journey. In a Hopfield landscape the explorer can get stuck in a local minimum, but even that is at least a valley somewhat like the correct answer. The shape of the landscape itself is static.

In a learning system the momentary shape of the landscape does not determine the one right answer, but is instead a source of information for changing the landscape to produce a better answer. Not only is the explorer looking for the global minimum, but he or she also needs useful bearings that will help redesign the landscape. Looking around, the explorer needs to know not only the elevation at that spot but which way the landscape tends — its slope.

It is possible to imagine a nightmare landscape — perhaps a valley, actually a narrow ravine, where movement either north or south gives the illusion of progress. Boxed in by steep sides the explorer follows a gentle downward slope, on and on and on. Is there a global minimum at the end of this? The sides are so steep that climbing them would take a discouraging amount of energy. But things are not improving very fast as the explorer follows the slope. The journey seems to stretch on forever. The ravine has become a trap. In the fall of 1989 Josh Alspector and Robert Allen were two explorers worried about just this nightmare.

The Canada geese waddling around on the shores of the pond outside Bellcore in Morristown, New Jersey, resemble very restless students today. The crisp fall air seems to amplify the honking from each V as it heads south. The earthbound geese look up from the reflected image of the research center almost as if they were measuring the aerial trend. It's impossible to tell from their expressions what these geese are thinking.

Behind the severe walls of the Bell Communications Research center, Alspector and Allen aim a much more random noise at a carefully constructed neural network chip. The process is akin to taking Albert Einstein to a Motley Crüe concert and strapping him down in the first row right up against the speakers. Alspector and Allen are hoping that their noise will teach their chip its lessons.

The two Bellcore researchers are a typical neural network team, multidisciplinary and ad hoc. Alspector has a Ph.D. in physics from MIT; Allen is an experimental psychologist from the

University of California at San Diego, that early hotbed of neural network research. At Bellcore, the central research laboratory for all the regional Bell telephone companies created in the breakup of AT&T, Allen works in the artificial intelligence group, Alspector in the VLSI (very large scale integration) chip area.

At many levels Alspector and Allen's work is profoundly counterintuitive. The two are blasting random noise at a very carefully designed neural circuit. Having built a very tiny bit of electronic brain, they spend their days shaking it up. Just the right amount of shaking, they believe, is the key to building a chip that learns. But why should adding randomness to their system produce stable learning? Alspector and Allen were convinced it would — but only if they could match the amount of noise they added with the geography of their system's landscape. The chips they began to build were actually explorations of the topography. What kind of valleys and hills did this landscape have? How likely were they to get trapped in a ravine? The amount of noise to add to the system depended on the answers to those questions.

After two years of software simulations, Alspector and Allen built a six-neuron, fifteen-synapse chip in the summer of 1988 that they hoped would answer some of these questions. Like Hopfield's flip-flop, their neuron was basically an amplifier with a threshold. Each one added up all the electrical currents from all the other neuron/amplifiers it was connected to. If the net input was greater than the threshold, it went from a low-voltage to a high-voltage state, sending current across the synapse.

But by adding modifiable, adaptive synapses, Alspector and Allen radically changed the nature of the Hopfield network. In the Hopfield network that calculated the best use of library assistants in shelving books, for example, information about the task went into the network either as currents of different strength to each amplifier or in the way connections among the amplifiers were specifically configured to represent the nature of the task. The paths of the wires in the network were selected so that no two assistants could be assigned the same task and each assistant was assigned only one. Essentially, this is a network constructed to perform only one computation and whose built-in structure depends on a clear understanding of the nature of the problem. *Because* the designer of the network already knows that no two assistants can do the same shelving task, the network can be wired to ensure that result.

Instead of specialized connections, Alspector and Allen designed adjustable synapses to connect their neurons. The current from neuron 1 flows to neuron 2 across a resistor that represents the synapse. Changing this resistance can strengthen, weaken, or even completely block the connection between two neurons, much like a light bulb can be dimmed by increasing the resistance in the dimmer switch. By adjusting the resistances in the appropriate synapses, Alspector and Allen can create the shelving network's wiring configuration. Other patterns of resistance can turn this same chip into a network to solve a different computational problem.

The biological synapse does all this adjustment at the level of chemical molecules and cell membranes. A single one of Alspector and Allen's synapses, on the other hand, uses 300 transistors. "The entire biological synapse is only a micron across," says Alspector. "To do something like the function of a synapse we have to use a few hundred transistors. No way we can fit those in one micron. The biological system operates on the molecular level, and we're stuck at the transistor level." The size of the synapses probably limits the size of the chip Alspector and Allen can build to a few thousand synapses. In mid-1990 Alspector and others at Bellcore built a chip that approached this limit with thirty-two neurons and 992 synapses.

The adjustable synapses also increase the problem of local minima. Unlike the Hopfield net, where the ball simply has to find the lowest valley in a preconstructed landscape, Alspector and Allen's chip first has to construct this landscape with the best configuration of hills and valleys and then get the ball into the global minimum. It does this by extending the trial and comparison method of Hopfield's 6 × 6 stacking assignment array. On each run in the learning mode, the final position of the ball is compared with what a "teacher" knows should be the correct position. This is done not by measuring a physical position but by comparing the energy levels of the existing and ideal landscapes. If the two don't match, the system applies a set of rules to make changes that *should* bring the two energy levels into closer alignment. Connections between synapses — weights as they are called in the neural network field — are strengthened when they contribute to correct answers and weakened when they contribute to incorrect ones following the procedures described for the machine by a learning algorithm.

Starting with a completely unconfigured landscape increases the kinds of problems the network can handle, but it also dramatically slows down the network and increases the local minima problem. If the ball falls into a local minimum here that isn't necessarily an approximate answer, it could be the result of a misconstructed landscape. Local minima also supply false information about how to reconfigure the topography. The last thing Alspector and Allen wanted their machine to do was construct a landscape based on a local minimum. What they needed was a way to eliminate or at least to minimize the chance that their machine would get trapped in a local minimum.

So they added random noise to their chip. Sitting next to the amplifiers, processors, transistors, and resistors of the neurons and synapses are tiny noise generators. These are Alspector and Allen's solution to the Hopfield network's tendency to settle into mis-

Alspector and Allen's thirty-two-neuron, 992-synapse chip. The noise generator is on the extreme right. Most of the chip's area is taken up by the synapses.
Photograph courtesy of Bellcore.

leading local minima. They are a way to push the ball uphill occasionally.

Like Hopfield, Alspector and Allen borrowed their method for treating computer states from the world of physical materials. At about the same time Hopfield applied spin glass mathematics to neural networks, Scott Kirkpatrick, working at IBM, suggested an analogy with annealing that could solve hard optimization problems on conventional computers. Actual physical annealing is a metallurgical technique for achieving uniform crystal structures, a material's lowest energy state, by careful melting and cooling. "Let's say you wanted to anneal damage in a silicon crystal that had broken into a lot of little pieces," explains Alspector. "If you heat it up and cool it down slowly, it will form a perfect crystal. If you do not cool it slowly enough, if you cool it too quickly, it will not form a perfect crystal. That is because certain domains freeze into their own local crystalline shape, preventing the whole, global crystal structure from forming." In annealing terms, if the system cools too quickly, you get local crystals, each of which is the most energy-efficient local state, but the whole system doesn't reach the most efficient global situation, a complete crystal that represents a global minimum.

In Alspector and Allen's chip, noise serves the same function as heat. In physical terms the two are actually identical, both being the addition of randomizing energy to a system. "If you add noise, enough noise, then every state becomes available for the network as a whole," says Allen. "And then if you cool it down slowly, it will cool to an optimal state of lowest energy." Alspector adds, "What is happening then is that in each one of these local interactions, the system has reached a state of local equilibrium with maximum efficiency. By introducing noise, you enable the system as a whole to reach equilibrium."

If you are having trouble understanding how noise helps the network produce a more accurate answer, once again visualize a ball and two valleys. Valley B is the deeper of the two, but it is separated from valley A by a hill. If our ball starts rolling from some random point on this landscape, it has about a 50–50 chance of winding up in either valley, since despite valley B's greater depth, both have about the same width. If we shake the whole system — that is, put random noise energy into it — the ball is more likely to move from valley A to valley B. Simply because valley B is deeper, it will take more energy to get the ball out of the bottom of that valley. If the shaking is gentle, the ball is many times more likely to move from A to B than vice versa, but any transition at all will be very rare. Most of the time the gentle shaking won't be enough to make the ball cross the hill. Rough shaking will move the ball over the hill frequently, but the violent shaking will be enough not only to move the ball from A to B but also to move the ball back from B to A.

The solution is to start rough and gradually get gentle. Rough shaking will generate a lot of movement from one valley to another. As the shaking gets gentler, at some point it will still be enough to move the ball from A to B but not from B to A. That amount of shaking will be the best compromise between the rough shaking that will ensure a transition and a minimal shaking that will ensure that the transition will never be the bad one from B to A.

All real systems have much more complicated, multidimensional energy landscapes than this one. Multiple valleys are separated by hills with dips, channels, ravines, sloughs, and other passageways of varying heights. Increasing the energy noise in such a landscape pretty much ensures that the ball will take one of these paths. But the complexity of the landscape makes it impossible to predict which path the ball will take or exactly how much noise is the optimum amount. Starting with a lot of noise and gradually turning it down may seem terribly unscientific, but right now it's the best way to solve this problem.

The noise was too noisy and not noisy enough on Alspector and Allen's six-neuron chip. There the noise generators worked by amplifying a tiny amount of noise to a much higher level. At that very high level the amplifiers in the noise generators themselves began to pick up the noise from each other. Instead of random noise going into each neuron, the noise became a uniform signal throughout the system. "The chip still worked, but this part of it did not work as well as we wanted it to," says Allen. "It seemed to work for very small problems, but in larger systems the noise would just overwhelm the signal. He and Alspector think they've solved the problem in their thirty-two-neuron chip by using a different method to generate the noise.

But if Alspector and Allen's noise generators solve one common Hopfield network problem, their use of adjustable synapses emphasizes a question central to the whole endeavor. The two researchers know that the brain uses adjustable synapses. Indeed, such synapses seem to be crucial to processing information in the brain and to learning and memory. But modifying the strengths among synapses eliminates the symmetry that all of Hopfield and Tank's proofs rely on. "We have programmable asymmetry on this chip," says Alspector.

Hopfield and Tank proved that a symmetric network will settle to an answer, but they gave up part of the richness of neural networks to do so. The only kind of problem a symmetric network can solve is one that settles to a fixed-point solution. The pattern must be static, the result fixed, the process ended. But what about computations that aren't static? Where the result is in constant dynamic motion and where the process doesn't come to an end but continues to evolve or depends on sequences and the relationships between them? "An asymmetrically connected system can settle to a fixed point, but it can also settle into a dynamic pattern," says Alspector. It can oscillate or show chaotic behavior. In fact, adding the kind of asymmetric-feedback connections that are common in the brain to a network almost guarantees chaotic oscillations.

But which more closely resembles a thought: a fixed-point solution or a chaotic journey around an attractor? According to Alspector, "It's not clear that settling to a static state is like a thought. It may be that an oscillating pattern is how to represent a thought."

No clear theory of how to understand machine "thought" emerges from these two kinds of networks. Hopfield himself sometimes seems ready to throw up his hands at the question. "I have no idea what meaning means," he admits.

But from these networks it is possible to get a glimmer of how meaning means and how such a system might yield a psychology. These networks are probabalistic, sensitive to initial conditions, innately bound to the flow of time. The brain may share these qualities.

Putting Hopfield and Tank's network and Alspector and Allen's learning chip side by side suggests another kind of temporal relationship. Suppose that each of Alspector and Allen's learning trials is seen as part of evolutionary learning. Each trial is a more or less successful network. The final network that results, the one that solves the problem, is then like the hardwired one built by Hopfield and Tank. The final landscape is produced by the interaction between the brain and the environment, a gradual discovery of how best to gather the sensory information and most quickly process it. Certain constraints will get built into the shape of that landscape. The hills and the valleys may be arranged so that certain answers, certain downhill pathways for our metaphoric rolling ball, simply aren't possible. Certain answers may be created as either/or pairs by that landscape. It's either the rabbit or the duck of the classic optical illusion.

This suggests that we may be born with landscapes that are already partially constructed. The basic shape of each landscape may reflect what our species knows about the world and its structure. Each landscape probably gets more specific with learning, and learning may even change the inherited shape during the lifetime of an individual. Nevertheless, it's likely that some of the neural connections that form this landscape are extremely resistant to change. Some are easily modified by learning; others we may be able to change only with great effort. Still others may not be modifiable by learning at all. The degree of mutability also probably changes as an individual ages.

All of this makes sense. All of it logically falls out of these two artificial networks. Whether or not any of it is an accurate model of thought, however, is another question. Answering that one, Jerome Feldman and George Lakoff think, requires building a system that is true both to neurobiology and to the characteristics of a complex human behavior such as language. An artificial system that works but that violates the rules of one or the other of these domains is headed down the wrong track.

8
SPACE, THE FINAL FRONTIER OF MEANING?

You can't expect a bowl of porridge to be smart.
— JEROME FELDMAN

Eric Knudsen is trying to eavesdrop on the brain. He wants to know what it says to itself about the outside world and what language it uses. At the moment, he believes that much of the brain talks "space." Or at least the brain of the barn owl does.

In Knudsen's Stanford University laboratory, a barn owl makes a rustling sound in its box and looks up at Knudsen from the floor. Wearing a pair of goggles over its big eyes, the fluffy seven-week-old looks like an explorer about take flight for the unknown. The costume fits the task at hand: the owl and Knudsen are cartographers out to map the unknown topography that lies inside the owl's head.

"Brain map" isn't just a metaphor for the forty-two-year-old Knudsen. He and others have shown that barn owls etch careful maps of sights and sounds onto thin layers of neurons. By combining maps in succession, much like Richard Howard's zip code machine does, the owl gradually builds up an accurate spatial image of the world.

The goggles are part of an experiment to study the way the maps combine. Fresnel prisms mounted in the goggles alter the owl's visual world by systematically displacing objects. A food reward two feet to the right of center might appear two feet to the left instead.

An owl can normally locate an object by sound alone to an accuracy of one to two degrees. Logically, displacing the owl's visual map shouldn't affect a spatial map derived from auditory information, but Knudsen has found that owls raised wearing the goggles systematically misjudge how to find objects using auditory information alone. "What we've found," he says, "is that it's vision that is telling the auditory system how to map space. It's always laid out the way the visual system tells it." As the young owl wears the goggles over a period of two to three weeks, the errors get bigger and bigger. The auditory map changes to respond to the optically displaced space from vision.

In every neural network discussed so far, the machine completes a pattern or looks for matches among patterns. The input into a zip code reader or the past tense machine or the Hopfield network is a carefully constructed and circumscribed pattern or data set. The answer, the output, results from some transformation

The barn owl in its goggles. The lenses over the owl's eyes shift space and lead to "mistakes" in the neural map the owl uses to locate a mouse from the sounds it makes in the dark.
Photograph courtesy of Eric I. Knudsen.

of that input, in much the same way that sounds are coded into electrical signals, then into digital zeros and ones, then back into electrical signals, and then sounds again in making and playing back a CD. The machine learns how to produce the correct transformations by adjusting thousands or tens of thousands of weights, but to do that, it must be able to compare its output with the correct answer and then make changes. Or a teacher must know the correct output and do the correcting. Trial after trial, the machine converges toward the answer as it learns how to map the transformation that turns input into output.

But how does the brain know the completed pattern that it seeks? It has no overt teacher but experience, and research in language acquisition demonstrates how difficult it is for experience to give a child or a machine a complete pattern of all possible outputs. Minsky and Papert put the question to those early perceptrons — how can a machine learn the complete pattern when it knows information out of only part of the structure? Mozer's Bach machine, if it is ever to equal Bach, will have to come up with some way to know global patterns from local information.

As long as we're thinking just about machines, the question has a practical answer that avoids epistemology. An engineer provides the global pattern. In the case of brains, or machines that learn, this leads to a choice between an agent who knows all and a mechanical process that builds the whole. Either God designed the brain or it designed itself. We have no other options.

It's easy, looking at the owl's brain, to understand how such a system could be engineered, Knudsen says. It's much harder to imagine such a system somehow organizing itself. "To get the map of space, you have to pick all the right values of cross-frequencies of all these different cues and bring them together on the right cell so that they vary systematically across space, even though the cues don't necessarily vary systematically," Knudsen explains. "How did the brain learn that it is very useful to compare the timing spikes from the two ears [as in the owl or Mead's artificial cochlea]? One can set it up easily to do that knowing that is what you want to do. But at a more fundamental level, how did the brain learn it wanted to do that?"

The answer, Knudsen believes, is that the brain never attempted to learn the complete patterns. It didn't try to analyze an object into all its constituent parts and then put it back together again, nor did it try to completely characterize a data set. It paid attention to bits, pieces, partial data — anything that worked to help the animal survive.

For example, as a first step the owl's brain seizes on just those qualities of the real world that will let it predict location from sound. The owl starts with an acoustic signal — a sound wave with frequency and amplitude only — and builds a map that systematically records those events.

The map in the owl's brain isn't that different from your common everyday road map. In neurobiological terms a map is an array of cells where a parameter changes systematically with movement across the array. A road map also meets this definition. It systematically maps miles or kilometers of roads, rivers, mountains, and so forth, against inches or centimeters of paper. Push your finger an inch to the left on the map and you've gone 5.6 miles left in real geographic space. Move your finger an inch to the right or up or down and you've traversed the same distance. If you could run your finger across a neural map, which for all intents and purposes is a map in just two dimensions, you would be moving across sound frequencies instead of miles.

Most maps, especially at the sensory periphery, chart only one parameter, probably for no other reason than that it's simpler that way. Representing multiple parameters on a single neuronal map can lead to problems of ambiguity and crosstalk. By and large the brain solves this problem in sensory systems by avoiding it.

As the maps in the owl's brain get farther and farther away from the sensory periphery, they change in character. In the early maps, called sensory maps, parameters and the way they change over the map surface directly reflect the sensory stimuli. The maps that represent the actual physical layout of the retina are of this kind. So, too, are the auditory maps that represent frequency.

As maps combine with maps on the way to finally giving the owl an accurate spatial representation of the world, a new kind of map called a derived or computational map starts to play a larger and larger role. A computational map still systematically represents a parameter, but now the parameter is one that the brain has created through its own computations. A computational map wouldn't represent frequency, for example, but instead would map differences in frequency. These subtractions, carefully plotted for each point in the cochlea, become the building blocks for the next computational process. In the barn owl, for example, the auditory map of space is the end product of two sensory maps and a number of computational maps.

Many of the maps along the way create partial representations of space. The qualities of the real world are represented at this stage as an inner mental thing. In what Knudsen calls the frequency map, for example, any neuron will only respond to a specific conjunction of frequency/timing and intensity differences that describes a small region of space. "That's not true of any of the earlier cells we've been talking about," says Knudsen.

> They respond to a particular cue, say three kilohertz, in all kinds of places. But when you put all the cues for a given location together there's only one place in space where the cell is going to respond. So at one end of the nucleus, cells respond to sounds directly in front of the animal. As you move back [in the nucleus] cells respond to sounds further on the side.
>
> Now that we've got a map, the next thing is trivial, and that's just putting the auditory map together with the visual map.

Signals from the separately derived visual map of space reinforce the auditory map of space and correct any errors. The owl's brain even has a complicated scheme for resolving errors, as Knudsen's work on young owls shows. For the first 200 days of the owl's life, the two maps remain plastic and capable of changing their interpretation of space. During this time the visual mapping of space has the upper hand; any discrepancies between the two maps are resolved in favor of the visual system. That only makes sense, Knudsen says, because vision is a more precise and reliable source of information. Owls that are reared with distorting prisms over their eyes learn a distorted spatial map, even though they have access to the correct information through their auditory system. If the lenses are removed before the owl reaches 200 days, the new correct visual information will force a remapping of the distorted auditory map that had been created.

Research shows that maps like these exist in owls, monkeys, rats, and human beings, among other species. Detailed sensory maps in the human brain represent our sense of touch, systematically matching points on our skin with neurons in a layer of the brain. Such a map doesn't merely duplicate sensory space, though. Territories on it that correspond to areas of greater sensitivity are larger. Fingers, for example, take up more room on the map than do similarly sized patches of skin on the back of the hand. Even at this lowly stage close to the sensory periphery, the brain is creating an inner representation that is not precisely the same as the objective, external world.

The best evidence for maps in the human brain comes from the primary regions of the cerebral cortex, the parts of the brain most directly concerned with visual, auditory, olfactory, somatosensory, and motor inputs and outputs. The secondary regions of the cerebral cortex process this information further, turning it into things like plans of motion. Yet another region, called the tertiary, or association, cortex, takes care of the most abstract and sophisticated of the brain's activity. Here, neuroscientists believe, the outside world is organized into general schemata and speech is understood and created.

At the moment, the nature of the tertiary "mind" is extremely unclear. The neurons that make up this part of the cortex are certainly similar to those in the primary cortex. The principles at their disposal — change in the membrane potential, the geography of dendritic trees, the chemistry of neurotransmitters and channels — don't seem very different from the tools used to process early sensory information. There are more long-distance connections and feedback loops in this part of the cerebral cortex than in the sensory periphery. But the substantial biological similarity need not correspond to a mental uniformity. The sensory periphery could rely on transformations of space, for example, to do its work. The tertiary cortex could use other kinds of principles, such as representations of logical rules. The kinds of mental processes that result from these parts of the brain certainly seem different in kind from the barn owl's ability to locate a mouse. Language, for example, often thought of as the most characteristic operation of this part of the brain as well as the mental operation that most clearly distinguishes our intelligence from that of animals, doesn't seem just to transcribe or map external reality. It can see a specific Fido and know it's an abstraction we call dog. And it can create imaginary abstractions, categories of things no human being has ever seen, like heaven or hell.

In the barn owl the final computational maps seem clearly derived from the much simpler maps of the sensory periphery, but in human beings the mental activities associated with the tertiary brain seem to be different in kind. Perhaps it would be better to speak of the human brain as if it were two, with different principles and possibly different sources of information. Thus, language might use the innate principles of a generative grammar, like that initially proposed by Noam Chomsky in 1957 in *Syntactic Structures*, that was somehow resident in the tertiary part of the brain.

Wait a minute, though, says George Lakoff, a linguist at the University of California at Berkeley. Language doesn't require a radically different mental system from that employed in the lowly sensory periphery. In fact, he says, the way we use and construct categories and other kinds of linguistic abstractions proves that "space" is the common material used for everything from seeing edges to giving language meaning. Rather than being based on some innate set of logical rules, language shows all the signs of being constructed out of our interaction with the world — just like the owl's map of auditory and visual space.

Lakoff didn't come easily to this position, including as it does a rejection of much of contemporary linguistic theory. His own career tracks the history of American linguistics over the last thirty years. He studied mathematics and literature as an undergraduate at MIT, the home of Noam Chomsky, generative grammars, and symbolic artificial intelligence. Chomsky reshaped linguistics by focusing attention on how people really learn language. The infinite variety of actual speech had to be generated by what he called a grammar.

According to Chomsky, a grammar is a set of abstract rule systems that together characterize what constitutes a well-formed sentence in a particular language. In this view the grammar of a language enables you, the speaker of that language, to put a word into sentences, to change it to refer to the past or future or present, to make it refer to single and multiple objects. This grammar contains a formal logic that lets the native speaker correctly put these word-symbols together in statements such as "Jack hit the ball." It also enables the speaker to generate variants such as "The ball was hit by Jack," and it rules out transformations that would turn "Jack went shopping" into "Shopping was went by Jack."

But you will notice that, so far, this system lacks any reference to what these word-symbols "mean." Using this linguistic model, we can analyze the logical structures of languages and predict what statements can be generated and what can't. But its very power derives from the way it has divorced syntax, the logical rules for generating language statements, from semantics, what the symbols mean.

After MIT Lakoff tackled this problem in generative grammar — how to put meaning back into this system. Lakoff's theory of generative semantics, first laid out in 1963, attempted to create a formal logic for semantics. Sentences were bundles of basic "meaning" units, such as "cause." This universally available stock of basic meanings could then be combined following a few simple rules. In effect, this turned meaning into a kind of very abstract syntax. The syntactical rules of a language, for example, would make certain kinds of meaning units possible and other kinds impossible.

That didn't satisfy Lakoff for long. The more he looked at language practice, the less adequate this theory seemed to be. In practice, meaning seemed to be situational. It depended on context and couldn't simply be deduced from first principles.

Model theory was one way out of that dilemma for both linguistics and artificial intelligence. Artificial intelligence practice had amply demonstrated that an intelligent machine needed to be told when to apply a specific rule. That led to the introduction of frames, schemata, and worlds. The artificial intelligence machine would be programmed to know that in a world where its task was building with blocks, a term like "on" or "big" had a specific meaning that was suited to that context. For such a machine, according to this linguistic theory, meaning resulted from mapping a set of symbols to a model world. The model itself and the mapping rules generated meaning. By this time at Harvard, Lakoff, along with Richard Montague and Barbara Partee, was one of the main proponents of model theory.

"So I did logic for a long time," says Lakoff, a short, slightly bearlike man with a ready delight in the world. "What I found was that there were half a dozen to a dozen real ways in which properties of logic showed up in language. Then I started to find that there were hundreds of ways that didn't work. And eventually, after I moved to Berkeley, I gave up on that idea."

Lakoff's shifts weren't occurring in isolation. Research in anthropology, physiology, and linguistics was throwing up problem after problem in the practice of real languages that showed exactly how problematic meaning was. The real puzzler, though, came in the form of experiments by cognitive psychologist Eleanor Rosch, which seemed to show that central colors such as blue had a cognitive meaning even in cultures that had no word for them.

To linguists who believed that a word is a symbol, this was extremely unsettling. To put meaning back in this system, Lakoff notes, linguists must say that these symbols refer to things in the real world. "Jack" in syntactic terms is a symbol defined by its role as subject of a sentence, noun of a certain class, and other like properties. "Jack" in semantic terms *means* because it points to a thing in the real world that is Jack.

That kind of mapping from symbols to external world works very well as long as the meaning of the symbol is very concrete. "Ball" is simple. We all know what a ball looks like. We can touch it, smell it, taste it, if we like. But what about relatively abstract terms like "ghost" or "heaven"? Well, here the reference is to an imagined world, some linguists argue. It means because it refers to an imaginary model world.

Accounting for all meanings of even a simple word like "on" requires gluing together an ever-larger number of model worlds. "On" the table clearly refers to a physical model world, but in "on time" the meaning of the word isn't the same. Here we have reference to a temporal model. What about the Dutch word "op," which is somewhat like the English "on." An object can be "op" the wall, but only if its entire surface is in contact with it. Nothing is ever "op" horizontally. Generating the meaning of words like "op" would seem to require culturally defined, culturally distinct model worlds.

Until the late 1960s evidence from anthropology seemed to support this cumbersome edifice. Research showed, for example, that colors were named arbitrarily, a result that meshed perfectly with a symbolic view of words as arbitrary markers for things in the outside world. In one standard bit of investigation, a researcher would go into a society and ask native speakers to point out the parts of the spectrum named by their basic color terms. From language to language the naming seemed arbitrary. Moreover, the boundaries between color terms differed. Two societies with different words for blue and green would also assign different bands of the spectrum to each term. And, even more convincingly, other societies wouldn't have the blue–green distinction at all.

The assault on the belief that color terms were arbitrary didn't require the development of new machineries or theories. Cognitive anthropologists Brent Berlin and Paul Kay simply rephrased the question that researchers had been asking. In their experiments they presented a collection of 144 paint chips to speakers of different languages. As long as they asked their subjects to point out the parts of the spectrum their language named, the responses seemed arbitrary. But when they asked their subjects to point to the best example of, say, "grue" — a name for a combination of blue and green — they got a central blue, not turquoise. No matter what color terms a language had, all human beings seemed to agree on what colors were most blue or most green or most red.

Eleanor Rosch learned of the Berlin-Kay results while she was in the midst of her own study of Dani, a New Guinea language with only two color terms: *mili* for dark-cool (including black, green, and blue), and *mola* for light-warm (including white, red, and yellow). Here was a society that posed an incredible challenge to the results of Berlin and Kay. Could Rosch duplicate their results with speakers of such a radically impoverished language?

Reproducing Berlin and Kay's test wasn't difficult. Confronted with the 144 chips and asked to pick the best example of *mola*, for example, Dani speakers picked focal colors, either central red, central white, or central yellow. None picked some mix of the three.

Rosch decided to take this test further. To what degree did the language, which had only two terms for color, determine the conceptual categories of Dani speakers? If language alone determined the conceptual categories, Dani speakers would have equal difficulty learning new words for colors whether the color term corresponded to central colors or to arbitrary divisions of the spectrum. In the early 1970s Rosch taught one group of Dani speakers arbitrarily chosen names for eight central colors. Another group was taught names for eight noncentral colors. Unequivocally, the group learning the central color names learned more quickly. They also remembered the names better. "These things have a cognitive reality even if there isn't a word for them. Isn't that cool?" Lakoff says, using his term of highest praise for an experiment that creates a new way of seeing a problem.

And indeed that's what Rosch's work did, not just in linguistics but for cognitive science as a whole. Her results, in fact, were a challenge to a way of understanding the world at least as old as Aristotle. In this view, which Lakoff labels the classical tradition, categories — basic concepts like dog, chair, mother, or patriot — are natural containers that exist in the world. Objects such as my dog, your dog, and Marge Schott's late, lamented Schottzie belong in this container because they all share certain properties in common. Despite its age, this view also underwrote contemporary theories of symbol manipulation. Symbols drew their meaning from their correspondence to the real world. Categories of symbols corresponded to categories in the real world.

Rosch focused attention on a troubling implication of the classic tradition. If categories are defined only by properties that all members share, then no members should be better examples of the category than any other members. Since all dogs that are in the category "dog" share all the traits of dogness, individual observers ought to regard all dogs as equally good examples of the category "dog." But some blues were better blues than others, her research showed. This phenomenon, called the prototype effect, suggested that certain members of a category were better members of the category than others. Some reds were more central to the category. They were prototypes of the category "red."

Rosch and other researchers found the prototype effect almost everywhere they looked. In some experiments subjects were asked to rate how good an example of a category various members were. When the category was "birds," for example, robins and sparrows always wound up more highly rated for birdness than ducks. They are seemingly more prototypical birds.

In another test subjects were asked to press a button indicating true or false in response to a category statement such as "A duck is a bird" or "A sparrow is a bird." The closer the example was to being a "central" bird, the faster the response time. The challenge was to explain why this prototype effect existed.

One possibility is that it reflects the structure of the category as it is represented in the mind. Looked at this way, prototypes might simply *be* mental representations. This fit in with the belief in Chomskian linguistics that the structure of language reflected the underlying psychological structure of the brain. If you could open up the skull and look at how the mind represents the category of bird, you would see a picture that very closely resembles a robin or sparrow, this view holds. Other members of the category are matched against that image and are included in that container to the degree that they have characteristics that overlap with those of the prototypical mental representation. Those with few overlaps would be weak members of the category.

This explanation leaves the classic tradition relatively intact. Categories are still objectively extant in the real world. Instead of a bundle of features that all members of the category share, the prototype defines the critical feature bundle that members of the category share in varying degrees. The 1970s saw many attempts to build artificial machine languages by specifying the important prototypes and then defining the rules that linked them with other members of a category.

Lakoff had become fascinated by categories. Certainly, any theory of linguistics and cognition would have to explain why the prototype effect existed — it had the character of a classic constraint, an experimental observation that any good theory would have to obey. But simply mapping the relationships of members of categories to the relevant prototypes seemed more an effort to save formalist linguistics than an explanation of language practice. Anthropology continued to turn up even more puzzling examples of the way some languages used categories. It might be time to rethink the whole question of semantic logic.

For instance, Dyirbal, an aboriginal language from Australia that Lakoff discusses in his 1987 book *Women, Fire, and Dangerous Things*, uses just four classes for all things. Whenever a Dyirbal speaker uses a noun it must be preceded by one of just four words: *bayi, balan, balam, or bala*. In his fieldwork R. M. W. Dixon, a linguistic anthropologist, carefully recorded the members of each Dyirbal class. *Bayi* included men, kangaroos, opossums, bats, most snakes, most fishes, some birds, most insects, the moon, storms, rainbows, boomerangs, and some spears. *Balan* included women, bandicoots (an Australian rat species), dogs, platypuses, echidna (spiny anteaters), some snakes, some fishes, most birds, fireflies, scorpions, crickets, the hairy mary grub, anything connected with water or fire, sun and stars, shields, some spears, and some trees. *Balam* included all edible fruit and the plants that bear them, tubers, ferns, honey, cigarettes, wine, and cake. And finally, *bala* included parts of the body, meat, bees, wind, yamsticks, some spears, most trees, grass, mud, stones, noises, and language.

Dixon refused to assume that this was simply an arbitrarily

memorized list. Looking at the four categories, he found a certain elementary order. *Bayi* was mostly composed of human males and animals, *balan* of human females, water, fire, and fighting. *Balam* contained mostly nonflesh food, and *bala* seemed designed to catch everything else. Superficially, these seemed like they might be natural kinds, the term that linguists and others use to designate a category that objectively exists in the external world, such as "Tree."

But Dixon found some deeper principles at work here. One, which Lakoff calls the domain of experience principle, explained some seemingly strange categorizations. Fishes belong in *bayi*, for example, because they are animals. Fishing spears, lines, and the like are also in that category because they are associated with fish.

Other categorizations are explained by the myths and stories of the society. Birds, being animals, should belong in *bayi*. Instead, they are part of *balan* because of a myth the Dyirbal speakers share that says most birds are the spirits of dead human females. Logically, they belong in the category with other female things. On the other hand, three species of willy-wagtails are believed to be mythical men, so they go in the *bayi* category, separated from other birds and from human females in the *balan* group.

Dixon noted that a single important property often would divide classes. Fishes are mostly in the *bayi* class with other animals. But stonefish and garfish are harmful, so they wind up in the *balan* class with other dangerous things.

These categories, then, are certainly not natural kinds. They don't independently exist in the external world but are instead created by Dyirbal speakers. Yet Lakoff insists that these categories aren't arbitrary. They may not reflect the preexisting order of the world, but they aren't random lumpings of objects, either. The linguistic category derives from the experience the Dyirbal speakers have with the world. The four categories mark what is important to *them* about the world and helps them survive in that world. Anyone who speaks Dyirbal needs to know that garfish and stonefish are dangerous.

To Lakoff categories are derived from the interactions of human beings with the world. These interactions are constrained in some ways by the biological properties of human beings. Central red may be central red because of the biological apparatus that human beings use to perceive color. Other categories are determined by physical interactions, such as the experience of fishing, and still others may have a source in social behavior, such as the Dyirbal myths. All, however, are constructed in this interaction.

If there are no natural kinds, as such, then the whole referential model of meaning seems likely to be false. Our words cannot simply refer to distinct classes of items in the world because such classes don't exist there. They are created by the specific quality of human interactions with the world. Human beings, in this view, resemble Brooks's Collection Machine. That machine, like a human being, doesn't simply map the external world. It sees only those things useful to the task at hand and orders the external world into the categories that are useful to picking up a can or stopping in front of a desk. It has no category for desk or chair or table, all categories that human beings "find" in the external world. Instead, it has the created category of "solid objects that have flat surfaces on top," which only exists because of the task engaging the machine.

If this view of categories and meaning is true, then language cannot be a closed formal system. It must constantly refer outside the system for meaning. Semantics isn't a single set of rules that determines how meaning is constructed. Instead, it involves the generation of meaning in many different systems — cultural, biological, experiential, to name just a few. In a formal system it should be possible to generate all the items in a class by following a set of rules. Writing implements include pencils and pens because of the rules of that class, and we can generate the subclasses pens and pencils by other rules that are inherent in the larger class. In real language, Lakoff maintains, that just doesn't happen.

Lakoff notes that Japanese, for example, has a classifier, *hon*, that groups together long, thin objects. Sticks are *hon*. Canes and pencils are *hon*. Candles, trees, and ropes are *hon*. The best examples of the category, as measured by response times and other tests, are rigid, long, thin objects. Thus, dead snakes and dried fish are both easily recognized as *hon*. So far this could be a natural kind, and it is certainly not impossible to imagine generating this set and its interrelationships through formal semantic rules.

But, as Lakoff notes, lots of other things are *hon*, too: martial arts contests, hits in baseball, shots in basketball, judo matches, rolls of tape, telephone calls, radio and TV programs, movies, letters, and medical injections.

Membership in this category, Lakoff has come to believe, is motivated in each case by a story. Martial arts contests use staffs or swords, which are long, thin, and rigid. Letters used to come in the shape of scrolls, which, rolled up, were long, thin, and rigid. Rolls of tape and movie film when unrolled are long and thin. Telephone calls come over wires. These stories explain why all these things belong together, but even all together they don't constitute a rule that can generate the members of this category. Things belong to the category in different ways. Some are close to the central meaning of *hon;* others are far away. And the pathways from the central meaning to the extended meaning of *hon* are many rather than one. Sticks and TV programs share no common properties; they wind up in the same category only because of a story that creates a chain. This is like that is like that is like that. To Lakoff this category seems to be organized by metaphor. Through the 1970s and 1980s, Lakoff, often in collaboration with Mark Johnson, explored the nature of language category metaphors, gradually coming to believe that they had a logic of their own.

In the *hon* category, for example, baseball bats are central members. Hit balls also belong, both because of their association with bats and because of the trajectory they form. It appears, however, that foul balls, pop flies, ground balls, and bunts aren't *hon* to native Japanese speakers, although here, too, there is a logic. The trajectories of the non-*hon* hits usually don't resemble the straight line of the home run or line drive. And in the one case where they might, foul balls, that form of batted ball is not a principal goal in hitting. The foul ball is logically outside the goal defined by the metaphor.

"Metaphors aren't just linguistic expressions," Lakoff says. "They're ways of understanding abstract concepts in general. There are metaphorical mappings throughout cognitive domains." Once the metaphor has been laid bare, he believes its logic can clearly be seen to organize categories and thoughts.

And Lakoff noticed something else about many of these metaphors and the way they make connections among objects. Often a metaphor involves spatial principles. One thing is like another because of some way a metaphor manipulates space or translates an action into a spatial quality. It seemed that the human experience of space, our day-to-day interaction with the physical world, was the raw material for much of the logic visible in language.

The pieces began falling together for Lakoff in the late 1970s. At the University of Buffalo Leonard Talmy was beginning to show that schematic mental images of spatial relations could be found in languages around the world. Spatial principles such as contained-in, bounded-by, paths, center-vs.-periphery, orientation, direction, and so on, structured mental schemata, Talmy said. In fact, they seemed to be at the core of the images we use to structure languages.

If language was based on these spatial relations, then its logic would largely be formed by them, Lakoff concluded. This fit with what he and Johnson were discovering about metaphors as they charted the ways they organized categories. "The things that kept coming up over and over again as we plotted out the details of the metaphors were spatial structures," says Lakoff.

Lakoff admits his conclusion is by no means certain or settled, but it does mesh very neatly with the neurobiological discovery of extensive topographic maps in the brain. Neural networks, both biological and artificial, could use these maps and various metaphoric transformations to compute spatial relations and thus understand everything from relatively simple categories such as "cat" to more abstract concepts such as "mother" and "on."

A system of maps and transformations could, for example, explain how we understand the use of "above" in a sentence such as "Her family will stop that marriage somehow; she is too far above him."

To Lakoff explaining this is relatively straightforward. We see that it says things about the relative social position of the two families. Depending on our own culture those things may include birth, wealth, breeding, or some combination of the three. Meanings in what he calls the social domain — the relationships between people and classes and the like — are structured by spatial metaphor. We see social classes as a spatial hierarchy, a pyramid, for example. We also have a wealth pyramid, with families arranged from the base of the poor to the pinnacle of the wealthy. And we have various spatial mappings that connect these two pyramids, since we recognize the possibility that breeding and wealth don't always go together and the two structures don't always coincide. One way to think about this view is to imagine spatial relationships as a kind of universal language that the brain uses no matter what specific language — social, moral, engineering, poetic — we are using at the moment. The exact nature of those spatial metaphors will vary from domain to domain, but all will use the human experience of space as the basic material.

Lakoff believes he can tie this mental language to the physical structure of the brain and its maps. In fact, Lakoff believes he must. Incorporating our knowledge of how the brain behaves is now crucial to forming linguistic theories. "What I'm saying is that you can't do linguistics without a cognitive model." For Lakoff that model of how a thought happens begins with the world, includes the perceptual apparatus of the individual human being, takes account of the essentially spatial experience we have with the world, and rests on evidence for topographical mappings in the brain. What results is a linguistic theory of meaning that draws together evidence from neurobiology — like the Hubel-Wiesel experiments showing orientation and direction sensitivity in individual neurons in the retina — and data from language practice, psychology, and elementary connectionism.

"A lot of linguists say I'm crazy," Lakoff says. But as far as he's concerned, it's obvious that the classic tradition doesn't work and his system does. "You look at it. You know it works. And the others [systems] don't." Not that everyone working in linguistics would see this "obvious" fact. The split is probably closer to 95 percent to 5 percent — with the 5 percent on Lakoff's side. "Cognitive science is broken up into all these branches that don't talk to each other. There's a branch of cognitive science called cognitive linguistics, which is what I do, and we take all this for granted and do this kind of work." On the other hand, "if you are doing generative linguistics, what we do [in cognitive linguistics] isn't linguistics. Linguistics is the study of symbolic logic."

"The [different] theories of linguistics make so many assumptions that they can't even be compared," says Lakoff. A generative linguist like Jerry Fodor, for example, assumes that language and thought are symbol manipulation and the symbols are uninterpreted, Lakoff says. That constrains his whole system. "We don't start there. And it turns out that not starting there we don't get there. We look at evidence that contradicts that."

With all these obstacles in the way of even basic communication among rival theorists, it's hard to imagine that debate can settle the question. But according to Lakoff, there is another way to test his and other theories: build each one into a machine and see if it can reproduce something we recognize as language competence. At the moment Lakoff is testing his system against the touchstone task proposed by his colleague Jerome Feldman. If it can perform this task, Lakoff will be safely on the way to resolving some of the deepest problems in linguistics.

Jerome Feldman works in a very clean, well-lighted place. It is also fashionably gray and extremely quiet. Except for a receptionist, this place, the International Computer Science Institute, which he directs, seems deserted. The windows of his office look out over the bay, away from the storefronts of Berkeley and the university. The towers of the Golden Gate Bridge and the fog-shrouded Marin headlands add a calming note. Here a scientist could sit and contemplate the immense scale and beauties of the physical world.

Instead, Feldman contemplates a puzzle. It isn't a particularly prepossessing puzzle, just a few simple pictures along with a few statements describing each one. But like such classic puzzles as the Gordian knot and Uther Pendragon's sword, this puzzle promises the world to whoever solves it. Specifically, whoever masters this puzzle will have unlocked the secrets of intelligence. Want to try your hand?

The challenge is straightforward: design a machine that can learn to describe what it sees. That's all. Feldman calls this a "touchstone task." Any artificial intelligence that can perform this task will embody the basic principles behind much of cognition. No machine that can't solve it can possibly be a serious explanation of how intelligence happens.

The task has just two parts. First, whatever machine you

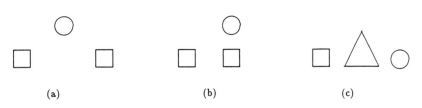

(a)   (b)   (c)

A touchstone puzzle: what does "over" mean? An artificial intelligence must be able to understand that in figure A the circle is "over" the two squares, but the squares are not "under" the circle. In figure B the machine must be able to understand that the circle is "over" just one of the squares, and in figure C, that the circle is "over" the triangle from the square.
Drawing courtesy of the International Computer Science Institute.

design will be given "examples of pictures paired with true statements about those pictures in an arbitrary natural language." The language could be English, French, or Chinese. The pictures aren't complicated. Just simple scenes containing up to four idealized geometric figures such as circles, squares, and triangles. A statement describing the scene might be "The square is bigger than the circle and above the triangle."

Second, "the system is to learn the relevant portion of the language well enough so that given a new sentence in that same language, it can tell whether or not the sentence is true of the accompanying picture." Given a sentence like "The square is to the left of the circle and below the triangle," the machine should be able to look at the picture and say, correctly, "True" or "False."

Despite its simplicity, the touchstone task requires a machine builder to solve all the problems bedeviling Lakoff and linguistics. The machine has to be able to learn the different spatial systems of the English "on" and the Dutch "op," just for starters. It will have to understand radically different grammars as well as radically different ways of conceptualizing spatial relations. To pass this test, a machine has to conquer the realm of abstract reason. According to Feldman, ". . . the system has to have a good theory of images and space; it has to have a good theory of language; it has to have a good theory of inference, because quite often a sentence will say something implicit about the picture; and obviously it has to have a good theory of learning." Arguably, the machine that passes this test will have demonstrated the central properties that we commonly say make human intelligence unique, even though anyone over the age of ten would probably regard the problem as trivial. "Put a little kid in any language environment, they learn. So if you got it right you should be able to have your program learn from examples," says Feldman.

Everything about Feldman's manner says that he hasn't a moment to spare from this effort. He never finishes a sentence — his conversation is a patchwork of thoughts, each one stitched to the next. As soon as he thinks the listener can complete the pattern of a sentence, he's off to another. And then he's up from the desk to check the fax machine. He's expecting comments on a critique of a paper he sent to Europe last night. Fishing around on his desk, he flings almost finished drafts of papers, slides from presentations, and government studies he helped prepare into the conversation.

Feldman shuttles back and forth between his two goals: solving this puzzle himself and getting the world to agree that this is the right puzzle to solve. Currently, the second goal is more important.

Feldman has worked hard to design his puzzle. He feels it is a truly neutral test — not prejudiced in favor of symbolic artificial intelligence, neural networks, generative linguistics, or any one of the dozens of other theories that purport to explain the nature of cognition. Yet he firmly believes that only one approach will solve it. When all the other claimants have tugged at the sword, cognitive science, which Feldman is betting is the right discipline, will step up and pull it from the stone with ease. But the demonstration will only be meaningful if he can get others to agree on the legitimacy of his touchstone.

In his own way what Feldman is proposing is a test that will perform the kind of hard-nosed analysis that Minsky and Papert applied to *Perceptrons* in 1969. It's not easy to tell from the first few stumbling steps if a rapidly developing science, especially one that is working from radically different principles from those of established science, represents a promising pathway or a dead end. What is the appropriate reaction to the Wright brothers' first flight, airborne for less than a minute, at Kitty Hawk? Is this a technology that with better engines, a greater understanding of lift, a different system for steering, would develop into a viable way for men to fly? Or is this a toy that no matter how much work the Wrights put in will remain a detour on the way to true manned flight?

He adds, "One of the nice things about the task, one of the things we claim, and I've said this publicly a number of times by now, is that none of the existing theories in linguistics or mathematics or connectionist learning or anything, comes close to being able to handle this little task. . . . I can tell literally anyone in thirty seconds what the task is. And none of our theories are remotely adequate for it."

Feldman thinks he knows how to go about solving his puzzle. "There is an approach that we're taking to the problem. And that is the same sort of, what we call structured connectionist models that I've been working on for years. You assume that you're going to need all of the good computational properties of neural systems. That you know that they are evidential, that they're redundant, that they learn, there's this whole list of properties."

But Feldman doesn't think the computational properties of

neural networks alone will be enough. What we know from linguistics and psychology and vision and computer science will also have to go into the recipe. And then to ensure that the result isn't simply some glutinous mass of overcooked but random ingredients, Feldman will call on the disciplines of cognitive science.

Feldman calls cognitive science a "science of converging constraints." "People invented the field [of cognitive science]," he says, "because they observed that there had been this fractionalization. People studying vision or language had done it from different angles and they had developed self-contained theories, which looked more or less okay from within that technical field. But when you looked [at them] from outside that field, they were sometimes just totally crazy. There were constraints that weren't being taken into account that somebody in a related field knew were fundamental."

For example, workers in artificial intelligence would propose building machine vision systems that required thousands of operations to go from the raw visual signal to the detection of an object. Experimental evidence seems to show that biological vision uses fewer than a hundred steps. So, cognitive science would argue, this artificial intelligence approach had clearly missed some important principle. Our knowledge of the biological system should eliminate certain approaches.

On the other hand, builders of neural networks, which at least lay claim to biological inspiration, would propose a system for performing visual computations. But a computer scientist using the principles of that science could clearly demonstrate that such a device could never compute the solution to a problem with that degree of complexity. "And so," says Feldman, "the idea was and is, if we take all these constraints seriously — what the physiologist says about vision as well as the psychologist and the computer vision person — we would sufficiently narrow down a set of possibilities so that we had a better chance of getting it right. I think that's a very simple, straightforward idea."

Feldman's perspective has evolved through the course of his own career in computer science: a Ph.D. in 1964 from Carnegie-Mellon University; associate director of the artificial intelligence laboratory at Stanford University; founding chairman of the computer science department at the University of Rochester; and now appointments at both the institute and at Berkeley.

His idea may be very simple and straightforward to him, but the principle it assumes is by no means universally accepted. Many "wet" neurobiologists don't believe computer science has much to tell them about how the brain must work. And many in the traditional artificial intelligence community simply reject the idea that their programs and machines should be constrained by the facts of biology.

Nor do all connectionists wholeheartedly believe in Feldman's principle. Feldman worries that after an initial gesture toward a synthesis that incorporated cognitive science, connectionism is ignoring the lessons of its own neurobiological roots. "There seems to have been a drift back. It's much more easy and natural for a group [of researchers] to say 'Isn't our stuff wonderful? Isn't it wonderful that we agree on all these assumptions?' Which is okay, except that the physical world isn't as compartmentalized as your discipline is, and if you want to get it right . . ." The rest of his statement is unspoken but clearly implied.

He also worries that neural network researchers have been seduced by the promise of programless computing. A lot of the appeal and commercial flash of neural networks comes from the promise that these machines will be able to learn everything and that programming won't be necessary. Not only can programming be done away with, but so can any worry about designing an initial structure for the network. The machine will learn that, too, or learn to do without one. The network can begin with randomly connected or fully connected neurons, and as it learns it will develop its own rules and its own internal structure. According to Feldman, there are neural network researchers who say, "Well, we don't have to do any of that: we're not going to have to worry about how the brain works or the properties of computation or the linguistic generalities which are true of the world's languages. We'll just build this brainlike net and we'll learn all that stuff."

The brain itself isn't unstructured mush, and Feldman would bet that any machine that can capture a fraction of the brain's properties won't start out as mush, either. He doesn't see how anyone who understands anything about computer science can possibly believe that any machine can learn all it needs to know — it would be overwhelmed by the possible alternatives. Just look at the history of neural networks so far, he argues. As young as the field is, there are already dozens of learning rules, all of which will work on different networks with very different patterns of connection among the neurons. Say you have a problem that you want a network to compute. Which learning rule and which structure should you pick? Asking the machine to learn the optimal combination would require it to work through every possible learning rule in all its meaningful variations and all possible structures. How long are you willing to wait while the machine grinds through the alternatives de novo?

"There's this huge space of possible learning rules and possible innate structures," says Feldman. The optimum degree of structure will depend on the particular learning rule used to solve the problem. And the optimum learning rule is, of course, dependent on the particular structure that has been evolved. Already, then, finding the best way to solve a problem as complicated as the touchstone task is difficult.

And, Feldman says, that still overly simplifies the problem. If it were just a choice of learning rules and structures, a two-dimensional plane would encompass the solution. But the problem is actually three-dimensional. The proper learning rule and structure, and the combination of the two, will depend on the specific task itself and the qualities of what Feldman calls the knowledge domain. Different tasks will require different structures. What we know about the brain says that's true. Says Feldman:

> One of the things that is very interesting is that parts of the higher levels of the cortex seem to have generally the same architecture. Which is very encouraging. But even then there's a lot of difference, and in the lower areas, which do most of the work, the architecture is very different. The vision system [has a structure] which is just radically, totally different [from other structures]. And that you would expect. Vision isn't much like moving your muscles.

It's easy to build an evolutionary argument to buttress that. A brain that responds to precise sensory cues, different in each sensory domain, would be more efficient and convey a survival advantage.

But how do we solve this problem in a multidimensional space defined by a multiplicity of learning rules, structures, and knowledge domains? If only there was a theory . . . but there isn't. If only there was a mathematical formula . . . but there isn't. Short of using up enough time to duplicate evolution's wandering course, is there nothing but trial and error? Fortunately, Feldman would whisper in your ear, there are converging constraints. What we know from neurobiology, psychology, physiology, linguistics, and other mental sciences will eliminate many of the points in this solution space. Evidence from one science or another rules them out, and the researcher can safely ignore those possibilities.

The information George Lakoff has collected on language practice makes up just such a set of constraints, one that is central to solving the touchstone task. According to Lakoff, language practice says that a formal symbolic approach cannot solve the touchstone task. The systems of spatial metaphors that do structure language are an essential ingredient to the solution. "This is the input that Jerry [Feldman] needs to get these spatial relation terms in languages around the world," says Lakoff. "He still needs something to do syntax and phonology and minor details like that," he jokes. "In terms of the basic semantics, though, this is what you need."

The touchstone task will show if Lakoff is right.

9

THE APPARENT REALITY
OF THE RISING FASTBALL

If you think of the world, the difficulty is not telling when
things are different, but telling when they are the same.

— ROGER SHEPARD

"You've seen this one, haven't you?" Roger Shepard is holding up
one of his collection of optical illusions. Retrieved from the pile that
is on its way to becoming his new book, *Mind Sights*, a commen-
tary on the role of the mind in perception, this one is a familiar
classic: at one moment a black drawing of a symmetrical candle-
stick, at the next two white faces in profile staring at each other.
Shepard hardly lets the drawing register, though, before he's digging through his cluttered Stanford office again. "How about this
one? See, it's a drawing of two tables from different perspectives.
When we see them as tables, our brain tells us that the top of this
one is longer. But look at the tops simply as parallelograms.
They're both the same size, aren't they? But your brain, which
knows they're tables, keeps denying it." The slight psychology professor pushes his gray mustache out just a little. "Now, why should
that be?"

Pen and ink drawings are only one of the many kinds of illusions Shepard studies just down the hall from David Rumelhart's
office. While Rumelhart is a new addition to Stanford's psychology
department, Shepard has been there for more than twenty-three
years. For even longer than that he has been designing experiments
devoted to understanding how we perceive and think.

"Stick your head in this box," nicely commands Michael
McBeath, one of Shepard's graduate students. This part of

Shepard's laboratory is devoted to studying a category of illusion called apparent motion, in which the brain is tricked into seeing motion where there is none. "See those four dots?" McBeath asks. On the computer's screen four dots in a diamond pattern flash in sequence. McBeath speeds up the flashing. Still the brain sees top dot, right dot, bottom dot, left dot, alternately — the four corners of the diamond. Faster, faster, until suddenly the diamond seems to become a circle. The screen seems to show not four dots flashing but one dot traveling in a circle.

"It happens at different speeds depending on the individual, but it always happens," says McBeath. "A related principle could explain the rising fastball," he adds, pulling out his 1990 paper, "The Rising Fastball: Baseball's Impossible Pitch." Shepard's fascination with the visual puzzle has apparently infected his student. Once physicists called the curveball impossible, McBeath explains, with the grin of the true enthusiast. No pitched ball could change direction once it left the pitcher's hand, they said. Without any force to act on it, the ball had to follow a straight path or one

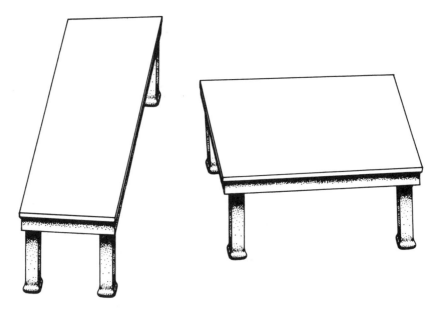

The brain turns these two identical parallelograms into tabletops of very different sizes and shapes.
Drawing from Roger Shepard, *Mind Sights*. Copyright © 1990. Reprinted with permission of W. H. Freeman and Co.

dictated by its initial velocity and gravity. Wind tunnel experiments, however, have actually explained most pitches — the curve, the late-breaking slider, and even the erratically fluttering knuckleball — as the product of the interaction of the baseball's seams and spin at speed thresholds that radically change the local aerodynamics around the ball. But the rising fastball remains a physical impossibility. Even though generations of batters swear that the game's hardest throwers fire a pitch that will jump up as it crosses the plate by as much as a foot, freeze-frame photography and aerodynamic tests so far fail to detect any measurable upward movement.

McBeath believes that the rising fastball is actually an optical illusion. "A pitched baseball is right at the edge of our perceptual abilities," he says. Nobody sees well enough to follow a ball all the way from the pitcher's hand to the catcher's glove. The human eye loses the ball at some point in its journey and then picks it up again as it crosses the plate. A great batter — a Ted Williams, for example — is able to follow the ball far longer than a poor hitter can, but all batters are actually guessing at the pitch's speed and location. Successfully hitting a baseball requires the brain to use visual clues, such as the speed at which the ball changes in size as it approaches the plate, to project the ball's location.

The rising fastball, McBeath theorizes, is the result of misjudging the ball's speed when it leaves the pitcher's hand. If the batter maintains the correct line-of-sight on the ball but thinks it's traveling slower than it is (a good possibility since most pitchers who own rising fastballs are the game's hardest throwers), he will project a trajectory that is inaccurate. Because at any moment he will think that the ball is farther away — because he has underestimated the speed of its approach — than it really is, he will predict a trajectory that is lower than the ball's actual course. Taxed beyond their perceptual limits, the eye and the brain lose the ball as it travels toward the plate. They "see" an imagined trajectory that must be combined with the more accurate perception of the path of the ball that the batter gains when it crosses the plate. At that moment the ball is correctly seen as higher than its earlier projected course. The brain accounts for this, says McBeath, by experiencing a hop that takes the ball from where the brain thought it was going to be to where it actually is.

What's the brain's alternative? Telling us it sees two balls —

one imagined on the wrong trajectory until the plate and then another at the right level crossing the plate? What leads the brain to the visual explanation called the rising fastball? For that matter, why do optical illusions exist at all?

Shepard and his students don't study these phenomena merely to explain them away. Optical illusions are clues to how the brain works. They are normal by-products of the brain's structures. They reflect the methods the brain has evolved to deal with the world, methods that have evolved because they serve us well under ordinary conditions. Any theory of how the brain works must show how optical illusions arise from the essential nature of the brain. Such a theory could also explain how the mind results from the physical brain. The mind would then no longer be a metaphor or a shorthand for all our mental processes but a phenomenon grounded in neurobiology. Scientists would be able to connect a mental entity, a thought about a category, for example, to a specific location and state of the brain. They would be able to translate Lakoff's spatial representations into patterns of activity in specific brain regions. Ah, they could point, see there. That's the pattern for a general cat; there's the one for Mr. Green's tabby.

Shepard's publications and his experimental data stretch back into the 1950s. He has been one of the most respected researchers in the psychology of perception for almost three decades, and it is clearly impossible to say that his work has been ignored or dismissed. Even so, the last few years have brought a definite change in Shepard's fortunes. He is suddenly immensely visible outside his field. He is an invited speaker at neural network meetings. Papers dense with mathematics attempt to turn his work into functions and maps. Shepard himself seems newly daring, publishing a challenging paper that deliberately invites a comparison with Sir Isaac Newton's *Philosophiae Naturalis Principia Mathematica*, one of the greatest works of Western science.

All this hasn't come from some new discovery that Shepard has made. Instead, it's largely the result of a new question posed to psychology by neural networks and the neurosciences. You in psychology study behavior and try to supply theories that motivate it, these brain sciences have said. We study the same brain on the level of neurons and neurotransmitters and brain areas. How do we tie our studies together? How do we explain even basic behavior, like the way we generalize, in terms of neurons and networks of neurons? Everybody suddenly wants to talk about Shepard's work because it suggests at least the outlines for connecting psychology to the microstructures of the brain.

Part of what is so intriguing about Shepard's work is that it adds up to the beginnings of a set of constraints, to use Feldman's term. Shepard's perceptual data outlines psychological principles that any microstructure must produce. The brain that emerges from Shepard's experimental data has a *very* distinctive character.

In all these illusions, says Shepard, the biological brain is clearly not a passive recorder of the scene that merely sketches a representation of what's out there. In the case of the candlestick/faces sketch, the brain seems to alternate between complete gestalts, switching from one way of seeing the entire image to another but never mixing the two. In the table/parallelogram problem, one gestalt, the "table context," seems to completely stymie the brain's ability to perceive the two flat parallelograms, which is "what is really out there."

In the other examples, the flashing dots and the rising fastball, the brain seems to have "a mind of its own" with its own internal logic. Fastballs jump. Flashing dots must become continuous circles. This brain seems to prefer some scenarios — those where fastballs jump — to others — those where fastballs are created and destroyed in different locations.

To Shepard these visual illusions are the result of a computational device of immense but not infinite power trying to make sense of the world. The brain is faced with bewildering complexity. Just consider simple problems like identifying an object from all possible points of view, under highly varied lighting conditions, and with the possible interference of other, occluding shapes. Or color constancy. Red must be red in bright sunlight, haze, and deepest shade.

Much of perception involves what a computer scientist calls "ill-posed problems," problems where the information available isn't sufficient to produce just one correct answer while rejecting all others. It is by no means a trivial task to decide that a table, now obscured by two boxes, is the same table that was in your living room a week ago. We can, of course, walk around the table to examine it more closely — Yes, it has the same legs as yesterday — but we don't usually need to do that. Standing in the doorway, we decide whether or not it's the same table at a glance.

Indeed, we must decide instantaneously, particularly if this isn't a table but instead an onrushing automobile, a nineteenth-century Parisian footpad, a Carthaginian war elephant, or a saber-toothed tiger. The dangers of the world give a significant evolutionary advantage to organisms, and brains, that can quickly and correctly perceive and avoid threats or recognize, find, and secure food, shelter, or allies. Reacting to evolutionary pressures, the brain has had millions of years to find ways to solve ill-posed problems quickly, or to find ways to correctly interpret the world when the information coming in is noisy or especially incomplete.

The brain didn't evolve to solve problems like these in all possible worlds, Shepard points out, just in one. Why is it that we can recognize and find our car in sunshine or shadow, but we'll walk right by it in a parking lot lit by sodium vapor lights? Simply because the brain solved the computational problem of recognizing color constancy by taking a fundamental shortcut. The brain and the eye, its front-end sensory input device, need to achieve color constancy in one specific world where the unchanging light emitted by the sun is modified only in a few specific ways by the earth's atmosphere.

Says Shepard:

> It's been found that there are three different types of cones in the human retina with three different photosensitive pigments, one responding more to the longer wavelengths of light, one to the medium, and one to shorter wavelengths. Well, why? To me the ultimate objective of the science of psychology, or the science of the mind, is not just to trace back properties to physiology but to ask why we are the way we are. And the only answer I can see for that is to go back and say: "If it's not arbitrary, there must be something about the world in which we've evolved that made it adaptive."

In the case of color, Shepard argues, three variables are enough to uniquely specify any color given the earth's sun and atmosphere. "There are just three degrees of ambient illumination on the earth having to do with things like the height of the sun in the sky, whether the light reaching the object is directly from the sun or whether you're just getting scattered light, which is the short-wavelength light that makes the sky blue, and whether the object is getting a lot of light or in deep shade. In order to achieve color constancy, in order to recognize the same object even though it's seen under different lighting conditions, we have to compensate for these three degrees of freedom in illumination, which means we have to separate the stimulus into three color portions."

That's by no means a trivial task, since it requires that each point in the visual world sampled by the retina be represented by three different receptors. But it certainly is a lot easier than building a computational system with an infinite variety of cones — one to compensate for each possible change in each wavelength in the visible spectrum — and not just the roughly 125 million receptors it actually uses.

This may all seem obvious when Shepard talks about light and a totally unconscious perceptual process like vision. But he believes that the principle extends throughout the brain's computational architecture and to interpretations of the world that seem less perceptual and more logical. As an example, he points to our innate, genetically inherited law of the conservation of objects. A series of experiments on apparent motion demonstrates the strength of this law.

An object in three-dimensional space, as long as it's rigid, unbending and untwistable, has only six degrees of freedom of position. Visualize a cube with a face painted on just one side. That cube can be moved about three different axes in space — the three degrees of freedom of location — left/right, up/down, and front/back. It also has three degrees of freedom of orientation — three ways it can be revolved on its axes. It can be rotated front to back, bringing the painted face from the front position to below, to the back side, and so on. The cube can also be rotated from left to right, or it can be corkscrewed on a diagonal axis. Specifying all six operations, and no more, is sufficient to uniquely position that cube in space, but only if it is rigid — if it can't be squashed into a parallelogram, for example — and only if the space remains three-dimensional.

Shepard's experiment, conducted with Sherryl Judd, started with twelve pairs of two-dimensional shapes. (The shapes were based on a series devised by Shepard's former student Lynn Cooper, now a professor at Columbia University.) Each pair consists of two identical shapes in different positions inside a circular field. The pairs follow simple rules of transformation: the second image in each pair was created by translation (movement in the two-

dimensional plane), scaling (one image is an enlargement or reduc-
tion of the other), rotation in the picture plane, reversal (one image
is a mirror image of the other), or rotation outside the plane (in
pair i, for example, we see the object turned on its edge).

Some transformations prevent alternative explanations. We
can imagine an escape from the two-dimensional plane of the
drawing to three-dimensional space or a transformation confined
to the two-dimensional plane that violates the objects' rigidity. The
first object in these pairs would have to shrink or grow to become
the second object; and in some pairs it would have to change shape.
A few instances would involve both size and shape changes.

Shepard and Judd showed each pair of images alternately to
observers and asked them how the two objects were related. In
their descriptions the observers preserved an object's rigidity
whenever possible, preferring to add another dimension to turn the
two-dimensional drawings into three-dimensional spaces. Pair d,
for example, was explained as movement from a distance in the left
background to a position in the right foreground rather than as
enlargement of the object. "Invariance in perceived size and shape
is achieved by liberating the transformation and the object from
the confines of the picture plane into three-dimensional space,"
Shepard wrote in 1984.

Shepard uses "invariance," a term from James Gibson's theory of ecological optics, to describe the results of his experiments.
Gibson, whose influential work *The Ecological Approach to Visual
Perception* appeared in 1979, stressed that as an organism moves
around in its environment, which itself is changing because of its
own dynamics, it perceptually experiences transformations in
actually unvarying objects. That perception of change is not always
useful to the observer's survival. Often the higher survival value
lies in perceiving the identity that is obscured by the seemingly
different views of the world. The key to the survival of the observer
is in finding ways to detect that identity, in knowing that the spot-
ted animal in the shade is the same hungry leopard that was in the
sun just a moment ago.

Gibson theorized that underlying those moment-to-moment
transformations are certain invariances, No matter what we see at
the moment, that tree is still there behind that passing truck. Seen
at noon or 7:00 A.M., from the roof of a house or a trench, close up
or far away, we still perceive it as the same tree. Gibson's radical

approach, one not universally accepted by perceptual psychologists and still not widely disseminated among workers in the neural network field, argued that an organism picks up sufficient invariances from the information available to all its sensory arrays to uniquely specify all significant events and objects in its environment.

It is not easy to grasp exactly what Gibson meant by an invariance. Clearly, it isn't some Platonic quality lurking in an object below its ever-changing surface. Your grandmother's face does

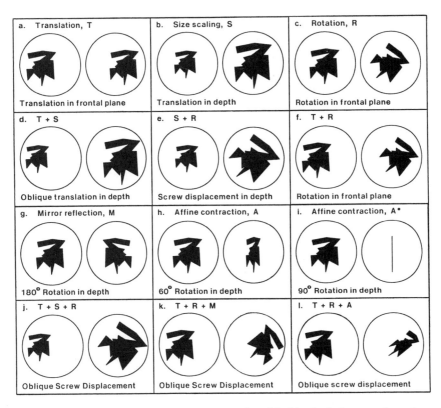

How would you explain these pairs? Shepard and Judd asked observers how the two objects were related. In figure a, for example, the object in the left-hand circle seems to have moved across the field. In some cases the observer had a choice of explanations. In figure b the transformation can be explained by saying that the object is enlarged or by assuming a third dimension and saying that it has moved from background to foreground. Explanations that keep the transformation confined to the two-dimensional plane of the picture are listed above each figure. Transformations that preserve the object's rigidity are listed below.

Drawing courtesy of Roger Shepard.

indeed look very different from moment to moment, and Gibson was not claiming that some invariant essence linked all those appearances. An invariance is not some quality inherent in the object. Instead, it describes some relationship between object and observer. Color constancy, for example, occurs not because we somehow build up a color such as red from cues in the object, but because of certain orderly relationships between the observer and the world that includes the object. The invariance of a grandmother consists in the limits to the transformations she can undergo in our world. A grandmother looks different close up and far away, but the changes produced by distance are generally predictable and constant.

Invariances, therefore, are constants constructed out of the observer's relationship with the world. Thus, it stands to reason that they can change as the observer's relationship with the world changes or, since we are talking about an evolutionary process, as the relationship changes from species to species or in the history of a species. A frog's visual invariances are not those of the human visual system, for example — not because the objects in the world are different, but because the frog interacts differently with the world. As Jerome Lettvin, H. R. Maturana, Warren McCulloch, and Walter Pitts put it in 1959, in one of the classics of computational neuroscience, "What the Frog's Eye Tells the Frog's Brain," the frog

> will starve to death surrounded by food if it is not moving. His choice of food is determined only by size and movement. He will leap to capture any object the size of an insect or worm, providing it moves like one. He can be fooled easily not only by a bit of dangled meat but by any moving small object. His sex life is conducted by sound and touch. His choice of paths in escaping enemies does not seem to be governed by anything more devious than leaping to where it is darker. Since he is equally at home in water and on land, why should it matter where he lights after jumping or what particular direction he takes? He does remember a moving thing providing it stays within his field of vision and he is not distracted.

It's a mistake to simply regard the frog's visual apparatus as more primitive than ours. Granted, the frog's eye lacks an equivalent to the human eye's fovea, that central zone of acuity that is more densely packed with receptors. And certainly, the frog's eye seems ill designed for recording an unmoving image. The neurons of the frog's visual system lapse into quiet in response to an unchanging visual pattern. If our understanding of the eye's task is that it is supposed to transmit an extremely detailed copy of the local distribution of light intensities in the world to the brain, then the frog's eye is a clear failure.

But suppose, suggest Lettvin, Maturana, McCulloch, and Pitts, that the eye is instead designed to detect certain patterns of light that correspond to certain relations in the real world. A spot of light has not only intensity but shape, size, edge, contrast, and curvature: the frog uses these features efficiently given its needs in the world. The frog's eye initially processes light in four main ways. A set of receptors and their neural connections react to a sharp border between contrasting light intensities. A second set of detectors reacts most strongly if an object with a curved boundary moves intermittently against a background. A third set reacts to moving boundaries in a wider area than the second set. A final set tells how much dimming occurs in an even wider area, weighted by distance from the center.

How does a hungry frog identify a bug? It's clear from its visual system that the frog doesn't build up the image of the bug by counting legs and body segments, looking for a thorax, comparing it to other categories such as dandelion fluff, and then flicking out its tongue. No, its second set of receptors and the processors attached to them seem to constitute a bug detector. They react most strongly when a dark object, smaller than the detector's receptive field (less than about three-eighths of an inch), enters that field, stops, and then moves intermittently. One invariant to a frog is therefore "bugness" in the same way that our invariants include three degrees of color invariance or the cues of looming (the degree to which an object changes in size as it approaches us).

To Gibson the ability of an organism to interact with its environment by moving through it and to actively seek information allowed it to find the necessary invariants. To Shepard Gibson's emphasis on the organism's interaction with the environment is an essential principle. But Shepard, more than Gibson, argues that some of the orderliness in the world has been internalized in the circuits of the brain. The brain, Shepard believes, often assumes order in situations where perceptual information about the outside world is ambiguous.

While he agrees with Gibson that evolution has pushed the brain toward the ability to extract invariants under favorable conditions, he thinks evolution has also pressured the brain to find ways of maximizing its performance under less than optimal conditions when it is impossible for an organism to find unambiguous invariances. Darkness, obscuring objects, brief glimpses, and noise are all part of our everyday perceptual world. We see the rising fastball, the circular dots, the three-dimensional pairs, because the brain's internal rules know that this is the way the world is most likely to be. Given ambiguous information or stretched to its perceptual limits, the brain chooses the interpretation that conforms to these internal rules.

In Shepard's model the brain is knowledgeable about the world. Driven by evolution, it has internalized certain constraints about the world in much the same way that a burrowing animal knows, without seeing the sun, when dawn approaches. That rhythm, based on a regularity of the environment, is internalized in the animal's biological clock. Our internal constraints and those of the burrowing animal so closely match the external world, says Shepard, that most of the time they are invisible to us. Only when the animal is deprived of sun, or when our brain is deprived of sufficient information from the external world, do these internal constraints become obvious. A phenomenon like a visual illusion, for example, where the brain has insufficient information, exposes the existence of those constraints.

The idea of internalized constraints has driven Shepard's work in two different directions. In one he continues devising experiments designed to reveal more of the brain's rules for making sense of the world. In the other he uses this insight to attack classic problems in psychology. The problem that has led him farthest toward a general theory of psychology is the question of how we generalize.

Generalization is a horrendously difficult job for a machine intelligence, Shepard knows, but he also believes it is probably the most important issue in neural network modeling. It has often been addressed by creating elaborate frames, that is, contextual rules that tell the machine what parameters to concentrate on in a specific instance in order to reach a relevant decision about sameness or difference. Many of the most accurate methods are built up through time-consuming feature extraction from the scene and then the manipulation of those features to eliminate differences that are unimportant in a specific context. Shepard couldn't help wondering if the brain might use some sort of internalized constraint to help solve this problem.

Color constancy or object identity, things we do all the time, are only special cases of generalization, Shepard points out. Our brain seems designed to detect invariances that can tell you that this is the same red Ford in the sunshine in front of you that you saw passing through shade on the distant hilltop. But how does it also tell you that this and the blue Chevy, the white Toyota, and the black Model T are all cars?

When Shepard begins to talk about generalization, he looks down at his gray sweater far more often, and his humor becomes self-deprecating. He is a little uncomfortable with what he is about to claim, but he also clearly enjoys tweaking the gods of science. His own theory of generalization was first laid out in a 1987 paper about as dense as a black hole entitled "Toward a Universal Law of Generalization for Psychological Science." "It's very difficult. I tried to punch a lot of ideas into a very limited space just to get it out there. Rather presumptuously it occurred to me that I should publish my proposed 'universal law of generalization' in 1987 because it was exactly 300 years after Newton published his *Principia* laying out the universal law of gravitation."

In this article Shepard theorized that generalization is a simple result of the connections in the brain working with one key internal constraint, what he calls the metric of similarity, that is derived from a species's experience in the world. In brief, Shepard posited that the brain represents objects as points in a psychological space in a way that makes those similar enough to be of the same natural kind fall into the same local region of that space. One region might correspond to "dog-ness," and representations of every dog will fall somewhere within it. Our perception of how closely things are related corresponds to the distance between two of those representations — between that of Lady the spaniel and Tramp the mutt. Things that are totally unlike dogs will fall into a different region. We know that a fireplug isn't a dog because it is far distant from the dog region. We know that bears and dogs are in some degree similar because the distance is relatively less.

This space is measured in units that are common to the perceiving species. In fact, they are created by that species's experience with the world. For a species whose survival depends on discriminating dogs from bears, the metric of similarity — the units that measure psychological space — would put a relatively great distance between the two. For one that only needs to comprehend dogs and bears as big animals, the psychological distance would be smaller; both dogs and bears might be found in the same region.

The metric of similarity is a species's scale of difference. It evolves through a species's interaction with the world, and it reflects the scale, textures, and kinds of interactions important to the organism.

Shepard's ideas of psychological space seem almost naturally to link up with neural network models such as Hopfield's and Rumelhart's that envision decision landscapes. "I think David Rumelhart and I have a very similar view about this," says Shepard about his colleague down the hall. Since building his past tense machine, Rumelhart has created more complicated models with more than two layers of neurons. Sandwiched between the input and output units is a hidden layer, which develops its own representation of the task at hand. Says Shepard:

> His idea, as I understand it, is that between the input units, which correspond to sensory cells in the receptor surface, and the output units, which control muscles, say, you have hidden units. As he's expressed it on occasion, the whole power of connectionist thinking is that this layer of hidden units can represent a psychological space. The mapping from the input to this hidden layer is just the psychological mapping that converts what is on our sensory surfaces into some representation that corresponds to what's out there in the world.

It is equally easy to think how one of Shepard's regions could be translated into Hopfield's scheme of valleys in a neural network's energy landscape, which is a physical metaphor for a mathematical abstraction called a solution space.

The best way to build up to this concept is to start with the straightforward Cartesian graph, the simple two-dimensional solution space you learned in junior high school. It has an x axis, the horizontal one, and a y axis, the vertical one. This two-dimensional space, actually a plane, defines all the possible answers in a system with just two degrees of freedom.

Let's say you are a scientist working to discover a way to stop apple worms from damaging apples. You've spent years gathering basic data on the problem. The data is of two sorts, the number of worms in an apple and the weight of the apple.

The solution space has just two dimensions, an X dimension labeled "worms" and a Y dimension labeled ounces. (Simple problems have simple solution spaces with just a few dimensions. Complex problems require spaces with far more dimensions.) Every possible solution to this problem lies somewhere on this plane. It is mathematical nonsense to imagine a solution that isn't on this plane. The only way to create a solution floating above the plane, for example, is to add another variable, say pounds of pesticide applied, to be considered before solving the problem.

A typical way to solve a two-variable problem is to graph all the data on hand and look for a pattern, maybe even a curve that mathematically describes the relationship between the variables. Each point you put down on your graph paper has two qualities: a number specifying the number of worms, along the x axis, and a number specifying the weight of the apple, along the y axis. You graph fifty points. The result is a straight line that begins at point 0 worms, 0 weight and runs upward from there. Looking at the line, you can see that point 2 worms, 4 ounces and point 4 worms, 8 ounces both lie on the line. Now you can write a mathematical equation that predicts this relationship, even for points you haven't graphed: $x = \frac{1}{2}y$. This is the second way to solve this problem, a second way to predict one variable from the other.

There is another way to get this solution, though, one that requires no calculations at all once the initial relationships have been discovered. You can systematically deform the solution space so that all the points have to fall along this line. One way to do this is to use a nonlinear scale along one or both of the axes, so that what had been a thin line in the earlier graph becomes an extremely broad band taking up almost all of the solution space. You can then solve your problem pretty much by throwing darts.

Think of the solution space as a multidimensional box with one dimension for each variable in the problem. Any point in that space is a possible solution to the problem at hand. Each point is defined by some value of each variable, so much x, so much y, so much z, and so on. A Hopfield landscape resembles this kind of space.

Carefully constructing this space, or if you prefer, deforming it, gets to be even more useful when the number of variables increases. In solving twenty- or thirty-variable problems, which require twenty- or thirty-dimension solution spaces, the space can be so warped that only the desired solutions fall out of the topology. A Hopfield network describes a solution space of this type, where the landscape makes certain states, or answers, extremely unlikely, and others easy to attain.

But is there any experimental evidence for this kind of psychological space and a metric of similarity? Theoretically, if there is, Shepard should be able to find a similar metric in an individual species no matter what perceptual task it is performing. There is certainly no dearth of raw data to examine. Researchers have been collecting data on categorization for decades in widely disparate species.

Shepard knew, though, that much of the data seemed to prove his theory wrong. Experiments on pigeons and other animals have enabled psychologists to establish orderly gradients of generalization for many species. A pigeon, for example, can be conditioned to peck a translucent key illuminated by light of a particular wavelength to get grain. Charting rates of response versus changes in the light's wavelength produces a graph that shows how close or far away from the original light's color any new light seems to be to a pigeon. The slope of that line — the amount of change in response time divided by the amount of change in wavelength — is called the gradient of generalization. It shows how much change in the stimulus is needed to cause a change in the rate or probability of response in that species for that task. Between 1955 and 1958 Shepard himself had established orderly gradients of generalization for humans, during learning that associated verbal responses with color chips.

All these results had one problem, however. In each, the response probability reliably decreased with an increase in the physical difference between the new stimulus and the training example. But the way it decreased, its rate, for example, not only varied from one species to another — as might be expected — but also according to stimulus dimension (such as hue or size) or sensory modality (such as vision, hearing, or touch) for a single species. The gradient of generalization was different in each case. The size of the units of difference varied so widely, it was extremely difficult even to compare the graphs. The metric of generalization in humans, for example, might be radically different in auditory and visual experiments, and even between visual experiments using shape and color.

But the idea of invariance suggested another way to look at this data. Instead of graphing responses against changes in particular physical characteristics of the object, the wavelength of light, for example, Shepard assumed that the animal in each of these situations was extracting an invariance from the situation and that that operation, whatever it might be, produced the gradient of generalization. Since the animal wasn't using a raw physical dimension of the stimulus as an indicator of difference, it didn't make any sense to use a change in that raw stimulus dimension as one of the graph's axes.

The animal was using some invariance, Shepard believed, to transform the physical stimulus into another quantity, much the way a mathematical function like $x = y^2$ maps 3 into 9, or $x = (y + 2)^2$ maps 3 into 25. Trying to graph the results of all these equations in one graph, without taking into account the transforming powers of different equations, produces an orderless jumble. The experimental data certainly confirmed that.

Pragmatically identifying each invariance and its mathematical form from psychological research was hopeless, Shepard knew, certainly for a single researcher with a limited life span. Pinning down Gibson's invariances had been a major occupation for an entire generation of psychologists and cognitive psychologists, and yet fewer than a handful had been convincingly identified. Shepard, on the other hand, was looking at data from widely disparate sensory modalities and widely varied stimuli within each modality.

Instead, Shepard decided to assume that he could work backward from the generalization data to reveal the unique mathematical function expressed by the invariance. If the generalization differences were the result of the operation of various invariances, perhaps he should use the amount of change in generalization as one scale of his graph. In line with his theory that generalization was mapped onto psychological space in some way that used distance to express difference, he decided to use distance in psychological space as his other scale.

Of course, he didn't have a way to apply a pair of calipers to psychological space. He didn't even have a clue about what psychological space should look like in rabbits, armadillos, or human beings. But his graphs could give him some hints. If he assumed that the world remained constant for all species, then an individual species would express its unique interaction with the world in the way it organized psychological space. If he tried to keep the curves described by the gradient of generalization similar from species to species, he would have to make changes in the scale that expressed distance. He would be forced to discover the foldings, distortions, and scales of psychological space that each species used.

Shepard found that he could produce almost identical curves for data as different as the ability of pigeons to differentiate spectral hues and the human ability to distinguish consonant phonemes. The curve was simple, approximating the simple exponential decay function. This indeed *looked* like a universal law of generalization.

Producing that simple curve, though, yielded intriguingly different kinds of psychological space. Accommodating the increase in generalization between the red and violet ends of the spectrum, for example, required only two-dimensional space, a geometry that reproduces the circular form of the Newtonian color circle. Generalization between tones separated by an octave required resorting to a three-dimensional space, and generalization involving a polygon with approximate central symmetry required four-dimensional space. This led Shepard to conclude that generalization is the discovery of whether a particular stimulus belongs in what he calls a consequential region, a "belonging" that is governed by the specific shape of that region in a psychological space that can itself vary in its dimensionality.

Shepard derives his exponential law of generalization from what he calls "simple arguments of probabilistic geometry." In the absence of other information, an individual of any species can do no better than to assume that nature has randomly chosen a region in the abstract psychological space of possible objects to be a "consequential region." Of course, the individual has no way of examining the layout of this psychological space, of graphing it, or understanding its organization. It simply is. Suppose that an individual finds a particular object to have an important consequence — for example, that it is edible or poisonous. In Shepard's scheme this means that the region corresponding to this consequence, though otherwise of still unknown location, size, and shape in psychological space, does overlap the point representing the object. The problem of generalization arises when the same individual now encounters another object that is more or less similar to the first. Does the second object also fall into that consequential region? Will it also be edible or poisonous? The closer the two objects are to each other in the space, the more likely they will both fall in the same consequential region. Shepard has shown that since the consequential region is finite, in this situation of minimum information, the probability that the second stimulus also falls within the consequential region falls off exponentially with the distance of the second object from the first in space.

"The space has been shaped, stretched, and compressed along different dimensions until it best serves us" in our search for natural kinds, says Shepard. "If we made lots of distinctions along some dimension that was never of any relevance to us, then presumably, through natural selection, that would get modified and that dimension would get compressed. If there was some other dimension where everything was scrunched up and we weren't making adequate distinctions, that dimension would get elongated." Psychologists like Shepard's Stanford colleague Mark Gluck have recently suggested several mathematical functions that might describe this space.

Thinking about space this way is also part of the modern transition from the world of Newton to that of Einstein. Newton's gravity was a force that operated on objects in the normal three Cartesian dimensions over time. Mass in the Einsteinian universe actually bends space. The planets and other objects move in the orbits that they do simply because they are moving on the straightest possible path in curved space/time. The way that space is bent, which can be described in a mathematical function, creates the possible motions of objects.

In his own writings and in his work with his mathematical collaborator Eloise Carlton, Shepard argues that psychological space is generally curved rather than Euclidean. Moreover, as in the general theory of relativity, the natural paths of motion in this psychological space correspond to the closest analogues of straight lines in a curved space, paths called geodesics.

But the most fundamental issue, according to Shepard, is not whether psychological laws will ultimately most resemble those of classical, relativistic, quantum, or any other physical theory, but whether psychological laws are universal in the sense that physical laws are universal. Through natural selection, Shepard believes, organisms are likely to internalize not only circumstances that are peculiar to their particular environmental niches, but also features that hold universally for the world in which all species have evolved. Such features include the three-dimensionality of physical space and the grouping of biologically significant objects into natural kinds. It is the existence of universal regularities such as these that Shepard sees as the ultimate source of any universal psychological laws.

Exactly what kinds of description and what kinds of laws are appropriate for the brain? A simple atomistic description seems less and less likely to be appropriate, even though that approach is the mainstream of 2,000 years of Western philosophy. Most frogs probably don't appreciate the situation, but their visual system presents an important challenge to some of the major schools of Western philosophy, not to mention many of the assumptions of artificial intelligence. The long atomistic, rationalist tradition that extends from Descartes, Leibniz, and Hobbes assumes that all phenomena, even mental ones, can be understood by breaking them down into their simplest primitive components. The goal of the great seventeenth-century rationalists was to find these components and the purely formal and logical rules that joined them together into the more complex compounds of the exterior and interior worlds. All reasoning, therefore, could be reduced to calculation, or in Leibniz's terms, the Calculus. Analysis would produce a kind of alphabet of facts, the simplest atoms of the world, that could then be recombined by a limited number of logical relations to produce and explain the world and all thoughts.

That same goal lies behind Russell and Whitehead's *Principia Mathematica*, their great attempt to reduce the world to logical operations expressed mathematically, Ludwig Wittgenstein's *Tractatus Logico-Philosophicus* (1922), and artificial intelligence. "AI," in the words of Hubert and Stuart Dreyfus, philosophers of science at the University of California at Berkeley, "can be thought of as the attempt to find the primitive elements and logical relations in the subject — man or computer — that mirror the primitive objects and their relations that make up the world." But that effort assumes that we can strip these atoms of all their relations, that at base they are context-free, linked by abstract rules. The grand project of artificial intelligence has been to find those atoms and the logical relations that govern them and to build a symbolic computer representation that captures that order.

But what if, as the frog suggests, the atoms can't be stripped of all context and association? In 1953, just as the foundations of artificial intelligence were being laid, Wittgenstein's previously published *Philosophical Investigations* repudiated his earlier *Tractatus* and the theory of atoms of fact. Facts can't be stripped of their context, Wittgenstein argued, because it is their context, their pragmatic use, that gives them meaning. In a frog's terms, a fly is not a set of facts connected by rules but a black dot that is good to eat. Reality can't be broken down into its constituent parts without a consideration of how that reality is used. "It makes no sense at all to speak absolutely of the 'simple parts of a chair,'" Wittgenstein wrote. "Chairness" has as much to do with how a chair is used, how it is encountered in everyday life, with its associations, as it does with the "facts" that most chairs have four legs — although some have fewer — and bottoms and backs — although some have none.

Neural networks don't magically escape or resolve this debate. In fact, they may intensify it. Shepard's theory may indeed lock global situations and local "facts" into a hermeneutic circle, like two snakes engaged in swallowing each other's tails. The researcher trying to understand the brain from outside the brain is confronted by a system that seems to have no beginning. The global space is created by the local facts, but the global space determines how the local facts will be applied and used. Where is the beginning thread in this fabric, the one that can be pulled loose to set it all unraveling? We can't measure the psychological space directly; it is only accessible to us through the local facts. How do we discover what elements of the external world the internal world is using in its construction project?

We can guess by doing thought experiments. This must be a critical clue that the brain uses, we can conclude by looking at behavior or the external world. We can then take our guesses and build machines that try to do what the brain does. If they succeed, we can dance with joy down the halls of our research laboratories.

But we can't conclude even from that success that we have hit upon the secrets that the brain uses. If, using edges and contrast, we build a machine that sees as well as the brain, can we assume that this is the way the brain works? Or have we simply built a different organism that uses some part of its own interactions with the world to do its own task as well as it can?

10
THANKS FOR
THE MEMORIES

It often happens that a man cannot recall at the moment, but can search for what he wants and find it. . . . For this reason some use places for the purposes of recollecting. The reason for this is that men pass rapidly from one step to the next: for instance from milk to white, from white to air, from air to damp; after which one recollects autumn, supposing that one is trying to recollect that season.

— ARISTOTLE, *De Anima*

Richard Granger has a bad cold. The thirty-eight-year-old mathematician can barely breathe, much less smell. Which seems appropriate, since Granger studies memories of smells.

The job of a rat's nose, says Granger, seems to divide naturally enough into parts, each of which seems to suggest a mechanism. To know about cheese from past experience, the rat needs some kind of memory. But that memory has to store both the specific cheese the rat has experienced and some category of cheese. And that is pretty tricky. As Roger Shepard points out, we don't see generalized cats or cheeses. We need to transform all those specific cheeses into a category called "cheese," and we also need to figure out a way to match the specific cheese experienced now with the generalized cheese. It would be helpful, too, if that scheme for categorizing was true to observed psychological behaviors, such as the prototype effect noted by Lakoff.

Building a machine to do this isn't likely to be simple. Each one of these mechanisms is pretty complicated. It's clear that such a machine would be a box or, worse yet, a series of boxes, as in Michael Mozer's and Rodney Brooks's machines, but each box would, in this instance, have to be capable of relatively complex discriminations and behaviors. For example, this machine will have to handle sensory input that is much more varied than the carefully constructed code that Mozer's BLIRNET perceived. This may take a while.

Unless, of course, Richard Granger's research is right. All these things — categories, representation, memory, and matching — are produced by one mechanism alone. In the model Granger built they all just naturally emerge as a part of memory. No one is more surprised than he is.

Using just a small portion of its brain, the olfactory bulb and a section of the neocortex, the rat can compute immensely complex things. From smell it can identify a cat it has smelled before, and possibly more impressively, it can tell that the smell of a never-before-smelled cat is still that of a generic cat. "You don't just sniff a thing and say it's x," says Granger. "There are a lot of things you know about x, not the least of which is what it's similar to and different from. What kind of thing it is." And then there are associations — learning to avoid traps even though they are associated with the smell of cheese, for example. Or mazes — rats can learn to run mazes by smell.

And so can the machine Granger has built. From odors it can distinguish cats from cheese, and it knows that a rose is a rose is a flower but is definitely not a daisy. It also knows that daisies and roses and lilacs are all flowers and all more like each other than any are like a cat, and it can remember what smells it has already encountered. But the machine does more, Granger believes. Indeed, it seems to demonstrate why some facts wind up as memories while others don't, and how the brain — rat or human — learns to generalize. And it seems to have a psychology that matches what researchers know about how pigeons, for example, organize the world when they generalize. Not bad for a machine that was designed only to test a theory of how synapses worked.

For the last six years Granger has worked with Gary Lynch at the Center for the Neurobiology of Learning and Memory at the University of California at Irvine to build a neural network out of all they knew about channels, neural transmitters, and cell membranes. Unlike Carver Mead or Michael Mozer, Granger and Lynch didn't begin with observed behavior or the study of a system. Unlike Richard Howard or Rodney Brooks, they haven't tried to engineer a solution by matching networks to tasks. Instead, they have worked from the lowest level they could reach, the micro-chemistry of the brain, and built their machine from those details level by level. They believe that whatever their machine does is caused by the properties of those basic chemical processes. The larger promise, they feel, is that other machines capable of equally complex behaviors can be constructed by following the micro-details of other parts of the brain — even if engineering them is too difficult and understanding their principles, for the moment, impossible.

Lynch has spent most of the last decade searching for a cel-lular mechanism that would explain memory. His job hasn't been made any simpler by scientists' inability to agree on what memory is or how and where it is stored in the brain. In the late 1940s and early 1950s Karl Lashley, a Harvard neuropsychologist, demon-strated that memory was not highly localized in the brain, destroy-ing the analogy between the concentrated and compartmentalized memory of a digital computer and human memory. Memory, it seems now agreed, is stored in changes in the brain's individual neurons. But how many neurons does it take to store one memory? The grandmother school, named after the theory that there is a single neuron in the brain that represents your memory of your grandmother, maintains that a single neuron can encode or repre-sent a memory. The distributed school, which at the moment is in clear ascendancy, claims that memories are spread out over a pool of neurons, each of which contributes to the whole. Even within that school, however, there is little agreement on how many neu-rons share a memory or how widely distributed they may be.

And then there's the question of how many kinds of memory there are. Larry Squire, a psychiatrist at the University of Califor-nia at San Diego, Endel Tulving, a psychologist at the University of Toronto, and others have clearly demonstrated the existence of at least two independent kinds of memory, sometimes called pro-cedural and factual. People with brain lesions who have forgotten such facts as whether they ever took piano lessons can still remem-ber how to play the instrument. Rats, Granger notes, can be taught to run mazes and to avoid certain behavior associated with tiny electric shocks, although they apparently remember each of these tasks with a different mechanism. Specific chemical antagonists introduced into the rat's brain will block one kind of learning and leave the other totally intact.

Any theory of what underlies memory has to explain at least three experimental observations: long duration, rapid induction or creation, and selectivity. Memories last a long time, potentially most of a human lifetime. They form quickly and without the need for repetition — we can remember scenes, events, and people even after just a single glimpse. Not everything gets turned into a memory, however. We remember our multiplication tables, but we don't remember the name of every person we've ever been introduced to. "At the least, you need to have something at the bottom that works quickly and that stays changed," says Granger. "It doesn't matter how many cells you've got, something has to stay changed."

In 1984 Lynch and Michel Baudry postulated that memory — actually, a specific type of memory called long-term potentiation — is created when messenger calcium sets off permanent changes in the structure of a synapse. Lynch and Baudry theorized that certain kinds of activity patterns, such as bursts of high activity at the synapse, change the electrical voltage on the target cell enough to allow the opening of NMDA receptors. These receptors, just one among many kinds on either side of the synapse, allow the passage of calcium into the postsynaptic dendritic spine. "That calcium goes in and does some mysterious thing," Granger says, "which is now widely suspected to be the activation of a protease, an enzyme, which in turn has some other mysterious effect, now widely accepted to be — I say this because these things have been hotly disputed over the last decade — changing the cytoskeletal protein inside the spine and therefore physically changing the surface membrane characteristics of the spine so that it is then more effective."

Lynch and Baudry argued that those physical changes would increase the effectiveness of the receiving synapse by revealing more of the AMPA receptors (the ones that actually chemically transmit the signals across the synapse) embedded in the cell membrane at the synapses. The next time a signal arrived at the sending synapse, it would release the same amount of neurotransmitter across the gap, but now, because more AMPA receptors were available to receive it, more molecules of the neurotransmitter would be captured and a stronger electrical signal would be created in the receiving cell.

Other than all the missing pieces required to fill in the "mysterious" parts of the process, the theory had one major problem. Scientists had long ago figured out how to get a brain cell to fire, but no one had yet managed to produce long-term potentiation in a real cell — one still in the brain. What kind of signal would induce the neuron not just to fire but also to produce the synaptic changes that the theorists said lay underneath memory? All three methods that produced synaptic change in the laboratory seemed unlikely candidates for the brain, to say the least. "Either you had to have an enormously high frequency stimulation of a target neuron. It was very unphysiological. It couldn't happen that way," says Granger. Or researchers had to inject chemicals that would increase the strength of the signal by knocking out all the inhibitory cells, which, says Granger, "was obviously something that the animal couldn't do itself." Or they could voltage-clamp the cell by inserting an electrode that would let them add voltage to it, and then additional "normal" activation would do the trick. "And so it remained a mystery what was going on in normal physiological activity. It was taken on faith that something must be but it wasn't known what," says Granger.

In the late 1980s John Larson, a postdoctoral student in Lynch's lab, added another piece of this picture. He suggested a way to explain chemically why not every signal creates a memory. He found that the timing of the electrical bursts that traveled through the neurons was crucial for producing long-term potentiation. The electrical signals could be very small, but if they arrived in a fixed, repeated rhythm, about 200 milliseconds (200-thousandths of a second) apart, long-term potentiation resulted.

These ideas haven't exactly gone down smoothly among neurobiologists. Lynch's brash personality and the professional animosity generated by his high profile in the media virtually guaranteed a stormy reception. Lynch is one of the few memory researchers, for example, to garner a glowing profile in the pages of the *New York Times Magazine*. But that aside, neurobiologists had traditionally believed that physical changes in cell structure, or brain plasticity, were limited to the early developmental stages of childhood. Now they were being asked to believe that brain plasticity extended far into adulthood, and they were uncomfortable with cell changes of this magnitude in adult animals.

Nor is the Lynch-Baudry-Larson hypothesis without challenge. Another school of memory research has focused on the side of the synapse that sends the signal, rather than the side that receives it, as the site of physical changes. Until results announced at a Cold Spring Harbor, New York, conference in 1990, the postsynaptic school seemed to be inching toward general acceptance, but at that meeting neurobiologists Richard Tsien of Stanford and Charles Stevens of the Salk Institute released new research findings that strongly buttressed the presynaptic case. At the moment the exact mechanism, or perhaps mechanisms, of long-term potentiation is still elusive.

Even John Larson's puzzle solving created new problems for understanding long-term potentiation and how it generates memories. Time suddenly seemed to be a crucial ingredient, and once they looked, Lynch and his colleagues began to discover time everywhere in the system. The two kinds of receptors, for example, operate on very different time scales. "The NMDA receptor channel is an immensely slow thing. It takes twenty milliseconds to open. A really long time on the scale we're talking about," says Granger, "especially compared to AMPA receptor channels, which can be opened in one millisecond." Excitatory neurons, units that send signals that tell the next neuron to fire, and inhibitory neurons, units that send signals that say don't fire, also show major timing differences. Inhibitory signals last for 100 to 500 milliseconds; excitatory signals for just about 20.

And then there was the biggest puzzle of all. The 200-millisecond interval needed to produce long-term potentiation exactly corresponded to the theta rhythm, the intervals between a rat's sniffs. Surely, there was a reason why rats took samples of smells by sniffing at exactly the same interval as was most effective for producing long-term potentiation.

To find out, the team decided to build a neural network model of this part of the rat's brain, a task that largely fell to Granger, the group's computer scientist. On a computer Granger would write a program, or more precisely a series of overlapping programs, that would simulate everything they knew about how this part of the rat's brain worked. Equations would duplicate the rate at which sodium moved across cell membranes and the very different rate for potassium. Other equations would preserve the timing differences between NMDA and AMPA receptors. Gradually, Granger built up the olfactory neocortex and the olfactory bulb. "You have to know the anatomy," says Granger. The olfactory neocortex is one of the simpler areas of the brain with just excitatory and inhibitory cells, but still Granger needed to know approximately how many of each and how they were connected.

"I was constantly trying to go to lower and lower levels," says

Granger. He hoped that all that fine detail would interact to form memory, even though he couldn't tell the machine how to perform that function. Granger certainly couldn't define the larger operation called memory, reduce it to rules, and put those into the machine. To use two terms often evoked by those who build artificial neural networks, Granger hoped that the system would *self-organize* all those finer details of anatomy and microbiology into a complex behavior without the researcher first discovering the rules governing the behavior and then programming them into the computer. The behaviors called memory and learning would *emerge* from that self-organization.

No one, not even Granger, was certain what this computer model of the rat's nose would do. He feared that nothing coherent would emerge. It wouldn't learn; it would recognize a rose as a rose on one run and as the scent of a lemon on the next. Maybe it would be too sensitive to minor changes, swinging wildly from one extreme to another. Maybe, worst of all, it wouldn't be able to remember anything. The biological research that Granger had put into the network might be insufficient to create lasting memories inside the machine. If these processes were correctly described and were the key ones that produced memory, then and only then would the model produce a simulated behavior that resembled what went on in the real animal. If key processes were missing or erroneously described, the computer model would fail.

Granger felt he had some leeway, but he didn't know how much. "You can build a radio a lot of ways," he says. "You can build it with tubes or transistors. You can give it a lot of different inputs, FM or AM, for example, and it will still be a radio. But you try to build it in some other ways and it won't be a radio."

Granger ran his model holding his breath. Results in hand, he tweaked it by adjusting some of his biological parameters. Then he ran it again. Adjusted again. Ran it, adjusted it, ran it once more. Finally, it seemed to demonstrate memory. Once exposed to the electrical signals that Granger knew represented a rose to a real rat, the artificial neural network would remember that pattern. The machine would correctly identify the next electronic smell of a rose as one it had smelled before.

But Granger's neural nose showed some rather unexpected behavior, too. If he let the machine take more than one "sniff" of each rose, the patterns would change with each one. The first time the machine experienced a smell, it actually didn't seem to learn anything. The pattern that Granger had initially labeled "rose" would only show up after the second sniff. On the next sniff of the same rose, the machine would generate an entirely different pattern, and the fourth sniff would yield yet another pattern. All other scents worked the same way. This was puzzling and also rather distressing. This wasn't much of a memory if it remembered the smell of a rose in six different ways.

Only when he compared the second and third sniff patterns from different kinds of scents did Granger develop a theory to explain what his nose was telling him. These weren't defective memories at all, he concluded. The neural network was creating categories of smells. After identifying the smell generally on the second sniff, the network would create a pattern narrowing the category on the third sniff. A fourth sniff would yield an even more explicit category of smell, maybe even a unique identification. It was as if the neural network had somehow figured out that a rose smelled sweet but that it also smelled flowery, and that, finally, it smelled only like a rose. The unique pattern for a rose was only produced after several sniffs and after the machine had created patterns that seemed to represent categories. As far as Granger knew, he hadn't told this computerized nose anything about categories of smells, and clearly the machine didn't have any independent knowledge of the real world. What was producing this behavior?

Granger finally concluded that this categorization was emerging not from any rules he had programmed into the machine but from the way the neurons in his artificial network were connected. Granger's network, like the brain, contained two different kinds of neurons. Excitatory neurons, when stimulated, produced a signal that would tend to make other neurons fire. Inhibitory neurons produced a signal with exactly the opposite effect. It urged neurons not to fire. A neuron receiving both excitatory and inhibitory inputs from all of its synapses would add up all these positive and negative signals and fire only if the sum exceeded some threshold value.

The first burst in Granger's neural rat activated both parts of the network. It first stimulated the excitatory target neuron. It also stimulated an inhibitory neuron that fed an inhibitory signal back toward the source of the excitatory signal. Because Granger had

preserved the timing and signal characteristics of inhibitory neurons in his simulation, the inhibitory neurons sent out stronger and
longer-lasting signals than excitatory neurons, and they quickly cut
off the effects of the first sniff. The inhibitory signal was so strong
it overwhelmed the excitatory signal. The neural rat couldn't even
identify the scent after this round, let alone memorize or categorize it.

Arriving just 200 milliseconds later, the next sniff elicited an
entirely different pattern of firing neurons. Now that inhibitory
neuron was exhausted from firing during the first sniff and
couldn't respond to this next round of signals. This time the burst
wasn't cut off early. With the inhibitory neurons inactive and recu-
perating, stuck in what is termed their refractory period, the
excitatory cells received enough of the burst to fire in a pattern
that represented the scent in a very general way. And since the
exhausted inhibitory cells couldn't cut off the burst, enough of the
signal reached the postsynaptic receptors to induce long-term
potentiation and produce memory.

With the next sniff, the model headed out into unexpected
territory. Because of how neurobiology told Granger to connect the
excitatory and inhibitory cells in this network, on the third sniff
inhibitory feedback combined with the exhaustion of the excitatory
neurons that had just fired to produce a new pattern. Even though
the input scent was the same, only neurons that hadn't fired a cycle
ago had the possibility of firing now. The neural network produced
a remainder, a narrower pattern that was a subset of the first, and
subsequent sniffs produced even narrower subsets. In effect, Granger reasoned, the neural network rat nose was going from a cluster
of excited neurons that represented sweet odors to a narrower cluster that represented floral odors to a still smaller cluster that represented a rose. Each sequential sniff produced a pattern that was
more specific to a particular odor. "We just couldn't believe it,"
he says.

The model also suggested a new way to think about the psychology of generalization and representation. Say you sit down in
a room much like his office, Granger begins. A commonsense view
of how you identify your location might be a sequence something
like this, he continues:

Oh, I'm in a room. Oh, I know it's Rick's office. Oh, I see he's cleared
off his desk today. In that order, boom, boom, boom. There is a

whole psychological literature on the rapidity with which people identify things at certain levels of description. It's termed a "basic-level" response. For instance, people are immensely faster to name a picture of a robin as a bird than they are to name it as an animal or to name it as a robin.

Explaining this creates tremendous problems for psychology and for traditional artificial intelligence. How does the "intelligent" machine, or the brain, know what level of representation is appropriate to the situation? How does the artificial intelligence know what it is supposed to know? Is it dealing with John as specific individual with specific traits, with John as Lithuanian, with John as carpenter, with John as Caucasian, or with John as father, or brother, or child? John is at one and the same time all of these, but only some of these traits are likely to be germane to any specific situation involving John. One artificial intelligence approach to solving this problem involves the creation of frames or schemata that specify for the machine the level of representation it should assume.

According to Granger:

> Representation is the big stumbling block for all of artificial intelligence and all of psychology. It certainly isn't the case that we've solved it. But our work raises an interesting question: what if there isn't a single unitary representation of things? What if instead things come arranged in hierarchies?

That would remove the tension between the ability to generalize and the ability to recognize specifics. Granger theorizes that the representation for a thing is a sequence. Our brain doesn't start the task of deciding how to represent some stimulus in the external world by asking what the appropriate frame is and then generate other representations from that by changing frames. Nor does it take that specific rose representation, extract common flower traits, and then compare them to some stored flower template to see if they match sufficiently to make a rose a flower — a process akin to how the zip code reader treats a 7. Instead, Granger's machine suggests, the brain encodes many levels of representation almost simultaneously from generalized category to unique identity. "You ride down that hierarchy to recognize the appropriate thing or to find the appropriate association, or more specific knowledge," says Granger. "And on and on and on. It's a tantalizing suggestion. And nothing more yet. We don't know where we'll go with it."

But again, from the rat's point of view beginning with the most general category makes good sense. "The last thing the rat wants to do is to begin with a unique representation of a particular cat smell and then have to run through a time-consuming matching and generalizing program until he recognizes that this unique smell also falls into the cat category," says Granger. "He'd get eaten while he was doing that."

Granger's model is still relatively small. "The size that we currently use has 500 inputs and 5,000 outputs, which is actually getting up toward realistic sizes. We're only a couple of orders of magnitude [100 times too small] off now," he says laughing. And it's slow even after doubling the memory in the Sun 4 workstations that run it. "Before that, one of these simulations of 10,000 cortical units and 800 bulb input units would run overnight. Now you can run the thing in a couple of hours." Still, the real rat's brain does this work in seconds or less.

But this machine and the model that runs on it have given Gary Lynch and Granger a new tool. Only recently have computers, and especially relatively affordable computers such as the Sun, become powerful enough to model systems as complex as the brain. Over the last decades neurobiology has made tremendous progress in understanding the ways the brain goes about its job down to the level of neurons, synapses, and dendrites and then to neurotransmitters and other parts of brain chemistry. But neurobiology's methodological strength has also been its weakness. It has been limited to what could be discovered by observing relatively small numbers of brain cells, often one at a time, and then trying to guess at the shape and significance of their interactions. Mathematics was able to offer only limited help in understanding the brain as a system. The nonlinear relationships, with thresholds, saturation limits, and timing sequences, quickly overwhelmed mathematicians' ability to solve for so many interdependent but complexly linked variables.

"I think the tool was required before these kinds of questions could get answers of any kind," says Granger, "but the goal [of understanding the microprocesses of the brain] has always been there. It's just that you had to get at it through experiment" using single-cell recording from animals during behavior. "The attempt has always been to spin a tale about how microprocesses give rise to behavior."

This tale of the brain's microprocesses has another point, too. If precise connections are the key to complex behaviors, how do the right connections get made in the developing brain? The brain, the immensely complex brain, begins as the single cell that is the origin of every human being. What engineers the final product?

11
MIND, ORGANIZE THYSELF

Mass communication is defined as the transfer, among
groups, of information that a single individual could not
pass to another.

— E. O. WILSON, *The Insect Societies*

Kenneth Miller says that he wound up studying the brain because
he's drawn to beauty. He wants to reveal the theoretical beauty of
the brain the same way a physicist reveals the beauty of the sub-
atomic world or the swirling complexities of interstellar dust
clouds. That desire is one so much more often expressed by physicists than biologists that it's no surprise to discover that Miller's
early training was in physics.

Miller's generation is the first one "trained in both biology and
theory," says Michael Stryker, Miller's dissertation adviser at the
University of California at San Francisco. With this background, it
just might be possible to produce a physics for the brain — a science with the mathematical beauty and the predictive power of
modern physics, but about neurons and synapses, behaviors, and
psychology, instead of atoms and quarks. The first place Miller has
picked to look for this beauty is in the growing brain.

Miller's scientific odyssey began during his first short, two-
year stay at Reed College in Oregon. "I quit school when I was
eighteen, which was 1972, the Vietnam War, my father died, and
other things," says Miller. "I quit because I felt there were things I
needed to discover."

Dropping out also rendered Miller's academic confusion moot,
for the moment. "I really loved theoretical physics. I loved the
beauty of it. But I thought the problems of biology seemed more interesting; they seemed more relevant; they seemed more juicy. How

do we think? Immunology. These are very practical questions that are very interesting. But I wasn't sure that I could find the same beauty in biology, so I went through a lot of real struggling."

Out of Reed, Miller worked for a year in commercial fishing and then joined a cooperative, the Hoedads, which worked on tree planting and forest conservation in Oregon. But he still kept debating his earlier decision. "I'd be planting trees and I'd be dreaming about physics and science. You know, you have a lot of time to think when you're planting trees eight hours a day." Finally, it just felt like it was time to go back to science. He finished his degree at Reed in a year and a half — "All I took was biology and physics" — and then realized he still couldn't pick between them.

Accepted into the Stanford physics department, he decided that this was perhaps his last chance to learn physics. At Stanford a course in neuroscience offered by Carla Shatz and Eric Knudsen seemed a way to unite biology and theory. It focused on the development of sensory systems, asking questions that Miller had tried to address during an abortive one-year fellowship at New York's Rockefeller University. "Shatz and Knudsen were the first people I ever talked to who really thought that [trying to do theory in neurobiology] was a good thing and that modeling was a good thing, and that biology needed modeling," he says. Shatz also sent Miller to talk with Michael Stryker at the University of California at San Francisco. She had worked with Stryker as a postdoctoral fellow in the Harvard laboratory of Torsten Wiesel and David Hubel, winners of the 1981 Nobel Prize in Medicine or Physiology for their work on the organization of the visual system. In Stryker Miller found someone who understood the importance of mixing experimental biology and theory.

Stryker had been trying to answer a question created by Hubel and Wiesel's discovery of extraordinarily detailed organization among the neurons of the visual system, How does the visual system wire itself in the developing brain? "The number of elements is so enormous and the precision is so amazing," says Stryker.

"Think of what has to be done to make a visual cortex," he says. "First off, the nerve fibers from the eye that carry information signals have to grow back to the right place in the brain, have to take the right route to get there, and have to find the structure where they're supposed to terminate. Of course, they have to recognize it, too.

"This is something that neurons do. It doesn't take a whole lot of information. There aren't that many structures in the brain, there aren't that many different potential pathways, and there's every reason to believe that those pathways and the target structures are actually marked by specific chemical labels." It's almost as if the developing neurons sniff their way to their targets. Yes, this neurochemical says, grow this way. No, not this way; I don't match your receptors, says another one.

But this establishes only the gross structure of the visual cortex, Stryker points out. "Once they get there, they have to arrange themselves, more or less in order, so fibers from one part of the eye go to one part of the cortex and those from another part of the eye go to the neighboring part of the structure. They have to coarsely arrange themselves into a topography, a map of the eye, that is aligned with a map in the cortex. In connection with the visual cortex, that's talking about maybe some million or so input fibers connecting to some hundreds of millions of cells.

"And the precision with which they connect in adult animals is close to perfect. If we're looking at fiber one-million-and-one, its terminals in the cortex are almost right next to the terminals from fiber one-million-and-two, and one-million-and-two is almost next to one-million-and-three. And the mapping isn't just specified according to the topography [of the retina], but also according to a couple of other parameters. Like whether [the cell in the retina] increases its activity for light on or light off and the orientation of edges. All of these kinds of precision don't appear to be there initially when the fibers grow in."

Hubel and Wiesel won their prize for showing, over the course of twenty years of experiments, the incredible complexity of structure in the visual cortex and relating that structure to perception. In the late 1950s neuroscientists were beginning to find the visual cortex a more and more troubling problem. Every year the anatomy seemed to get more complicated. In this part of the cerebral cortex — the two-millimeter-thick plate of cells that covers the cerebral hemispheres — scientists were identifying an ever-larger number of anatomically distinct visual areas. What had been three to four known visual areas in the 1950s had grown to include more than a dozen by the 1970s. (Neuroscientists now know of about two dozen such areas.) Anatomists claimed that the cells in each of these areas differed in shape and connections. As far as researchers toiling away in the world's best laboratories could discover, however, all this anatomy seemed to have no function.

The very front end of this system seemed clear enough. Cells in the retina would respond to the presence of light (called an "on" stimulus) or its absence (called an "off" stimulus). Retinal cells would clearly fire in the presence of one or the other stimuli, but not all would respond to every stimuli. Individual cells would only respond to a specific stimulus. And the stimulus had to be located in the right place in the visual field.

The visual cortex and the lateral geniculate (the visual structure in the brain intermediate between the retina and the visual cortex) showed an obvious anatomical structure of multiple layers that seemed well matched to this sort of visual mapping. A first layer might create a map that preserved the details of the retinal map. Other layers could be imagined to map, plate to plate, to each other. The only problem was that investigators couldn't get the cells of the visual cortex to fire at all in response to stimulation of the retina — the stimuli that produced activity in the retina seemed to have no effect. Yet researchers knew that a patient with a damaged visual cortex couldn't see. How could cells that didn't respond to light be crucial to vision?

Hubel and Wiesel took their own crack at solving this puzzle in 1958. Using the standard single-cell recording method of the time, they were able to listen in on a single neuron in the cortex of a cat through a microelectrode. As Hubel described it years later, "We tried everything short of standing on our heads to get it to fire." Nothing worked for the first five hours. They shone light into the retina; they projected black spots and white spots. But except for the occasional spontaneous firing, there was no reaction from the neuron. Simply because it seemed to be generating slightly more of a response, they began to concentrate on the black spot, created by pasting a black dot on a glass slide. "Eventually we caught on," wrote Hubel. The shadow of the edge of the slide as they put it into the projection holder, not the spot itself, was producing the response, and only when the shadow crossed one part of the retina and only if the edge was oriented in one particular direction. If all the conditions were met, the neuron fired like a machine gun. Omit just one, direction, say, and it was silent.

That was just the beginning. Over the next two decades, the Hubel-Wiesel team, including at one point Stryker and Schatz, mapped the complex organization of orientation sensitivity in the cortex. Cells were also sensitive to the direction of movement, it turned out, and even to the orientation of the edge. Hubel and Wiesel discovered simple neurons that fired only when the proper stimuli fell into their receptive fields. Simple "on" cells, for example, would respond only to an "on" bar of light that fell in their "on" receptive field. A bar of light in an "off" region would create no response. A bar of light passing from an "off" region to an "on" region would lead to firing.

They also found complex neurons that would look for either an on or off stimuli in a much larger region and respond to either kind of bar anywhere in that region.

But Hubel and Wiesel also discovered that the features that led to firing in these neurons were the basis for other kinds of maps in the visual cortex. Cells from the same eye were grouped together in alternating bands — or more precisely columns if you considered the depth of the cortex — called ocular dominance columns. Cells with similar orientation preferences also formed groups. At each 0.05 millimeter the preferred orientation of the cells shifted by about 10 degrees. The whole orientation sequence began again at about every 0.9 millimeter, a distance that let the groups map the entire 180 degrees of possible orientation. Ocular dominance patterns repeated every 0.7 to 0.8 millimeters. The two maps, ocular dominance and orientation, didn't seem to be closely related. "It is as though the cortex were diced up in two completely different ways," Hubel wrote. These columns show up clearly in stained sections of monkey and cat brains.

Hubel and Wiesel's results preserved and indeed strengthened the idea that the visual cortex mapped external visual reality, but they changed the meaning of that metaphor. If even simple cells in the visual cortex had receptive fields so that they received input from hundreds of rods and cones, then a single simple cell didn't map just a single point on the retina. A bar oriented at 60 degrees and shown only to the left eye will produce firing in only every other ocular column (left columns only) and only in those columns sensitive to 60 degrees (one out of every 18). (The pattern is actually not quite this clear since columns show substantial overlap.) That still produces a map, but it's not simply topographic in the three dimensions of the visual cortex.

Hubel and Wiesel suggested ways that this organization related to the brain's processing of visual signals. For example, orientation-specific groups are either/or choices (although the choices are muddied because of the variation in response). A bar is either at 60 degrees or at 70 degrees or 80, and so on, but not at more than one. Clearly, the choice of 60 degrees should inhibit the other alternatives. Inhibitory connections in the visual cortex are very local. By positioning alternatives next to each other in narrow bands, local inhibition can effectively produce winner-take-all solutions to orientation problems.

The effort to lay out the relationship between that organization and the way the brain "sees" visual signals still occupies neurobiologists and neural network modelers. So, too, with another question Hubel and Wiesel addressed: is this organization innate or is it somehow created as the brain interacts with the outside visual world?

The two researchers collected two kinds of evidence. First, they ran deprivation experiments with cats and macaque monkeys. In one experiment they covered one eye of the infant monkey or rendered the visual world extremely blurry by covering one eye with an obscuring lens. In every case involving an infant monkey, the development of ocular dominance columns was affected. The

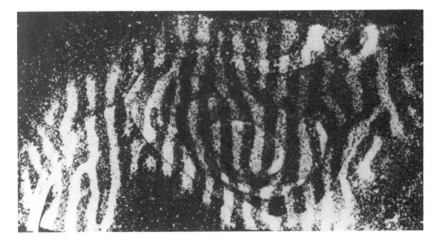

Ocular dominance columns in the visual cortex. Bright columns representing the left eye are separated by the dark columns of the right eye.
Reprinted with permission from Hubel and Wiesel, *Proceedings of the Royal Society*, 1977.

columns from the covered or blurry eye shrank in size; the columns from the other eye grew correspondingly larger. A decrease in information from the left eye resulted in small left columns and big right columns. Restoring normal vision after the period of developmental plasticity — a period extending from birth to about five or six weeks of age in cats — did not restore the normal pattern in the ocular dominance columns.

In other experiments Hubel and Wiesel covered both eyes of an infant monkey. If experience could shift the size of the columns in monocular vision, what would total deprivation do? Some experiments seemed to indicate that without light no structure would develop, but the results were inconclusive. It was hard to study newborn animals. Most experiments before those of Hubel and Wiesel had been conducted on young animals that had been raised in the dark until they were big enough to be studied conveniently. But Hubel and Wiesel felt this didn't prove anything about the innate structure of the visual cortex. After all, those structures could have been present at birth and then decayed while the animal was kept in darkness.

Hubel and Wiesel conducted their study on animals that were just one day old. Even a day-old macaque showed nearly mature responses: cells in the cortex had fewer synapses and a sparser dendritic tree than in a normally raised adult, but ocular and orientation columns were already present. Although they clearly noted that the evidence was subject to interpretation, Hubel and Wiesel concluded that the organization of the visual cortex was innate, and that the change in the ocular dominance columns of visually deprived individuals, as Hubel wrote in 1988, "was mainly due to a deterioration of connections that had been present at birth, not to a failure to form because of a lack of experience."

That answer didn't satisfy Stryker, even while he worked in their laboratory. "In my scientific work as a graduate student," he says, "I started out assuming that Hubel and Wiesel were wrong about this innate organization. I was really interested in how activity could organize things. At that time I thought activity meant experience. Try as he might, though, as long as he looked at monkeys and kittens that were old enough to see, Stryker could only confirm Hubel and Wiesel's results. "They turned out to be exactly right [about] the very limited role for experience in producing normal organization."

But eventually he started to ask a slightly different question: what if there is a kind of activity in the brain that precedes experience? "I think no one realized at the time that neural activity can play a role long before there is visual experience.

"As early as Hubel and Wiesel looked, many of the features of the organization of the visual system appeared to be innate. They were present as soon as they looked." But in separate experiments after they had left Hubel and Wiesel's lab, Stryker and Shatz looked even earlier, in visually immature cats. Stryker examined newborn cats that hadn't yet opened their eyes; Shatz studied fetal cats. In each experiment Shatz and Stryker set out to block all neuronal activity in the cats' visual system. "At that time," says Stryker, "we weren't even certain that there was activity in utero, but we set out to block any that there was."

Injecting a neurotoxin from the Japanese puffer fish, Stryker shut down all activity in his infant cats' visual systems. Everything appeared to develop normally except that the connections from the two eyes failed to sort out in the lateral geniculate; they were completely intermingled. The visual organization that Hubel and Wiesel had discovered was thus not innate after all. But, as they had reported, it wasn't dependent on visual experience, either. The organization was the result of completely internal, spontaneous activity in the visual system. Now all Stryker or Shatz had to do was explain how this internal activity produced what were clearly organized maps in the visual cortex and the lateral geniculate.

The story, as best as Stryker could piece it together, went like this. In development the visual system gets organized in two stages. First, the neurons in the lateral geniculate organize themselves into layers. About four to five days later the two eyes form ocular dominance columns in the visual cortex. The two stages happen at different times in the development of different species. In the human and the monkey the organization is about 90 percent complete by birth. In the cat the organization of the cortex takes place postnatally, during the first few days while the kitten's eyes are still closed. In the ferret, which has an even shorter gestation period than the cat, both stages occur after birth.

Fetal neurons do fire. Without stimulus from any experience. Spontaneously. In fact, all neurons do. The rate is much slower than with experience, but that spontaneous firing, Shatz and Stryker were forced to conclude, is the only activity that might help organize the cortex in fetal monkeys, cats, or ferrets. It wasn't at all clear to Stryker, however, how spontaneous firing could produce an organized map.

Random spontaneous firing wouldn't do the trick, obviously. The randomness wouldn't provide any information about the position of cells in the retina that would help cortical neurons to know where the signals were coming from. It turns out, though, that spontaneous firing isn't random. It does encode some information about location. "Even in the dark, even in utero, neighboring ganglion cells, the cells in the retina that send information to the brain, are active," says Stryker, "and this dark discharge has information in it, because two cells that are next to each other will tend to fire together, whereas cells that are far apart from each other won't tend to fire together. And the cells in the two eyes won't tend to fire together. This information could be used to set up a map. If you strengthen connections between cells that tend to fire together, and if you weaken ones that don't fire together, and if the initial pattern of input is one where neighbors are active together but more distant ones aren't active together, that has all the information in it you need to construct a perfectly precise topographic map."

At least in theory. But going from experiments that showed that blocking this spontaneous activity prevented the development of normal organization in the visual cortex, to showing how these few firings, each containing only a tiny bit of information, could create normal dominance columns was a tremendous leap. "We knew that there was spontaneous activity, that this spontaneous activity had information in it, and that the brain could, we thought in a vague hand-waving sense, make use of this information to organize connections in the nervous system," says Stryker.

But so little information is involved that Stryker worried that it might not be sufficient.

> It turns out that for one type of retinal ganglion cells, for example, better than 80 percent of the spikes of the cell occur in association with the spike in one of its six nearest neighbors. That doesn't look very impressive, if you just concentrate on one pair. Even if 100 percent of the spikes occurred in association with [spikes in] one of its six nearest neighbors, you'd see only about 20 percent correlation in any pair, which doesn't seem like very much.

That much correlation is sufficient, though, if the system runs over enough time. By around 1975 David Willshaw and Christoph von der Malsburg had demonstrated, in a general way, that the kind of columns and patterns seen in the visual cortex could be generated by correlated activity. To explain how this comes about, Stryker likes to use a story Jerome Lettvin told him while he was at MIT.

In the early years of astronomy in the seventeenth century, scientists were busily mapping and timing the movements of the stars in an effort to unravel the mechanics of the universe. Scientists across Europe shared observations. This gave them a bigger mass of data to use, but it also introduced variations into the data due to the different reaction times of individual observers. Big books listed the personal factors for each astonomer so that data from different observers could be compared. More than any other scientists, astronomers were intensely aware of the limits of human reactions and performance.

One day Christian Huygens (1629–1695), a Dutch mathematician and physicist who was the first to use pendulums in clocks and who was the first to interpret correctly the rings around Saturn, was walking down the street. The story goes that he wandered by a clockmaker's shop, and he noticed that on this big stone wall in back of the shop there were fifty to one hundred clocks. All of them had pendulums swinging, and all of the pendulums were either exactly in phase or exactly counter-phase. Huygens knew that there's just too much variance in human performance, that even astronomers couldn't start up those pendulums so that they were perfectly in phase or perfectly out of phase. So he asked the clockmaker to stop a few clocks and watched him while he started up the pendulum, wondering how he got it so that they were all exactly synchronized with each other. And the clockmaker just started them up at random.

Huygens realized that all these pendulums were oscillators that just barely vibrated the wall on which they were all mounted. Given a sufficient amount of time, all it took was a tremendously weak coupling to produce organized activity. With enough time, such a system would self-organize, producing an orderly behavior that was not accounted for by any global influence on the system, such as the clockmaker's guiding hand.

"So we knew in a kind of vague general way that self-organization could, in principle, produce patterns that are somewhat like the ones we see in the visual cortex," says Stryker, "but we were really stuck in getting any use out of these ideas biologically." He wanted to prove that the actual biological information observed in spontaneous firing would produce the biologically observed dominance columns found in the visual cortex. He also wanted to know what controlled the size and spacing of the columns. What told the visual cortex where to end one patch and begin another? And he wanted to do it in a way that would produce predictions that could be tested in biological experiments. What Stryker really wanted was a mathematically rigorous model that would tell him how the parts of the system fit together and that would generate predictions that could be tested against results from actual experiments. What he wanted was a "physics" for the brain.

Stryker didn't find the existing models very helpful. They were too abstract. There wasn't any straightforward way to relate the elements of the model to any biological measurements. In the model put together by Leon Cooper at Brown, for instance,

> they have things that they call neurons. . . . But they don't have properties like any neuron. In their model a single neuron can have both positive and negative effects on its neighbors, whereas real

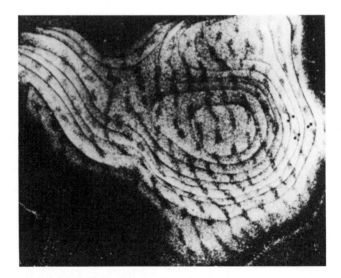

The bright ocular dominance column stripes representing the normal eye almost overwhelm the thin dark stripes from the closed eye in this picture of the visual cortex. Compare it with the previous illustration of normal development.
Reprinted with permission from Hubel and Wiesel, *Proceedings of the Royal Society*, 1977.

neurons are only excitatory or inhibitory. You can't do any experiments and say that they [these models] are right or wrong. They can always say, "Well, no, you didn't interpret it right. You haven't made the right correspondence between our abstract computational element and real neurons." Most of the neural network work, in relation to the brain, is pretty vague. People do a few simulations, get something that looks a bit like the brain, and leave it.

Stryker knew he wanted more in a model than that; he had even as an undergraduate. At the University of Michigan he had gravitated from mathematics to philosophy in his junior year. "I'd always been interested in how we think and how the brain works. As I did more and more philosophy, it became clearer and clearer to me that the real questions, as far as I was concerned, about how the mind worked were empirical questions." As far as he could see, the outstanding philosophical questions about the mind had been solved, an opinion that would probably come as a shock to many philosophers. By the time Stryker left Michigan, he wanted to do neuroscience.

Stryker's questioning of Hubel and Wiesel's theory of an innate order in the visual cortex was based on more than just a desire to confound his elders. The discovery of the genetic code in the 1950s had promised to solve the basic problem of development: how did the body — including the brain — know how to develop from egg to maturity? In the first rush of postdiscovery excitement, it looked like the double helix would be the answer — the directions for development were mapped in the genetic code. However, as researchers gradually began to estimate the amount of information that could be stored in the spiraling DNA in all our genes, a clear mismatch emerged. The human being, which will eventually be complete with arteries and veins, a musculoskeletal system, and nerves that reach into all parts of the body and terminate in the brain, begins as a single cell. Until we knew the mechanisms of the genetic code, it was possible to assume that all this growth, which must occur in a precise temporal order and result in a precise topography, could be specified by that code acting as a giant blueprint. Some piece of information could say, "Nerve number 456 it's now time for you to grow to muscle number 284A." Information would simply specify that the nerve was to grow so far this way, so far that way, and so forth. More information would specify other connections and how the nerve would hook up with other nerve cells and how it would function. The search for chemical markers that would translate this genetic information into a precise template has successfully shown that a part of the process works this way.

But all of development can't be controlled this way. The genome simply doesn't, and can't, contain enough information to completely specify all the precise connections that must be made in development. It now seems that the general shape of the template is specified beforehand by the information in the genome, and that the final precise connections are the result of self-organization by the various systems and subsystems. The dynamics of the system create the necessary order, just as the subtle vibrations in the stone wall created precise order in the swinging of Huygens's randomly started clock pendulums. The difficulty lies in specifying both the precise dynamics involved and their interactions.

While still in the physics program at Stanford, Kenneth Miller began talking with Stryker once a month about the possible nature of these system dynamics. Soon he was working in Stryker's laboratory at the University of California at San Francisco every day. [Stryker became his dissertation adviser after Miller made the formal shift from physics to neurobiology. Shatz was the departmental liaison with Stanford.] The model Stryker had already developed was similar to the one Miller had been working on in his head for a couple of years. He, too, believed that a Hebb synapse could be the basic building block. Add in the right degree of local excitation and inhibition, and "you think that should do the trick," says Miller.

Stryker and Miller's resulting neural network model is a very straightforward three-layer system. Two layers represent the lateral geniculate, one responding to each eye. A third layer represents the visual cortex. They believe that just three parameters will create ocular dominance columns in the cortex sheet.

First, Miller and Stryker specify the four functions that describe the correlation between the input from different points in the geniculate. The four functions state the likelihood that four points in the two eyes will fire together.

Second, an additional function describes the initial connectivity in the network. Called the arbor function, it describes the treelike shape of the connections from the lateral geniculate to the visual cortex. From the point of view of a single neuron in the geniculate, this is the fan-out of its connections, the number of neurons in the next layer that this single cell touches.

The last parameter describes interactions across the cortex. It specifies the degree of local inhibition and excitation among cortical cells.

"We knew that we could study this with computer simulations," says Stryker. "When Ken came in and we sat down and wrote the differential equations for the model, there was no question that we could let it grow in the computer."

Miller didn't want to just build a simulation, though. "I came in with this prejudice from physics that you begin by analyzing the model," he says. The problem with a simulation is that you have no idea what parameter is responsible for what. To understand the system, Miller wanted to specify the mathematical relationships that connected its parts. But he quickly found the system impossible to penetrate with his traditional tools. "There were limits that I just couldn't cross with pure analysis." The final method is a combination of simulation, biology, and mathematical analysis.

Using the university's access to the National Science Foundation's supercomputer, Stryker and Miller ran their simulation and then changed the parameters and ran it again. Some values didn't produce anything resembling the cortex's ocular dominance columns. For example, eliminating all correlations between neighboring cells in the retina prevented any clustering. Eliminating intracortical interaction turned cortical cells into isolated individuals. Other sets of parameters, however, not only produced clusters but clusters that looked like ocular dominance columns.

But this was still largely a black box. Parameters went in and columns did or didn't come out. There wasn't any way to predict the result for any set of parameters except by running the model. Some parameters that Stryker had expected would control the development of the organization, for example, turned out to be far less important. "At the start my expectation was the spread of the correlation function would determine the width of the patches. In fact, that's basically wrong."

Joseph Keller, who had been Miller's dissertation adviser while he was in the physics department, gave them crucial insight into their opaque model. Miller had started by trying to write simple linear equations to describe the system, even though he didn't believe they were correct. He knew the system had to be nonlinear in some way; otherwise, it wouldn't result in stable patterns. Solving complex systems of nonlinear equations with our current mathematics is difficult and often impossible. The relationships between the variables change depending on their respective magnitudes. For example, in a nonlinear system, if variable A was 3 and went to 6, variable B would also double. But if variable A was larger, if the system had run longer, it might double from 3,000 to 6,000. Variable B, however, might increase by only a very slight increment. This makes calculating the final condition of a nonlinear system almost intractable. The most common method is to find a way to approximate the nonlinear relationships by linear equations under certain circumstances — or to model the system on a computer.

Keller, who specializes in the problems of characterizing complex systems, suggested that Miller stop worrying about the final state of the system. The most robust initial states would set the basic features of the final state during the system's early history. Specifically, Keller recommended a technique called linear stability analysis as a way to approximate the system. This approach begins the analysis at a very early point in the system's history and looks at the initial patterns and their growth. It will work only if those early patterns grow so fast that they dominate any later nonlinear functions. Miller and Keller both believe that to be the case in their dominance model.

The system behaves like a mountain poised for an avalanche. All it takes is a slight vibration to send snow cascading down with a force far greater than the slight perturbation that set it in motion. "That's the basic idea of linear stability analysis," says Miller.

In this case, instead of a snow-covered mountain, you have a whole pattern in the cortex. "It's unstable. A very small perturbation [happens] and then it will break in some periodic way." The classic way to predict the final state of the system after the perturbation has played out is to look at that first moment of instability and ask which patterns start growing and which one grows the fastest. "And that's the pattern that should dominate." Looking at the first moments will give a picture of the final pattern, without the need to figure out the interactions between all the patterns set in motion by the initial perturbation. Most of these patterns will die out, overwhelmed by the one that grows the fastest. Of course, all this assumes that the nonlinearities that become more pronounced as the system ages will also be overwhelmed by the fastest-growing pattern. It's a big assumption, given our knowledge, or lack of knowledge, of how the brain works, but it does give Miller and Stryker a way to produce mathematical solutions that can be experimentally checked against actual biology. The biology will in effect tell them if the assumption is justified.

"It turns out," says Miller, "that this idea that the fastest-growing pattern should overwhelm the others is not always true. I mean, it's a naive thought. As things get big and nonlinear, you could get a complete reorganization, which is driven by the nonlinear interactions." However, "To me, it's hard to imagine that this system will completely reorganize." A reorganization would require that the biological system waste all it has invested in its organization up to that point, and Miller doesn't think that's likely given the nature of biological systems. But this point, too, is testable with the model.

The linear instability analysis even provides a kind of commonsense way to understand why the visual cortex self-organizes into columns. Begin with the parameters of the model and a randomly organized visual cortex. At this moment all neurons in the visual cortex receive roughly equal signals from both the left and the right eyes. They are equally connected to both eyes through the very bushy arbor. That represents the system's initial stability, and if the activity in the visual cortex were also random and continued to be random, the cortex would remain in that state.

But that random state isn't stable. Neighboring cells are more likely to fire together, disrupting the randomness of the cortex. Spontaneous activity in the cortex itself produces simultaneous firing between neighbors, and that tends to strengthen the synapses between them. The initial state is likely to give any single cortical neuron more left or right input, even if by just a tiny amount. While the overall distribution is random, no single cortical neuron is likely to be precisely and exactly balanced between right and left. If one eye is just slightly more successful in activating an individual cortical neuron, the synapses connecting that neuron with the retina of the successful eye are gradually strengthened. Those with the unsuccessful eye are gradually weakened and finally excluded.

The two eyes wage an intense competition for each cortical neuron. Like the visual cortex as a whole, each individual neuron is initially balanced between the two eyes, and that balance is unstable. As with a ball pushed off a peak, the tipping of the balance toward one eye is at first almost unnoticeable, but it rapidly picks up speed. At first, says Miller, "they kind of fight it out without any pattern getting too big. You get a pattern of a few cells in a row where the right eye has gotten ascendancy and they are all acting upon each other, and then, whew, they take off." Virtually invisible a moment before, the pattern suddenly jumps into prominence.

The flow of battle shows up clearly in Stryker and Miller's simulations. In the illustration below, ocular dominance columns develop after fewer than eighty iterations of the model. At $T=0$, the initial random state, almost all cells receive equal input from both right and left eyes. $T=10$ doesn't change the situation much. But between $T=20$ and $T=30$, the segregation quickly divides the field.

The size and period of the ocular dominance patches also result from competition. The initial random state is a mixture of patterns. Mathematically, any simple curve, an ellipse, for exam-

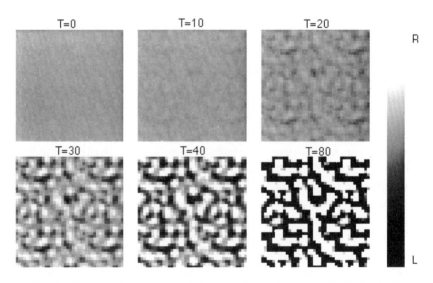

Ocular dominance columns emerged from Stryker and Miller's simulation in fewer than eighty iterations when signals from the two eyes competed. The model also reproduced the experimental effects of monocular deprivation seen in the previous photograph.
Photograph courtesy of Kenneth D. Miller.

ple, can be rewritten as the sum of a number of different curves, the French mathematician Fourier proved. If you think again of Huygens's wall of clocks, each clock has an individual vibration that together adds up to the whole vibration. Each individual vibration is a wave with an amplitude determined by many factors, including how the clock is attached to the wall, but mainly by the size of the clock and its pendulum. Each individual vibration also has a wavelength determined by the pendulum's swing. When all these vibrations (since they have both an amplitude and wavelength, it is safe to call them waves) are added together, some cancel each other out, some add to others. The result is a dominant wavelength.

So, too, in the cortex. When the random state is disturbed by the first spontaneous activity, some of the component sine and cosine waves grow and some diminish. The resulting dominance pattern represents the sine wave of the winning pattern. This has led Miller to suggest that the decline of plasticity in adult animals isn't totally due to a loss of the ability of individual neurons to add new synapses and rearrange interneuronal connections. Michael Merzenich, among others, has shown that the loss of a finger, for example, even in an adult, can lead to a limited remapping of the sensory map in the cortex. The area representing the sense of touch in the missing finger shrinks, and areas representing the remaining fingers enlarge to some limit, now estimated at about 600 to 700 angstroms. Plasticity, Miller argues, may not be a property of young neurons that is gradually lost as the cells age. Instead, it may be due to the relative instability in early development of what will later become the final dominant pattern in the cortex. Rearrangement to preserve that pattern may be possible even in the adult, but its overthrow in favor of a new organization may be impossible. The existing pattern may simply have too much inertia; it damps out all competing influences before they can grow large enough to challenge its sway.

Stryker and Miller's model is part of a growing emphasis in neurobiology and neural network modeling. Like the work of Richard Granger and Carver Mead, their model pays attention to the interaction of numbers of neurons over time. Models have grown large enough and sophisticated enough to show exactly what happens when many very simple units with a few rules of interaction exist in a dynamic system that changes over time. We already know that system-wide properties that are very different from the characteristics of individual neurons can emerge from these interactions. They might even hold the key to troubling concepts such as attention, consciousness, and mind.

It is an irony that a brain able to understand jokes might appreciate that, just at the time when neurobiologically detailed models like these have been delivering such intriguing results, neurobiologists have begun to provide experimental evidence that threatens some of the basic assumptions of neural network theory. The new mass of neurobiological detail doesn't say that the theory is wrong, only that it is too simple. By failing to put enough real detail in the system, these models may be failing to tap into the full power of the brain. The single neuron is a far more powerful and complex thing than Donald Hebb ever imagined, this evidence says. In those details lurk the promise of immensely more powerful networks and a real understanding of the brain — if anyone can manage to put them all into a single model.

12

ASSUMPTIONS, ASSUMPTIONS

I just read this paper by a neuroscientist that I found really annoying. He says, "Well, let's use backpropagation [in this model] even though we know it's not biological."

— MURIEL ROSS

Truth can at any moment become its opposite.

— ALEXANDER THEROUX, *An Adultery*

By 1990 it should have been clear that everyone — network builders and neurobiologists — had underestimated the neuron for decades. No one had really gone looking for this incredibly complicated and tremendously powerful neuron. It just kept showing up, uninvited, on researchers' doorsteps. Many hoped it would quietly go away again.

In 1986 Muriel Ross didn't know that she was about to open her door to this intruder. Ross had heard of neural networks, but they seemed peripheral to her work. She just wanted to understand why what she saw under her electron microscope wasn't what the textbooks described. How could she know that answering that question would lead her into a strange new world?

It all began with a bet Ross made with herself. Either her research on the macula was terribly wrong or all the textbooks were. The macula, a tiny part of the ear that tells us which way is up, was a thoroughly studied and, so the textbooks said, well-understood part of the nervous system. Textbooks listed two types of hair cells in the patch that made up the macula. Type I cells connected to the ends of cranial nerve fibers at a bulblike terminal, called a calyx, that looked like a tulip. These nerve fibers took signals from the type I cell to the central nervous system. Type II cells connected slightly differently, with the small, buttonlike terminals of other nerve fibers, but they too sent signals back to the central nervous system through their own system of connections.

At least that was what the textbooks said. "The first place any of those signals was integrated [the textbooks said] was in the central nervous system, and that was perfect, that was it," Ross remembers. According to the texts, the macula shared that pattern with all the rest of the nervous system. The peripheral organs of vision, smell, or touch collected information about the outside world and then passed it back to higher brain centers, where most of the work of processing that information was done.

Except that after 4,000 electromicrographs, Ross couldn't find the independent type II connections with the central nervous system. She could see the type II cells send collateral branches over to lean against the calyces, but she couldn't find the predicted independent pathways from the type II cells that supposedly took signals from those cells to higher centers for processing. Her photographs seemed to show that the type II cells were only connected to calyces or nerve fibers ending in calyces. They didn't directly transmit anything to higher brain centers.

Ross is an extremely calm and unassuming scientist. Her first reaction was to doubt her own micrographs. "So I went back to the literature, and I said that if I find even one [published] electron micrograph that really shows that the innervation to the type II cell leaves the macula and goes out to the central nervous system, I will pursue my original research project. But otherwise, I'm going to start sectioning this tissue and looking at it because I don't believe that this [description] is correct."

Ross didn't find that one piece of contrary evidence; she would have to build the correct picture by collecting her own data. To capture all the detail of the macula, she shaved thin slices from prepared rat tissue and then photographed each one with an electron microscope. It took at least 370 sections to slice through a nerve fiber's receptive field. As her techniques improved, she could slice through larger portions of the macula in 570 sections. Soon she was overwhelmed with data.

Ross knew that a two-dimensional drawing couldn't capture enough detail. Even a static three-dimensional reconstruction would be inadequate. It would only show the outermost layer of a section. What Ross needed was something much more like an animated macula that would rotate to show each side and even split apart to show its interior.

Ross's fascination with animation as an analytic tool had begun, innocently enough, a little more than fifteen years before. She was then a hardworking research scientist at the University of Michigan studying the vestibular system, which is used for balance and orientation.

During a sabbatical at Oxford, Ross "interacted a bit with this fellow from the United States who was working at Oxford and also had his own computer business. They were beginning to model molecules and things like that, and I felt that surely we could use the computer to reassemble the tissue sections that I had made into a three-dimensional model. And he said, 'Oh, sure, that can be done.'" But back at Michigan, she couldn't line up the computer power and the programming talent she needed. Just a hint of frustration seeps out in Ross's voice. She could see that maybe this new tool would enable her to look inside this system, but she couldn't get her hands on it. The vestibular system just wasn't very sexy.

In mammals the vestibular systems work to keep the animal oriented in space as it moves, and especially to keep the eyes targeted while the head is moving. The liquid-filled inner ear canals sense the rotation and angular acceleration of the head. Another organ, the one that Ross wound up studying, uses the macula, a patch of sensory hair cells in the ear, to detect linear acceleration. In effect it is a gravity receptor.

Fortunately, the National Aeronautics and Space Administration had both the computer power she needed and an intense, practical interest in the systems that Ross wanted to study. Something unpleasant was happening to astronauts when they went into space. Weightlessness was affecting the human gravity receptors and making about half the humans shot into space ill, some extremely so, with what resembled intense motion sickness. NASA knew that Russian cosmonauts who experienced extreme distress on a first space shot would show many fewer symptoms in a subsequent voyage. Apparently the body could adapt, and that suggested that the right training program might be able to reduce or eliminate the symptoms entirely. When the agency invited Ross to join its Ames Research Center in Mountain View, California, she jumped at the chance. It took just a year and a half of forty-hour weeks for Ross and her staff to build their first three-dimensional reconstruction on the space agency's IRIS graphic computer.

The great Warner Brothers or Disney animators would feel right at home with Ross's animation. Building the reconstruction wasn't that different from making an animated cartoon. Every fifth slice of the rat macula would be photographed under the electron microscope at 1,600 times magnification. Those photos were blown up to 4,000 times and then traced onto acetate sheets. Stacking all those sheets would have reconstructed the macula as a pile of acetate. Bugs Bunny is just such a stack of main character,

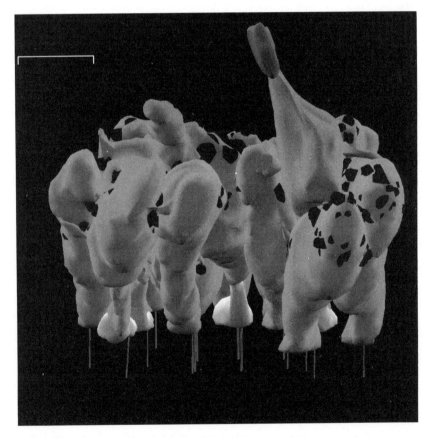

A few neurons from the macula in 3-D. The stereocilia, type I and type II cells, and calyces are all clearly visible.
Photograph courtesy of Muriel D. Ross and Rei Cheng, NASA.

second character, background, and so forth, all drawn onto individual acetate sheets, piled up, and then photographed frame by frame. Instead of turning the acetate sheets into film, however, Ross's team digitized them and fed the results into a computer, which could then reassemble the macula, rotate it, or reveal its interior on command.

For such a small organ, the macula shows an extremely complex structure. It begins by turning acceleration into nerve signals. The otoconial complex, made up of a gel and crystallite particles embedded in the gel, moves in response to head movement. The macula itself is firmly attached to the bone of the ear and moves with the head. The relative motion of the particles and the gel bend tiny threadlike structures that grow from the surfaces of the hair cells. These structures, grouped into bundles, turn that bending into electrochemical signals that indicate the direction and magnitude of acceleration.

The accepted wisdom declared that direction was something that the higher brain areas calculated from the relatively raw information passed along by the hair cells. But if the type II cells weren't passing anything along directly and were instead talking to the same nerve fibers as the type I cells did, that couldn't be true. Ross's rejection of the traditional biology left her with a deeper puzzle. How did direction get calculated?

Computer animation was supposed to reveal at least part of the answer, but that first reconstruction just kept raising more questions. Ross had begun by tracing where the axons and dendrites began and ended and what neurons were connected to what other neurons. The connections, she noticed, weren't the same even for all type I or type II cells. Some were on the calyx, others on dendritic arms far away from the calyx. Unlike the textbook drawing, her sections indicated that type II hair cells connected only with the terminals that also connected with type I cells and not directly with the central nervous system. Also, one type II cell typically connected with more than one terminal.

As she added more detail to her model, she began to notice a kind of geographical pattern emerging. Hair cells of both types, and their connections with each other and "deeper" layers of neurons, were actually grouped. Stimulating the ends of the hair cells in the macula didn't produce independent responses from each hair cell or a general response across the entire field. Instead, groups of hair cells responded together. In these receptive fields a group of cells would all respond most strongly to motion in a particular direction. Another group would be tuned to respond to a different direction. Each group of type I and type II cells was linked by synaptic connections into a network. Typically, a type II cell would connect with the terminals of one to four neighboring groups. The receptive fields even had a kind of organization: they were all generally oval in shape, but the three types Ross identified differed in the degree to which that oval was elongated.

But what did all this detail mean? How was the macula using this geography to detect the direction of motion and its magnitude? If it was. Because Ross had to admit that she had no direct evidence that this organization served a functional purpose. She had a lot of hard data and an increasingly complete three-dimensional picture, but she didn't really have a framework for understanding how this structure could be telling the animal what it needed to know about direction and gravity. When in doubt, collect more data points. The model kept growing.

Soon after she arrived at NASA, Ross sat down to read a book on information technology. "It was a book commissioned by some group so that two big experts could tell people what information technologies meant to society," she remembers. "And I only read the first chapter because as it began to describe what they called an information technology I said, 'That's my macula. That's what it is.' So I came back and I went to work over the weekend on writing a paper, and when I came back in on Monday, I started talking with my staff." They in turn talked about her insight with other NASA staffers over lunch. "And pretty soon I had young people knocking on my door bringing me all types of papers on neural networks. Now, I had taught this stuff for years and years, but we never used that term. I began to get lots and lots of papers to read and it became more and more exciting."

Putting the two approaches together, Ross concluded that the structure of the macula didn't simply collect information from the outside world and pass it on to the central nervous system for processing. Even a region like the macula, both tiny (about the size of a period in humans) and at the very end of the nervous system, was producing and processing information-carrying signals. The way type I and type II hair cells were connected was in some manner crucial to that information processing.

The first clue to what kind of information device this was

came from the arrangement of the threads, called the stereocilia, that emerge from the hair cells to detect the motion of the crystallite particles in the gel. The stereocilia are grouped into bundles, called tufts, of about sixty to eighty. The stereocilia in each tuft are arranged in rows of increasing height. Some fifty to one hundred tufts are in turn organized into a hexagonal array at the top of each hair cell. Conventional wisdom had a ready explanation for that shape. Hexagons pack very efficiently. This is just a way to get a lot of tufts in a small space.

"The man I originally hired for the image analysis work [Wilson Orr] had a background in signal processing," Ross remembers. One day she happened to mention the hexagonal nature of these things to him and to Dale Mugler, a visiting scholar at Ames. Orr asked if she knew the twenty-year-old work proving that hexagonal spacing is the most efficient array for signal processing. Looking at the literature, Ross became convinced that the macula worked like radar.

But it wasn't like the familiar system that uses a rotating dish. Instead it simulated the fixed antenna of a phased-array radar. That type of radar works by splitting up the single wave received from an object into differing waves. Those waves are then put back together again to create a single beam whose character now reveals direction. The macula condenses the typical 100-foot antenna of the radar down to the hexagons of the stereocilia. Ross, Orr, and Mugler believe that the different lengths of these hairs work to create a unique, direction-specific signal for each receptive field. Longer stereocilia will delay the signal more, creating a predictable pattern of delay that depends on how the motion strikes the gradual incline of the stereocilia. Motion that is exactly aligned with the incline, striking the shorter stereocilia first, will produce a series of delays that corresponds exactly with the heights of the threads. Motion from the opposite direction will create a different pattern of delays, as it strikes the longer stereocilia first. These shifts in phase between the signal from one stereocilium and another indicate direction.

Up to this point much of what Ross had discovered could properly be filed under reinventing the wheel. She had applied signal processing theory and neural network principles to revise the accepted wisdom of how a specific system, the macula, works. But her discovery that these theories illuminated the structure of this part of the nervous system periphery couldn't really be termed surprising. In light of the existing explanations for how the cochlea worked, for example, it would have been surprising if the macula didn't show these traits. In the late 1980s Ross's findings amounted to the discovery of a traditional neural network in the macula. She had established that the way the neurons were connected was the key to the macula's ability to calculate direction. If she had started with a neural network approach, she might have arrived at this point sooner. That was the cost of Ross's roundabout path to her now very fruitful research.

But Ross's relatively late self-education in these theories also had a benefit. Being unfamiliar with the theoretical framework, her model is grounded only in observed detail. Slice after slice, she has recorded exactly what she sees. It's a painstakingly experimentalist approach, but one that seems in keeping with Ross's character.

Ross has relatively little visibility either on the neural network scene or in the larger world of neuroscience. Working at NASA, she's out of the ebb and flow of neural network politics at Stanford, Berkeley, and San Diego, even though they are virtually at her door. Her methods, based on computer animation, are unusual in this field, where most computer simulations crunch numbers and represent the interactions between neurons as mathematical functions.

Even after her discovery of the neural network structure of the macula, Ross continued to add detail to her reconstruction. Why not? There was still more biological information in the system. For example, the nerve fibers connecting hair cells and other neurons aren't all alike. Some are coated with myelin, the nervous system's natural insulator around signal-conducting fibers, all the way to the calyx. Others have short unmyelinated segments, and still others, long uninsulated stretches. If all these patterns of connection, distances, and wiring sizes were important enough to picture, they were clearly also important to the dynamics of the system. Her graphic reconstruction could show the geography of the array of neurons in the macula, but it couldn't show the signal processing that goes on in the cable. Yet. That required building a model that could show this new level of detail and then embedding it in the geographic model.

Just as Ross has tried to characterize types of neurons and the way they typically connect with other neurons, she is now trying to characterize nerve fibers. This involves using what are called compartment models to lay out the character of the wires from synapses to cell body as a linear path. Rather than concentrating on the physical geography of the system, a compartment model maps the events in the signal's life. Each compartment is, in fact, defined by an event — a fiber leaving the calyx or a change in myelination. The detail is potentially horrendous. "We may have to create a compartment for each synapse," says Ross, "That may sound crazy, but I don't see any other way to understand what is happening to each signal." She's worried that all this information will soon overwhelm her computers. But the IRIS machines keep getting more powerful as new models come out, and there is always the possibility of moving the model to a supercomputer like the Cray — all to create a model of a section of the nervous system smaller than a pinhead.

In adding compartment models to her system Ross went a step beyond the traditional assumptions behind most neural network models. Most modelers assume that each neuron is a very simple computational device, an assumption that has been a central tenet of neural network research since the development of McCulloch and Pitts's theories in the 1940s. According to this standard theory, individual neurons are simple linear threshold devices, much like transistors. The power of the brain comes from hooking up billions of these very simple units into a single network.

That assumption has long been supported by research in neurobiology. The "neuron doctrine," which traces its history back to the 1880s, holds that the brain and the nervous system are composed of individual units, neurons, which are connected only at specific points. For decades neurobiology concentrated on the aggregate action of these simple, discrete units. Only recently have neurobiologists been able to "see" deeply enough into individual neurons to discern the details of these units. Their work, like that of Ross, seems to show that the neuron is actually far different from the simple unit assumed by modelers and much neurobiology. The simple neuron, say experimental neurobiologists such as Gordon Shepherd, theorists such as Wilfrid Rall, and computational neuroscientists such as Thomas Brown, more closely resembles the microprocessor of a computer with hundreds of independent nonlinear operations being performed at once in the branching network of the dendritic tree.

The neuron doctrine has worked well enough for most of this century, and assumptions that work "well enough" are hard to disprove. At some point during whatever passed for science education when you went to school, you heard the story of how Galileo dropped different objects off the tower at Pisa. Up until that time, everyone had believed objects fell at different rates depending on their weight. By observation, the story says, Galileo saw that this wasn't true. All objects fell with a constant rate of acceleration no matter what their weight. This discovery laid the groundwork for Newton's formulation of a universal law of gravitation.

There's just one problem with that story: it's impossible. (The story of the experiment at Pisa is itself a tall tale invented by one of Galileo's disciples.) Galileo couldn't have observed a constant rate of acceleration for all objects. On earth, in our atmosphere, objects do fall at different rates. Air resistance, a specialized case of friction, guarantees it. No, Galileo's "discovery" came despite, not because of, observation. A leap of intuition carried him beyond what he observed. Assume, Galileo might have said, a world without friction or air resistance. *Then* how would bodies fall?

The entire field of neural networks was built upon a similar leap of intuition, or more precisely, two leaps. First, assume, as Donald Hebb supposed, that somehow neurons that fire together strengthen the connection between them. Second, assume that neurons are boxes that connect with other boxes across narrow synaptic gaps. Ignore all the confusing details such as the branching dendrites or the fluids that bathe the neurons. *Then* what kind of computation could a network of such boxes perform?

Researchers in the field knew that either assumption could have been enormously wrong. Most concern focused upon the first. What kind of mechanism could explain the kind of strengthening that Hebb postulated between neurons? Neurobiologists and psychologists knew the problem wasn't nearly as simple as Hebb's statement of it implied. We didn't learn or remember everything, they pointed out. What was required was some mechanism that allowed neurons to fire and to sometimes learn. The neuron had to have some way to discriminate between things to be learned and things simply to be passed on to the neighboring neurons.

The second was much less worrisome. It largely assumed what neurobiology assumed about the neuron: that for all intents and purposes, the neuron behaves as if it were a simple point unit that generates a spike that encodes information, much like a telegraph signal uses dots and dashes to represent its message. As Gordon Shepherd, a Yale University neuroscientist who has been part of the effort to revise this dogma, writes, "One of the basic tenets of neuroscience, handed down from the classical era of Ramon y Cajal and [Charles Scott] Sherrington at the turn of the last century, is that the neuron has a relatively simple functional organization, in which the dendrites receive synaptic inputs, and the axon sends the output of the neuron, by means of impulses that travel down the axon and activate output synapses in the axon terminals." This simple plan implied that all neurons are similar input-output devices. It isn't the characteristics of the units that are important but the way they are hooked together into networks.

In 1943 Warren McCulloch and Walter Pitts used this image of the neuron to re-imagine the brain as a computational device. Hebb's work, while it emphasized the role of the synapse in learning and memory, still treated the neuron as a simple summing unit. Signals of different strengths travel down the dendrites to the soma, where they are added, and then they are transmitted to other neurons through the axon. The character of the dendrites and axons as wires doesn't matter, nor does the spatial distribution of the synapses and the arms of the dendrites. All the computational work is done at the soma, where all the signals are added. The power of the brain results from linking together all these simple computational units, all these neurons, into networks.

This view of the neuron certainly simplifies the task of building neural networks. In fact, without this assumption, simulating neural networks on computers wouldn't have been possible at all until very recently — any higher level of detail would have simply overwhelmed then existing machines. Current commercial networks designed to run on personal computers or on simple workstations are only possible because of this assumption about what the neuron is like.

But as neuroscience has learned how to see the neuronal structures of the brain in finer and finer detail, this assumption has produced a troubling quandary. Tracing the dendrites and axons in detail has shown that most synapses are far out on extended dendritic networks that look like trees. If the neuron is a simple summing device, efficient design requires that these synapses, the points where signals are input, be as close as possible to the cell body where they are to be added. That maximizes speed and accuracy, and it eliminates the leakage from long dendritic wires. The actual geography of biological neurons is just the opposite, however. The brain has either adopted what Gordon Shepherd characterizes as a very inefficient system — it wouldn't be going too far to call it a stupid design choice — or the neuron isn't the kind of processor the traditional view thinks it is.

If computational neuroscience — the study of the computational processes of the brain as if the details mattered — has a founding spirit, it is Wilfrid Rall, now at the National Institutes of Health in Bethesda, Maryland. Rall started to reveal the computational complexity of the neuron in the early 1960s by tracing the outlines of the first cracks in the traditional neuronal model, which had begun to appear a decade earlier. In 1954 researchers found the first inhibitory feedback circuit in the brain. Built around the Renshaw interneuron, named after Birdsey Renshaw of Rockefeller University, who had postulated its existence, this was a new kind of circuit in the brain. A collateral branch from a motor neuron axon in the spinal cord synapses onto the Renshaw interneuron. That cell (called an interneuron because it mediates the action of two neurons) then completes the circuit through a very short axon that makes an inhibitory synaptic connection back onto the original motor neuron. In effect, it makes up a very small circuit, what Pasko Rakic in 1976 would call a local circuit and what Gordon Shepherd in 1978 would label a microcircuit.

The discovery was fascinating and puzzling. What was the purpose of this local circuit in the general scheme of the brain? One obvious possibility was that the neurons in the circuit were doing some kind of local signal processing before sending information to higher centers of the brain. Did more local circuits of this sort exist?

The olfactory bulb, an ovoid structure attached to the front part of the brain that relays signals between the olfactory receptors in the nose and the olfactory cortex, seemed a promising landscape for the search. The input and output layers of the bulb are clearly separated, a rarity in the nervous system. A researcher could easily stimulate an individual pathway. And the three types of cells in the bulbs are arranged in very clearly delimited layers.

One of these types of cells in particular, the granule cell, posed a thorny problem. It seemed to act as an interneuron in connection to the mitral cells of the bulb. The mitral cells send long axons to the olfactory cortex and are clearly the pathway that olfactory information takes toward the higher processing centers of the brain. The granule cell, on the other hand, sends out two long dendrites in opposite directions, and as far as the researchers could tell, it had no axon at all. If the traditional view of the neuron was true, a neuron without an axon could have no output; in fact, it could have no way to pass along any signal to another neuron. Yet one team of researchers in the Oxford University laboratory of Charles Phillips believed that the granule neuron made up a local inhibitory circuit, like that made by the Renshaw interneuron in the spinal cord.

In 1962 Gordon Shepherd moved from Phillips's Oxford laboratory, which he had joined fresh out of medical school, to Rall's laboratory at the National Institutes of Health. Rall, a physicist by training, had already begun his pioneering studies of dendrites. Unlike most neuroscientists then, he hadn't been happy assuming that the dendrites were simply undifferentiated and passive wires between the cell bodies, which did all the work. He had already discovered that the electrical currents set up by the synapses flow throughout the dendritic tree, and that the currents and the potential changes in the membranes are affected by the geometry of the trees and by the electrical properties of the dendrite.

Rall's method, now known as compartment analysis, was to divide the dendrite into "events," places where signals were added together, which he called local summing sites. Each synapse, each spine, each branch of the dendrite, was such a local site, and each site represented a compartment of the dendrite that could be characterized by its electrical and physical properties. The passage of the electrical signal down the dendrite to the cell body, and the strength it had when it got there, was predicted by the properties of all these compartments.

Shepherd and Rall began applying this technique to the recordings Shepherd, Phillips, and T. P. S. Powell had made of the mitral and granule cells. Working backward, they constructed a model that fit the observed pattern of electrical signals. It said that the arrival of an impulse in the mitral cell triggered excitatory synapses between the secondary dendrite of the mitral cell and the spines on the dendrite of the granule cell. This input depolarized the granule cell, and that in turn activated inhibitory synapses back from the granule cell to the mitral cell. The model exactly reproduced the long-lasting inhibition in the mitral cell they had seen in Phillips's laboratory.

The results were unorthodox, to say the least. Here two neurons formed a circuit without any axon at all; nothing went to the cell body for summation. All the information was extremely local: it included only what the few parts of the dendrite knew. And yet the result was long-lasting inhibition in the entire cell. Dendrites talked to dendrites. Local circuits could be extremely local. Significant processing went on in the farthest reaches of the neuron without any involvement by the core. In 1965 Thomas Reese and Milton Brightman actually identified the synapses predicted by the model in photographs they took with an electron microscope. Further research showed that such dendrite-to-dendrite circuits were extremely common in the olfactory bulb.

The world didn't beat a path to Rall and Shepherd's door. As late as 1978 Shepherd could write, "For many research workers the existence of dendrondendritic circuits has been difficult to reconcile with traditional notions of neural organization based on circuits formed by axons." Shepherd and Rall, together and then independently, haven't waited for acceptance, though. After showing that dendrites could form microcircuits and that the properties and geometries of dendrites matter, they have shown that dendritic spines and the synapses at the heads of these spines can form local processing units, too. Neurons, they argue, are merely an intermediate processing level whose properties are determined by the interactions of much smaller units. This view hasn't gone down easily in the neural network community.

Computational neuroscience exists in a tense relationship with neural network research. The results of the cooperation have been enormously fruitful, but neither camp really trusts the other. The neural network emphasis on model building and computer simulations has provided some of the basic tools used in computational neuroscience. Employing these software models, neuroscientists can experiment with the effects of changes that they can't yet detect in biological systems. Yet they are impatient with the models that many network builders use. Some models are so unbiological that the biologists bridle when a network architect refers to a computational unit as a neuron. The neurobiologists have adopted as allies some modelers, like Terry Sejnowski and Carver Mead, who are trying to use the principles of real biology in their networks. But for the rest of the neural network community, the neurobiologists have a thinly disguised contempt that has done little to disseminate their point of view.

In return, many neural network builders shake off the biological argument. Researchers like Richard Howard and David Rumelhart argue that neural networks don't have to be that biological. Basic principles are enough. What difference does it make whether a network uses accurate models of neurons or neuronlike units that approximate the computational functions of many dendrites, somas, and axons in one mathematical function?

This question has gained a whole new urgency as a result of the successful search for a mechanism that would account for the Hebb synapse. The entire field of neural network research breathed a sigh of relief when, in the mid-1980s, several laboratories — Charles Stevens's and Thomas Brown's key among them — identified and described the NMDA receptor in the neural membrane. This receptor was the Hebb synapse, each reported. The first crucial assumption of neural network theory was true. Only a few researchers noticed that this same discovery meant that the neuron did not behave like a simple summing unit.

According to the Salk Institute's Charles Stevens, the results throw down a challenge to all neural network models. "I would claim that the experimentalists such as myself would say that there is a fundamental problem with neural network theory. There is a fundamental difference between the way the neuron works in the brain [and the way it is modeled in an artificial network]. It's not a detail. It's a fundamental difference. It doesn't mean that neural networks aren't valuable, but it does mean that they aren't brains."

The NMDA receptor, one of two classes of receptor on the neuronal synapse, seems to be the mechanism that produces long-term potentiation. It explains how correlated signals strengthen the connections between individual synapses. Briefly, the NMDA receptor is not involved in the normal transmission of signals across the synaptic gap. That falls to another class, the AMPA receptors. The NMDA receptor only goes into operation when the sum of all the signals reaching the postsynaptic membrane across the synaptic gap is especially large.

Most of the time, the conjunction of signals at the synapse is strong enough to depolarize the membrane and send a patch of depolarization traveling down the dendrite toward the cell body or soma, but it isn't strong enough to overcome the higher threshold of the NMDA receptor, which is kept closed by a special magnesium blocker. Occasionally the depolarization of the postsynaptic membrane is enough to push over this threshold and clear the blocker. At this point the NMDA receptor sets in motion a series of calcium-modulated events that permanently changes the behavior of the synapse. (Exactly what events depends on whether Lynch, who points to changes in the postsynaptic membrane, or Stevens, who favors the presynaptic side, is right.) Hebbian learning has taken place.

But Stevens says this clearly isn't anything like a simple addition. "The fundamental assumption of all the neural network models," he says, "is that at every synapse you have a weight that modifies the input. That weight can change, but at a given point in time it is fixed for that cell. It is determined." But in the NMDA mechanism that is precisely what doesn't happen at a synapse. Weights, says Stevens, aren't determined or fixed. The weight for each input varies with the course of all the other inputs.

It helps to concentrate on just one input, call it A, from neuron 1 to neuron 2. According to neural network theory, the input is increased or decreased at each synapse by a weight. That weight has a fixed value, created by the operation of some rule, for example, the Hebb rule. Let's say that the firing of neuron 1 is only moderately correlated with the firing of neuron 2, so that weight A, at 0.5, is not too high and not too low. That means that any input A from neuron 1 to neuron 2 will be multiplied by 0.5. Another input, call it B, which is much more closely correlated with neuron 2, has a higher weight, say 1.0. These weights can be modified as the system changes or as it learns more about the correct correlation between the two neurons.

But the NMDA channel doesn't work that way. On two different occasions input A can have the same weight but produce a totally different effect on the postsynaptic NMDA receptors. In the first case, suppose that it arrives with other signals that don't sufficiently depolarize the membrane. No NMDA action occurs. In a second case, the other inputs are different and push the postsynaptic membrane over the threshold. Input A, the same input, with what is called the same weight, will have a totally different outcome, says Stevens.

"What is unique about NMDA channels that is different from every other kind of channel is that their effectiveness depends jointly on two things. First, it depends on the amount of neuro-transmitter that is released and the sensitivity of the synaptic membrane, that is, on the synaptic weight. But [second] it also depends on the total input to this cell," says Stevens. This is a strangely paradoxical kind of computer, Stevens points out, in which the weights are not set once and for all; their effect depends on the total inputs, on the momentary signal context created by all the inputs. The individual neuron is the only place in the brain that knows what all these inputs are; in that sense the neuron is an independent unit and the computation is completely local. But that local computation is determined by the state of all the neurons in its surrounding group, which can number anywhere from 1,000 to 10,000. From that point of view, the local computation is determined by the global state — which is, of course, only the set of all the local computations.

This isn't the end of the story, either, says Stevens. This is just one of the many types of "learning" mechanisms in the brain. He is currently trying to pin down the exact place where synaptic change happens in long-term potentiation. He and Richard Tsien of Stanford advocate changes in the presynaptic side of the gap. Roger Nicoll of the University of California at San Francisco and Gary Lynch argue for postsynaptic changes. In the process of deciding this question, Stevens has studied a lot of other kinds of synaptic change. In many of these cases the mechanisms aren't the same as in long-term potentiation. Some strengthen the connections across a synapse when the signals are correlated. Others turn up what Stevens calls the volume control in the entire system. In that case, he says, one group of neurons says let's strengthen this whole other group of synapses. Other mechanisms strengthen synaptic connections on the basis of use, not correlation.

This kind of complexity is a two-edged sword. In the first place, it isn't surprising. In fact, our metaphor of the machine suggests that this is only natural. Complex behaviors, and the brain certainly produces those, are the result of complex machines. We produce more and more complex behaviors in a machine, a computer, for example, by adding more and more parts in more and more complex structures. It seems logical to us, for example, that a program to figure a spreadsheet should require more lines of code and more routines and subroutines in its program than one that simply adds a string of three-digit numbers.

Such a perspective applied to something like Muriel Ross's

effort at machine building yields a rather daunting result, however. What if it takes a supercomputer to model just the details of the macula? Then how many supercomputers will it take to model the way all the elements of the vestibular system work together with touch and vision, assuming that other supercomputers can model those senses? Room upon room filled with computer upon computer to model one brain section after another. Someday the end comes, far in the future, after all the earth's economies have been devoted to producing supercomputers for decades on end. At that moment some finite collection of machines duplicates all the brain's systems. But there is no understanding in that, merely copying. It will not stand as science, if by science we mean an understanding of the basic principles that are represented in this detail. No one studying or using such a machine would know what principles organized it or which details were essential to its operation or which could be left out. Like the brain, it would be a black box mystery. Maybe those who argue for a simpler kind of neural network with a neuronlike processor summing inputs are right.

We believe complexity can be reduced to principles. Standard neural network theory is an example of that, and so is much of physics, especially physics before the quantum age. From this point of view, we say that we can explain and indeed produce the incredible variety of chemical compounds in the world by combining fewer than 110 basic elements. The characteristic of those, in turn, can be explained by the arrangement of a few kinds of particles, electrons, protons, and neutrons. We know that those particles themselves are not irreducible physical entities, but are instead composed of other, more basic particles. But on the level of much of chemistry, electrons, neutrons, and protons are adequate explanations. Can we not find a similar level for explaining the operations of the brain?

In physics we have long assumed that the behavior of visible matter can be explained by — in fact, is caused by — the behavior of identical smaller units. Explanations in physics have pushed from atoms to electrons-neutrons-protons to ever-smaller and more basic particles. All of our physical universe may finally be explicable in terms of four basic particles. Biology in general and neurobiology in particular increasingly seem to be understandable in a similar way, in terms of the interaction of chemical transmitters, receptors, antagonists, and microchannels.

But there is some evidence that biological systems don't work exactly this way. They have this curious information problem. Take the great example of "particle" biology, the genetic code. Not all the material twisted into the four-base sequence that makes up DNA is meaningful. It is misleading to think of this material as making up a message as in Morse code, where every dot and dash is information in the message, or even as in this sentence, where most of the letters are directly related to the sense of the whole. Researchers in the human genome project now know that there is a lot of scrambled genetic material interspersed between the meaningful parts of the code. This material, as far as we can tell now, doesn't tell any part of the system to do, not to do, speed up, or slow down anything.

Which is extremely curious, because biological systems seem to have massive information deficits. When compared to physical systems, as John Hopfield notes, they are immensely more information-intensive. A rock, for example, is a fairly complicated physical object, since it has a lot of unrelated local structures that each require some information to specify them. The details of a particular rock — its mineral composition — represent the consequences of a long and detailed evolution. Hopfield estimates that it takes about a hundred bits of information to generate a particular piece of rock equivalent, for all macroscopic intents and purposes, to another piece of the same kind of rock.

Describing how to make a cat from its chemical components is far more complex. In fact, Hopfield estimates it requires far more than the one million bits of information in the cat genome. "A genome containing one million bits is large enough to describe a bacterium, but not a cat." On the one hand, the amount of information necessary to specify the state of a piece of biological matter such as a cat is hugely greater than an equivalent mass of geological matter requires. Hopfield estimates that the difference is on the order of thousands or millions of times more. On the other hand, the genome, the blueprint for the machine, isn't capable of carrying this amount of information.

The relationship of parts to the whole — and the related question of how the whole is produced at all — is one of the grand puzzles of biology. Biological systems often go to elaborate lengths to produce carefully differentiated units, such as neurons with different learning mechanisms or sperm with detailed inheritance, only to kill off most of those information-bearing individual units. They often show an incredible, seemingly profligate redundancy. Thousands of offspring crawl out of eggs and only a dozen reach adulthood. Millions of neurons die as the brain organizes itself in the early stages of development. The global functioning of the whole seems dependent on the characteristics of individual units, but not upon the survival of a specific unit. Engineered machines are clearly not built this way. We don't build Chevys with twenty-four sparkplugs and assume that six of those will function correctly and the rest will die.

But the fact that complexity doesn't quite play out the same way in biological systems as it does in machines suggests an alternative scenario to a world with rooms full of supercomputers duplicating the function of the macula. Maybe a biological system that exhibits complex behaviors doesn't need to be structurally complex in the same way a machine does. Brooks's Collection Machine has already hinted at that possibility. Two efforts to build neural models that more fully incorporate known biological details show that the metaphors of physics and machines may be misleading descriptions of the brain.

One of Gordon Shepherd's Yale colleagues, Thomas Brown, and Christof Koch of the California Institute of Technology, have used the precisely determined physical and chemical characteristics of individual receptors, and the actual spatial geography of synapses, spines, and dendrites, to simulate just a single neuron, but one with 2,000 synapses. When they present this neuron with sets of random input patterns, groups of synapses compete to represent them. Some win by chance when their individual characteristics, such things as where they fall on a dendritic branch, make them and the current pattern a better match.

In effect, they survive and other groups don't. The brain gets carefully organized representations of patterns from the outside world, without precisely engineering any group to match that world. Redundancy makes competition possible, and competition leads to the careful representation of information. This process is fully deterministic, given the character of the input and the structure of the neuron. And yet the rule that picks a specific group is not a reductive summary or a list of principles. The rule for who wins and who loses is nothing less than the complete list of all data in the input set and the complete description of each synaptic group. There isn't any simpler description of the rules of this competition than the system itself.

Brown and Koch's simulated dendritic tree begins with a computational model of a Hebb synapse, incorporates it into a model of a whole neuron, and then gives that neuron a structured set of inputs. As the model runs, the neuron learns. It organizes its activations to represent the correlations in the input space. So far, there is nothing at all unfamiliar about Brown and Koch's work. Nothing, at least, until Brown flashes a slide of the model, called MOSAIC, on the screen. This doesn't look at all like the boxes and lines that usually represent a neuron and its branches. Brown and Koch began MOSAIC by modeling a specific neuron, one from the hippocampus, and all its geometry. "These little protuberances are called dendritic spines," says Brown to the audience at the 1990 NIPS conference. "The Hebb synapses would terminate on this dendritic spine where it will release a transmitter that will cause a current to flow which will change the voltage here. So our biophysical model of the Hebb synapse is basically a model of this spine." The model contains equations that represent the chemical and electrical properties of the NMDA and AMPA receptors. Other equations represent the physical qualities of the spine and the dendritic shaft.

Brown and Koch have radically increased the ratio of synapses to neural bodies, while preserving the time components of the network. According to Brown, "There are about twenty thousand of these spines per neuron." In their system, as in Carver Mead's chips, it takes time for signals to pass from point to point, and each specific time is determined by the physical qualities of the dendritic cable and by the distance between all these spines and cables. "If the processing element is a point [as it is in most neural models], then there is no analog to the spatial aspect of this dendrite. In contrast, in our dendrite space is an essential part of the computation it performs," says Brown. "This neuron is not isopotential," he adds, which means that there are differences in voltage all along the dendrite from the head to the shaft and down the shaft. Any single local current is the result of local interactions between incoming signals and local circuits of spines and synapses. All these local currents affect the signal as it moves toward the cell body. This is not a passive cable.

"What we wanted to understand was what happens when you

put a realistic Hebb model together with a realistic neuronal model. What kinds of things happen, what kinds of things might you see?" says Brown. To do that you need some very accurate anatomy; you have to know what the electrical properties are at every point along the dendrite. To create that picture, Brown and Koch applied Rall's compartment methods. "We have some estimates of electrical properties and what we then do is take the anatomy and chop it up into little pieces, each of which you can think of as being iso-potential." Brenda Claiborne of the University of Texas supplied the precise anatomical detail necessary for the model. Using a computer microscope system that she developed, she can break down each neuron into a set of 3,000 data points, each representing a length, a diameter, and a conductivity. According to Anthony Zador, a graduate student working on this project with Koch and Brown, "Ultimately we want to know what is the computational capability of a neuron."

To enable MOSAIC to run the dynamics of this system in reasonable times, Brown and Koch had to simplify their spine model to include just 200 synapses. No one knows exactly what the input to the hippocampus, a higher brain structure implicated in memory storage, looks like. "Some of the more senior people call the hippocampus the black hole," says Zador. "Researchers go into it and never emerge. It does something important, that we know." The team uses a set of patterns, each one containing some neurons firing together, as input. "In some vague sense we're imagining that it represents dog or blue or happiness," says Zador, "but we're not worrying about that. All we're assuming is that some neurons are firing together."

As Brown runs his videotape of one simulation, some of the synapses turn blue, a sign that they are getting weaker. Others strengthen, turning yellow or green. The network of synapses gradually settles toward a stable pattern: some synapses go dark; others brighten. Usually the synapses along an entire branch go dark or light together. Order gradually forms out of what was once randomness. After a number of trials the patterns no longer change. "We go through all the patterns and we call that a trial and we go through lots of trials and we watch these self-organize," says Brown.

That organization finally emerges from a kind of competition among the synapses, with the results determined by the electrotonic properties of the dendrites and the geometry of the branches. The patterns themselves are randomly chosen and presented. Some fit the existing geometry better than others and grow. Others fit badly and die. As the tape rolls, one pattern flickers out. "This one happens to be a loser," says Brown. "It starts off with this average value. It starts to lose, except for this little cluster, which is strengthened. Then even this cluster starts to get weaker. By trial eleven this pattern produces almost no response in the neuron. If we left it longer, it would produce no response."

Another random pattern begins on the tape. "Here's a winner. The same number of synapses. The same conductances. But just by chance this one has more favorable electrotonic relationships. And this one strengthens right away. Even on the first trial. By trial eleven almost all of these are strengthened. This result is extremely robust. We don't have to tweak things at all to have the neurons lock onto a subset of the available inputs. In addition to winning overall or losing overall, you find clusters, subsets of these patterns, that win. Sometimes it will be two or three clusters."

Brown cheerfully admits that he really can't explain what principles are behind this self-organization. There are simply too many random parameters at work here. Some variables, like the electrotonic structure, he knows are important. The kind of membrane and the distribution of the synapses make a very big difference. Using a slightly different form of the Hebb rule completely changes the response in a given electrotonic environment. There are several ways of implementing the rule, and Brown doesn't know which is biologically correct. In fact, he says, maybe he should use different rules for different kinds of neurons.

Nor is Brown quite sure exactly what one of his stable patterns represents. His model seems to suggest a way to unite biology with theories of representation and perhaps psychological space. The properties of spines and dendrites might create something like a choice of possible consequential regions for Roger Shepard's categories. The match between a particular category and a particular set of synapses might occur through competition, with the structure of the category looking to find the best match among available geometries. Brown and Koch don't suggest that their model works this way, but certainly it offers an interesting medium for that kind of speculation.

At another conference just six months prior to Brown's

presentation of MOSAIC to his peers in November 1990, Gerald Edelman, then director of the Neurosciences Institute at Rockefeller University in New York City and winner of the 1972 Nobel Prize for Physiology or Medicine, ran a videotape very similar to Brown's. In a series of machines named after Charles Darwin and Alfred Russel Wallace, the great English naturalist who proposed his own theory of evolution at about the same time as Darwin, Edelman illustrated a similar kind of competition that could explain how the brain completes its wiring during development.

Edelman won his Nobel for untangling the chemical structure of gamma globulin, a crucial step in understanding the function of antibodies in the immune system. He then turned his attention to the nervous system and began to analyze a series of mechanisms that explains how neurons grow toward their eventual proper positions. In developing from a unicellular egg, a human being has to gradually create new kinds of cells — brain cells, muscle cells, bone cells — and put them in the right places. To create the central nervous system, one of the more complicated wiring jobs, the developing human must generate all the different kinds of neurons and connect them in exactly the right order. An individual nerve fiber, for example, must often grow over, under, and around before finding its proper connection. That pathway cannot be coded in the genetic material. A map telling every neuron exactly how to grow is far too complex to be carried in the limited code of our DNA. Instead, Edelman explained at the conference, a complex of chemical markers and receptors sets the route.

That work left Edelman with another question, though. How does the brain create neuronal structures that are precisely matched to the processing required of the outside world? Presumably, the connections of a network have to be very accurately constructed to perform the precise computation needed. One neuron out of place and the answer comes out wrong. But Edelman knew that the brain's developmental mechanisms are not precise enough to generate that kind of accuracy. The brain is simply not capable of hooking itself together with the kind of precision an engineer might use in designing a machine capable of discriminating such fine differences in color or such tiny increments of distance.

Edelman was also intrigued by another aspect of the developmental process. If the brain followed a largely hardwired pattern in development, how could it deal with new kinds of experience?

Learning could obviously take care of things like the meaning of green and red traffic lights, but what about bigger changes in the external world? What about the changes required by a world that moved at sixty miles per hour instead of at a walking pace? How is it possible that essentially the same brain is able to make sense of the world of the Roman senator, the Renaissance lady, and the modern fast-food worker? Whole new categories of experience have appeared and disappeared in those ages, yet the time period is far too short to produce any major structural changes in the brain. So where does this flexibility come from?

Edelman's machines and his theory are built around a principle he calls neuronal group selection. According to this theory, the brain consists of numerous roughly equivalent neuronal groups. During development the brain generates a number of largely redundant groups, each of which is potentially capable of handling a cognitive task such as representing "senator" or "justice." Each is slightly different because of the sloppiness inherent in the biological information system, but now that sloppiness and redundancy are strengths instead of weaknesses. In a process akin to the one in Brown and Koch's model of the neuron, experience creates a kind of competition in the brain between these roughly equivalent groups. The one with the structure that best matches the experience in question winds up as the one used by the brain.

The connection between this theory and evolution isn't apparent until you watch the machines work. Here competition and extinction are clearly the dominant principles. Competing patterns grow, wiping out some of their competitors until the field is divided among just a few patterns. As the machines run trial after trial of their experience set, most of these patterns gradually die out, too. Finally, just one is left.

Each one of these neuronal groups represents a rough equivalent of an organism with a unique genome. Instead of an external ecosystem, each group strives to survive in the artificial world of the input pattern. The one that survives is the neuronal group/organism best suited to the current experience pattern. Using an energy function, Darwin looks for the most efficient way of representing this experience. Neuronal groups that can't pass this energy threshold aren't allowed to compete again in the system's next generation/trial. They die.

These are, of course, machines, and they are clearly artificial.

Yet the evolutionary metaphor that best describes their behavior is not mechanical but biological. The relation of part to whole is not that of the well-designed watch, nor is the efficiency of this system that of Occam's razor. Reductionist explanations are certainly still possible, but they seem to have limits. At some level an explanation of the causal principles of the system is a description of the system.

It is not yet clear whether systems like Edelman's or Brown and Koch's are a way out of the toils of complexity that loop out from Ross's macula. If the brain can't contain an internal blueprint of all its connections, maybe artificial machines shouldn't strive to do so either. If the brain is the product of some interplay of genetic code, chemical markers, and competition, maybe artificial brains should be constructed in the same way. Maybe the key to building this kind of machine lies in abandoning the machine metaphor's definitions of design, efficiency, and structure, and thinking about organization and structure in terms suggested by another metaphor. Maybe thinking about this artificial brain requires thinking in the terms of a new field, one called artificial life by some scientists.

13
SURVIVAL OF THE SMARTEST

You believe in a God who plays dice, and I in complete law and order.

— ALBERT EINSTEIN

David Ackley, David Stork, and Chris Langton are all field biologists — of a very artificial sort. Ackley watches protohumans try to dodge carnivores long enough so they can evolve intelligence. Stork gives birth to generations of computer algorithms, ruthlessly kills those that aren't good at recognizing typefaces, and lets the others have sex. Langton constructs virtual ants that march across his desktop, building intricate colonies as they search for food. At the least, these three men believe, life, death, and evolution can teach us how to grow neural networks ideally matched to specific tasks. And these principles can tell us why the brain exists and reveal the organization of all life.

David Ackley doesn't look like God. In an ill-fitting suit that could use a press, he looks like he could sell whole life. But create it? — no chance. Today, though, at a session of the International Joint Conference on Neural Networks, Ackley is giving an eyewitness account of the scene in a primitive world as simple beings struggle for survival.

"This world is very simple really," Ackley says. A giant plain takes up most of it. A mountain range runs along two edges. Plants dot the landscape, and trees form a small forest in the south. Carnivores and man-things roam the plains searching for food. Occasionally the man-things become a meal for the carnivores.

Neither species is very smart. The carnivores are mostly appetite, but they can't climb trees and they don't see very well. A protohuman doesn't have to be very far away to be almost invisible. The humanoids can climb trees for safety. But most of their existence is spent looking for food and water, eating, and making more humanoids. They have two major advantages over the more powerful beasts. Some evolve and pass on changed genes and new abilities to the next generation. Others learn new skills during their lifetimes.

"That's about it," Ackley says. "There are a few more rules, about how fast plants grow and how quickly carnivores reproduce and when they die, but basically that's the program."

Program? All of this world takes place inside a computer, like some giant video game. Just as the rules of Nintendo determine how high the Mario brothers can jump, so Ackley's rules animate his characters' actions. With a press of the execute key, he can set this world in motion.

Generation after generation the humanoids are born, grow, reproduce, and get eaten. The population swells near ready sources of shelter, food, and water, overwhelms these resources, and dies back. Occasionally a generation evolves something new, and it pushes beyond the mountains, gets more organized about avoiding carnivores, or discovers that the beasts can't climb trees. Or something they learn changes the basic dynamics of the game. It's as if the Nintendo player, having grown tired of level 1, were to reset the machine for level 2. The humanoids, like the Mario brothers, are now capable of new behaviors, but the rules of the landscape and for the carnivores remain the same. Then the population of the plains grows to new levels. A kind of evolution guides this system, although it, like the world in which it operates, has been radically simplified.

"Now, we can stop this at any time and look inside the heads of our humanoids. We can see what they've been learning," says Ackley. The brains of these humanoids, it turns out, contain a mixture of the predictable and the surprising.

"For instance, even if we start with exactly the same initial conditions and exactly the same rules, we almost never wind up with the same result. There's just enough randomness in the system to assure that." Most individual humanoids die out quickly. In fact, most populations rapidly head for extinction. Individuals survive initially by luck: they happen to be in the right place at the right time. In one run, because the carnivores and the humanoids at first interact pretty much at random, a guy will miss being eaten and will discover a successful tree-climbing behavior. In another run, that same humanoid will get eaten before he learns anything. That behavior won't get discovered for another generation or two, by which time the beasts will have eaten a lot more humanoids.

All that makes good sense to Ackley. It's the relationship between learning and evolution that has left him scratching his head. Ackley and his colleague Michael Littman compared five strategies. Two strategies relied upon populations that could neither learn nor evolve, while the other three assumed populations that could either learn or evolve or, in one case, do both.

Not surprisingly, the strategy that allowed both learning and evolution did the best by far. The average population using both those abilities survived for 80,707 generations. Ackley was amazed to discover that the strategy that allowed evolution but not learning did only slightly better than one of the strategies that allowed neither. The average learning but nonevolving population survived for just 1,564 generations, while an average population that neither learned nor evolved survived for 1,562 generations. Biasing the humanoids so that they spread themselves uniformly across the world — but still neither learned nor evolved — pushed the average survival to 6,560 generations. Evolution, it seems, is highly overrated — at least for humanoids inside a computer program at Bellcore.

Ackley and Littman think they have an explanation for these strange results, and they detailed it in a paper they wrote together, "Learning from Natural Selection in an Artificial Environment." Since most humanoids die quickly in this harsh world, most populations that do develop descend from a single individual. Genetic recombination can have little effect; random mutation in a uniform population won't discover many new rules, handy or not.

What the researchers would love to explain is why some populations do so much better than others that are following the same strategy. Is it all chance? And how does the nature of the artificial world affect the way these five strategies perform? Does the world itself have a dynamic that leads to these results? Ackley and Littman found that decreasing the plant density and increasing the range of the carnivore vision as the world aged — so that survival was easier at first but became harder as time went on — seemed to make evolution relatively more important than learning, at least in comparison to the original static world.

When Ackley presented this same work in February 1990, at the Santa Fe Institute's conference on artificial life, he got peppered by other questions. What rules did the learning group develop that the evolving group didn't? Did Ackley examine what would happen if the evolving group started with those learned rules, too? Ackley had to admit that he hadn't yet tracked down exactly why a few groups outperformed their betters. If there were rules they knew, he hadn't yet been able to find any that made the crucial difference when he popped them into the heads of other populations. He was also working on a completely different possibility. Maybe it wasn't what the humanoids knew but when they knew it. Maybe the key wasn't the rules but the dynamics of the entire system.

Ackley's work belongs to the tradition of evolved models, often called genetic algorithms after one type of learning rule used to construct such a system. Genetic algorithms, a school of computation most closely identified with John Holland, are designed to "solve" systems through artificial evolution. Genetic algorithms are one way to grow efficient computer programs to solve problems that confound more traditional methods for designing programs. They replace a human software engineer, who is asked to understand the problem and create a program to solve it, with a model that evolves the best program for solving the problem.

A system that uses genetic algorithms begins with some kind of fitness function. Each entity in this system consists of a computer program for solving the task at hand that is initially designed by an engineer, and a two-part genetic algorithm, which sets the rules of reproduction for surviving programs. Typically, the genetic algorithm includes a mixing function, which allows for the exchange of information between algorithms — the equivalent of sex between two sets of computational procedures — and some random change generator — the equivalent of genetic mutation — which produces random change in the program between generations.

Each computer program entity is measured against the fitness function. Those programs that pass the threshold are allowed to reproduce, yielding a new generation similar to their parents but with some random changes as well as some differences that occur as a result of the mixing of information between two programs. Programs that don't pass the threshold "die." Each generation, its solutions, the measurement against fitness, the death or reproduction of a new generation, and so on, are modeled in a computer. Hundreds of generations can be compressed into tiny amounts of computer time, allowing the program to simulate the eons of time that biological evolution employed to design complex and efficient ways to solve problems.

The attraction of genetic algorithms and evolved systems for neural network researchers and neurobiologists should be obvious. Here is a way to grow a complex system like the brain without having to understand every single connection and how it relates to the final product, a fully developed owl, rat, rabbit, or human brain. Genetic algorithms, in fact, have found ready applications in these "brain" sciences. Some neural network researchers are using them to configure the connections in their networks. Some neurobiologists are using them to explain how the brain completes its own organization during development.

David Stork, for example, uses a similar kind of evolution to grow neural networks that recognize different typefaces. Stork, who was recently spirited away from Stanford University to join a new neural network research program at Ricoh's Menlo Park, California, corporate research center, knew that one way to do this would be to develop an algorithm to recognize one typeface and then tinker with it to see how many others it would recognize. He could then design another algorithm for a different family of typefaces. Instead, he has decided to evolve systems that recognize each typeface and then compare them, looking for common traits that he can include in a vision system.

"Simulating evolution itself is fraught with difficulties," says Stork. "But it has some things to recommend it. Genetic algorithms are like stochastic searches, only instead of having just one system searching an energy landscape, you have many simultaneously searching. One may find a good niche, a good local minimum, and it will survive better than another system that has found a local minimum that isn't as close to the global minimum. Those that are best will survive." In other words, instead of designing a simple algorithm, using the best insights available on how to perform a task, and then hoping it can find the minimum in the energy landscape, the researcher designs many good algorithms, allows them all to search, and then allows the best of those to reproduce and mutate into new generations of algorithms that search the landscape and themselves reproduce.

Stork adds some of his own tricks to Holland's model of a genetic algorithm. "What we're working on is incorporating neural networks and genetic algorithms so that you have a population of neural networks all reproducing and competing." To do that, he says, you have to include genetics, certainly, but you also have to add learning to the system. And that involves building something like an artificial organism.

Stork's mathematical organism includes "genes" that encode the possible synaptic connections in a neural network. "You've got a very long gene of ones and zeros representing in a complicated way the connection strengths." If the neural network uses more than one layer, each layer can be represented in a separate gene. Other genes can be used to represent other parts of the system, such as a representation scheme or an output device.

Employing the classic sort of genetic algorithm with a stringent fitness function, almost no organisms will survive. To live to reproduce, they have to know exactly the right pattern to solve the task, and almost none do. (This classic type of algorithm does resemble one current evolutionary model, which proposes that evolution consists of long periods of relative stability in a species punctuated by brief moments of change.) "So it would take a very long time for a population of these to ever survive," says Stork. "You need many, many of them to begin with before you have even one or two that get it right. One way to think of it is that it's a haystack with a needle in it that represents the exact proper set of synaptic weights necessary for survival. Now, if you start with a genome that's wrong, it's like reaching into a haystack and grabbing a straw. No, that's not the needle. You have to keep going back to see if you can grab the needle."

But change the fitness rule and introduce learning, and the process gets much faster. "If an organism is near the proper synaptic weights, it could learn enough to survive." The initial weights would still be wrong, and using only the original weights, the organism couldn't perform the task. It wouldn't be allowed to reproduce. But, Stork says, the weights could be close enough so that a few learning trials could produce the correct combination. "If you allow learning, more networks survive," and the more learning, Stork feels, the faster the entire population will evolve. To him, this system seems to represent the actual biological solution. When a baby is born, nature doesn't expect it to be able to read A, B, C, D, and E. "A very stringent survival or fitness function would say that the baby can only survive if it gets all five letters correct," he says. Instead, nature allows for learning. If the baby can learn to recognize these letters, it will survive and get a chance to pass on its genes.

Midway through a late November morning, there isn't much life, artificial or otherwise, stirring in Los Alamos, New Mexico. An occasional pickup truck pulls up to the supermarket. A few cars wait to take a turn at the McDonald's drive-through window. The town sits in quiet splendor on top of three sheer finger mesas, each one cut off from the other. The exposed rock faces blushing in shades of red sandstone, the black-green of the pines, the endless clear blue of the almost cloudless sky, make this a breathtakingly beautiful place.

Human history was transformed here in 1945. The street signs alone are enough to make anyone shiver. "Trinity" the main drag is called. Out at the national laboratory in the energy museum, exhibits on medical lasers sit next to models of the first atomic bombs, which made this town briefly famous forty-seven years ago.

Right next to the museum, at the Center for Nonlinear Studies, Chris Langton watches a colony of artificial ants, "vants," he calls them, for virtual ants. The life forms that Langton works with at his computer often resemble those that Stork and Ackley have created, but his reasons for studying them are much different. His goal is not a better algorithm or an improved neural network. Langton is trying to understand how the kind of organized structure we call life came to be. In the process he has developed some theories about the place of the brain in the universe. "An ant colony is a wonderful analogy for the brain," he says, propping his cowboy boots up on his battered desk.

Within the confines of his computer, the vants search their environment, meet other vants, and reproduce to create new vants. "You start off the system with a bunch of randomly specified ants and give them a few simple rules, such as what to do when they meet other ants and so forth."

The fitness function is also extremely basic. "You can just say that they survived. Did they get enough to eat? Real organisms aren't faced with some complex set of differential equations for finding a fitness function out there that they're trying to hill-climb on [in some kind of solution landscape]. Real organisms have to eat and produce offspring and garner resources and allocate them back into the gene pool." With these rules and that fitness function, Langton starts his ants in motion.

The screen is a swarming mass of motion as vants move about and colonies grow. Even with just a few rules, the vants form patterns with a startling complexity. Paths grow across the screen, curl in on themselves, and die. Colonies form L-shaped blocks and then reassemble themselves into other patterns. Patterns seem to snowball. The interaction of two vants, for example, creates a dense pattern that wanders across the screen until it meets another structure. That meeting produces an even more complex pattern. Over and over again shapes and geometries grow out of the disorder and then dissolve back into it, some quickly and some after long periods of relative stability.

Langton just sits there and smiles. Where are these patterns coming from? his cocked eyebrow asks. "This, to me, explains vitalism. This is how you can be both a vitalist and a mechanist at the same time. The vitalist idea is that you have some kind of mysterious organizing principles that operate at a very high level and that dictate the behavior of the parts. That moves the parts of the body around. Otherwise it's just mush." To the vitalists that organizing principle is a separate material, sometimes called spirit, sometimes mind, sometimes God. "If you took away the physical material, you would still have this organizing principle. It's outside of the material. It's some sort of quintessence, some kind of fifth stuff that's not earth, air, fire, and water. Now look what you get here," says Langton pointing to the screen. Only local rules. No vitalism need apply.

What's going on in Langton's computer, despite the absence of carbon or DNA, is "virtual life." At least it is to Langton, who points out that neither the standard dictionary definition of the term nor the traditional commonsense view is very useful. Webster's *New World Dictionary* describes life as "that property of plants and animals which makes it possible for them to take in food, get energy from it, grow, adapt themselves to their surroundings, and reproduce their kind: it is the quality that distinguishes a living animal or plant from inorganic material or a dead organism."

Why does that definition limit life to just plants and animals? Langton asks. Everything it describes can be performed by other kinds of systems, too. Thermodynamic systems use energy to grow, for example, and they certainly can be said to adapt to their environments. No, this definition is still bound up with the idea of vitalism, what Langton defines as "the notion that life was an extra something necessary over and above the detailed organization of a material organism."

"When you think about dynamic structure, you begin to start to think there are a lot of things that are analogies with life. Life is more of a pattern in space-time than it is a set of particular physical things," he says. It isn't a question of the particular things, but of the behavior of the structure of these things. The key feature of life is the properties of the interactions between parts, not the properties of the parts. "That's where the life is in a cell. The molecules aren't alive. It's the pattern of activity that the whole cell goes

"Living" by only a few simple local rules, Langton's vants create complex, shifting patterns of activity.
Photograph courtesy of Chris Langton, Los Alamos National Laboratory.

through because of the local interactions and the way that the local interactions set the stage for other local interactions."

In his introduction to the published proceedings from the first Santa Fe Institute conference on artificial life, Langton wrote, "To animate machines, therefore, is not to 'bring' life to *a* machine; rather it is to organize a population of machines in such a way that their interactive dynamics is 'alive.'" [Emphasis is in the original.]

Focusing on the entire organism obscures the way nature works, Langton believes. "What it seems that nature has done in evolution, the way that it has discovered new functionality, really increased the complexity of something, is not by making individuals more and more and more complex; it's by finding new collections of individuals, finding that a collection of individuals as a group will do something that's useful as a group and that often just depends on the properties of the individual behaviors, not so much what they're made of."

Langton knows that vants aren't at all like neurons, and he isn't arguing that they are. But he isn't really interested in the specific character of vants or neurons. What he's after is the dynamics of a system in which very simple independent units interact with each other by following a few very simple rules. The rules are somewhat biological since they reflect the reality of an ant's behavior. However, the vant colony could represent any complex system — neurons, perhaps.

Langton believes that the way this class of biological system behaves can explain the way the brain works and, indeed, why a brain like ours exists at all. But unlike a neural network researcher, Langton, who splits his time between the center and the Santa Fe Institute (a more theoretically inclined think tank set up by some of the senior people from the Los Alamos laboratory a few years ago), isn't primarily interested in the brain.

"I guess the easiest way to describe what I'm interested in is this notion of the emergence of higher-level properties from collections, large aggregates of fairly simple parts, and how these emergent properties often form new individuals at a higher level." To Langton the parts can be the molecules of liquids, schools of fish, ant colonies, individual cells, or the brain. He and his coworkers want to understand complex systems. "Things like economies, things like the immune system, things like life, things like intelligence."

Only from a very specific point of view are economies, immune systems, and intelligence the same kind of thing. Most of us treat the world as if it had just two kinds of order, each very different. One kind is deterministic. In these situations everything seems to follow rules. The entire system is completely predictable. No matter how many times we run such a system, the results will be the same, as long as we don't change the initial conditions. The whole is predictable. Behavior is determined.

Deterministic systems are ruled by linear dynamics, it was thought. Linear systems could be described by relatively simple rules. The amount of light reaching a surface was inversely proportional to the square of the distance between the light source and the surface, for example. The rules were called linear since the relationships they described remained the same for all conditions of the system. The inverse proportion rule for light held whether the distance was one inch or twenty light-years.

The other kind of order we commonly assume is probabilistic. Often such a system and the process of understanding it is called stochastic. This is a kind of statistical order, an order on the average. We can't predict the result of any specific coin flip, but we can predict the result over time of a series of coin flips.

Probability is a way to deal with extreme complexity that doesn't readily resolve into linear rules. The results of a coin toss might be predictable if we could understand all the causal elements and the way that they interrelate. We would have to develop a way to include everything from velocity of toss to room temperature to wear on the coin. Each one of these variables, furthermore, probably has a different effect on the result depending on the state of the other variables. The wear on the coin, for example, might be more important when the velocity of the toss is high. The relationship between each of these variables is likely to be nonlinear. They can't be described by simple rules like that of inverse proportion over the entire range.

This rough division of the world into deterministic and stochastic has taken a severe beating during the last twenty or thirty years. Nonlinear systems that are so complex that they seem to be random or probabilistic, it turns out, can be deterministic. Very simple systems that are seemingly lacking in complexity and are seemingly linear, it also turns out, can actually show complex and nonlinear behavior.

All it takes is a simple electronic hand calculator to explore this world. (The following example is laid out in more detail in Ian Stewart's book, *Does God Play Dice?*) Let's limit our starting values for this exploration to any value between zero and one. Take the number 0.54321, for example, and the simple function $1/X$. This just tells the calculator to divide 1 by X, initially 0.54321. On the first go-round, this gives 1.840908673. On the second, $1/1.840908673$ turns out to be 0.54321. The system is perfectly orderly. It alternates between the same two values. Such a system is called periodic. It's what we might expect from such a simple system. After all, it has just one variable.

A slightly more complicated system, such as $X^2 - 1$, also shows a simple order. Again, start with 0.54321. The answer is said to cycle between -1 and 0. After about ten repetitions, each alternate answer is close to either 0 or to -1.

But take another simple equation $2X^2 - 1$. The addition of a 2 certainly shouldn't change the behavior of the system that much. Start with 0.54321 again. The result is anything but a minor difference. The regular cycles of $X^2 - 1$ disappear. Instead, an uneven oscillation appears, seen in the figure opposite.

This simple equation is actually even stranger than it seems, Stewart points out. If you were to write a general program for the equation $KX^2 - 1$, where K is any number, you would find an extremely wide universe of behaviors. For example, when $K = 1.4$, the answer cycles through sixteen different values. $K = 1.5$ produces a pattern that resembles $K = 2$, and as K increases from 1.51 that disordered pattern remains. But suddenly, at $K = 1.75$, the pattern reverts to a simple cycle of three, going from 0.744 to -0.030 to -0.998 and then repeating.

Like the more complicated traveling salesman problem, this simple equation creates a landscape with features called sinks, sources, saddles, and limit cycles. As a map of the solution space of the equation, this landscape predicts the pattern of answers produced by the equation from any given starting point, just as the landscape of a Hopfield network determines the settling of a network from its initial state. The "flow" of an equation, over time, is indicated by curved lines, as in the accompanying figure on page 274. A starting point such as 0.54322 for X and 1.75 for K, which for the purposes of drawing a two-dimensional portrait, we will redefine as Y, falls somewhere on one of these curves. The first iteration, the answer the first time we apply this equation, falls also on that curve, as does the result of the second iteration, and so on. The different patterns that result from the equation are expressed in this picture as different kinds of curves. Thus, for example, starting points that produce a limit cycle fall on one of the closed circles. A sink, which would be called a minimum in the Hopfield-Tank landscape, represents a starting point that yields just one value no matter how many iterations. Sources are the opposite of sinks: values move away from this point with each iteration. Saddles represent values that are stable but that slide off quickly into either sources or sinks.

These four kinds of features account for many kinds of order, but they don't explain the quasi-order shown in the oscillations that result from $2X^2 - 1$ when $X = 0.54321$. Those oscillations never exactly repeat, but neither are they completely random. A number of sciences have developed to study these kinds of behaviors. Chaos science, for example, has shown that the seemingly orderless pattern of $K = 2$ has an order that employs a different kind of attractor than the traditional sinks, sources, saddles, and limits. These chaotic attractors, called strange attractors to distinguish them from the traditional four, can produce many kinds of order.

The larger field that encompasses both artificial life and chaos is called complexity science. One of its jobs is to explain how order can emerge from the interaction of simple parts. Systems exhibiting this kind of interaction are often called self-organizing, since the order seems to stem from the interactions of the system's units rather than from some outside principle or template. Often complexity science shows that such a system is the result of one emer-

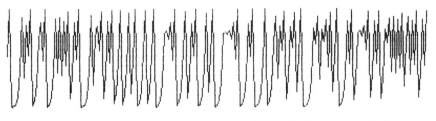

Graphing the results of repeated calculations of $2X^2 - 1$ shows a seemingly random pattern. Chaotic dynamics actually order this system.

gent system being built on top of another, with the behaviors of the first system becoming the primitives that form new behaviors in the second.

Doyne Farmer, until recently one of Langton's colleagues and the former leader of the complex systems group at Los Alamos, believes that this kind of structure is a crucial principle for many biological systems. He calls the brain "a supreme example of a self-organized state" that is built out of relatively primitive agents. Adding layers of emergent systems on top of other emergent systems is "probably the key to why our brains are so powerful," says Farmer. "In phylogeny you see a progression from simple little brains to very complex brains, each stage building on the previous stage, so you're building on an emergent property. You have emergence heaped on top of emergence heaped on top of emergence.

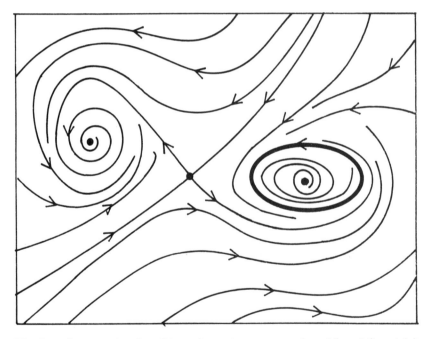

The flow of an equation describing a dynamic system can show (*from left to right*) a circular sink, a saddle where currents cross, a limit cycle (the dark circle), and a source. These four kinds of features make up the traditional attractors common to nonchaotic systems.

I view the artificial life movement as saying, Okay, let's forget about all these details, let's just try and pin down what makes that kind of open-ended emergence possible."

Complexity suggests that many human biological structures — the immune system, for example — share this kind of organizational logic. Each antibody type interacts with on the order of a thousand other antibody types. "So your immune system is actually a very highly interconnected web," says Farmer. That's a very controversial idea, he adds, because it pushes the locus of computation and learning in the immune system from inside the individual cell out into the network as a whole. "Where's the seat of computation in the immune system?" he asks. "Does computation exist entirely inside of individual lymphocytes, which behave independently of other lymphocytes? The alternative view is that lymphocytes strongly interact with each other and that the properties of the immune system are a result of the population of lymphocytes." That's the same as asking whether the brain is a set of individual, extremely smart neurons or a connected network where the connections to each other matter a lot. "It's obvious in the brain that their connections matter a lot," says Farmer. "My personal view is that something similar occurs in the immune system." The analogies between the immune system and the brain seemed even clearer to Farmer after he began building connectionist models of the immune system about five years ago.

Making these kinds of connections between extremely different physical systems is the meat and potatoes of complexity science. It is also the justification for the movement known as artificial life. The reasoning goes something like this: Figuring out what are the important principles of complex systems isn't easy. Part of what obscures these universal features is the paucity of examples in the real world. When we study economics, we can only study existing economic systems. When we want to know how socialism or capitalism or Marxist-Leninism works out, we have only one real world history to look at. And if we're studying a system like evolution, the situation is even worse. We have only one evolutionary past to consult. How can we draw valid conclusions from that? Since real life offers too small a sample, the artificial life movement says, just create more evidence, more alternatives for testing theories and deriving them, in the artificial world inside a computer. "Then we'd be able to say what is universal to all of those paths and what's just accidental," says Chris Langton. "All life on the earth uses the same genetic code. Is that because that genetic code is somehow a universal property of life or is it just an accident?"

Biology has traditionally used the history of organisms as a way to separate the accidental from the universal. But that story-telling actually obscures cause and effect, Langton believes. Saying that trilobite A came before trilobite B doesn't tell much about the universal properties of life.

That is why, for example, it is better to study artificial systems — and lots of them — than brains. "I mean," says Langton, "the neural net people are sort of tied to brains. We get to look at a lot of biological phenomena that are examples of emergent behavior in aggregates and things where you get collective behavior." He feels that studying just the brain, that one example of a complex system, again threatens to obscure the universal point.

Life, Langton believes, is a special kind of dynamic system, one that is perched on the edge of phase transitions, like those between the ordered crystals of ice and the less ordered molecules of water. Located between phases and using a solution space filled with strange attractors, the system that we call life can bounce back and forth between frozen and active states. Slight changes in initial conditions can end life or set it spinning in a new orbit that represents a new species or an evolutionary dead end. Only such a dynamic system can produce the stability and the sensitivity to slight changes in conditions that seem to define life across all of Langton's artificial organisms.

Life is such a complex system that it must be located at such a boundary between the periodic and the chaotic, Langton feels. "I concentrate on those dynamical systems that have a full range of behaviors, from totally ordered crystals to totally disordered hot gases. When you look at where they exhibit the most complicated behavior, it's in the vicinity of a phase transition actually." If you created a map of solution space that contained all the possible dynamic systems that could be alive, some would be too stable. They would be trapped in limit cycles, for example. Some would be too unstable. They would swing so wildly that an organism couldn't hold its structure from generation to generation. For life to be as dynamically complex as it seems to be, with the exact mixture of stability and instability that characterizes it, it must be a dynamic system very precisely located in that solution space so that it balances between too much order and too little.

"Structure is information," says Langton. You need a periodic structure to create information, but you need a dynamic structure in order to express new information. "Where," he asks, "can you have structure and have it be dynamic instead of static? It's at this transition point."

Like life itself, the brain seems to show this balance between stable patterns that contain old information and new patterns that hold new thoughts. When we learn something, Langton points out, we don't completely scramble all we know. The mind remains mostly stable, but it isn't static. It can't finally resemble those neural networks that settle to a point attractor. Settling is stasis. Death.

Have you ever thought about why a high fever leads to hallucinations? Langton asks. If the brain is a system poised on this transition between periodic order and chaos, all it may take is a little more heat to push it into a region with much less order. "Assume that the brain is sitting in exactly this sort of complex region. The temperature is being maintained at ninety-eight point six. It may be that the reason for keeping it there is that if it's a little hotter, you're just too much in the chaotic regime. You can't do useful thinking when you have a fever." Nor, as Langton points out, when the brain's temperature sinks. Hypothermia, the dangerous cooling of the body, leads to seizures — "in other words, very oscillatory behavior. The brain just spikes repeatedly over and over again." It may be that balancing act between stability and change that makes us intelligent.

Wild and unorthodox? Certainly. But no stranger than the very odd results that have come out of some of the world's top neuroscience laboratories within the last few years. The balance between periodic order and chaos may indeed explain consciousness, the mind, and maybe even individual thoughts. Such a theory certainly suggests a new way to build an artificial brain.

14

THE MIND AT LAST

Sticking an electrode in and looking for consciousness is a tricky business.

— CHARLES GRAY

In the beginning is the chaos of neural activity, which is already present in the womb when the brain is no bigger than a grain of rice. Is the brain then conscious? Is consciousness caused by conception, by birth, by feeding, or exercise, or education? These questions seem to mock us.

— WALTER FREEMAN

During the winter of 1989 Charles Gray and his coworkers in Wolf Singer's laboratory in Frankfurt may have discovered consciousness.

Since September 1986 Gray had been at work in Singer's lab at the Max Planck Institute for Brain Research studying the development of the columns in the primary visual cortex of cats, exactly the same problem that has occupied Kenneth Miller, Michael Stryker, and Carla Shatz. Gray was trying to explain an observation that had initially shown up in a small quantity of data collected by Laurence Mioche, who had worked in the laboratory before he arrived. Mioche had been recording from electrodes implanted in the orientation columns of the visual cortex. To get clean signals from single cortical neurons, she used filters to eliminate the background noise. At regular intervals she removed the filter to get a base record of the entire field potential, the average electrical activity of all the neurons near this electrode. These periodic checks made sure that all the equipment was functioning and that the filter wasn't introducing spurious signals into the recordings.

Gray, though, noticed a strange fleeting pattern in the recordings made during this equipment test. Occasionally, over periods of a little less than half a second, the electrical current across the entire field oscillated in a regular wave pattern with a frequency from forty to sixty hertz. Then it broke up in a confusion of competing waves. When Gray arrived, he found the data suggestive. His initial calculations seemed to indicate that all the neurons in a single field might be organizing themselves for a moment into a single synchronous pattern. Since the existing data was so sketchy, though, he set to work to collect more and to analyze the nature of these patterns.

And what if neurons in a large area of the brain did fire synchronously? What would that mean? Gray knew that interpreting the results would be even more difficult than finding the patterns. The list of behaviors waiting for neurobiological mechanisms was a long one. Maybe these patterns would reveal how the brain represented an idea; maybe one of these patterns *was* an idea. Or maybe the brain locked into synchronous behavior when it paid attention to something. Or maybe it was consciousness itself — whatever that might be.

Gray also wondered what these alternations between synchronous order and disorder might mean about how the brain worked. To us, when we think about our thoughts, they feel stable, ordered, fixed. But what if they aren't? The patterns Gray was looking for suggested that the brain might indeed be balanced between periodic order and chaos. A thought might be some kind of dynamic pattern, like the course traced out over time by the bob of a pendulum, rather than a fixed set of activated neurons.

Oscillations had shown up in other, earlier experiments. As early as the 1930s researchers had described neuronal rhythms in the brain. Stimulating a brain area, such as the olfactory receptor sheet, provoked both a burst of response from individual neurons and a rhythmic wave of activity that could be recorded in the field potential of the olfactory area. That rhythmic wave began at about the same time as the stimulus-produced burst, but it outlasted both the burst and the presence of the stimulus. A single stimulus, it seemed, produced both a static pattern of neuronal firing and a wave of activity.

Rhythmic patterns were initially identified in the olfactory bulb and the pyriform cortex (the part of the cortex involved in smell) in amphibia, fish, and a variety of mammals, including humans. Similar rhythms were later discovered in the somatosensory and visual areas of humans, cats, and monkeys. The characteristic frequencies of these rhythms varied from area to area between twenty and sixty hertz, and in all cases their onset was linked to a stimulus and their presence was most obvious when the subject was engaged in some behavioral task. No one before Gray, however, had seen any of the distinct rhythmic waves related to a stimulus temporarily come together to make up a single synchronized wave, a process called phase-locking.

Even before the evidence of phase-locking, these oscillations had posed a challenge: what purpose, if any, did they play in the brain's work? Walter Freeman, a neurophysiologist at the University of California at Berkeley, had firmly established the existence of oscillations in the olfactory cortex. In the olfactory cortex system, Freeman showed, this oscillation is involved in discriminating odors. He went on to argue that oscillations also played a role in the visual cortex. Wolf Singer wondered whether he and Gray had found something like a visual sniff.

But Singer also wondered whether this might not be the solution to the "binding problem," one of the crucial unsolved puzzles in understanding the brain. Researchers have discovered neurons and systems of neurons that fire in response to visual stimuli such as edges, movement, contrast, and orientation. They are convinced that somehow the brain builds those responses to individual features into objects. But what lets the brain bind all the right stuff and none of the wrong stuff together?

How the brain selects only the appropriate features to build up an object is a tremendous puzzle, says Gray, who now runs his own laboratory at the Salk Institute in La Jolla. His laboratory there is so new that in October 1990, some equipment still sits in crates. Other pieces have not yet arrived. Reaching into his desk, Gray readily puts his hand on two transparencies. This is his favorite illustration of the binding problem, one shown to him initially by Wolf Singer.

The two sheets are covered with short black lines. "Just turn away for a second," Gray says, as he overlays the two sheets and backs them up with a solid white piece of paper. The combined sheets look like a random jumble of lines. Each sheet "is just a set of lines that I have drawn by hand." Then he moves the bottom transparency, sliding it in a randomly chosen direction under the other sheet, and suddenly, a triangle pops out of the random lines.

Until the beginning of that movement, the triangle made up of lines on the bottom transparency was lost in the stationary mass of lines created by both transparencies. It only appeared when the lines on the bottom sheet went into motion and the lines on the top remained motionless. "As soon as relative motion occurs, they just pop out like that. It's probably not even important exactly where you're looking at the moment: your visual system can segregate out the figure." Somehow the brain connects only those lines that are in motion to form the image of a triangle.

The first stages of the recognition process are well understood, says Gray. Individual neurons respond to elements in the random scene, such as edges, line segments with certain directions, and the like. At this point they react in precisely the same manner to lines on either transparency. They have no reason to separate what will be background from what will be the triangle figure.

With motion, though, the neurons somehow divide into two different patterns of activation, one of which still represents the random lines of the top sheet and the other of which now "sees" the triangle on the bottom sheet. Gray wants to know how the response of the neurons firing in reaction to the elements that make up the triangle "bind" together into a single figure. They are all still embedded in the same network. The neurons that before were firing in response to the ground are still firing. Some new neurons that only respond to motion now fire for the first time, but neurons that fired in response to edges, contrast, and oriented line segments in the lines that now seem to belong to a triangle still fire. "The neurons that respond to the coherent part need to identify themselves in some way," says Gray. "But the possibility of establishing the relationships has to be there latently and not really expressed until the stimulus is present."

About ten years ago Christoph von der Malsburg, then at the Max Planck Institute, made an almost despairing suggestion. Maybe, the theoretician wished, the neurons involved with a single object might briefly synchronize their activity. (A similar idea had also been proposed in 1974 by one of Donald Hebb's colleagues, Peter Milner of McGill University.) Von der Malsburg hypothesized that assemblies of neurons, separated by large distances in the brain, might fire at the same time. This synchronicity would distinguish the neurons in this assembly from all the other neurons that were also firing either randomly — without any rhythm — or perhaps with a different rhythm. The shared rhythm would flag these neurons, telling the brain that their firings all related to a single object.

Von der Malsburg's theory added another language to the brain's repertoire. "Rather than just using the total amount of activity of the neurons, you also utilize their selective temporal interactions with other neurons," says Gray. "That was the idea, but as far as he [von der Malsburg] was concerned, he was pretty pessimistic about finding a mechanism that would do that." The necessary experiments would be like finding a needle in a haystack. "You go into the brain with an electrode and you're able to pick up maybe five cells," Gray says. A researcher would have to get pretty lucky in order to put that electrode down next to two neurons that were following the same rhythm at the precise moment when they were showing that behavior.

But maybe the researchers in Singer's laboratory had gotten lucky and blundered upon a trace of von der Malsburg's synchronized pattern. Singer and Gray went to work mapping the exact extent of the synchronized activity and its cause.

Gray was in many ways the perfect colleague for this work. As a graduate student, "I had been very strongly influenced by Walter Freeman at Berkeley," says Gray. After years of research, Freeman had firmly established the role of oscillation in smell. His conviction that oscillation also played a role in the rest of the brain, though, was regarded with skepticism. Freeman "had been proposing that this rhythmic activity that he had seen in the olfactory system would also be present in the neocortex. He had been working with the assumption that the olfactory system was a simple model of the neocortex. It seemed like a reasonable idea to look at. But we didn't go into this with the idea that here's von der Malsburg's theory, here's Freeman's prediction, and let's bring these two together and simply go look for this. We said that oscillations are an interesting phenomenon, and we do have this problem that the visual system really is a parallel processor and somehow has to bring all this together." Phase-locking individual oscillations into a synchronized pattern would be one way to pull off that trick.

Using a network of electrodes to record the EEG, the pattern of electrical activity generated by an area of the brain, Freeman had discovered distinctive rhythms in the olfactory lobe. A perfectly quiet rabbit, one sitting still and breathing purified room air, shows a characteristic rhythm in its EEG. "When he breathes inward through the nose, you get this kind of high-frequency burst," says Gray. "It's pretty easy to see. If you just pinch his nostrils shut, both of the rhythms go away." By using as many as sixty-four electrodes, spaced 0.5 millimeter apart, over the surface of a substantial part of the olfactory bulb (about 20 percent), Freeman could record the spatial pattern of activity and extrapolate it over that entire brain region. He discovered that large collections of neurons show the same rhythm. At a time when many neural network researchers held that a percept was encoded in the firing of just one neuron, or in the firing of a small number of neurons, Freeman argued that the coordinated pattern of an entire population of neurons was a smell.

Performing an experiment on the visual cortex of a kitten that was analogous to Freeman's olfactory work, as Singer and Gray were trying to do, was incredibly difficult. The structure of the visual cortex and the nature of visual stimuli are both much more complex. Gray had to shine small, carefully oriented bars of light onto the kitten's retinas. "We used the standard Hubel and Wiesel type of approach. We identified the location in the visual field where the cells respond, and then we used a light bar of a particular orientation, moving it in a particular direction at a certain velocity."

The patterns that Singer and Gray, now joined by Peter König and Andreas Engel, did see were fascinating. Gray could actually watch the signals begin to mesh. "These responses would start; they would coalesce; they would phase-lock in. That would last for a certain number of cycles, and then as the stimuli left the receptive fields or it changed, the reaction changed. They rapidly shift out of phase or do their own separate thing." At one moment the oscillations would be a clashing pattern of waves, all of the same height and frequency, but out of phase. One wave's trough would match the shoulder of another wave, for example. Then suddenly the waves would all march in phase-locked step, trough to trough, shoulder to shoulder. The signals synchronize very quickly, within fifty to one hundred milliseconds, Gray says. Typically, they stay phase-locked for fifty to as much as eight hundred milliseconds under experimental conditions, and then they'll fall out of phase and become unrelated.

The character of this mechanism matched several well-established biological constraints. For example, the brain very quickly creates coherent objects from a multitude of neuronal responses and erases them just as rapidly. "A requirement for any mechanism that you want to use to identify things that belong together is that it be quick and that it probably shouldn't last too long," says Gray. "It has to synchronize quickly, get the job done and then break down and get out so that it can establish other relationships with other neurons in the network. So you should be able to see quite a dynamic fluctuation."

Gray, Singer, and their colleagues devised an experiment to test another known constraint. They reasoned that a "binding" mechanism should show a preference for connected stimuli. In this experiment the researchers located two cell groups with separate receptive fields that were arranged so that they could be stimulated independently with two bars of light or with a single long bar. The strongest synchronization resulted if a single bar stimulated both fields simultaneously. If the stimulus was two independent bars of light with identical orientation and movement direction, the synchronization became weaker. It disappeared completely if the light bars moved in opposite directions over the receptive fields. It certainly looked like this could be a coherency detector.

The next experiment tried to measure exactly how far synchronization extended in the visual cortex. The first tests had involved only relatively nearby groups of cells. Could Gray and Singer discover synchronized oscillations across larger distances? Experiment by experiment, they pushed to larger and larger distances. First, they found it between the columns that Hubel and Wiesel had identified as the major structural element in the visual cortex, then between collections of columns, called hypercolumns, at distances between seven and nine millimeters.

That result was both significant and surprising. It meant that the synchronized wave patterns were not the result of control signals. They couldn't be since the synchronized activity covered a greater distance than any possible connecting cable stretched. The synchronized activity had to be the result of the properties of the network itself. This global pattern self-organized out of the local interaction of individual neurons. Gray calculates that the participating neurons are covering somewhere between 10 and 15 percent of the visual field. "It really indicates that cells that are looking at two different locations can communicate in a coherent way. That's really the most exciting implication."

Because of that implication Gray and Singer's find puts new life into one of the oldest debates of neuroscience. How many neurons participate in a thought or in a simple cognitive step? At the one extreme, the microscopic one-thought/one-neuron position of researchers such as Horace Barlow seems less and less tenable. The fact that human memory and cognitive abilities degrade gradually with injury seems to argue against a brain constructed around individually unique neurons. If that were so, the death of a single neuron, a relatively frequent occurrence, would wipe out a memory or interrupt a cognitive chain.

At the other extreme, the macroscopic position has claimed that large areas of the brain participate in the storage of a memory or the performance of a cognitive task. From his measurements of the EEG, which is a form of the "noise" of the bulb as it does its work, Freeman argues that a smell is represented by the neuronal activity of the entire olfactory bulb.

The brain lacks sufficient long-range connections to coordinate this kind of large ensemble, the opponents of this view have pointed out. Now, with Gray and Singer's evidence, it seems clear that the brain can conduct coordinated activity without the need for direct long-range communication. The question of how a mental entity corresponds to its biological counterparts has become even more problematic.

Other researchers have confirmed the results from Singer's laboratory and extended the synchronization to even greater distances. For example, another German group has shown synchronized activity in two entirely separate cortical areas, V1 and V2, in the cat, says Gray. After he left Singer's lab to set up his own at the Salk Institute, Gray says, Singer, König, Engel, and Andreas Kreiter went on to demonstrate synchronized activity between corresponding cortical areas in the two separate hemispheres of the brain.

Such experimental results don't guarantee that all these synchronous oscillations mean anything, Gray cheerfully admits: "One of the main criticisms of the work has been that this sort of rhythmic activity simply represents an epiphenomenon of cortical networks. It's like the redness of hemoglobin. It's wonderfully red, but the redness isn't used for anything." The brain's oscillations may be just as meaningless.

Some neural network researchers, however, think that this data might point the way to understanding the big issues of cognition, those involving the whole brain. The oscillations are some of the first evidence that the brain's networks may self-organize into dynamic systems that can express information. This could be the step beyond the static feature detection networks that seem to work so well for some tasks at the sensory periphery. It could be the basic mechanism for attention or even consciousness.

Gray steers away from making such a leap, but CalTech's Christof Koch has deliberately launched himself into that very thin air. In 1990 he coauthored a paper with the Salk Institute's Francis Crick that speculated that these synchronized oscillations could be the basis for a "neurobiological theory of consciousness."

"What do we mean when we say we are conscious beings?" Koch asks.

> In the most general terms we mean we are aware. We have a lot of trouble defining what that means precisely. We know lots of things that we aren't aware of. We gather a lot of sensory perceptions that we aren't aware of. Awareness seems to mean some kind of process that brings things to a level of the brain where we can articulate them and where we know that we are thinking about them.

Momentarily synchronous oscillations that link columns and sections of the brain for a moment before dissolving might be the cause of that awareness, says Koch. "There's lots of other, nonsynchronous activity in the brain, but maybe we're only conscious of the synchronous activity."

Koch doesn't expect any experimental evidence to vindicate this view soon. "It's probably wrong, I'd guess, at some really obvious level that we don't know anything about yet," he says. Nevertheless, the paper is designed to change the kind of questions neural network researchers and neurobiologists ask about the brain and intelligence. Koch hopes it will force modelers and neurobiologists to talk about the nature of mental events. "There has been this very strong prohibition in America, due to the very strong influence of Skinner and the behaviorist school, not to talk about consciousness. It's like religion and ideology. For them a phenomenon like blind sight would not be a legitimate source of study since they only care what the behavior is."

That phenomenon, blind sight, is one of the human brain's most thoroughly studied puzzles, one that is intriguing in its own right and that also offers a wealth of information about how the brain must work. Explaining blind sight is a major challenge to any theory of cognition.

Blind sight is found in human patients with brain lesions. On first examination, a neuroscientist often concludes that the lesion has destroyed the patient's ability to see an object in one half of the visual field. A ball presented to the right visual field, for example, is easily recognized and reported by the subject, but the same ball in the left visual field might as well be invisible. The patient doesn't seem to see the object at all and when asked to describe it, can't. A typical reply is "What ball?"

But a slightly different test reveals an entirely different picture. The patient with the lesion is now asked to guess what color the ball is that is present in the seemingly nonfunctional visual field. The patient denies that anything is there, but if the researcher insists, saying, "Just go ahead and guess," the patient, who can't *see* anything, picks the correct color with an accuracy that far exceeds chance. From patient to patient, researcher to researcher, the results are strikingly similar. The brain lesion seems to have impaired not sight per se but the ability to consciously know what is seen. As such it seems to be related to other neurological cases where patients who can't remember ever learning to play the piano — and who in fact deny that they can play — actually show a kind of unconscious memory that enables them to perform.

"I'm aware, you're aware, but this patient isn't aware of what goes on in the left part of his visual field," Koch says. "The point is that we can now start constructing theories of consciousness [to account for things like blind sight]. We can now start deciding what are the elements that we need. What has to be explained? What do we know already? This is the more general point of our paper. That it's time to start asking these questions, that you can now ask some very hard-core, materialist questions about it. The outline of the thing is available now. And particularly now that Francis's name is connected with it, it will get a hearing."

Crick and Koch have quite consciously proposed a theory that even in its first steps goes far beyond von der Malsburg's hypothesis or anything that Gray or Singer have themselves felt comfortable with speculating. "We said that it solved the binding problem and directly related to attention. It would be the neuronal equivalent of attention," says Koch.

Their 1990 paper builds on a metaphor that Crick proposed

in 1984: the attentional spotlight. He hypothesized that the brain only pays attention to the elements that are lit up by this spotlight. "The story is really more complicated, but that is the bottom line," says Koch.

Synchronized oscillations could be the mechanism that underlies this metaphor, Koch believes. Let's say that a monkey is looking at a scene with objects, colors, and motions, but it isn't really attending to anything in particular. All these features will be detected. They will cause neurons to fire. Motion, for example, will result in firing in MT, the area of the monkey's brain specialized for motion, while the color or hue of an object will cause neurons in another part of the cortex, V4, to fire. "These guys are all excited and they oscillate," says Koch, "but they aren't phase-locked; they randomly oscillate." Then the monkey decides, for behavioral reasons, to pay attention to just part of the scene, say the moving banana. "Now that the monkey has decided to attend to this location," says Koch, "the idea is that at the single-cell level the firing of this single cell would be phase-locked with the firing of that cell. And this cluster of cells would be synchronized with that cluster of cells." The "motion" neurons firing in MT would be connected to the "yellow" neurons in V4 to represent the moving banana. Only the cells that represent the attended banana would oscillate synchronously. "That would be the normal expression of attention, and that in turn induces short-term memory."

Anything that explains attention will also have to explain short-term memory, Koch believes. "If you think about it, it's very intuitive. You cannot attend to something without putting it in short-term memory. And you cannot put something in short-term memory without attending to it. There really are two things you have to explain, attention and short-term memory. Long-term memory is really not required.

"You can look at patient HM, for example," says Koch, referring to one of the classic case studies of cognitive functioning in patients with serious brain lesions. Presumably because of surgery conducted in 1957 to control his intractable epilepsy, HM has lost some kinds of memory. "You look at him and he seems perfectly normal. You ask him what day it is and he has no idea. He guesses. And when you tell him he says, 'Aha.' Then you ask him a minute later and he again has no recollection. He guesses randomly. Long-term memory enriches our lives immensely; without it we're poor beasts almost. But to all intents and purposes, you are still perfectly conscious if you only have short-term memory."

Crick and Koch suggested in their paper that oscillations could cause both attention and short-term memory. "We said that the neuronal expression of attention at the single-cell level is oscillation and at the same time this oscillation, by various biophysical mechanisms, induces short-term memory in these cells." The two are still up in the air over exactly what those biophysical mechanisms might be. "You put these things in short-term memory, and that can mean either of two things: either that these cells persist in firing over a half a minute, let's say, or that you strengthen the synapses for a short time so that if you return to them you can remember the pattern."

According to this theory, the brain has two kinds of global code, as well as all the local activity among individual neurons. A movement that is seen, but not attended, will produce firing and perhaps oscillations — but the oscillations will not be synchronized on the global level. Attended movement will result in synchronized oscillations. "This explains a very nice paradox," says Koch, the one exhibited in both patient HM and blind sight. "We're saying that there are two kinds of neuronal firing. One cell can fire and induce another cell to fire, and we're not aware of it. We're aware of only a special type of firing, the phase-locked firing."

Koch, who calls his field computational neuroscience, and the other neuroscientists just beginning to explore the possible meaning of global patterns in the brain, know that they have to speak about their work with extreme precision. Our everyday language constantly threatens to expand their hypothesis about specific mechanisms in one brain area into grandiose claims about the entire brain. For example, it's certainly legitimate to try to relate these phase-locked oscillations to certain kinds of internal mental states, such as awareness or attention. But once we start theorizing about specific internal mental states, it's hard not to wind up talking about that vague concept we call mind. "Mind" is exactly what generations of philosophers have called the phenomena these oscillations may explain. But is the mind equivalent to the patterns created by neuronal networks on this global level?

"There's always been this distinction," says Koch. "There's the brain, the wet mass of a hundred billion neurons and their connections. And then there's the mind. It's almost like the distinction between the body and the soul. We have instinctively for centuries maintained that there was this nonphysical thing, which we certainly could neither explain nor even identify, that did the thinking, had the thoughts, contained our psychology, was our personality. We've pushed deep enough into the brain, now, so that it really looks like maybe this mental thing doesn't exist. Our mind really is just a phenomenon of all that wet stuff.

"I think that's true. I think that from an objective, scientific point of view one can only conclude that neurons are all there is," he says. "But, you know, I don't think this should take away any of the wonder. It certainly hasn't diminished my sense of admiration for how logic or speech or Beethoven comes out of these tiny things. I also don't think we've begun to understand exactly how complicated this system is. The more we know about neurons, for example, the more details we have to include about this biological computer to get it to work. We're going to keep adding those details, I'm certain."

But experiments to gather those details will have to wait, at least in Charles Gray's laboratory, while researchers try to make sure that phase-locked oscillations actually exist. As much as Koch wants to believe, he himself questions what the evidence really shows. "The evidence, one has to be quite honest about it, is that the oscillations are to some extent phase-locked. That's the most remarkable thing about it, that neurons up to twelve millimeters away can be phase-locked. But you have to be very careful when you talk to these guys Singer and Gray and the like because what they're really saying is phase-locked on the average. It's not, unfortunately, what I really wanted, which is that every time you have a spike here you have a spike there at the same time. Sometimes they come earlier, sometimes they come later, but on the average they come at the same time. The question is to what extent can a locked oscillation on average be exploited by the brain?"

Gray has heard these criticisms and more, and he worries about them. Eliminating some of the uncertainties is the purpose behind the experiments he is just now starting. One problem with the data that he collected in Singer's lab is that it primarily came from anesthetized animals. As subjects these animals are certainly easier to work with in such complicated tests, but since they aren't actively exploring their environment — since, in fact, they don't show any behavior — it is impossible to connect any specific neuronal pattern with any event. "We still don't know if the animal is using it [the phase-locked oscillations] for any kind of visual discrimination; we can't really assign any functional significance to it," says Gray.

After all, as Gray notes, one of the reasons that oscillations and synchrony were ignored for so long after these principles were discovered in the brain is that they occur most commonly in situations where they don't seem to have any behavioral significance. "Several well-known things lead to synchrony in the brain," he says. "The first is sleep. The other one is certain types of anesthetic agents. Those are the two things that lead to widespread and really robust synchrony between large areas of the brain. I think those results led to the general feeling that synchrony is detrimental to information processing." Like the engineers who tried to get oscillations out of their electronic systems because the noise got in the way of the information-carrying signals, neurobiologists have tended to regard this class of oscillation as incapable of carrying any meaningful information. Too, most neural network models have been built around systems that settle to a stable point attractor. They have been constructed to avoid conditions that could lead to oscillatory behavior.

But Gray feels that the kind of synchronous oscillations he's studying are very different from the other kinds of oscillatory patterns found in the brain. He says these waves are at a much higher frequency than those that characterize sleep, for example, and they are also much more fleeting. "The synchrony is very specific depending on what stimulus is present and it's very transient." He believes it occurs and breaks up so quickly that the formation and disruption of the synchronous patterns could themselves carry information.

Gray's new experiments require training awake monkeys to pay attention to only one attribute of an object — such as motion — and to one particular condition — such as the absence or presence of motion. "Whenever an object moves relative to the background and relative to the observer, all the features that make up the object move together as a coherent structure. That sort of coherent motion is an extremely powerful cue for object recognition."

"You can ask an animal when there are two features out there and when they start moving, do they move coherently or do they move as separate objects? And you should be able to get a yes or no answer. And then you can look under those conditions to see what the interactions are between the neurons that are being activated by the two stimuli. And so you should be able to draw a correlation between the animal's activity in the world and the activity in the cortex." Or at least, says Gray, that's the hope.

The results that have come out of the labs of Singer and others, and the intense interest now being directed at oscillations, is a kind of vindication for Walter Freeman, although no one who knows Freeman would really expect him to admit heaving a sigh of relief. He has been out on a limb of his own making for so long, decades now, that he seems comfortable playing the role of the lone voice of truth. Since the early 1980s, he has hammered away at one scientific community after another, whether composed of neural network makers, psychologists, or his own colleagues, neurophysiologists. The brain is not as simple as you think, he keeps saying. Individual neurons are not the units of cognition, he nags. Thoughts are not equivalent to stable energy states, he preaches. Feedback has to be added to the system. Oscillations are the key to brain function. Now other labs have shown that his position actually may be right and the orthodoxy wrong. One of his students, Charles Gray, has helped find experimental evidence that has put oscillations front and center in the research agenda.

Of course, anyone who knows Freeman isn't exactly surprised to hear he thinks Gray and Singer have missed the point because they still see the trees and not the forest. According to Freeman, they can't explain how the brain can "read" their phase-locked feature detectors. Twelve years ago he proposed a phase-locking hypothesis for olfaction and six years later proved it untenable. Freeman predicts this will happen in vision, too, within the next five years.

It's impossible to miss Freeman, either striding across the Berkeley campus or at scientific meetings. With his white hair, gentle manner, and slightly stooped but still very tall frame, he could pass for an elder statesman. His work certainly has earned him that stature. His decades of research on the olfactory system have clearly established the role of oscillations in that part of the brain and linked it to the sniffing, exploring behavior of animals such as rats and rabbits. The experimental work that he has produced during his thirty-two years at Berkeley is a massive, ingeniously and rigorously constructed refutation of the classic stimulus response model of the brain.

Freeman takes a kind of quiet satisfaction in pointing out that what most "reflex" experiments — studies of conditioning like those of Pavlov on dogs — show isn't that an animal's behavior can be expressed as a sum of the responses to stimuli, but that animals can control the behavior of researchers. He has written:

> Researchers spend, or should have spent, small fortunes on the care, feeding, and housing of their subjects; they tailor the equipment and tasks to the capabilities of the species; familiarize and train them, and then sit waiting for them to deign to stop eating, licking, grooming, or just looking around long enough for the experimenter to get in a CS [conditioned stimulus] for a controlled trial; all this can go on for weeks. What is lost in all this is the fact that these animals are continually producing behaviors from within by anticipating external stimuli to guide or pace their actions. These behaviors express internally generated activity of the nervous system and are not deterministic responses to stimuli.

Freeman has shown that only when the animal is motivated and only when the specific stimulus has some meaning for the animal, such that it acts on the stimulus, do odor-specific patterns form in the olfactory bulb. The same stimulus presented to an unmotivated animal doesn't lead to any observable changes in the system. The brain's own internal states play an active role in the recognition of even something as basic as a smell. The brain, intrinsically, is an active agent designed to explore its environment, Freeman has concluded.

If Freeman were willing simply to let this substantial body of experimental work speak for itself, he could easily rest on his laurels. But he is convinced that the physiology he has uncovered adds up to a portrait of the brain, and that this portrait is radically different from that sketched by most of his peers. If Freeman is right, many of them are wrong, and he insists on telling them so. It is not uncommon for him to rise after a scientific paper, come to the microphone, and begin his comments with "I think this is basically wrong." There are certainly members of the neural network community who wouldn't mind if Singer and Gray's research turned out to be wrong if it would mean that Freeman wasn't right.

Freeman, for his part, often gives the impression that he believes that much of neural network theory and neurobiology is founded not so much on truth as on convenience. Neurobiologists and cognitive scientists believe in the reflex model because it promises to make the brain into an easily analyzable machine. Neurobiologists concentrate on the feed-forward networks in the brain while ignoring the feedback loops, because it's easier in the former case to connect a stimulus to a response. Neural network modelers concentrate on these same feed-forward networks because the mathematics of networks using feedback loops is so difficult. Adding feedback makes networks unstable. They don't settle into energy minima or maxima, but instead show patterns that repeat in cycles or, even worse, patterns that *almost* repeat with time.

But just because these facts are inconvenient doesn't mean we should ignore them, Freeman says. That would mean choosing to disregard the majority of the brain's behavior. And Freeman isn't exactly subtle about reminding his colleagues of their scientific duty.

Freeman has been around scientists for so long that he's developed a rather unusual perspective on the practice of science. His father was a neuropsychiatrist, and Freeman himself has spent more than thirty years in the trenches. Most scientists want the world to be a place where their tools work, Freeman says. "You know the joke about the MIT grad student's prayer?" he asks. "'Dear God, please make the world linear, stationary, and Gaussian.'" Until very recently the tools of our science could only handle a limited amount of complexity. They were designed to fit a linear world where systems begin in stable initial conditions and change in some way that can be readily described by a system of equations to reach some stable end state. Science that fits that conception of the world has a built-in advantage over science that doesn't.

"Old ideas die hard," Freeman says. For examples he reaches no further than the microchemistry of his own field. For a long time all the textbooks used a theory called the Bernstein hypothesis that relied on calculations of the potassium gradient to explain the workings of the cell membrane of a neuron. "It was known to be incorrect when it was first published," he says. It had been disproved experimentally even before the original paper appeared in print, and it was disproved repeatedly after it appeared. "Nevertheless it was the mainstay of teaching and research for fifty years. It was simple, understandable, and good enough." The current model, the Hodgkin-Huxley equations, aren't that much better, he says. They just added a sodium channel to the earlier theory's potassium gradient. All the experimental evidence shows that the membrane is much more complex than that, says Freeman. "We know it's untrue," but because the model is mathematically tractable and will yield answers that are good enough, it, too, has become the accepted theory. "We haven't had decent models of cerebral cortex. That's what I think I provide."

You can understand the flavor of Freeman's model from one simple characteristic: "The brain is always in action, neurons are always firing, even when there is no outside stimulus. That activity, the patterns that it sets up and the changes between the kinds of patterns, are what holds meaning." This is far different from the static network that settles to an answer by following some fixed landscape. Those networks can't explain the brain's peculiar mix of stability — we do remember things — and change — we do learn new things, and sometimes what we learn causes us to reorganize what we already know.

The brain's constant neuronal activity is the medium for reconciling these two opposites. The brain is a constantly shifting dynamic system, more like the flow of a fluid where patterns emerge and disappear than like a static landscape. Meaningful patterns are dynamically poised between sudden changes, and they constitute the internal "mental" structures of the brain. Each individual pattern has many potential routes for change that are at any moment determined by the character of the dynamic system, which itself is subject to change. A slight change in initial conditions can push a pattern tracing out one wing of a figure eight into the other wing. Where most network modelers see meaning in the orderly settling of their networks toward steady states, Freeman sees meaning in the waves, oscillations, and rhythms, and, in fact, in the chaotic dynamics that change the course of these patterns in response to outside stimuli.

Freeman isn't shy about pushing the implications of this model. For example, he sees the seemingly constant tendency of human beings to interpret the world in terms of cause and effect as a result of the brain's basic operation. The active brain follows a process that resembles a causal chain, and our inclination to see the world in these terms is a reflection of that characteristic. Paradoxically, he argues, chaotic dynamics, a science whose nature can be summed up by noting that it describes deterministic systems that appear to be random, ensures that we will never be able to understand the processes of the brain in causal terms.

Freeman hasn't always thought this. A model turned his own world upside down in 1983.

After years of recording patterns from the olfactory bulb, Freeman felt it was time to try to model this system in order to study the patterns he had observed. Were there correlations between behavior and the patterns? Did the patterns themselves have any kind of meaningful order? Building a model would also let Freeman see what kinds of distances and connections were involved.

The model was a way to test the most controversial assumption that Freeman had made. His method was built on simultaneously recording the EEG from large areas of the olfactory bulb. This gave him a picture of the changes in the electrical field for the whole ensemble of neurons. Other researchers questioned the relevance of Freeman's data, however, arguing that the EEG washed out the important information being carried by the firings of individual neurons. The information existed at the level of individual neurons, and Freeman's ensemble recording couldn't recover that behavior at all. In response Freeman argued that sensory information does indeed exist in single neurons, but that perceptual information coexists in the neuronal ensembles that the EEG measures.

Freeman had sorted the data for his model using adaptive filters, like those that inspired Bernard Widrow's work thirty years earlier. The filters would separate the meaningful information in the pattern from the random signal — the static in the telephone line — that had no meaning.

In 1983, to check that his filters were operating correctly, Freeman added randomly generated artificial noise to correspond to the noise he had seen in actual biological systems. He carefully ran a different randomly generated noise through each channel in the model. The model behaved as expected, but its output differed from the output of the bulb as shown by the EEG. Instead of simply canceling out, the EEG noise generated patterns in each channel. His analysis of the patterns shocked Freeman. "The noise, so called, was the same on all the channels with variations that had fooled us all these years into thinking it was independent." What Freeman had been assuming was meaningless random noise looked like it had a structure that could carry information.

His experimental tools seemed to have led him completely astray. Most physiological studies used anesthetized animals. In these animals the firing of individual neurons seemed directly correlated to a stimulus — a bar of light shown on the retina resulted in spike trains in the neural units. It seemed clear that the information was encoded in the temporal pulses produced by individual neurons, much as the information in a telegraph signal is encoded in dots and dashes.

Experiments with awake and normally responding animals produced a very different picture. A stimulus would produce unit activity with a variability that was almost uninterpretable. To counter that, researchers averaged their data and locked that average response to a stimulus. Most of what they actually observed they discarded as noise, just as Freeman had set out to do. However, if there were patterns in this welter of varying response, then maybe stimulus-locked averaging wasn't the correct procedure, and maybe the response of an individual neuron wasn't the important carrier of information.

Freeman rushed back to the biological data. Once he knew what to look for, this kind of coherent pattern showed up clearly over the whole olfactory bulb, not just in limited sections. That in itself was puzzling. Could this huge ensemble of neurons be the important unit to study? The conventional research agenda concentrated on individual neurons or on the interactions of much smaller networks. In his data, though, it looked like every neuron in the entire olfactory bulb was playing a role in discriminating each odor.

It wasn't surprising that Freeman has missed seeing any pattern in this "noise" for so long. Both engineering and information processing had told Freeman what a signal had to look like: it would be regular with easily described repetitions and variations; it would return to a baseline at some interval that would give the variation meaning; it would repeat itself at some interval. Scientists and engineers would be able to measure the distance between repetitions. It would also be linear — a change in initial conditions would produce a predictable change in the final condition.

The patterns Freeman was now seeing looked nothing like that. They were aperiodic. Often Freeman saw patterns that seemed similar, but they wouldn't recur at regular intervals, and while similar, the waveforms would never be exactly the same. Noise, the model drawn from engineering, simply didn't fit this biological system. The analogy from artificial information systems to the biological one didn't hold. In fact, he concluded, it had blinded him for years. "It did tremendous harm by imposing a false dichotomy. I spent twenty years looking for a signal and not finding it because it was aperiodic. It looked like what we think noise looks like."

But there was order here. The patterns clearly weren't random. At times they seemed to wander around a point, almost repeating themselves. And then they would suddenly switch into a completely different figure. Some of the switches between patterns, too, seemed to be related to the regular sniffing cycle of the rabbits that Freeman used in his experiments. Patterns clearly present during inhalation would disappear during exhalation, only to appear again during the next inhalation, as long as the stimulus odor remained the same.

Freeman realized that chaotic dynamics could explain what he was seeing. His EEG recordings surveyed the electric field potential created by a huge number of neurons. Each recording was a picture of the state of that group. Sequential recordings would show how that state changed over time.

The dynamics of the system seemed distinctly chaotic. When Freeman correlated his recordings with the odors he was using as stimuli, he discovered that it didn't take a big change in the odorant presented to the rabbit to cause an immense shift in pattern. The oscillation related to the new odorant wouldn't simply be a variant of the former pattern. It would be a completely different trace. Even when the odorants were closely related, the resulting traces would be radically different. This system was incredibly sensitive to small changes in initial conditions, a key sign of chaotic dynamics.

Freeman found another telltale sign. Repeating a rabbit's exposure to the same odorant after letting it sniff something different, even filtered air, would not produce exactly the same pattern. Smelling amyl at two different times produced patterns that were clearly related but not exactly the same. They seemed to be organized around attractors in the landscape, tracing a course around one like a comet traces a course around the sun. Each reappearance of amyl was characteristic, but not identical.

A chaotic system is extremely sensitive to initial conditions. "A very small stimulus can cause it to jump into a new condition," says Freeman. Chaos seems to explain the behavior of a pile of sand, for example. Add one grain and the pile gets just one grain bigger. Add another and another, and at some point the linear addition creates a totally new behavior. The sand slides in a miniature avalanche. It turns out that chaotic dynamics can find patterns here and explain why the sand pile's behavior changes so radically at this point. Clearly, chaotic dynamics is extremely provocative for someone trying to explain how the brain can discriminate between very subtle changes in the external environment.

Freeman's new vision wasn't exactly greeted with hosannas. In 1985 his major research grant was up for renewal, and Freeman wrote his plans to study chaos into his proposal. It came as somewhat of a shock when, after twenty years of support from the National Institutes of Mental Health, the proposal was approved but not funded. "They felt that maybe I was going overboard with this idea of chaos and that maybe I ought to go look at unit activity or something," he says. The proposal eventually got funded on a technicality. It had initially been sent to the wrong committee.

Freeman admits that in retrospect he isn't too surprised. After all, he sums up his own reaction in 1983 to his discovery in one word: dismay. "It meant there are no analytic solutions." The brain may be understandable, but it definitely won't be understandable in the ways that the solar system is understandable. It won't be reducible to mathematical relationships, although it may be possible to model it using mathematics. "It goes back to something von Neumann wrote and that was published posthumously," Freeman says. "'The language of the brain [is] not the language of mathematics,'" Freeman quotes. "'Whatever the system is, it cannot fail to differ considerably from what we consciously and explicitly consider as mathematics.'" Researchers who declare that their subject defies solutions can expect to have some funding difficulties.

To understand Freeman's vision, it helps to use a Hopfield network as a starting place. In that network the system settles toward an energy minimum, and that is the answer. In Freeman's world the landscape is set up so that there is no settling. The dynamics of the Hopfield landscape are constructed around the four traditional attractors. The alternatives in this landscape are either steady movement toward a sink and eventual settling there; steady movement away from a source; repeated circlings around a limit cycle in a periodic pattern that repeats at regular intervals; and a saddle between higher and lower features. To construct a useful Hopfield landscape, a neural network builder usually tries to arrange the topography so that the system will settle into a sink — ideally the globally deepest one.

The dynamics of Freeman's brain can include all these traditional attractors as well as strange attractors. Strange attractors give chaotic systems strange dynamics. They do provide order, pattern, and structure, but the order is not periodic and it is often extremely difficult to perceive. In fact, the structure of a chaotic dynamic system is no less determined by the inputs than is the structure of a periodic system. The pattern here isn't random. A specific chaotic system will always show the same kinds of order as long as the initial conditions are the same.

But this chaotic order, while deterministic, isn't linear or predictable. Chaotic systems may revolve around an attractor, like a traditional system revolves in a limit cycle, but it will not trace exactly the same path each time. The curves the system traces over time will show the resemblances of a family, not of identical twins.

A single system can show behavior that ranges from the regular and predictable to the ordered unpredictability of chaos to seemingly complete disorder. (Please note the caveat of "seemingly." Only decades ago systems that are now clearly chaotic were also thought to be without order. The apparent disorder of any specific system may not be in the physical world but result from our scientific tools.)

Chaotic systems have a strange kind of stability, one that bears only a slight resemblance to the classical idea of equilibrium. In the brain, says Freeman, "the system is not at equilibrium. That is a false image." In Freeman's solar system the planets don't follow the same path in each trip around the sun. If you traced the path of one of Freeman's planets over time, its track might bear some resemblance to the classical elliptical orbit part of the time. It would trace an approximation of the same path each time, but never exactly the same one. That is a kind of stability, though. Chaotic systems don't simply wander all over space. They settle into a pattern around an attractor. The famous pattern called the

Lorenz attractor, after its discoverer, Edward Lorenz, shows exactly this kind of stability.

But chaotic systems can also show a kind of immense, regular instability. In some attractors of the type plotted by Lorenz, the system can simply trace one wing of the butterfly over and over again and then suddenly flip over into the other wing. The pattern around a strange attractor can be thought of as a collection of potential paths, all of which are available to the system under some conditions.

Chaotic dynamics give the brain a tremendous set of tools. The system belongs to the class that Chris Langton likes to study, those balanced between rigid order and apparent randomness. The brain has access to a kind of stability that includes a library of potential variations that can each result from relatively minor changes. The flavor of the human brain — how easy it is for a human being to learn something new versus how easy it is to remember something old — may be the result of the balance in this specific dynamic system between stability and change.

Freeman says that he can imagine two different ways for the brain to use chaos. His first thought was that the various parts of the brain, the olfactory bulb or the visual cortex, for example,

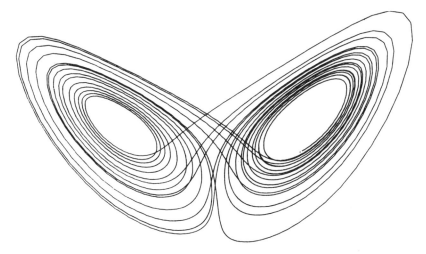

The famous butterfly attractor discovered by Edward Lorenz. The system cycles around the two lobes. Freeman wonders if this dynamic state could be a model for a thought.

would maintain a separate chaotic attractor for each stimulus. That view, which might be called the grandmother attractor theory, ran into immediate difficulties. Once the system has settled into a pattern around one attractor, how can it ever move to another? This kind of brain would wind up with a limited collection of very fixed ideas. The only way out of this that Freeman can see is some kind of reset mechanism that turns the brain off, or into a learning mode that frees the brain to seek new attractors.

Right now, Freeman prefers to believe that each brain area, rather than each stimulus, has an attractor. This global attractor in each brain area has to be much more complex and operate in many more dimensions than does a simple stimulus attractor. The possible pattern around that attractor isn't a simple shape such as a torus (roughly a doughnut) but rather a shape with multiple wings in multiple dimensions, each branching out from the attractor. The initial conditions, the specific odorant in the case of the olfactory bulb, pushes the system into one wing or the other of the attractor cycle. Freeman associates the restriction of the system to that wing with a specific spatial pattern of amplitude in the common chaotic waveform of the oscillation he records in his EEGs. It is the representation of the stimulus in the brain, the pattern that the brain understands as a specific smell, such as rotting fish or a blooming rose.

This system also needs to take into account the continued change in the brain itself. Since the brain is always growing, always changing, as a result of new experience and continued development, the dynamic system itself is ever shifting. Not only does brain activity move among different parts of an individual attractor, but also the attractors themselves change. The brain "has no attractors in the mathematical sense," Freeman says.

This represents a change from a "building block" metaphor to one of an "instruction set." This brain doesn't begin with feature detectors that result in partial representations that are put together into percepts. As Freeman wrote in 1989,

> Most cortical physiologists will continue to believe until they die that cortical percepts are assembled from visual primitives that are expressed in the discharge of point, edge, and bar "feature detectors" in visual cortex, perhaps in much the way that a cartoonist thinks he constructs an image of a face from lines, curves, and shaded surfaces.

Rather than being the building blocks of precepts, in Freeman's brain raw sensory data serve as an instruction set. Incoming data place the brain in the proper basin of attraction. They define a range of possible patterns around a specific attractor, and the chaotic pattern around that attractor then immediately replaces the raw sensory data with a global pattern of brain activity. A yellow onion smell may be an approximate figure eight extending to the left of an attractor. A red onion smell might be a similar figure eight extending from the attractor, but this time to the right. How can anyone imagine that the brain uses feature-detector neurons and derives logical pictures for anything? Freeman asks. All the biological evidence says that these detectors guide the brain to the appropriate attractors and then are replaced by mental percepts. It is not a logical process, but then most of brain function is prelogical, says Freeman.

Freeman has not proved that any of this is true. His theory indeed explains his data and certain behaviors of the brain, and that is realistically all that can be expected, he points out. As Bertrand Russell and Alfred North Whitehead showed years ago, axioms cannot be proved, only deductions from them. Freeman's new paradigm for the brain will stand if it can resolve some of the baffling complexities and blind alleys that bedevil the current view of the brain's operations. On the other hand the EEG may, as Richard Granger and others believe, measure the wrong thing, a shadow of the brain's operation with all the meaningful data wrung out. Freeman may be guilty of extrapolating an explanation that is true for the olfactory system to other parts of the brain that behave in very different ways. Chaos may be no more than a faddish theory. It may be possible to produce the kinds of behaviors that Freeman explains with chaos by other means. Stephen Grossberg believes that his series of ART networks can generate the necessary behaviors without using chaos. Although feedback loops are obviously a necessary part of any brain explanation, to this point Freeman's evidence doesn't show that chaos is the only possible dynamic that can explain the brain.

Freeman's theory, even if it is wrong, does draw us back to thinking about the nature of the brain, as expressed both in its structure and in its behavior. As he has collected more and more data that he believes buttress his vision, his own writings have changed in tone. In the last few years they have become no less combative, but they seem more willing to consider the philosophical implications of what Freeman thinks he knows. "You tend to worry about the bigger problems when you get older," he says.

Heraclitus and Kant slip easily into his conversation in 1991. In a dynamic system built around chaotic attractors, "it's like Heraclitus said, not only can't you put your foot in the same river twice, you can't have the same thought twice, either." In Freeman's system the same thought can't ever be expressed by the same exact pattern around a strange attractor, let alone by the firing of exactly the same neurons. That throws such concepts as identity and knowledge up for grabs. Freeman understands this, and he enjoys it. "Basically the animal is never the same twice. If you look at the same brain over even very short intervals of time when it is looking at what we commonly call the same stimulus, the brain isn't the same. It doesn't react the same. It doesn't produce the same patterns."

That, says Freeman, drives the engineers crazy. They can't accept a system that doesn't represent the same image in the same way twice. How can you build something — an object recognizer — when the code keeps shifting? he asks. If the brain doesn't generate stable patterns, it can't be the map that gives meaning to the symbols that represent things, Freeman says. "That means that stable map has to be somewhere else. But there is no stable map anywhere." One of the trickiest problems his system suggests is figuring out what the brain means by the same thought. If the patterns are always different, how much sameness and of what kind do they have to have for the brain to recognize the smell of amyl on two different trials?

Could it be that objects are ultimately unknowable? If the raw sensory data disappear so early on, to be replaced by shifting patterns that are purely internal, how can we be said to know what is outside our mind? "We can't know objects completely," Freeman says. "How can you say you know an object, except to the extent that you can interact with it?"

Freeman thinks the world may be as inscrutable as the brain. In 1990 he wrote:

> Chaotic behavior emerges from the nonlinear interaction of its parts, and global behavior in the system cannot be reduced to or deduced from knowledge about the characteristics and interactions among individual components. It appears to us as likely that during the next decade or so machines will be constructed that will display

useful traits heretofore restricted to biologic intelligence, and the irony will be that we will be unable to understand their processes in causal terms.

That doesn't mean we won't try, of course. In fact, Freeman thinks that the construction of our brain means we must. Time and cause and effect, he believes, are embedded in the biological brain. The exact state of the neuronal network is created by the past. Attention and expectation seem to be real behaviors in our brain that determine what we will perceive and express in that network. They represent our anticipation of our future needs. The interactions of the brain, the motor-sensory system, and the limbic system correspond to an internal flow of time. "Consciousness," writes Freeman, "bears the imprint of both the recent past and the expectation of future action, real or imagined."

Even though the search for a cause of our own intelligence and consciousness *may* be doomed to frustration, we nonetheless can't escape forming a posse and riding out into the unknown landscape. We believe in cause and effect because our brain is built around a time-bound connection between commands, priming, feedback, and confirmation. This is the ultimate essence of our relationship to the world. We may be seeking the cause of ourselves because the brain "feels" the world in that way. It would be ironic if we sought this ultimate goal at the command of a biological entity that will itself inevitably frustrate that search.

NOTES ON SOURCES

This book is based on the words and research of scientists in disciplines ranging from neurobiology to computer science. More than forty researchers patiently explained their work to me in interviews conducted from September 1988 through August 1991. Other material comes from the writings of these and other researchers. I have tried to clearly attribute the sources of quotations in the chapters themselves. In these notes I have simply noted the dates of those interviews. When a chapter draws heavily on a published work, I have often cited that work by title there, and I mention it below. A full citation will be found in the bibliography. In these notes I have also included published works that inform the general argument of a chapter.

The reader who is interested in pursuing any of these topics further will find other references in the bibliography.

PROLOGUE
I interviewed Federico Faggin and Carver Mead, separately and together, in San Jose and Pasadena on October 7, 1988; May 15, September 26, and December 2, 1989; and March 8, 1990. My information on Synaptics' early chips comes from published patents.

CHAPTER 1
The scene sketched here occurred at the 1990 Neural Information Processing Systems conference held in Denver, Colorado, from November 26 to 29, 1990. Papers describing Golomb's, Pomerleau's, Moore's, and Keesing's networks can be found in *Advances in Neural Information Processing Systems*, vol. 3 (1991).

Robert Hecht-Nielsen did not attend this conference. I interviewed him in his office at HNC in San Diego on December 5, 1989.

The quote from Thomas Kuhn is found on page 5 of Kuhn's *The Structure of Scientific Revolutions*, (1970).

CHAPTER 2

The presentation of the Adaline that I witnessed took place at the International Joint Conference on Neural Networks in Washington, D.C., on January 20, 1990. I interviewed Bernard Widrow in his Stanford office and got another demonstration of the Adaline on December 6, 1989. Widrow's 1960 paper with Hoff, "Adaptive Switching Circuits," is reprinted in *Neurocomputing: Foundations of Research* (1988).

I interviewed Carlos Tapang in his home office on September 25, 1989.

Marvin Minsky and Seymour Papert's 1969 *Perceptrons* was annotated by them in 1972 and expanded with an epilogue for the 1988 edition. Minsky's *The Society of Mind* is the best statement of his agents of mind theory. Papert's ruminations on perceptrons appear in his essay "One AI or Many?" in *The Artificial Intelligence Debate: False Starts, Real Foundations* (1988). His quote is found on pages 4–5. "Making a Mind Versus Modeling the Brain: Artificial Intelligence Back at a Branchpoint," by Hubert L. Dreyfus and Stuart Dreyfus in that same volume, provided a useful, brief history of the early development of artificial intelligence.

Frank Rosenblatt's work on the perceptron and its connections with the brain and psychology is best put forth in his *Principles of Neurodynamics: Perceptrons and the Theory of Brain Mechanisms* (1961). His 1958 essay "The Perceptron: A Probabilistic Model for Information Storage and Organization in the Brain" is reprinted in *Neurocomputing: Foundations of Research* (1988).

Donald Hebb's key work as far as neural network researchers are concerned is *The Organization of Behavior* (1949).

Herbert Simon and Craig Kaplan, "Foundations of Cognitive Science," and Allen Newell, Paul S. Rosenbloom, and John E. Laird, "Symbolic Architectures for Cognition," both in *Foundations of Cognitive Science* (1989), provided a useful context for the development of various approaches in artificial intelligence.

CHAPTER 3

I interviewed David Rumelhart in his office at Stanford on June 25, 1990; James McClelland in his office at Carnegie-Mellon on March 5, 1990; Geoffrey Hinton in his office at the University of Toronto on February 27, 1990; and Terry Sejnowski twice at the Salk Institute, on December 15, 1989, and on October 22, 1990.

The key text for the work of the PDP Group is the 1986 two-volume set *Parallel Distributed Processing: Explorations in the Microstructure of Cognition* (Vol. 1: *Foundations* and Vol. 2: *Psychological and Biological Models*). The past tense machine is described in "On Learning the Past Tenses of English Verbs," in volume 2. Hinton's pre–PDP Group period is represented by *Parallel Models of Associative Memory* (1981), which also includes alternative approaches to connectionist networks.

Terry Sejnowski and Charles Rosenberg's NETtalk is described in "NETtalk: A Parallel Network That Learns to Read Aloud," *Complex Systems* 1 (1987), and "Learning and Representation in Connectionist Models," in *Perspectives in Memory Research and Training* (1988). Some of Sejnowski's more philosophical ruminations on the nature of neural computation can be found in a joint paper with Christof Koch and Patricia Churchland, "Computational Neuroscience," *Science* 241 (September 9, 1988), and in Churchland and Sejnowski, "Perspectives on Cognitive Neuroscience," *Science* 242 (November 4, 1988).

The quotation from Ellen Markman that opens the chapter can be found on pages 11 and 12 of her book *Categorization and Naming in Children: Problems of Induction* (1989). Other material by Markman is from the same source. W. V. O. Quine's "Gavagai" example is discussed by Markman on pages 19 and 20.

Steven Pinker edited a special issue of *Cognition* (vol. 28, 1988) that included his critique with Alan Prince as well as other articles examining connectionist assumptions. The Pinker and Prince essay is "On Language and Connectionism: Analysis of a Parallel Distributed Processing Model of Language Acquisition." My understanding of Pinker's own work on language learning comes from his 1989 book *Learnability and Cognition*. M. D. S. Braine's exchange with his child is quoted on page 13 of that book. I used Pinker's essay "Language Acquisition," in *Foundations of Cognitive Science* (1989), for background on the status of language acquisition theory.

An interesting critique of NETtalk from a connectionist perspective is David Stork, "Sources of Neural Structure in Speech and Language Processing," in *Progress in Connectionism* (in press).

CHAPTER 4

I interviewed Richard Howard twice, once over the phone in November 1988 and once at his laboratory on October 5, 1989. At that time Yann Le Cun showed me the current version of the zip code reader at work. I have pieced together the gradual evolution of the zip code reader from J. S. Denker, et al., "Neural Network Recognizer for Handwritten Zip

Code Digits," in *Advances in Neural Information Processing Systems*, vol. 1 (1989); Denker, et al., "Automatic Learning, Rule Extraction, and Generalization," *Complex Systems* 1 (1987); and Yann Le Cun, et al., "Backpropagation Applied to Handwritten Zip Code Recognition," *Neural Computation* 1 (Winter 1989).

I interviewed Ben Yuhas at the 1990 Neural Information Processing Systems conference held in Denver, Colorado, on November 28, 1990. His work is described in Yuhas, et al., "Neural Network Models of Sensory Integration for Improved Vowel Recognition," *Proceedings of the IEEE* (October 1990). I also interviewed Alex Waibel at Carnegie-Mellon on his neural network approach to speech recognition on March 5, 1990. I found that interview extremely helpful and the work extremely interesting. I regret that Waibel's work didn't make it into this book.

CHAPTER 5

The core of this chapter is based on a series of interviews with Carver Mead and Sylvie Ryckebusch. I first interviewed Mead, with Federico Faggin, in October 1988 at Synaptics in San Jose. Other interviews, either at Synaptics or CalTech, took place on September 26 and December 2, 1989, and on March 7, 1990. My two interviews with Ryckebusch were on September 26, 1989, and March 7, 1990, both at CalTech. The scene in Mead's lab is a composite of two visits, that of September 26, 1989, and March 7, 1990.

For descriptions of particular networks by Mead, his students, and collaborators, I drew on *Analog VLSI and Neural Systems* (1989), and a collection that Mead edited with Mohammed Ismail, *Analog VLSI Implementation of Neural Systems* (1989). For Mead's sense of computational metaphor I drew on the introduction in the first of those volumes. I used Chapter 15 of that volume, written with Misha Mahowald, for background on silicon retinas, and Chapter 16, written with Richard Lyon, for background on electronic cochleas. In the second volume I used "Circuit Models of Sensory Transduction in the Cochlea" by Mead and John Lazzaro; "A Chip That Focuses an Image on Itself" by Tobi Delbrück; "Cooperative Stereo Matching Using Static and Dynamic Image Features" by Mahowald and Delbrück; and "Adaptive Retina" by Mead for background on the work by this group.

Ryckebusch's work is described in Ryckebusch, Bower, and Mead, "Modeling Small Oscillating Biological Networks in Analog VLSI," in *Advances in Neural Information Processing Systems*, vol. 1 (1989), and in Ryckebusch and Mead, "Analog VLSI Models of Oscillatory Biological Neural Circuits" (undated preprint).

The neurobiology in this chapter is from David Hubel, *Eye, Brain, and Vision* (1988); *Neurobiology* by Gordon Shepherd (2d edition, 1988); *The Synaptic Organization of the Brain,* edited by Shepherd (3d edition, 1990); and Kandel and Schwartz (eds.), *Principles of Neural Science* (2d edition, 1985).

Two other interviews helped me put Mead's work on neural networks in perspective: one with Paul Mueller at the University of Pennsylvania on February 22, 1990; and one with Dan Hammerstrom at his company Adaptive Solutions on March 12, 1990, about alternative approaches to neural computation.

CHAPTER 6

I interviewed Michael Mozer at the Neural Information Processing Systems conference on November 28, 1990, the day after his presentation of his Bach machine. Mozer graciously shared the then unpublished manuscript of his book, now published by MIT Press, *The Perception of Multiple Objects: A Connectionist Approach* (1991). Material on neglect dyslexia is drawn from Mozer and Marlene Behrmann, "On the Interaction of Selective Attention and Lexical Knowledge: A Connectionist Account of Neglect Dyslexia," *Journal of Cognitive Neuroscience* 2 (Spring 1990).

I interviewed Rodney Brooks in his office at MIT on December 6, 1990. The tour of the robots and the chance to watch Attila on the bench are owed to Colin Angle. For background I have drawn on Brooks's articles: "Elephants Don't Play Chess," *Robotics and Autonomous Systems* 6 (1990); "Intelligence Without Representation" (preprint, 1986); "A Robust Layered Control System for a Mobile Robot," *IEEE Journal of Robotics and Automation,* RA-2 (March 1986); and "A Robot That Walks: Emergent Behaviors from a Carefully Evolved Network," *Neural Computation* 1 (Summer 1989).

I have drawn Daniel Dennett's comments on intention from two books, *Brainstorms* (1980) and *The Intentional Stance* (1989). The summary of his thought that appears here owes more to the earlier work, especially the introduction and the essay entitled "Intentional Systems."

The bee experiment of James and Carol Gould is described on page 247 of Cheney and Seyfarth, *How Monkeys See the World* (1990).

My reporting on Bruce McNaughton's research draws on a presentation he gave at CalTech on March 7, 1990, and his articles "Neuronal Mechanisms for Spatial Computation and Information Storage," in *Neural Connections, Mental Computation* (1989), and "Hebb-Marr Networks and the Neurobiological Representation of Action in Space" (with Nadel), in *Neuroscience and Connectionist Theory* (1990).

CHAPTER 7

Dennett's quote is from p. x of *Brainstorms* (1980). His comments on the physical basis of thought are from that same volume.

I interviewed John Hopfield at CalTech on September 25, 1989. I have drawn on a wide variety of Hopfield's and Tank's published work, especially Hopfield's "Dynamics and Neural Network Computation," *International Journal of Quantum Chemistry: Quantum Chemistry Symposium* 24 (1990), and "Neural Networks and Physical Systems with Emergent Collective Computational Abilities," *Proceedings of the National Academy of Sciences* 79 (1982). Tank and Hopfield, "Collective Computation in Neuronlike Circuits," *Scientific American* 257 (December 1987), and Hopfield and Tank, "Computing with Neural Circuits: A Model," *Science* 233 (August 8, 1986), were also valuable.

I interviewed Josh Alspector and Robert Allen at Bellcore in October 1988. I interviewed Alspector again on April 22, 1990.

CHAPTER 8

I interviewed Eric Knudsen in his office at Stanford on July 19, 1990. My description of Knudsen's work on the computational maps in the brains of barn owls relies most heavily on his articles "Sensitive and Critical Periods in the Development of Sound Localization," in *From Message to Mind: Directions in Developmental Neurobiology* (1988), and "Computational Maps in the Brain" (with du Lac and Esterly), *Annual Review of Neuroscience* 10 (1987).

George Lakoff lays out his argument for the spatial and metaphorical basis of language in *Women, Fire, and Dangerous Things: What Categories Reveal About the Mind* (1987). I have relied on this work for my description of research by Kay and Berlin, Rosch, and Dixon. I interviewed Lakoff in Berkeley on March 15, 1991.

My understanding of the course of modern linguistics draws from Lakoff both in reading and conversation; from Chierchia and McConnell-Ginet, *Meaning and Grammar: An Introduction to Semantics* (1990); and two works by Noam Chomsky, *Language and Mind* (1972) and *Language and Problems of Knowledge* (1988).

The touchstone task is described in Feldman, Lakoff, Stolcke, and Hollbach Weber in an unpublished paper, "Miniature Language Acquisition: A Touchstone for Cognitive Science" (1990). I interviewed Feldman at the International Computer Science Institute on March 9, 1990. I have used his essay "Neural Representation of Conceptual Knowledge," in *Neural Connections, Mental Computation* (1989), for further background on representation and constraints. For background on contrary views I have drawn on J. A. Fodor, *Representations* (1981), and Fodor and Pylyshyn, "Connectionism and Cognitive Architecture: A Critical Analysis," *Cognition* 28 (1988).

CHAPTER 9

I first interviewed Roger Shepard at Stanford on March 21, 1990; a second, shorter interview took place on July 25, 1990. On that same day I interviewed Michael McBeath, who gave me a tour of the laboratory and conducted my exposure to apparent motion. McBeath's article "The Rising Fastball: Baseball's Impossible Pitch," was published in *Perception* 19 (1990). I have used Shepard's "Ecological Constraints on Internal Representation," *Psychological Review* 91 (October 1984), and "Internal Representation of Universal Regularities: A Challenge for Connectionism," in *Neural Connections, Mental Computation* (1989), as a summary of the earlier part of his work. "Toward a Universal Law of Generalization for Psychological Science" appeared in *Science* 237 (September 11, 1987). My characterization of Mark Gluck's work on psychological space is drawn from his poster at the 1990 Neural Information Processing Systems conference and from a short conversation with him there. The extensions of Shepard's work at the end of the chapter rely on a personal communication of April 30, 1991.

The article by Lettvin, Maturana, McCulloch, and Pitts, "What the Frog's Eye Tells the Frog's Brain," is reprinted in *Embodiments of Mind* (1965).

The characterization of AI by Hubert and Stuart Dreyfus is from page 18 of their essay "Making a Mind Versus Modeling the Brain," in *The Artificial Intelligence Debate* (1988). Many other neural network researchers have explored the way the brain may manipulate geometry and space. I interviewed Shun-ichi Amari on this topic on January 18, 1990.

CHAPTER 10

I interviewed Richard Granger twice: December 1, 1989, and October 23, 1990. He had a cold on the former occasion.

The following are additional sources for my description of the memory model and for the activities and theories of Gary Lynch's group at the University of California at Irvine: Granger, Ambros-Ingerson, and Lynch, "Derivation of Encoding Characteristics of Layer II Cerebral Cortex," *Journal of Cognitive Neuroscience* 1, no. 1 (1989); Granger, Whitson, and

Lynch, "Asymmetry in Cortical Networks Enhances Hierarchical Structuring," *Biological Cybernetics* (September 1989); Lynch, "Induction of Synaptic Potentiation in Hippocampus by Patterned Stimulation Involves Two Events," *Science* 232 (May 23, 1986), and *Synapses, Circuits, and the Beginnings of Memory* (1986); Lynch and Baudry, "The Biochemistry of Memory: A New and Specific Hypothesis," *Science* 224 (June 8. 1984), and Granger, Baudry, and Larson, "Cortical Encoding of Memory: Hypotheses Derived from Analysis and Simulation of Physiological Learning Rules in Anatomical Structures," in *Neural Connections, Mental Computations* (1989).

Charles Stevens was kind enough to discuss at length the status of research into the mechanisms of long-term potentiation and the differences between the postsynaptic and presynaptic schools. I interviewed Stevens at the Salk Institute on October 25, 1990.

My understanding of the types of memory is based upon Tulving and Schacter, "Priming and Human Memory Systems," *Science* 247 (January 19, 1990); and two works by Larry Squire, "Mechanisms of Memory," *Science* 232 (1986), and *Memory and Brain* (1987). In addition, I interviewed Squire on October 22, 1990, in his office at the Veterans Administration Hospital on the campus of the University of California at San Diego.

CHAPTER 11

I interviewed Kenneth Miller at the University of California, San Francisco on March 20, 1990. I also interviewed Michael Stryker on March 8, 1990, in his office there.

For descriptions of their model I drew upon Miller, Keller, and Stryker, "Ocular Dominance Column Development: Analysis and Simulation," *Science* 245 (August 11, 1989), and Miller, "Correlation-Based Models of Neural Development," *Neuroscience and Connectionist Theory* (1990).

My account of David Hubel and Torsten Wiesel's experiments that laid out the structure of dominance columns is based on Hubel, *Eye, Brain, and Vision* (1988). The discovery of edge detection is found on page 69. In addition, I used Hubel and Wiesel, "Functional Architecture of Macaque Monkey Visual Cortex," *Proceedings of the Royal Society of London (B)* 198 (1977); "Receptive Fields of Single Neurons in the Cat's Striate Cortex," *Journal of Physiology* 148 (1959); and "Brain Mechanisms of Vision," *Scientific American* (September 1979).

Michael Merzenich's evidence for neural reorganization is reported in Merzenich, et al., "Progression of Change Following Median Nerve Section in the Cortical Representation of the Hand in Areas 3b and 1 in Adult Owl and Squirrel Monkeys," *Neuroscience* 10 (1983).

CHAPTER 12

I interviewed Muriel Ross twice at Ames, once on September 22, 1989, and once on March 23, 1990. In addition, I saw a video of her animation at work at the International Joint Conference on Neural Networks in June 1989. The history of her system and its current details can be found in Ross, Dayhoff, and Mugler, "Toward Modeling a Dynamic Biological Neural Network," *Mathematics and Computer Modelling* 13 (1990); Ross, Cutler, Meyer, Lam, and Vaziri, "3-D Components of a Biological Neural Network Visualized in Computer Generated Imagery, Part 1," *Acta Otolaryngol* 109 (1990); and Ross, et al., "3-D Components of a Biological Neural Network Visualized in Computer Generated Imagery, Part 2," *Acta Otolaryngol* 109 (1990).

I used Wilfrid Rall's "Cable Theory For Dendritic Neurons," in *Methods in Neuronal Modeling* (1989), as my introduction to his work.

My history of the development of neural computation is largely reconstructed from Gordon Shepherd, "Microcircuits in the Nervous System," *Scientific American* 238 (February 1978), and from two interviews with Christof Koch on December 1, 1989, and October 23, 1990. I also used two of Shepherd's articles: "A Basic Circuit of Cortical Organization," in *Perspectives in Memory Research* (1988), and "The Significance of Real Neuron Architectures for Neural Network Simulations," in *Computational Neuroscience* (1990); as well as Shepherd (ed.), *The Synaptic Organization of the Brain* (3d edition, 1990). In that volume Shepherd and Koch, "Introduction to Synaptic Circuits," was especially useful.

Besides my interviews with Koch, my description of the MOSAIC model and the work in Thomas Brown's lab is drawn from an interview with Anthony Zador at Yale on March 26, 1991; Brown's presentation of MOSAIC in November 1990 at the Neural Information Processing Systems conference in Denver; and the article by Zador, Koch, and Brown, "Biophysical Model of a Hebbian Synapse," *Proceedings of the National Academy of Sciences* 87 (September 1990).

My description of Gerald Edelman's work is drawn from a lecture he gave at the 1990 International Joint Conference on Neural Networks and the following of his published works: "Cell-Adhesion Molecules: A Molecular Basis for Animal Form," *Scientific American* (April 1984); *Neural Darwinism* (1987); *The Remembered Present* (1990); and *Topo-*

biology: An Introduction to Molecular Embryology (1988); as well as Reeke, Finkel, Sporns, and Edelman, "Synthetic Neural Modeling: A Multilevel Approach to the Analysis of Brain Complexity," in *Signal and Sense: Local and Global Order in Perceptual Maps* (1990).

John Hopfield's remarks on the complexity of biological and physical systems are from Hopfield, "Physics, Computation, and Biology" (in press). For a contrasting view that relates quantum effects to the sources of noncomputability in the brain, a view that Hopfield explicitly rejects, see Roger Penrose, *The Emperor's New Mind: Concerning Computers, Minds, and the Laws of Physics* (1989).

The quotations from Charles Stevens on the NMDA receptor and its implications for neural networks are taken from my interview with him on October 25, 1990.

CHAPTER 13

David Stork introduced me to the role of genetic algorithms in neural network systems. I interviewed him on September 22, 1989, and then again at the 1990 International Joint Conference on Neural Networks. My understanding of his work at Ricoh is the result of conversations at the 1990 Neural Information Processing Systems conference.

My description of David Ackley's model is drawn from his presentation at the 1990 International Joint Conference on Neural Networks.

I interviewed Chris Langton and Doyne Farmer at the Los Alamos National Laboratory and a taco stand on November 30, 1990.

All work in genetic algorithms seems to trace its way back to John Holland. I used his *Adaptation in Natural and Artificial Systems* (1975).

My general understanding of chaos comes from a reading of James Gleick's *Chaos* (1987), of course, and Crutchfield, Farmer, Packard, and Shaw, "Chaos," *Scientific American* 255 (1986). I used Ian Stewart, *Does God Play Dice? The Mathematics of Chaos* (1989), to understand the mathematics underlying these dynamic systems. His examples of the calculator-produced systems begins on page 18.

I drew heavily on Langton (ed.), *Artificial Life: Santa Fe Institute Studies in the Sciences of Complexity*, vol. 6 (1989), for background on artificial life, and on Langton's introduction to that volume for his philosophical approach to his work.

CHAPTER 14

I interviewed Charles Gray on October 22, 1990. The evidence for phase-locked oscillations is presented in Gray, Engel, König, and Singer, "Mechanisms Underlying the Generation of Neuronal Oscillations in Cat Visual Cortex," in *Induced Rhythms in the Brain* (in press); "Stimulus-Dependent Neuronal Oscillations in Cat Visual Cortex: Receptive Field Properties and Feature Dependence," *European Journal of Neuroscience* 2 (1990); "Temporal Properties of Synchronous Oscillatory Neuronal Interactions in Cat Striate Cortex," in *Nonlinear Dynamics and Neural Networks* (in press).

I interviewed Christof Koch in his office at CalTech on December 1, 1989, and October 23, 1990. Crick and Koch laid out their theory of consciousness in "Towards a Neurobiological Theory of Consciousness," *The Neurosciences* 2 (1990).

I interviewed Walter Freeman three times: in June 1989 at the International Joint Conference on Neural Networks; on December 2, 1990; and on March 13, 1991. I have tried to piece together the development of Freeman's body of work from those three interviews and his publications: *Mass Action in the Nervous System* (1975); "On the Fallacy of Assigning an Origin to Consciousness," in *Machinery of the Mind* (1990); "A Physiological Hypothesis of Perception," *Perspectives in Biology and Medicine* 24 (Summer 1981); "Changes in Spatial Patterns of Rabbit Olfactory EEG with Conditioning to Odors" (with Schneider), *Psychophysiology* 19 (1982); and "How Brains Make Chaos in Order to Make Sense of the World" (with Skarda), *Behavioral and Brain Sciences* 10 (1987).

Stephen Grossberg's critique on the necessity of chaos can be found in Skarda and Freeman along with other critiques of Freeman's chaos theory.

I found Patricia Churchland's book *Neurophilosophy: Toward a Unified Science of the Mind-Brain* (1986) useful in focusing the argument of this chapter. I interviewed Churchland at the Salk Institute on October 22, 1990.

BIBLIOGRAPHY

Ackley, David H. "Associative Learning via Inhibitory Search." In *Advances in Neural Information Processing Systems*, vol. 1, edited by David S. Touretzky. San Mateo, Calif.: Morgan Kaufman, 1989.

Alkon, Daniel L. "Memory Storage and Neural Systems." *Scientific American* 261 (July 1989): 42–51.

Alkon, Daniel L., and J. Farley, eds. *Primary Neural Substrates of Learning and Behavioral Change*. New York: Cambridge University Press, 1984.

Allman, William F. *Apprentices of Wonder: Reinventing the Mind*. New York: Bantam, 1989.

Ambros-Ingerson, José; Granger, Richard; and Lynch, Gary. "Simulation of Paleocortex Performs Hierarchical Clustering." *Science* 247 (March 16, 1990): 1344–1348.

Anderson, James A. "Cognitive and Psychological Computation with Neural Models." *IEEE Transactions: Systems, Man, and Cybernetics* 13 (1983): 799–815.

Anderson, James A., and Hinton, G. E. "Models of Information Processing in the Brain." In *Parallel Models of Associative Memory*, edited by G. E. Hinton and James A. Anderson. Hillsdale, N.J.: Lawrence Erlbaum, 1989.

Anderson, James A., and Rosenfeld, Edward, eds. *Neurocomputing: Foundations of Research*. Cambridge: MIT Press, 1988.

Ballard, Dana H. "Cortical Connections and Parallel Processing: Structure and Function." *Behavioral and Brain Sciences* 9, no. 1 (1986): 67–120.

Ballard, Dana; Hinton, G. E.; and Sejnowski, T. J. "Parallel Visual Computation," *Nature* 306 (1983): 21–26.

Barlow, Robert B., Jr. "What the Brain Tells the Eye." *Scientific American* (April 1990): 90–95.

Baudry, Michel, and Lynch, Gary. "Glutamate Receptor Regulation and the Substrates of Memory." In *Neurobiology of Learning and Memory*, edited by Gary Lynch, James L. McGaugh, and Norman M. Weinberger. New York: The Guilford Press, 1984.

Baum, Eric B., and Haussler, David. "What Size Net Gives Valid Generalization?" *Neural Computation* 1 (Spring 1989): 151–160.

Bear, M. F.; Cooper, L. N.; and Ebner, F. F. "The Physiological Basis of a Theory for Synapse Modification." *Science* 237 (1987): 42–48.

Berger, Peter L., and Luckman, Thomas. *The Social Construction of Reality.* New York: Doubleday, 1966.

Bern, Marshall W., and Graham, Ronald L. "The Shortest-Network Problem." *Scientific American* 260 (January 1989): 84–89.

Bliss, T. V. P., and Dolphin, A. C. "Where Is the Locus of Long-Term Potentiation?" In *Neurobiology of Learning and Memory,* edited by Gary Lynch, James L. McGaugh, and Norman M. Weinberger. New York: The Guilford Press, 1984.

Brooks, Rodney A. "Elephants Don't Play Chess." *Robotics and Autonomous Systems* 6 (1990): 3–15.

———. "Intelligence Without Representation." Preprint. Artificial Intelligence Laboratory, MIT, 1986.

———. "A Robot That Walks: Emergent Behaviors from a Carefully Evolved Network." *Neural Computation* 1 (Summer 1989): 253–262.

———. "A Robust Layered Control System for a Mobile Robot." *IEEE Journal of Robotics and Automation* RA-2 (March 1986): 14–23.

Byrne, John H., and Berry, William O., eds. *Neural Models of Plasticity.* San Diego, Calif.: Academic Press, Inc., 1989.

Campbell, Jeremy. *The Improbable Machine.* New York: Simon and Schuster, 1989.

Cheney, Dorothy L., and Seyfarth, Robert M. *How Monkeys See the World.* Chicago: University of Chicago Press, 1990.

Chierchia, Gennaro, and McConnell-Ginet, Sally. *Meaning and Grammar: An Introduction to Semantics.* Cambridge: MIT Press, 1990.

Chomsky, Noam. *Language and Mind.* Cambridge: MIT Press, 1972.

———. *Language and Problems of Knowledge: The Managua Lectures.* Cambridge: MIT Press, 1988.

Churchland, Patricia S. *Neurophilosophy: Toward a Unified Science of the Mind-Brain.* Cambridge: MIT Press, 1986.

Churchland, Patricia S., and Sejnowski, Terrence J. "Neural Representation and Neural Computation." In *Neural Connections, Mental Computation,* edited by Lynn Nadel, Lynn A. Cooper, Peter Culicover, and R. Michael Harnish. Cambridge: MIT Press, 1989.

———. "Perspectives on Cognitive Neuroscience." *Science* 242 (November 4, 1988): 741–745.

Cooper, L. A. "Demonstration of a Mental Analog of an External Rotation." *Perception and Psychophysics* 19 (1976): 296–302.

———. "Mental Rotation of Random Two-Dimensional Shapes." *Cognitive Psychology* 7 (1975): 20–43.

Cooper, L. N.; Lieberman, F.; and Oja, E. "A Theory for the Acquisition and Loss of Neuron Specificity in Visual Cortex." *Biological Cybernetics* 33 (1979): 9–28.

Cowan, Jack D., and Sharp, David H. "Neural Nets and Artificial Intelligence." In *The Artificial Intelligence Debate: False Starts, Real Foundations,* edited by Stephen R. Graubard. Cambridge: MIT Press, 1988.

Crick, Francis. *What Mad Pursuit: A Personal View of Scientific Discovery.* New York: Basic Books, 1988.

Crick, Francis, and Asanuma, C. "Certain Aspects of the Anatomy and Physiology of the Cerebral Cortex." In *Parallel Distributed Processing: Explorations in the Microstructure of Cognition,* vol. 2, edited by D. E. Rumelhart and J. L. McClelland. Cambridge: MIT Press, 1986.

Crick, Francis, and Koch, Christof. "Towards a Neurobiological Theory of Consciousness." *The Neurosciences* 2 (1990).

Crutchfield, James P.; Farmer, J. Doyne; Packard, Norman H.; and Shaw, Robert S. "Chaos." *Scientific American* 255 (1986): 46–57.

Denker, J. S.; Gardner, W. R.; Graff, H. P.; Henderson, D.; Howard, R. E.; Hubbard, W.; Jackel, L. D.; Baird, H. S.; and Guyon, I. "Neural Network Recognizer for Handwritten Zip Code Digits." In *Advances in Neural Information Processing Systems,* vol. 1, edited by David S. Touretzky. San Mateo, Calif.: Morgan Kaufman, 1989.

Denker, J. S.; Schwartz, D.; Wittner, B.; Solla, S.; Hopfield, J.; Howard, R.; and Jackel, L. "Automatic Learning, Rule Extraction, and Generalization." *Complex Systems* 1 (1987): 877–922.

Dennett, D. C. *Brainstorms: Philosophical Essays on Mind and Psychology.* Cambridge: MIT Press, 1980.

———. *The Intentional Stance.* Cambridge: MIT Press, 1989.

Dreyfus, Hubert L., and Dreyfus, Stuart E. "Making a Mind Versus Modeling the Brain: Artificial Intelligence Back at a Branchpoint." In *The Artificial Intelligence Debate: False Starts, Real Foundations,* edited by Stephen R. Graubard. Cambridge: MIT Press, 1988.

Dudek, F. Edward, and Traub, Roger D. "Local Synaptic and Electrical Interactions in Hippocampus: Experimental Data and Computer Simulations." In *Neural Models of Plasticity,* edited by John H. Byrne and William O. Berry. San Diego, Calif.: Academic Press, Inc., 1989.

Eckhorn, R.; Reitboeck, H. J.; Arndt, M.; and Dicke, P. "Feature Linking via Synchronization Among Distributed Assemblies: Simulations of Results from Cat Visual Cortex." *Neural Computation* 2 (Fall 1990): 293–307.

Edelman, G. M. *Neural Darwinism.* New York: Basic Books, 1987.

———. *The Remembered Present.* New York: Basic Books, 1990.

———. "Topobiology." *Scientific American* 260 (May 1989): 76–88.

———. *Topobiology: An Introduction to Molecular Embryology.* New York: Basic Books, 1988.

Edelman, G. M., and Reeke, G. N., Jr. "Selective Networks Capable of Representative Transformations, Limited Generalizations, and Associative Memory." *Proceedings of the National Academy of Sciences* 79 (1982): 2091–2095.

Farmer, J. Doyne. "A Rosetta Stone for Connectionism." *Physica D* 42 (1990): 153–187.

Feldman, J. A. "A Connectionist Model of Visual Memory." In *Parallel Models of Associative Memory,* edited by G. E. Hinton and J. A. Anderson. Hillsdale, N.J.: Lawrence Erlbaum, 1981.

————. "Neural Representation of Conceptual Knowledge." In *Neural Connections, Mental Computation*, edited by Lynn Nadel, Lynn A. Cooper, Peter Culicover, and R. Michael Harnish. Cambridge: MIT Press, 1989.

Feldman, J. A., and Ballard, F. H. "Connectionist Models and Their Properties." *Cognitive Science* 6 (1982): 205–254.

Feldman, J. A.; Lakoff, George; Stolcke, Andreas; and Hollbach Weber, Susan. "Miniature Language Acquisition: A Touchstone for Cognitive Science." Unpublished paper. International Computer Science Institute, 1990.

Finkel, Leif H.; Reeke, George N., Jr.; and Edelman, Gerald M. "A Population Approach to the Neural Basis of Perceptual Categorization." In *Neural Connections, Mental Computation*, edited by Lynn Nadel, Lynn A. Cooper, Peter Culicover, and R. Michael Harnish. Cambridge: MIT Press, 1989.

Fodor, J. A. *The Language of Thought.* Cambridge: MIT Press, 1979.

————. *Modularity of Mind.* Cambridge: MIT Press, 1983.

————. *Representations.* Cambridge: MIT Press, 1981.

Foster, Tom C.; Castro, Carl A.; and McNaughton, Bruce L. "Spatial Selectivity of Rat Hippocampal Neurons: Dependence on Preparedness of Movement." *Science* 244 (June 30, 1989): 1580–1582.

Freeman, Walter J. *Mass Action in the Nervous System.* New York: Academic Press, Inc., 1975.

————. "On the Fallacy of Assigning an Origin to Consciousness." In *Machinery of the Mind*, edited by E. Roy John. Boston: Birkhauser, 1990.

————. "A Physiological Hypothesis of Perception." *Perspectives in Biology and Medicine* 24 (Summer 1981): 561–592.

Freeman, Walter J., and Schneider, W. "Changes in Spatial Patterns of Rabbit Olfactory EEG with Conditioning to Odors." *Psychophysiology* 19 (1982): 44–56.

Freeman, Walter J., and Skarda, Christine A. "How Brains Make Chaos in Order to Make Sense of the World." *Behavioral and Brain Sciences* 10 (1987): 161–195.

Fukushima, K., and Miyake, S. "Neocognitron: A New Algorithm for Pattern Recognition Tolerant of Deformation and Shifts in Position." *Pattern Recognition* SMC-13, no. 5 (1984): 455–469.

Gallagher, Michela. "Current Perspectives on Memory Systems and Their Modulation." In *Neurobiology of Learning and Memory*, edited by Gary Lynch, James L. McGaugh, and Norman M. Weinberger. New York: The Guilford Press, 1984.

Gallistel, Charles R. *The Organization of Learning.* Cambridge: MIT Press, 1990.

Gardner, Howard. *The Mind's New Science: A History of the Cognitive Revolution.* New York: Basic Books, 1985.

Gazzaniga, Michael S. "Advances in Cognitive Neurosciences: The Problem of Information Storage in the Human Brain." In *Neurobiology of Learning and Memory*, edited by Gary Lynch, James L. McGaugh, and Norman M. Weinberger. New York: The Guilford Press, 1984.

Gelperin, Alan; Tank, David W.; and Tesauro, Gerald. "Olfactory Processing and Associative Memory: Cellular and Modeling Studies." In *Neural Models of*

Plasticity, edited by John H. Byrne and William O. Berry. San Diego, Calif.: Academic Press, Inc., 1989.

Gibson, J. J. *The Ecological Approach to Visual Perception.* Boston: Houghton Mifflin, 1979.

———. "Ecological Optics." *Vision Research* 1 (1961): 253–262.

Gilder, George. *Microcosm: The Quantum Revolution in Economics and Technology.* New York: Simon and Schuster, 1989.

Gleick, James. *Chaos: Making a New Science.* New York: Viking, 1987.

Gluck, Mark A., and Rumelhart, David E., eds. *Neuroscience and Connectionist Theory.* Hillsdale, N.J.: Lawrence Erlbaum, 1990.

Golomb, B.; Lawrence, D.; and Sejnowski, T. J. "Sexnet: A Neural Network Identifies Sex from Human Faces." In *Advances in Neural Information Processing Systems*, vol. 3, edited by Richard Lippmann, John Moody, and David S. Touretzky. San Mateo, Calif.: Morgan Kaufman, 1991.

Gould, Stephen Jay. "What, If Anything, Is a Zebra?" In *Hen's Teeth and Horse's Toes.* New York: Norton, 1984.

Granger, Richard; Ambros-Ingerson, José; and Lynch, Gary. "Derivation of Encoding Characteristics of Layer II Cerebral Cortex." *Journal of Cognitive Neuroscience* 1, no. 1 (1989): 61–87.

Granger, Richard; Ambros-Ingerson, José; Staubli, Ursula; and Lynch, Gary. "Memorial Operation of Multiple, Interacting Simulated Brain Structures." In *Neuroscience and Connectionist Models*, edited by Mark Gluck and David Rumelhart. Hillsdale, N.J.: Lawrence Erlbaum, 1989.

Graubard, Stephen R., ed. *The Artificial Intelligence Debate: False Starts, Real Foundations.* Cambridge: MIT Press, 1988.

Gray, Charles M.; Engel, Andreas K.; König, Peter; and Singer, Wolf. "Mechanisms Underlying the Generation of Neuronal Oscillations in Cat Visual Cortex." In *Induced Rhythms in the Brain.* edited by T. Bullock and E. Basar. In press.

———. "Stimulus-Dependent Neuronal Oscillations in Cat Visual Cortex: Receptive Field Properties and Feature Dependence." *European Journal of Neuroscience* 2 (1990): 607–619.

———. "Temporal Properties of Synchronous Oscillatory Neuronal Interactions in Cat Striate Cortex." In *Nonlinear Dynamics and Neural Networks*, edited by H. G. Schuster and W. Singer. In press.

Grossberg, Stephen. "Adaptive Pattern Classification and Universal Recoding. Part 1: Parallel Development and Coding of Neural Feature Detectors." *Biological Cybernetics* 23 (1976): 121–134. Reprinted in *Neurocomputing: Foundations of Research*, edited by James A. Anderson and Edward Rosenfeld. Cambridge: MIT Press, 1988.

———. "How Does a Brain Build a Cognitive Code?" *Psychological Review* 87 (1980): 1–51. Reprinted in *Neurocomputing: Foundations of Research*, edited by James A. Anderson and Edward Rosenfeld. Cambridge: MIT Press, 1988.

Grossberg, Stephen, ed. *The Adaptive Brain.* Vol. 1: *Cognition, Learning, Reinforcement, and Rhythm.* New York: Elsevier, 1987.

———. *Neural Networks and Natural Intelligence.* Cambridge: MIT Press, 1988.

Hammerstrom, Dan; Leen, Todd; and Means, Eric. "Dynamics and VLSI Implementation of Self-Organizing Networks." Draft paper, March 12, 1990.

Hebb, Donald O. *The Organization of Behavior.* New York: Wiley, 1949.

Hinton, G. E. "Implementing Semantic Networks in Parallel Hardware." In *Parallel Models of Associative Memory,* edited by G. E. Hinton and J. A. Anderson. Hillsdale, N. J.: Lawrence Erlbaum, 1981.

Hinton, G. E., and Anderson, J. A., eds. *Parallel Models of Associative Memory.* Hillsdale, N.J.: Lawrence Erlbaum, 1981.

Hinton, G. E., and Nolan, S. J. "How Learning Can Guide Evolution." *Complex Systems* 1 (1987): 495–502.

Hofstadter, D. R. "Artificial Intelligence: Subcognition as Computation." In *The Study of Information: Interdisciplinary Messages,* edited by F. Machlup and U. Mansfield. New York: Wiley, 1983.

———. "Lisp: Lists and Recursion." In *Metamagical Themas.* New York: Basic Books, 1985.

———. "Waking Up from the Boolean Dream, or, Subcognition as Computation." In *Metamagical Themas.* New York: Basic Books, 1985.

Holland, John H. *Adaptation in Natural and Artificial Systems.* Ann Arbor: University of Michigan Press, 1975.

Hooper, Judith, and Teresi, Dick. *The 3-Pound Universe: The Brain — From the Chemistry of the Mind to the New Frontiers of the Soul.* New York: Dell, 1986.

Hopfield, John J. "Dynamics and Neural Network Computation." *International Journal of Quantum Chemistry: Quantum Chemistry Symposium* 24 (1990): 633–644.

———. "Neural Networks and Physical Systems with Emergent Collective Computational Abilities." *Proceedings of the National Academy of Sciences* 79 (1982): 2554–2558. Reprinted in *Neurocomputing: Foundations of Research,* edited by James A. Anderson and Edward Rosenfeld. Cambridge: MIT Press, 1988.

———. "Neurons with Graded Response Have Collective Computational Properties Like Those of Two-State Neurons." *Proceedings of the National Academy of Sciences* 81 (1984): 3088–3092. Reprinted in *Neurocomputing: Foundations of Research,* edited by James A. Anderson and Edward Rosenfeld. Cambridge: MIT Press, 1988.

———. "Physics, Computation, and Biology." In press.

Hopfield, John J., and Tank, David. "Collective Computation in Neuronlike Circuits." *Scientific American* 257 (December 1987): 104–114.

———. "Computing with Neural Circuits: A Model." *Science* 233 (August 8, 1986): 625–633.

———. "Neural Architecture and Biophysics for Sequence Recognition." In *Neural Models of Plasticity,* edited by John H. Byrne and William O. Berry. San Diego, Calif.: Academic Press, Inc., 1989.

Hsu, Feng-hsiung; Anantharaman, Thomas; Campbell, Murray; and Nowatzk,

Andreas. "A Grandmaster Chess Machine." *Scientific American* 263 (October 1990): 44–50.

Hubel, David. *Eye, Brain, and Vision.* New York: Scientific American Library, 1988.

———. "Vision and the Brain." *Bulletin of the American Academy of Arts and Sciences* 31 (1978): 17–28.

Hubel, David, and Wiesel, Torsten. "Functional Architecture of Macaque Monkey Visual Cortex." *Proceedings of the Royal Society of London (B)* 198 (1977): 1–59.

———. "Receptive Fields of Single Neurons in the Cat's Striate Cortex." *Journal of Physiology* 148 (1959): 574–591.

———. "Receptive Fields, Binocular Interaction and Functional Architecture in the Cat's Visual Cortex." *Journal of Physiology* 160 (1962): 106–154.

Hurlbert, Anya C., and Poggio, Tomaso. "Making Machines (and Artificial Intelligence) See." In *The Artificial Intelligence Debate: False Starts, Real Foundations,* edited by Stephen R. Graubard. Cambridge: MIT Press, 1988.

———. "Visual Information: Do Computers Need Attention?" *Nature* 321 (June 12, 1986): 651–652.

Johnson, George. *In the Palaces of Memory.* New York: Knopf, 1991.

———. *Machinery of the Mind: Inside the New Science of Artificial Intelligence.* New York: Times Books, 1986.

———. "Memory: Learning How It Works." *New York Times Magazine* (August 9, 1987): 16–21.

Johnson, R. Colin, and Brown, Chappell. *Cognizers: Neural Networks and Machines That Think.* New York: Wiley, 1988.

Johnson-Laird, P. N. "Cognition: Connections and Controversy." *Nature* 330 (November 5, 1987): 12–13.

———. "Mental Models." In *Foundations of Cognitive Science,* edited by Michael I. Posner. Cambridge: MIT Press, 1989.

Kandel, Eric R. *Behavior Biology of Aplysia.* San Francisco: W. H. Freeman, 1979.

———. *A Cell-Biological Approach to Learning.* Bethesda, Md.: Society for Neuroscience, 1978.

———. "From Metapsychology to Molecular Biology: Explorations into the Nature of Anxiety." *American Journal of Psychiatry* 140 (1983): 433–442.

———. "Small Systems of Neurons." *Scientific American* 241 (1979): 66–76.

Kandel, Eric R., and Hawkins, Robert D. "Steps Toward a Cell-Biological Alphabet for Elementary Forms of Learning." In *Neurobiology of Learning and Memory,* edited by Gary Lynch, James L. McGaugh, and Norman M. Weinberger. New York: The Guilford Press, 1984.

Kandel, Eric R., and Schwartz, James H., eds. *Principles of Neural Science.* 2d ed. New York: Elsevier, 1985.

Kesner, Raymond P. "The Neurobiology of Memory: Implicit and Explicit Assumptions." In *Neurobiology of Learning and Memory,* edited by Gary Lynch, James L. McGaugh, and Norman M. Weinberger. New York: The Guilford Press, 1984.

Klose, Monika, and Bentley, David. "Transient Pioneer Neurons Are Essential for Formation of an Embryonic Peripheral Nerve." *Science* 245 (September 1, 1989): 982–984.

Knudsen, Eric I.; du Lac, Sascha; and Esterly, Steven D. "Computational Maps in the Brain." *Annual Review of Neuroscience* 10 (1987): 41–65.

Knudsen, Eric I., and Knudsen, Phyllis F. "Sensitive and Critical Periods for Visual Calibration of Sound Localization by Barn Owls." *Journal of Neuroscience* 10 (January 1990): 222–232.

Knudsen, Eric I., and Konishi, M. "Mechanisms of Sound Localization in the Barn Owl (Tyto Alba)." *Journal of Comparative Physiology* 133 (1979): 13–21.

———. "A Neural Map of Auditory Space in the Owl." *Science* 200 (1978): 795–797.

Koch, Christof. "Review of Neural and Brain Modeling." *Nature* 335 (September 15, 1988): 213–214.

Koch, Christof; Luo, Jim; Hutchinson, James; and Mead, Carver. "Optical Flow and Surface Interpolation in Resistive Networks: Algorithms and Analog VLSI Chips." California Institute of Technology preprint, July 4, 1989.

Koch, Christof, and Segev, Idan, eds. *Methods in Neuronal Modeling.* Cambridge: MIT Press, 1989.

Kohonen, Teuvo. *Associative Memory: A System-Theoretic Approach.* West Berlin: Springer-Verlag, 1977.

———. *Content Addressable Memories.* New York: Springer-Verlag, 1980.

———. *Self-Organization and Associative Memory.* New York: Springer-Verlag, 1984.

Konishi, M. "Birdsong: From Behavior to Neuron." *Annual Review of Neuroscience* 8 (1985): 125–170.

Kuhn, Thomas S. *The Structure of Scientific Revolutions.* 2d ed. Chicago: University of Chicago Press, 1970.

Kuperstein, Michael. "Neural Model of Adaptive Hand-Eye Coordination for Single Postures." *Science* 239 (March 11, 1988): 1308–1311.

Lachter, J., and Bever, T. G. "The Relation between Linguistic Structure and Theories of Language Learning — A Constructive Critique of Some Connectionist Learning Models." *Cognition* 28 (1988): 195–247.

Lakoff, G. *Women, Fire, and Dangerous Things: What Categories Reveal About the Mind.* Chicago: University of Chicago Press, 1987.

Langton, Christopher G., ed. *Artificial Life: Santa Fe Institute Studies in the Sciences of Complexity,* vol. 6. Redwood City, Calif.: Addison-Wesley, 1989.

Larson, John, and Lynch, Gary. "Induction of Synaptic Potentiation in Hippocampus by Patterned Stimulation Involves Two Events." *Science* 232 (May 23, 1986): 985–988.

———. "Role of N-Methyl-D-Asparate Receptors in the Induction of Synaptic Potentiation by Burst Stimulation Patterned after the Hippocampal Theta Rhythm." *Brain Research* 441 (1988): 111–118.

Larson, John; Wong, D.; and Lynch, Gary. "Patterned Stimulation at the Theta Frequency Is Optimal for the Induction of Hippocampal Long-Term Potentiation." *Brain Research* 386 (1986): 347–350.

Lashley, Karl. "In Search of the Engram." *Society of Experimental Biology Symposium. Number 4: Physiological Mechanisms in Animal Behavior.* Cambridge: Cambridge University Press, 1950.

Lazzaro, John, and Mead, Carver A. "A Silicon Model of Auditory Localization." *Neural Computation* 1 (Spring 1989): 47–57.

Le Cun, Y.; Boser, B.; Denker, J. S.; Henderson, D.; Howard, R. E.; Hubbard, W.; and Jackel, L. D. "Backpropagation Applied to Handwritten Zip Code Recognition." *Neural Computation* 1 (Winter 1989): 541–551.

Lettvin, J. Y.; Maturana, H. R.; McCulloch, W. S.; and Pitts, W. H. "What the Frog's Eye Tells the Frog's Brain." In Warren S. McCulloch, *Embodiments of Mind.* Cambridge: MIT Press, 1965.

Li, Z., and Hopfield, J. J. "Modeling the Olfactory Bulb and Its Neural Oscillatory Processings." *Biological Cybernetics* 61 (1989): 379–392.

Linsker, Ralph. "Self-Organization in a Perceptual Network." *IEEE Computer* 21 (March 1988): 105–117.

Livingstone, M. S. "Art, Illusion, and the Visual System." *Scientific American* 258 (1988): 78–85.

Lynch, Gary. *Synapses, Circuits, and the Beginnings of Memory.* Cambridge: MIT Press, 1986.

———. "What Memories Are Made Of." *The Sciences* 25 (September/October 1985): 38–43.

Lynch, Gary, and Baudry, Michel. "The Biochemistry of Memory: A New and Specific Hypothesis." *Science* 224 (June 8, 1984): 1057–1063.

Lynch, Gary; Granger, Richard; Baudry, Michel; and Larson, John. "Cortical Encoding of Memory: Hypotheses Derived from Analysis and Simulation of Physiological Learning Rules in Anatomical Structures." In *Neural Connections, Mental Computation,* edited by Lynn Nadel, Lynn A. Cooper, Peter Culicover, and R. Michael Harnish. Cambridge: MIT Press, 1989.

Lynch, Gary; Granger, Richard; and Larson, John. "Some Possible Functions of Simple Cortical Networks Suggested by Computer Modeling." In *Neural Models of Plasticity,* edited by John H. Byrne and William O. Berry. San Diego, Calif.: Academic Press, Inc., 1989.

McBeath, Michael. "The Rising Fastball: Baseball's Impossible Pitch," *Perception* 19 (1990): 545–552.

McClelland, James L., and Rumelhart, David E. "An Interactive Activation Model of Context Effects in Letter Perception, Part 1: An Account of Basic Findings." *Psychological Review* 88 (1981): 375–407. Reprinted in *Neurocomputing: Foundations of Research,* edited by James A. Anderson and Edward Rosenfeld. Cambridge: MIT Press, 1988.

———. "An Interactive Activation Model of Context Effects in Letter Perception, Part 2: The Contextual Enhancement Effect and Some Tests and Extensions of the Model." *Psychological Review* 89 (1982): 60–94.

McCormick, David A. "Membrane Properties and Neurotransmitter Actions." In *The Synaptic Organization of the Brain.* 3d ed., edited by Gordon Shepherd. New York: Oxford University Press, 1990.

McCulloch, Warren S., and Pitts, Walter H. "How We Know Universals: The Perception of Auditory and Visual Forms." In Warren S. McCulloch, *Embodiments of Mind.* Cambridge: MIT Press, 1965.

———. "A Logical Calculus of the Ideas Immanent in Nervous Activity." In Warren S. McCulloch, *Embodiments of Mind.* Cambridge: MIT Press, 1965.

McNaughton, Bruce L. "Long-Term Synaptic Enhancement and Short-Term Potentiation in Rat Fascia Dentata Act Through Different Mechanisms." *Journal of Physiology* 324 (1982): 249–262.

———. "Neuronal Mechanisms for Spatial Computation and Information Storage." In *Neural Connections, Mental Computation,* edited by Lynn Nadel, Lynn A. Cooper, Peter Culicover, and R. Michael Harnish. Cambridge: MIT Press, 1988.

McNaughton, Bruce L.; Barnes, Carol A.; and Rao, G. "Presynaptic Versus Postsynaptic Control Over Long-Term Synaptic Enhancement." In *Neurobiology of Learning and Memory,* edited by Gary Lynch, James L. McGaugh, and Norman M. Weinberger. New York: The Guilford Press, 1984.

McNaughton, Bruce L., and Nadel, Lynn. "Hebb-Marr Networks and the Neurobiological Representation of Action in Space." In *Neuroscience and Connectionist Theory,* edited by Mark A. Gluck and David E. Rumelhart. Hillsdale, N.J.: Lawrence Erlbaum, 1990.

Markman, Ellen M. *Categorization and Naming in Children: Problems of Induction.* Cambridge: MIT Press, 1989.

Marr, David. "Simple Memory: A Theory for Archicortex." *Philosophical Transactions of the Royal Society (B)* (1971): 23–81.

———. *Vision: A Computational Investigation into the Human Representation and Processing of Visual Information.* San Francisco: W. H. Freeman, 1982.

Marr, David, and Poggio, T. "Cooperative Computation of Stereo Disparity." *Science* 194 (1976): 283–287.

Mead, Carver. *Analog VLSI and Neural Systems.* Reading, Mass.: Addison-Wesley, 1989.

———. *Introduction to VLSI Systems.* Reading, Mass.: Addison-Wesley, 1980.

Mead, Carver, and Ismail, Mohammed, eds. *Analog VLSI Implementation of Neural Systems.* Boston: Kluwer Academic Publishers, 1989.

Mervis, C., and Rosch, E. "Categorization of Natural Objects." *Annual Review of Psychology* 32 (1981): 89–115.

Merzenich, M. M.; Kaas, J. H.; Wall, J. T.; Sur, M.; Nelson, R. J.; and Felleman, D. J. "Progression of Change Following Median Nerve Section in the Cortical Representation of the Hand in Areas 3b and 1 in Adult Owl and Squirrel Monkeys." *Neuroscience* 10 (1983): 639–665.

Miller, Donald L., and Pekny, Joseph F. "Exact Solution of Large Asymmetric Traveling Salesman Problems." *Science* 251 (February 15, 1991): 754–761.

Miller, G. A. "The Magical Number Seven: Plus or Minus Two. Some Limits on Our Capacity for Processing Information." *Psychology Review* 9 (1956): 81–97.

Miller, Kenneth D. "Correlation-Based Models of Neural Development," In *Neuroscience and Connectionist Theory,* edited by Mark A. Gluck and David E. Rumelhart. Hillsdale, N.J.: Lawrence Erlbaum, 1990.

————. "Derivation of Linear Hebbian Equations from a Nonlinear Hebbian Model of Synaptic Plasticity." *Neural Computation* 2 (Fall 1990): 321–333.

Miller, Kenneth D.; Keller, Joseph B.; and Stryker, Michael P. "Ocular Dominance Column Development: Analysis and Simulation." *Science* 245 (August 11, 1989): 605–615.

Minsky, Marvin. *The Society of Mind.* New York: Simon and Schuster, 1988.

Minsky, Marvin, and Papert, Seymour. *Perceptrons.* Cambridge: MIT Press, 1969 (revised 1988).

Mozer, Michael C. *The Perception of Multiple Objects: A Connectionist Approach.* Cambridge: MIT Press, 1991.

Mozer, Michael C., and Behrmann, Marlene. "On the Interaction of Selective Attention and Lexical Knowledge: A Connectionist Account of Neglect Dyslexia," *Journal of Cognitive Neuroscience* 2 (Spring 1990): 96–123.

Mugler, D. H., and Ross, M. D. "Vestibular Receptor Cells and Signal Detection." *Mathematics Computer Modelling* 13 (1990): 85–92.

Nadel, Lynn; Cooper, Lynn A.; Culicover, Peter; and Harnish, R. Michael, eds. *Neural Connections, Mental Computation.* Cambridge: MIT Press, 1989.

Nadel, Lynn, and Wexler, Kenneth. "Neurobiology, Representations, and Memory." In *Neurobiology of Learning and Memory,* edited by Gary Lynch, James L. McGaugh, and Norman M. Weinberger. New York: The Guilford Press, 1984.

Newell, Allen. "Physical Symbol Systems." *Cognitive Science* 4 (1980): 135–183.

————. *Unified Theories of Cognition.* Cambridge: Harvard University Press, 1990.

Newell, Allen; Rosenbloom, Paul S.; and Laird, John E. "Symbolic Architectures for Cognition." In *Foundations of Cognitive Science,* edited by Michael I. Posner. Cambridge: MIT Press, 1989.

O'Keefe, J., and Nadel, L. *The Hippocampus as a Cognitive Map.* Oxford: Oxford University Press, 1978.

Packard, Norman H. "Intrinsic Adaptation in a Simple Model for Evolution." In *Artificial Life: Santa Fe Institute Studies in the Sciences of Complexity,* vol. 6, edited by Christopher G. Langton. Redwood City, Calif.: Addison-Wesley, 1989.

Papert, Seymour. "One AI or Many?" In *The Artificial Intelligence Debate: False Starts, Real Foundations,* edited by Stephen R. Graubard. Cambridge: MIT Press, 1988.

Penrose, Roger. *The Emperor's New Mind: Concerning Computers, Minds, and the Laws of Physics.* Oxford: Oxford University Press, 1989.

Pinker, Steven. *Learnability and Cognition.* Cambridge: MIT Press, 1989.

————. "Language Acquisition." In *Foundations of Cognitive Science,* edited by Michael I. Posner. Cambridge: MIT Press, 1989.

Pinker, Steven, ed. *Visual Cognition.* Cambridge: MIT Press, 1985.

Pinker, Steven, and Prince, Alan. "On Language and Connectionism: Analysis of a Parallel Distributed Processing Model of Language Acquisition." *Cognition* 28 (1988): 73–193.

Poggio, Tomaso. "Vision by Man and Machine." *Scientific American* 250 (April 1984): 106–116.

Poggio, Tomaso, and Koch, Christof. "Synapses That Compute Motion." *Scientific American* 256 (May 1987): 46–52.

Posner, Michael I., ed. *Foundations of Cognitive Science*. Cambridge: MIT Press, 1989.

Pylyshyn, Zenon W. *Computation and Cognition*. Cambridge: MIT Press, 1984.

Rall, Wilfrid. "Cable Theory for Dendritic Neurons." In *Methods in Neuronal Modeling*, edited by Christof Koch and Idan Segev. Cambridge: MIT Press, 1989.

Reeke, George N., Jr., and Edelman, Gerald M. "Real Brains and Artificial Intelligence." In *The Artificial Intelligence Debate: False Starts, Real Foundations*, edited by Stephen R. Graubard. Cambridge: MIT Press, 1988.

Reeke, George N., Jr.; Finkel, Leif H.; Sporns, Olaf; and Edelman, Gerald M. "Synthetic Neural Modeling: A Multilevel Approach to the Analysis of Brain Complexity." In *Signal and Sense: Local and Global Order in Perceptual Maps*, edited by G. Edelman, W. Gall, and W. Cowan. New York: Wiley, 1990.

Ristau, Carolyn A., ed. *Cognitive Ethology: The Minds of Other Animals*. Hillsdale, N.J.: Lawrence Erlbaum, 1991.

Roitblat, Herbert; Moore, Patrick; Nachtigall, Paul; and Penner, Ralph. "Natural Dolphin Echo Recognition Using an Integrator Gateway Network." In *Advances in Neural Information Processing Systems*, vol. 1, edited by Richard Lippmann, John Moody, and David Touretzky. San Mateo, Calif.: Morgan Kaufman, 1991.

Rosenblatt, Frank. *Principles of Neurodynamics: Perceptrons and the Theory of Brain Mechanisms*. Washington, D.C.: Spartan Books, 1961.

Ross, Muriel D.; Cutler, Lynn; Meyer, Glenn; Lam, Tony; and Vaziri, Parshaw. "3-D Components of a Biological Neural Network Visualized in Computer Generated Imagery. Part 1." *Acta Otolaryngol* 109 (1990): 83–92.

———. "3-D Components of a Biological Neural Network Visualized in Computer Generated Imagery. Part 2." *Acta Otolaryngol* 109 (1990): 235–244.

Ross, Muriel D.; Dayhoff, J. E.; and Mugler, D. H. "Toward Modeling a Dynamic Biological Neural Network." *Mathematics Computer Modelling* 13 (1990): 97–106.

Rumelhart, David E. "The Architecture of Mind: A Connectionist Approach." In *Foundations of Cognitive Science*, edited by Michael I. Posner. Cambridge: MIT Press, 1989.

———. "A Multicomponent Theory of the Perception of Briefly Exposed Visual Displays." *Journal of Mathematical Psychology* 7 (1970): 191–218.

Rumelhart, David E.; Hinton, G. E.; and Williams, R. J. "Learning Internal Representations by Error Propagation." In *Parallel Distributed Processing: Explorations in the Microstructure of Cognition*. Vol. 1: *Foundations*, edited by David Rumelhart and James L. McClelland. Cambridge: MIT Press, 1986.

Rumelhart, David E.; McClelland, James L.; and the PDP Research Group, eds. *Parallel Distributed Processing: Explorations in the Microstructure of Cog-*

nition. Vol. 1: *Foundations.* Vol. 2: *Psychological and Biological Models.* Cambridge: MIT Press, 1986.

Ryckebusch, Sylvie; Bower, James M.; and Mead, Carver. "Modeling Small Oscillating Biological Networks in Analog VLSI." In *Advances in Neural Information Processing Systems,* vol. 1, edited by Richard Lippmann, John Moody, and David S. Tourtezky. San Mateo, Calif.: Morgan Kaufman, 1989.

Ryckebusch, Sylvie, and Mead, Carver. "Analog VLSI Models of Oscillatory Biological Neural Circuits." California Institute of Technology preprint, n.d.

Sacks, Oliver. *The Man Who Mistook His Wife for a Hat and Other Clinical Tales.* New York: Perennial Library, 1987.

Searle, John R. "Is the Brain's Mind a Computer Program?" *Scientific American* 262 (January 1990): 26–31.

Sejnowski, Terrence J. "Neural Populations Revealed." *Nature* 332 (March 24, 1988): 308.

Sejnowski, Terrence J.; Koch, Christof; and Churchland, Patricia S. "Computational Neuroscience." *Science* 241 (September 9, 1988): 1299–1306.

Sejnowski, Terrence J., and Rosenberg, C. R. "NETtalk: A Parallel Network That Learns to Read Aloud." *Complex Systems* 1 (1987): 145–168.

———. "Learning and Representation in Connectionist Models." In *Perspectives in Memory Research and Training,* edited by Michael Gazzaniga. Cambridge: MIT Press, 1988.

Sejnowski, Terrence J., and Tesauro, Gerald. "The Hebb Rule for Synaptic Plasticity: Algorithms and Implementations." In *Neural Models of Plasticity,* edited by John H. Byrne and William O. Berry. San Diego, Calif.: Academic Press, Inc., 1989.

Shepard, Roger N. "Ecological Constraints on Internal Representation: Resonant Kinematics of Perceiving, Imagining, Thinking, and Dreaming." *Psychological Review* 91 (October 1984): 417–447.

———. "Internal Representation of Universal Regularities: A Challenge for Connectionism." In *Neural Connections, Mental Computation,* edited by Lynn Nadel, Lynn A. Cooper, Peter Culicover, and R. Michael Harnish. Cambridge: MIT Press, 1989.

———. *Mind Sights.* New York: W. H. Freeman, 1990.

———. "Stimulus and Response Generalization: A Stochastic Model Relating Generalization to Distance in Psychological Space." *Psychometrika* 22 (1957): 325–345.

———. "Toward a Universal Law of Generalization for Psychological Science." *Science* 237 (September 11, 1987): 1317–1323.

Shepard, Roger N., and Cooper, L. A. *Mental Images and Their Transformations.* Cambridge: MIT Press, 1982.

Shepard, Roger N., and Judd, S. A. "Perceptual Illusion of Rotation in Three-Dimensional Objects." *Science* 191 (1976): 952–954.

Shepard, Roger N., and Metzler, J. "Mental Rotation of Three-Dimensional Objects." *Science* 171 (1971): 701–703.

Shepherd, Gordon M. "A Basic Circuit of Cortical Organization." In *Perspectives in Memory Research and Training*, edited by Michael Gazzaniga. Cambridge: MIT Press, 1988.

―――. "Microcircuits in the Nervous System." *Scientific American* 238 (February 1978): 92–103.

―――. *Neurobiology*. 2d ed. New York: Oxford University Press, 1988.

Shepherd, Gordon M., ed. *The Synaptic Organization of the Brain*. 3d ed. New York: Oxford University Press, 1990.

Shepherd, Gordon M., and Koch, Christof. "Introduction to Synaptic Circuits." In *The Synaptic Organization of the Brain*, 3d ed., edited by Gordon M. Shepherd. New York: Oxford University Press, 1990.

Shepherd, Gordon; Woolf, Thomas; and Carnevale, Nicholas T. "Comparisons Between Active Properties of Distal Dendritic Branches and Spines: Implications for Neuronal Computations." *Journal of Cognitive Neuroscience* 1 (1990): 273–286.

Simon, Herbert, and Kaplan, Craig. "Foundations of Cognitive Science." In *Foundations of Cognitive Science*, edited by Michael I. Posner. Cambridge: MIT Press, 1989.

Smolensky, Paul. "Connectionist Modeling: Neural Computation/Mental Connections." In *Neural Connections, Mental Computation*, edited by Lynn Nadel, Lynn A. Cooper, Peter Culicover, and R. Michael Harnish. Cambridge: MIT Press, 1989.

―――. "On the Proper Treatment of Connectionism." *Behavioral and Brain Science* 11 (1988): 1–23.

Squire, Larry R. "Mechanisms of Memory." *Science* 232 (1986): 1612–1619.

―――. *Memory and Brain*. New York: Oxford University Press, 1987.

Stewart, Ian. *Does God Play Dice? The Mathematics of Chaos*. Cambridge: Basil Blackwell, 1989.

Stork, David G. "Is Backpropagation Biologically Plausible?" *Proceedings of the International Joint Conference on Neural Networks*, vol. 2, June 1989.

―――. "Self-Organization, Pattern Recognition, and Adaptive Resonance Networks." *Journal of Neural Network Computing* 1 (Summer 1989): 26–42.

Tapang, Carlos. "The Significance of Sleep in Memory Retention and Internal Adaptation." *Journal of Neural Network Computing* 1 (Summer 1989): 19–25.

Thompson, R. F. "The Neurobiology of Learning and Memory." *Science* 233 (1986): 941–947.

Tulving, Endel, and Schacter, Daniel. "Priming and Human Memory Systems." *Science* 247 (January 19, 1990): 301–306.

Turing, A. M. "Computing Machinery and Intelligence." In *Computers and Thought*, edited by E. A. Feigenbaum and J. Feldman. New York: McGraw-Hill, 1963.

von der Malsburg, Christoph. "Self-Organization of Orientation Sensitive Cells in the Striate Cortex." *Kybernetik* 14 (1973): 85–100. Reprinted in *Neurocomputing: Foundations of Research*, edited by James A. Anderson and Edward Rosenfeld. Cambridge: MIT Press, 1988.

Von Neumann, J. *The Computer and the Brain.* New Haven: Yale University Press, 1958.

Waibel, Alex. "Modular Construction of Time-Delay Neural Networks for Speech Recognition." *Neural Computation* 1 (Spring 1989): 39–46.

Waibel, Alex; Hanazawa, T.; Hinton, G.; Shikano, K.; and Lang, K. "Phoneme Recognition Using Time-Delay Neural Networks." *IEEE Transactions on Acoustics, Speech and Signal Processing* 37 (March 1989): 328–339.

Weinberger, Norman; McGaugh, James L.; and Lynch, Gary, eds. *Memory Systems of the Brain.* New York: The Guilford Press, 1985.

White, Halbert. "Learning in Artificial Neural Networks: A Statistical Perspective." *Neural Computation* 1 (Winter 1989): 425–464.

Widrow, Bernard, and Hoff, Marcian E. "Adaptive Switching Circuits." In *1960 IRE WESCON Convention Record.* New York: IRE, 1960. Reprinted in *Neurocomputing: Foundations of Research,* edited by James A. Anderson and Edward Rosenfeld. Cambridge: MIT Press, 1988.

Wiener, Norbert. *Cybernetics, Or Control and Communication in the Animal and the Machine.* Cambridge: MIT Press, 1961.

Wilson, H. R., and Cowan, Jack D. "Excitatory and Inhibitory Interactions in Localized Populations of Model Neurons." *Biophysical Journal* 12 (1972): 1–24.

Wilson, Stewart W. "The Genetic Algorithm and Simulated Evolution." In *Artificial Life: Santa Fe Institute Studies in the Sciences of Complexity,* vol. 6, edited by Christopher G. Langton. Redwood City, Calif.: Addison-Wesley, 1989.

Winograd, Terry. "Frame Representations and the Declarative-Procedural Controversy." In *Representation and Understanding: Studies in Cognitive Science,* edited by D. Bobrow and A. Collins. New York: Academic Press, Inc., 1975.

Yuhas, Ben P.; Goldstein, Moise H., Jr.; Sejnowski, Terrence J.; and Jenkins, Robert E. "Neural Network Models of Sensory Integration for Improved Vowel Recognition." *Proceedings of the IEEE,* October 1990.

Zador, Anthony; Koch, Christof; and Brown, Thomas. "Biophysical Model of a Hebbian Synapse." *Proceedings of the National Academy of Sciences* 87 (September 1990): 6718–6722.

INDEX

Ackley, David, 261–264, 267
Adaline, 20, 28–32, 36–37, 60
adaptive learning. *See* learning
Adaptive Solutions, Inc., xviii, 12–13, 43
AI. *See* artificial intelligence
airplanes, 75, 178
algorithms, 48–49, 96, 139, 145, 150, 153
  backpropagation, 14, 39–40, 49, 235
  genetic. *See* genetic algorithms
  for typeface recognition, 261, 265
  for Wiener solution, 27
Allen (robot), 119, 120
Allen, Robert, 151–157
Alspector, Josh, 12, 151–157
ALVINN (Autonomous Land Vehicle in a Neural Network), 4–5
ambiguity, 42, 112
AMPA receptors, 207, 209, 249, 255
Anderson, James, 46, 47
Anderson, Janeen, xiv
Angle, Colin, 120–123
animation, computer, 237, 238–239, 242
annealing metaphor, 150, 155
ants, artificial (vants), 261, 267–269, 270
apparent motion, 184, 187, 189
arbor functions, 228–229, 231
Aristotle, 204
ART architectures, 14, 38, 303
artificial ants (vants), 261, 267–269, 270
artificial brain, 277
artificial evolution, 264–267. *See also* evolution; genetic algorithms
artificial intelligence (AI), 9, 15, 32, 63, 105, 202. *See also* neural networks, artificial

biology as seen in, 180
birth of, 21, 25
complex behaviors and, 38–39, 125–126
Defense Department and, 10–12
expert systems, 38–39
local vs. global information and, 115, 129
model theory and, 166
recursive principle and, 35
representation as stumbling block for, 213
robots and, 117–126, 129
rules in, 51–52, 105, 202–203
schemata and frames in, 41–42
symbolic, neural networks vs., 8–9, 21–24, 33, 35, 39–40, 42, 89
unconscious mental processes as seen in, 50
Artificial Intelligence Laboratory (MIT), 23, 117. *See also* Massachusetts Institute of Technology
artificial (virtual) life, 260, 269, 274, 275–276
associative memory. *See* memory, associative
asymmetrical networks, 150, 157
AT&T, 15, 38, 74, 78, 79, 105, 152
AT&T Bell Laboratories, 12, 75
atoms of fact, 202–203
attention, 133, 234, 286, 287, 305
  MORSEL and, 129–136
  multiple mechanisms for, 135–136
  oscillations and, 288, 289
Attila (robot), 121–123
attractors, 300–301, 302, 303, 304
  Lorenz (butterfly), 301
  strange, 274, 276, 300, 301, 304
auditory system. *See also* macula
  in barn owl, 109–112

auditory system (*continued*)
  maps in, 160, 162–163
  vestibular system and, 237, 252
  vision and, 87–92
Autonomous Land Vehicle in a Neural
  Network (ALVINN), 4–5
awareness. *See* consciousness
axons, xv, xvi, xvii, 7, 81, 101, 102,
  103, 245, 249
  local circuit and, 247, 248
  traditional view of neurons and,
    247, 248

Bach, Johann Sebastian, 114, 115,
  116, 161
Bach machine, 114–116, 161
backpropagation, 14, 39–40, 49, 235
barn owl
  brain of, 159–160
  ear of, 109–112
  maps in, 161–164
basic-level response, 213
Baudry, Michel, 207, 208
bees, 116–117
behavior(s), 17, 99. *See also*
    intelligence; psychology; *specific
    behaviors*
  in collections of individuals, 270
  complex, complexity of structure
    producing, 125–126, 251, 254,
    272
  determinism and, 271
  explanations for, 18, 45, 117, 124,
    186–187, 252
  intelligence shown by, 106, 113,
    116, 117–118, 124, 125, 127–
    129
  multiple mechanisms for, 135–136
  neuroscience and, 186–187
  rules and, 52, 53, 125
  seen as result of brain processes,
    18–19, 46, 113, 186–187
  self-organization and, 210
behaviorism, 53, 286
Behrmann, Marlene, 134, 135
Bellcore (Bell Communications
  Research), 12, 87, 151–152, 153
Berkeley, George, 34
Berlin, Brent, 168
Bernstein hypothesis, 294–295
binding problem, 280–281, 284, 287
biology, biological systems, x, 17, 18,

158, 216–217, 231, 257. *See
  also* neural networks, biological
  complexity of, 64, 253–254
  as information-intensive, 252–253
  mind and, 186
  neural network theory and, 7, 14–
    16, 19, 32, 39, 40–41, 47, 76,
    80, 109, 150, 179, 180, 234,
    248–249
  neuron doctrine and, 243–244
  robotics and, 118
  universal properties and, 276
blind sight, 286–287, 289
BLIRNET, 130–131, 132–133, 134,
  205
Boltzmann, Ludwig, 43
Boltzmann machine, 42–43, 88, 150
Boolean logic, 105, 148
brain, ix, xiv, xv, xix, 16, 17, 32, 93–
  94, 112–113, 129, 137, 277. *See
  also* neural networks, biological
  assumptions about processes of, 76
  of barn owl, 159–160
  behaviorist view of, 53
  binding problem and, 280–281
  blind sight as clue to processes of,
    286–287
  "building block" vs. "instruction
    set" metaphors for, 302–303
  causal chain in, 295–296
  cerebral cortex of. *See* cerebral
    cortex
  computational tools of, 104–105
  computer compared with, xvii–xviii,
    6–7, 8, 15, 19, 25, 35, 41, 80,
    96, 130, 138, 141–142, 206,
    252, 254
  as dynamic system, 304
  evolutionary development of, 94,
    107, 181, 186, 188, 194, 258–
    259
  ill-posed problems and, 187–188
  immune system compared with, 275
  internalized constraints in, 193–
    194, 195
  lesions in, 18, 41, 287, 288
  mathematics as metaphor for
    processes of, 96–97, 299
  memory storage in, 285
  neuronal group selection and, 259
  optical illusions as clues to structure
    of, 186, 187, 194

oscillations in, 278–280, 281–286, 288–289, 290–291, 292
pattern matching in, 82
physics for, 216, 226
place of, in universe, 267, 276
plasticity and, 208, 222, 233
power of, 79, 94, 234, 243, 245, 275
as proof that networks work, 40–41
reverse-engineering of, xv, 94
self-organization of, 217–218, 221, 222–233, 254, 275, 286
stability vs. change in, 277, 295, 301–302
structural flexibility of, 258–259
synchronous order vs. disorder in, 279
tertiary cortex of, 164–165
time and, 111–112, 140, 142, 157
as tool to study itself, 79
understanding of, 6, 68–69, 214–215
Braine, M. D. S., 54
Brainstorms (Dennett), 137
Brooks, Rodney, 117–119, 120, 121, 123–125, 126–127, 129, 172, 204, 205, 254
Brown, Thomas, 14, 15, 243, 249, 254–258, 259, 260
bus, multiplexing, 81

calcium, 100, 207
California Institute of Technology (CalTech), 13, 38, 40, 94, 98, 108, 109, 138, 254, 286
calyx, 236, 239, 242, 243
candlestick/faces illusion, 183, 187
Carlton, Eloise, 201
carnivores, in Ackley's model, 261–263
categories, categorization, 5, 9, 45, 73, 85, 169–173, 198, 205. *See also* generalization
children's learning of, 73–74
feature maps and, 83–84
pattern matching and, 81–83
prototype effect in, 169–170, 204
smell and, 204, 211
Categorization and Naming in Children (Markman), 73–74
cats, 280, 285
genome of, 253

visual cortex of, 219, 220, 221, 222, 223–224, 278, 283
cause and effect, 295, 305
central nervous system, 63, 123, 236, 240. *See also* nervous system
creation of, 258
central pattern generators, 95
cerebral cortex, 164, 233, 295. *See also* visual cortex
chaos, chaotic systems, 19, 148, 149, 150, 157, 296, 298–299, 300–302, 303, 304–305
brain temperature and, 277
instability in, 301
periodic behavior vs., 276–277, 279
stability in, 300–301
strange attractors and, 273–274, 276, 300, 301, 304
children:
categories learned by, 73–74
languages learned by, 49, 52, 73, 161
Chomsky, Noam, 53, 62–63, 165, 169
Claiborne, Brenda, 256
clock pendulums, 225, 228, 233
cochlea, 162, 242
artificial, 109–111, 112, 115, 161
cockroaches, walking of, 94, 95, 96, 106–107
cognates, biological, 97
cognitive science, 175, 178–180
psychology. *See* psychology
Collection Machine, 117, 120, 121, 123–125, 126, 172, 254
color constancy, 187, 188–189, 192, 195
color names, 167–168
compartment analysis, 247, 256
compartment models, 243
complexity, 148, 270–271, 274–275. *See also* chaos, chaotic systems
computation, xiv, 11, 15, 16, 41–42, 47, 48, 94, 96, 105–106. *See also* thinking, thought
brain's tools for, 104–105
connectionism and, 47
flip-flop circuits and, 142
in Hopfield network. *See* Hopfield network
in immune system, 275
parallelism and, 48
psychology and, 147

computation (*continued*)
  time factor in, 105, 111–112
  vision and, 98
computational (derived) maps, 162–163
computational neuroscience, 246, 248, 289
computer(s):
  associative memory in, 48, 139, 140
  electrical states in problem-solving process of, 140
  neural networks simulated on, 7, 40, 78, 108, 245, 248
  neurons compared with, 243
  traditional digital, 6–7, 8, 25, 103
computer science, 17, 18, 35, 97, 180
  mathematics as language of, 96–97
congenital medical disorders, 5
connected stimuli, binding problem and, 284
connectionism, 24, 47, 49–50, 180. *See also* neural networks, artificial
Connection Machine, 108, 121
consciousness (awareness), 234, 278, 286, 287, 289, 305
  neurobiological theory of, 286
consequential region, 200–201
conservation of objects, 189
consistency, 34
Cooper, Leon, xviii, 12, 226
cortex. *See* cerebral cortex
Crick, Francis, 46, 47, 62, 132, 286, 287–288, 289

DARPA (Defense Advanced Research Projects Agency), 12, 39
Dartmouth College, conference at, 25
Darwin (machine), 258, 259
De Anima (Aristotle), 204
Deep Thought, 9
Defense Department, U.S., 10–12
Delbrück, Max, 98
Delbrück, Tobi, 105
dendrites, dendritic trees, xv, xvi, xvii, 7, 81, 103, 243, 249, 257
  calcium and, 207
  electrical charge and, 102, 103
  of granule cell, 247
  in local circuit, 248
  in MOSAIC model, 254, 255, 256

and neurons as simple devices, 244, 245
  timing and, 105
Dendros machines, 21, 37–38, 43
Dennett, Daniel, 117, 137
Department of Defense, U.S., 15, 23, 38, 39
derived (computational) map, 162–163
Descartes, René, 147–148, 202
determinism, 105, 271, 272, 296, 300
development, human, 227–228, 258–259
DeWeerth, Steve, 105, 107–108
distributed representation, 70
Dixon, R. M. W., 170–171
DNA, 98, 227, 253, 258
Does God Play Dice? (Stewart), 272
dolphins, 4
Dreyfus, Hubert, 202
Dreyfus, Stuart, 202
Dyirbal, 170–172
dyslexia, neglect, 134–135

ear, 105. *See also* auditory system
Ecological Approach to Visual Perception, The (Gibson), 190
Edelman, Gerald, 258–259, 260
edge detection, 97, 107
EEGs, 282–283, 285, 296–297, 298, 302, 303
electrical signals, in neurons, 100–104
Elman, Jeffrey, 49
emergence, 52, 125, 210, 271, 275
energy landscapes. *See* landscapes
entropy, 43
equation, "flow" of, 273
equilibrium, 300
evolution, 5–6, 7, 8, 18, 19, 188, 258, 259–260. *See also* learning
  artificial (evolved model), 261–267. *See also* genetic algorithms
  of brain, 94, 107, 181, 186, 188, 194, 258–259
  collections of individuals and, 270
  invariances and, 192, 194
  landscapes and, 157–158
  learning vs., 85
  optical illusions and, 186
  robotics and, 118
  stability vs. change in, 266

time element in, 146
universal properties and, 276
excitatory connections, xvi, 104, 131, 209, 211, 212, 228, 229, 247
"exclusive or" pattern, 67–68
expectation, 305
expert systems, 38–39
eye. *See* visual system

faces/candlestick illusion, 183, 187
Faggin, Federico, xiii–xv, xvii–xix, 12, 97
Farmer, J. Doyne, 274–275
fastball, rising, 184–186, 187, 194
feedback, 294, 303, 305
feed-forward networks, 294
Feldman, Jerome, 46, 158, 159, 176, 177–182, 187
ferrets, visual cortex of, 223–224
fever, 277
filters, 26–27, 296. *See also* Adaline
finite state machines, 123, 124–125
fitness function, 264–265, 266, 268
fixed-point solution, 157
flashing dot illusion, 184, 187, 194
flip-flop circuit, 142, 149
"flow" of equation over time, 273
Fodor, Jerry, 175
Ford Motor Company, xviii, 78
Fourier, Jean Baptiste Joseph, 233
Freeman, Walter, 278, 280, 282–283, 285, 292–305
Frege, Gottlob, 34
frog, visual system of, 192–193, 202, 203

Galileo, 244
gender identification, 5
generalization, 23, 30, 59, 60, 67, 73, 87, 113, 194–201, 205, 212–214. *See also* categories, categorization
consequential region in, 200–201
gradients of, 198–200
invariance and, 195, 199
metric of similarity and, 195–196, 198
smell and, 204
"genes," artificial, 266
genetic algorithms, 6, 264–267
fitness function in, 264–265, 266, 267, 268

mixing function in, 264
random change generator in, 264
genetic code, 227–228, 253, 258, 276
Genghis (robot), 120, 121, 122
Gibson, James J., 137, 190–192, 193, 194, 199
global information, local information vs., 115, 129, 203, 251
Gluck, Mark, 201
Gödel, Kurt, 34, 42
Goldstein, Moise, 88
Golomb, Beatrice, 5
Gould, Carol, 116
Gould, James, 116
Graf, Hans Peter, 79
grammar, 9, 50, 51, 52
children's learning of language and, 52–56
generative, 165–166
grandmother cells, 70, 206
Granger, Richard, 204, 205–215, 233, 303
granule cell, 246–248
gravity, 201, 244
macula and, 237, 240
Gray, Charles, 132, 278–286, 287, 290, 291–292, 293
Grossberg, Stephen, 13–14, 38, 303

hallucinations, 277
Hammerstrom, Dan, 12, 43
hardware, 80
division between software and, 7, 35
hearing. *See* auditory system
Hebb, Donald, 9–10, 40–41, 234, 244, 245, 250, 256, 257, 281
Hebb synapse, 9–10, 11, 41, 100, 228, 249, 255
Hecht-Nielsen, Robert, xviii, 3, 12, 14, 15
Heraclitus, 304
Herbert the Collection Machine, 117, 120, 121, 123–125, 126, 172, 254
hexagonal spacing, 241
hidden layers, 67–68, 69, 84, 85, 86, 196
Hillis, Danny, 121
Hinton, Geoffrey, 46, 47, 49, 79, 134, 150
hippocampus, 255, 256

HNC, xviii, 12, 14, 15
Hodgkin-Huxley equations, 295
Hoff, Ted, 27, 31, 32
Holland, John, 266
homogeneous network, 68
honeybees, 116–117
Hopfield, John, 21, 38, 39, 42, 138,
    140–147, 149–150, 155, 157,
    196, 253
Hopfield network, 14, 42, 138–151,
    152, 153, 154, 156, 157, 160,
    196, 198, 272, 299–300
Howard, Richard, 12, 15, 75–81, 83,
    84, 85, 87, 105, 159, 205, 249
Hubel, David, 41, 86, 104, 175, 217,
    218, 219–223, 227, 283, 284
Hume, David, 34
Huygens, Christian, 225, 228, 233
hypercube, 36, 37
hyperplane, 36
hypothermia, 277

IBM, 12, 150, 155
identity, 304
ill-posed problems, 187–188
immune system, 271, 275
incompleteness theorem, 34
infantile hypercalcemia, 5
information, structure as, 277
information processing, noise and,
    291
information technology, macula and,
    240
inhibitory connections, xvi, 104, 131,
    208, 209, 211–212, 221, 228,
    229, 246, 247, 248
Intel Corp., xviii, 12, 42, 43
intelligence, 15, 19, 33, 113, 129,
    164, 271, 305. See also artificial
    intelligence; behavior
  behavior as indication of, 106, 113,
    116, 117–118, 124, 125, 127–
    129
  in animals, 126–129, 164
  intention and, 116, 117, 118
  robots and, 117–118, 123–125,
    126, 127
  stability vs. change in, 277
  touchstone task and, 176–177
  Turing test and, 114, 115, 116
intention, 116, 117, 118, 126
internalized constraints, 193–194,
    195

interneuron, 246, 247
invariance, 190–192, 193–194, 195,
    199
ions, 100, 101, 102–103

Jackel, Larry, 79
Japanese language, 172–173
Johns Hopkins University, 46, 49, 88,
    89, 90
Johnson, Mark, 173, 174
Judd, Sherryl, 189–190, 191

Kant, Immanuel, 34, 304
Kay, Paul, 168
Keesing, Ron, 5–6
Keller, Joseph, 229–230
Kepler's Laws, 51
Kinsella, Kevin, xviii
Kirkpatrick, Scott, 155
knowledge, 304
Knudsen, Eric, 109, 159, 160, 161,
    163, 217
Koch, Christof, 254–257, 259, 260,
    286–290
König, Peter, 283, 285
Kohonen, Teuvo, 57
Kohonen associative memories, 14,
    57
Konishi, M., 109
Kuhn, Thomas, 3, 16

Lakoff, George, 158, 165, 166, 167,
    168, 169, 170, 171, 172–176,
    177, 182, 186, 204
lamprey, 94, 95
landscapes, 138, 150–151, 152, 153–
    154, 155–156, 157–158, 266.
    See also Hopfield network
  limit cycles in, 272, 273, 274, 300
  saddles in, 272, 273, 274
  sinks in, 272, 273, 274, 300
  sources in, 272, 273, 274
Langton, Chris, 261, 267–271, 274,
    276–277, 301
language, 9, 17, 18, 50, 52, 158,
    164–176. See also linguistics;
    speech
  categories and, 169–173
  children's learning of, 49, 52–56,
    73, 161
  as closed formal system, 87–88,
    172
  Dani, 168

Dyirbal, 170–172
    grammar and. *See* grammar
    Japanese, 172–173
    logic in, 166, 173
    maps and, 164–165, 167, 170, 172,
        173–175
    meaning in, 165, 166–167, 172
    metaphors in, 173, 174–175, 182
    touchstone task and, 176–177, 178,
        182
Larson, John, 208
Lashley, Karl, 206
lateral geniculate, 219, 223, 228
Lazzaro, John, xvii, 111
learning, xv, 6, 7–8, 32, 33, 41,
        52–53, 60, 80, 150, 153, 157,
        180–181. *See also* evolution;
        memory
    in Adaline, 20, 30–31
    algorithms and. *See* algorithms
    backpropagation and, 39–40
    of categories, 73–74
    in children, 49, 52, 73–74, 161
    in Dendros, 37
    evolution vs., 85
    fitness function and, 266–267
    in immune system, 275
    landscapes and, 157–158
    of language, 49, 52–56, 73, 161
    neglect dyslexia and, 134–135
    in perceptrons, 22, 23
    randomness and, 152
    self-organization and, 210
    stable patterns vs. new patterns in,
        277
    in tapped-delay lines, 26–27
    in zip code reader, 84–85
Le Cun, Yann, 14, 79, 85, 86–87
leeches, 94
Leibniz, Gottfried Wilhelm, Baron
        von, 202
Lettvin, Jerome, 192, 193, 225
life, 267, 276–277
    artificial (virtual), 260, 269, 274,
        275–276
    definition of, 269–270
    phase transitions in, 276
    universal properties in, 276
limit cycles, 272, 273, 274, 300
linear stability analysis, 230–231
linear systems, 148, 149, 271, 294,
        300
linguistics, 17, 18, 45, 51–52, 63,

131–132, 165–166, 175–179,
    180. *See also* language
    behaviorism and, 53
    cognitive, 175
    connectionism and, 50
    generative, 175
    model theory and, 166
    speech and, 87–88
LISP, 119
Littman, Michael, 263
lobsters, 94
local circuits, 246, 248
local information, global information
    vs., 115, 129, 203, 251
local minima problem, 153–154
local summing sites, 247
locust, 95
logic, 7, 9, 33, 34, 36, 50–51, 105,
        113, 146, 148, 166, 173, 202.
        See also linguistics
    and assumptions about brain
        processes, 76, 77
    Boolean, 105, 148
long-term potentiation, 207–209,
        249, 251
Lorenz attractor, 301
lymphocytes, 275
Lynch, Gary, 205–207, 208, 209,
        214, 250, 251

McBeath, Michael, 183–185
McClelland, James, 46, 47, 49, 51,
        52–53, 55, 56–62, 64, 65, 67,
        71, 73, 129, 130
McCulloch, Warren, 6, 192, 193, 243,
        245
machines, 149
    as metaphor, 147–148, 251, 254,
        260
machine vision, 81
McNaughton, Bruce, 127–128
macula, 235–243, 252, 254, 260
maps, mapping, 63, 196
    auditory, 160, 162–163
    in bees, 116–117
    computational (derived), 162–163
    definition of, 162
    frequency, 163
    generalization and, 199
    language and, 164–165, 167, 170,
        172, 173–175
    NETtalk as, 69–70
    in owls, 159–160, 161–162

maps, mapping (*continued*)
  in rats, 127
  in robots, 119–120, 123, 125
  sensory, 162, 163–164, 233
  vision and, 112, 160, 163, 220,
    223, 224
  in zip code reader, 83–84
Markman, Ellen, 45, 73–74, 131
Massachusetts Institute of Technology
    (MIT), 13, 23, 24, 25, 40, 54,
    117, 151, 165, 166, 222
matching, 205
mathematics, 96–97, 214. *See also*
    logic
  as metaphor for brain processes,
    299
  nonlinear systems and, 230
Mead, Carver, xiii–xv, xvii, xviii–xix,
    12, 15, 21, 43, 93–94, 95, 96,
    97–99, 100, 104–105, 106, 107,
    108, 109, 111, 112, 161, 205,
    233, 248–249, 255
meaning, 165, 166–167, 172, 295
memory, 28, 113, 157, 204–214, 205
  in Boltzmann machine, 43
  in brain, xviii, 18
  cellular mechanisms and, 206
  degradation of, 285
  factual, 206
  as localized, 206
  long-term, 288–289
  long-term potentiation, 207–209,
    249, 251
  procedural, 206
  short-term, 288–289
  of smells, 204–205, 209–214
  storage of, 206
  types of, 206, 207
memory, associative, 47, 48, 57, 59,
    139–140. *See also* Hopfield
    network
  in networks, 42
Merzenich, Michael, 233
metaphors, 173, 174–175, 182
metric of similarity, 195–196, 198
microcircuits, 246, 248
microprocessors, xvii, xviii, 97
Miller, Kenneth, 216–217, 228–233,
    278
Milner, Peter, 281
mind, ix, 50, 137, 234, 268, 289–290
  causal principles of, 51–52

  nature of, 53
  optical illusions and, 186
Minsky, Marvin, 13, 22–24, 32, 33,
    36, 37, 38, 39, 40, 42, 67, 73,
    161, 178
Mioche, Laurence, 278
MIT. *See* Massachusetts Institute of
    Technology
mitral cell, 247, 248
model theory, 166
monkeys, 280, 291
  visual cortex of, 220, 221–222,
    223–224
moon explorer, 121
Moore, Patrick, 4
MORSEL, 129–136
MOSAIC, 255, 256, 258
motion, apparent, 184, 187, 189
Mozer, Michael, 114–116, 129–136,
    161, 204, 205
Mugler, Dale, 241
multiple-layer networks, 21–22, 23,
    37–38, 40, 49
multiple objects, MORSEL and, 129–
    136
multiplexing bus, 81
muscle action, repetitive, 95
myelin, 242, 243

National Aeronautics and Space
    Administration (NASA), 237–
    238, 240, 242
National Institutes of Health, 246,
    247
nerve fibers, 7, 243, 258. *See also*
    axons; dendrites, dendritic trees
nervous system, 63, 123, 236, 240,
    242, 243, 246
  creation of, 258
Nestor, Inc., xviii, 12, 13, 78
NETtalk, 64–72, 74, 84, 115, 137–
    138
neural networks, artificial, ix–x, xiv–
    xv, xvii, 47, 78. *See also* neurons,
    artificial; *specific machines and
    topics*
  abstraction in, 226–227
  and assumptions about neurons,
    244–245
  biological reality and, 7, 14–16, 19,
    32, 39, 40–41, 47, 76, 80, 109,
    150, 179, 180, 234, 248–249

brain compared with, 10, 14, 15
commercial applications of, 78
computational neuroscience and,
248
computer models of, 7, 40, 78, 108,
245, 248
as connectionism, 47. *See also*
connectionism
convenient theories and, 294
defining, 6–9
dictionary of functions for, 99
facts and, 203
generalization as important issue in,
194–195. *See also* generalization
"genes" in, 266
local vs. global information and,
115, 129, 203
machine metaphor and, 148
meaning in, 295
multiple-layer, 21–22, 23, 37–38,
40, 49, 266
multiplicity of structures and
learning rules for, 180–181
and neuron as simple summing
device, 245
as paradigm shift, 16, 17, 19
as parallel distributed processing,
47–48
reductionist explanations and, 252–
253, 260
revival of interest in, 40–41
self-organization of, 210
structure matched to task in, 6, 76,
181, 206
structures for, 87, 180, 181, 265
symbolic artificial intelligence vs.,
8–9, 21–24, 33, 35, 39–40,
42
"thoughts" of, 137–138
two natures of, 16
types of architecture for, 48
neural networks, biological, 9, 98–
105. *See also* brain; neurons,
biological
associative memory in, 139–140
neuronal imperfections and, 95
number of neurons and, 80, 81
psychology and, 186–187. *See also*
psychology
representation and, 70, 71, 72–
73
specialized networks in, 76

neurobiology. *See* biology, biological
systems
neuronal group selection, 259
neurons, artificial, xiv, xv, 7, 19, 96,
235. *See also* neural networks,
artificial
biological neurons vs., 249
categorization and, 211
connections between layers of, 48,
80–81
as map elements, 70
number of, 37–38, 40, 81–82
representation and, 70, 71
synapse competition and, 254–258.
See also synapses, artificial
types of, 48, 211. *See also*
excitatory connections; inhibitory
connections
neurons, biological, xv, 6, 18, 47, 63,
96, 98, 113, 142, 235, 290. *See
also* neural networks, biological
artificial neurons vs., 249
binding problem and, 280–281
complexity of, 234, 243, 246–248
computational capability of, 256
data points of, 256
development of, 258–259
early study of, 70–71
electrical pulse of, 100–104
imperfections in, 95
main features of, xvi
memory storage and, 206
numbers of, in computations, 80,
81, 285
perception and psychology as result
of, 46
plasticity and, 233
potassium channels in, 100–104,
294–295
representation and, 99
self-organization of, 217–218, 254,
258
as simple summing device, 243–
246, 249
sodium channels in, 100–104, 294–
295
specificity of response in, 41
spontaneous firing of, organization
and, 223–224, 226, 231, 233
synapses and. *See* synapses,
biological
synchronized firing of, 278–280,

neurons, biological (*continued*)
    281–286, 288–289, 290–291,
    292
  thought and perception explained
    by, 47
  three-dimensional connections of,
    80, 81
  time and, 140, 233–234
  types of, 211. *See also* excitatory
    connections; inhibitory
    connections
neurotransmitters, 102–104, 207, 251
Newell, Allen, 25, 121
Newton, Isaac, 50, 186, 195, 201, 244
Newtonian physics, 17–18
Nicoll, Richard, 251
NMDA receptors, 207, 209, 249–251,
    255
noise, 19, 26, 82, 83, 91, 151, 152,
    154, 155–156, 296–298
  information vs., 291
  structure in, 297
nonlinear systems, 230–231, 272, 304

object recognition, 187–196, 291–
    292
ocular dominance columns, 220, 221–
    222, 223, 226, 228, 229, 231–
    233, 284
olfactory system, 209, 236, 279, 280,
    282–283, 292, 298–299, 303,
    304
  memory and, 204–205, 209–214
  olfactory bulb in, 209, 246–248,
    279, 285, 293, 296–297, 301–
    302
optical illusions, 183–187, 194
optimization problems, 38, 143, 149–
    150
  shelving example, 143–145, 152,
    153
  traveling salesman example, 138–
    139, 143, 273
order, 58–59, 60, 273–274, 301
  brain temperature and, 277
  deterministic, 271, 272
  periodic, chaos vs., 279
  probabilistic, 271–272
orientation sensitivity, in cortex, 219–
    221
Orr, Wilson, 241
oscillation, 149, 150, 157, 273, 277,

    278–280, 281–286, 288–289,
    290–291, 292
owl, barn. *See* barn owl

Papert, Seymour, 13, 22–24, 32, 33,
    36, 37, 38, 39, 40, 67, 73, 121,
    161, 178
paradigms, 16
paradigm shift, neural networks as,
    16, 17, 19
parallel distributed processing, 47–48,
    50, 51
*Parallel Distributed Processing:
    Explorations in the
    Microstructure of Cognition*, 46–
    47
Parallel Distributed Processing (PDP)
    Group, 46–47, 48, 49, 62
parallelism, 48, 80, 119
Parallel Models of Associative Memory
    (Anderson and Hinton, eds.), 46
parallelogram/table illusion, 183, 184,
    187
past tense machine, 49, 52–62, 64,
    65, 66–67, 115, 129, 160
pattern associator, 57–58, 59–60, 66–
    67
pattern generators, repetitive motion
    and, 95
pattern matching, 81–83, 160–161
pattern recognition problems, 33
PDP (Parallel Distributed Processing)
    Group, 46–47, 48, 49, 62
pendulums, clock, 225, 228, 233
perceptrons, 21–23, 31–33, 36–37,
    150, 161
Perceptrons (Minsky and Papert), 13,
    22–24, 36, 38, 67, 178
periodic order, chaos vs., 276–277,
    279
phase-locking, 280, 282, 283, 288,
    289, 290, 291, 292
phase transitions, 276
Phillips, Charles, 247, 248
*Philosophiae naturalis principia
    mathematica* (Newton), 186,
    195
Philosophical Investigations
    (Wittgenstein), 203
phylogeny, 275
physical symbol system hypothesis, 25
physics, 50, 64, 216–217

for the brain, 216, 226
reductionist explanations in, 252
pigeons, 198, 200, 205
Pinker, Steven, 54, 55, 60–62, 73, 74, 131
Pitts, Walter, 6, 192, 193, 243, 245
planets, 201
  Kepler's Laws and, 51
plasticity, brain, 208, 222, 233
Platt, John, xiv
Pomerleau, Dean, 4–5
potassium, in neurons, 100–104, 209, 294–295
Prince, Alan, 60–62, 73
Principia Mathematica (Russell and Whitehead), 34, 202
probability, 271–272
programs, programming, 7, 9, 23, 33, 52, 105, 124, 180
  genetic algorithms and, 264
  self-organization and, 210
pronouncing words. *See* NETtalk
prototype effect, 169–170, 204
psychological space, 195–203, 257
psychology, 17, 18, 32, 45, 49–50, 51–52, 53, 72, 113, 157, 194.
  See also behavior
  computational basis for, 147
  mind and, 290
  neurosciences and, 186–187
  representation as stumbling block for, 212–213
pyriform cortex, 279

Quine, W. V. O., 73, 74, 82

rabbits, olfactory system of, 282–283, 292, 298
radar, phased-array, 241
Rall, Wilfrid, 243, 246, 247–248, 256
rats, 292
  in buried-food tests, 128–129
  mazes run by, 127–128, 205, 206
  smell-memory in, 204, 205, 209–214
reading:
  attention and, 132
  NETtalk and. *See* NETtalk
reason, reasoning, 50–51, 63, 202
receptors:
  AMPA, 207, 209, 249, 255
  NMDA, 207, 209, 249–251, 255

recursive principle, 35
"reflex" experiments, 293, 294
refractory period, of inhibitory neurons, 212
relativity, 17–18, 50, 201
Renshaw, Birdsey, 246
Renshaw interneuron, 246, 247
representation, 71–73, 205, 212–213, 257. *See also* maps, mapping
  distributed, 70
  relative, 71–72
reshelving books, as optimization problem, 143–145, 152, 153
resistors, 153
retina, xv, 22, 97, 98, 99, 105, 132, 162, 188, 189, 218, 219, 220, 224, 231, 297
  artificial, 29, 107–109, 130
Ricoh Co., Ltd., 5, 12
rising fastball, 184–186, 187, 194
robots, 117–126, 129
Rosch, Eleanor, 167, 168–169
Rosenberg, Charles, 64–66, 68, 69, 70
Rosenblatt, Frank, 21–22, 23, 24, 31–32, 33, 36, 37, 40
Ross, Muriel, 235–243, 251–252, 260
rules, 9, 33, 50–51, 53, 60, 80, 105, 124, 125, 141. *See also* algorithms; grammar; programs, programming
  context and, 202–203
  determinism and, 271
  for pronouncing words, 66
  self-organization and, 210
Rumelhart, David, 13, 14, 21, 39, 45–46, 49–53, 55, 56–62, 64, 65, 67, 71, 73, 124, 129, 130, 183, 196, 249
Russell, Bertrand, 34, 202, 303
Ryckebusch, Sylvie, 94–96, 99–100, 106–107, 150

saddles, 272, 273, 274
Salk Institute, 5, 46, 49, 62, 209, 249, 280, 285, 286
San Diego, University of California at, 46, 50, 151–152, 242
Santa Fe Institute, 270–271
schizophrenia, 18
science:
  cognitive, 175, 178–180

science (*continued*)
  convenient theories and, 294–295
  paradigms of, 16
Searle, John, 116
sea slugs, 70, 94, 95, 99
second derivative, 97
seizures, brain, 277
Sejnowski, Terry, 5, 21, 46, 49, 62,
  64–66, 68–70, 71–73, 84, 88,
  137, 248–249
self-organization, 19, 210, 225, 228,
  256–257, 274, 284
  of brain, 217–218, 221, 222–233,
  254, 275, 286
semantics, 166, 172
sensors, 120, 121, 124–125
sensory maps, 162, 163–164
sensory systems, 112
sequential processes, 50–51
SEXNET, 5
sexual characteristics, 5
Seymour (robot), 120, 121
Shatz, Carla, 217, 220, 223–224,
  228, 278
shelving books, as optimization
  problem, 143–145, 152, 153
Shepard, Roger, 183, 184, 186–190,
  191, 193–196, 198–203, 204,
  257
Shepherd, Gordon, 243, 245, 246,
  247–248, 254
signal filters, 26–27, 296. *See also*
  Adaline
signal processing:
  local circuits and, 246
  macula and, 241, 242
Simon, Herbert, 25, 41, 121
Singer, Wolf, 132, 278, 280, 282, 283,
  284, 285, 287, 290, 292, 293
single-cell studies, 41, 219
single-layer perceptrons, 21, 23
sinks, in landscapes, 272–274, 300
Skinner, B. F., 53, 286
sleep, 291
smell. *See* olfactory system
Smolensky, Paul, 46
sodium, in neurons, 100–104, 209,
  295
software, 8, 80, 81, 105, 141, 248.
  See also programs, programming
  division between hardware and, 7,
  35
  genetic algorithms and, 264

solution space, 196–198, 273, 276–
  277
soma, 103, 245, 249
somatosensory areas, 280
sonar, 119, 120
sources, in landscapes, 272, 273
space, curving of, 201
space, psychological, 195–203, 257
specialized structures, 8, 19, 76
speech, 87–92, 112, 164. *See also*
  language; NETtalk
spin glass theory, 38, 39, 138, 150,
  155
squids, 70
Squire, Larry, 206
static feature detection networks, 286
stereocilia, 241
Stevens, Charles, 209, 249, 250–251
stochastic order, 271–272
Stork, David, 5, 6, 261, 267
strange attractors, 273–274, 276,
  300, 301, 304
structure(s), 85, 87, 105, 180–181,
  265
  complex behaviors and, 125–126,
  251, 254, 272
  learning and, 33
  task matched to, 6, 76, 181, 206
Structure of Scientific Revolutions,
  The (Kuhn), 3, 16
Stryker, Michael, 216, 217–218, 220,
  222–229, 231–233, 278
swimming, 94, 95
symbols, 169, 175
symmetrical networks, 150, 157
synapses, artificial, xviii, 81, 211. *See*
  also synaptic weights
  in Adaline, 37
  adjustable, 152–153, 156–157
  competition among, 256–258
synapses, biological, xv, xvi, xviii, 7,
  11, 41, 47, 63, 81, 102, 103,
  105, 142, 247, 248, 249–250,
  251
  adjustable, 156–157
  competition among, 254–255
  Hebb, 9–10, 11, 41, 100, 228, 249,
  255
  memory and, 207, 208–209
  and neurons as simple devices, 244,
  245–246
  plasticity and, 233
Synaptics, Inc., xiii, xiv–xv, xviii, 12

synaptic weights, 29–30, 49, 66, 153, 161, 251
    in Adaline, 30, 31, 36, 37
    evolution and, 266–267
    in NETtalk, 68, 69
    in past tense machine, 66–67
    in speech recognition, 91
    in tapped-delay lines, 26, 27
    in zip code reader, 84
synchronized oscillations, 278–280, 281–286, 288–289, 290–291, 292
Syntactic Structures (Chomsky), 165
syntax, 166
Syntonic Systems, 20–21, 43
Szu, Harold, 13

table/parallelogram illusion, 183, 184, 187
Talmy, Leonard, 174
Tank, David, 38, 39, 138, 140–145, 149–150, 157. *See also* Hopfield network
Tapang, Carlos, 20–21, 37–38, 42, 43–44
tapped-delay lines, 26–27
templates, 83, 84, 213
tertiary cortex, 164–165
thinking, thought, 41, 63, 113, 137, 157, 175, 186, 285. *See also* computation
    mind and, 290
    multiple physical states and, 137–138
    in neural networks, 137–138
    strange attractors and, 304
    synchronous oscillations and, 279
time, 105, 140, 142, 146, 157, 233–234, 255, 305
    as computational tool, 111–112
    evolutionary, 146
    "flow" of equation over, 273
    long-term potentiation and, 208, 209
    memory and, 212
touch, 236, 252
touchstone task, 176–177, 178, 181, 182
Tractatus Logico-Philosophicus (Wittgenstein), 202, 203
transistors, xv, xvii, 99, 153
traveling salesman problem, 138–139, 143, 273

trial and error, 19
Tsien, Richard, 209, 251
Tufts University, 117
Tulving, Endel, 206
Turing, Alan, 34–35, 96, 114
    universal machine of, 34–35, 96
Turing test, 114, 115, 116
typefaces, recognition of, 261, 265

uniqueness, 131
Universal Turing Machine, 34–35, 96

vants (virtual ants), 261, 267–269, 270
vector computation, 128
very large scale integration (VLSI), 97, 98, 152
vestibular system, 237, 252
vestibulo-ocular system, 108
virtual ants (vants), 261, 267–269, 270
virtual (artificial) life, 260, 269, 274, 275–276
visual cortex, 218–226, 228–233, 278, 280, 283, 284, 301–302
visual system, 71, 76, 98, 105, 179, 181, 192, 236, 252, 280. *See also* retina; visual cortex
    blind sight and, 287
    edge detection and, 97, 107
    of frog, 192–193, 202, 203
    grandmother cells in, 70
    hearing and, 87–92
    mapping and, 112
    self-organization of, 217–218
    vestibulo-ocular system and, 108
visual maps, 160, 163
vitalism, 268, 269–270
VLSI (very large scale integration), 97, 98, 152
von der Malsburg, Christoph, 224–225, 281–282, 287
von Neumann, John, 6, 41, 50, 148, 299

walking, 94, 95, 96, 106–107, 113
Wallace, Alfred Russel, 258
weights. *See* synaptic weights
Werbos, Paul, 14
Whitehead, Alfred North, 33–34, 202, 303
Wickelfeatures, 61, 70
Wickelphone system, 61, 129

Widrow, Bernard, 20, 21, 22, 23, 24, 26–33, 36–37, 40, 49, 60, 91, 296
Widrow-Hoff rule, 30
Wiener, Norbert, 26
Wiener solution, 26, 27, 30–31
Wiesel, Torsten, 41, 86, 175, 217, 218, 219–223, 227, 283, 284
Willshaw, David, 224–225
Wittgenstein, Ludwig, 202, 203

word recognition, MORSEL and, 129–136

Yuhas, Ben, 87–92

Zador, Anthony, 256
Zilog, Inc., xvii
zip code reader, 74, 75–87, 159, 160, 213